ISHI THE LAST YAHI

ISHI THE LAST YAHI
A DOCUMENTARY HISTORY

Edited by

Robert F. Heizer and Theodora Kroeber

UNIVERSITY OF CALIFORNIA PRESS

BERKELEY   LOS ANGELES   LONDON

University of California Press,
Berkeley and Los Angeles, California
University of California Press, Ltd.,
London, England
Copyright © 1979 by
The Regents of the University of California
First Paperback Printing 1981
ISBN 0-520-04366-9
Library of Congress
Catalog Card Number: 76-19966
Design by Dave Comstock
Printed in the United States of America

08   07   06   05   04
14   13   12   11   10   9   8   7

The paper used in this publication meets the
minimum requirements of ANSI/NISO
Z39.48-1992 (R 1997) (*Permanence of Paper*). ∞

As one of the editors of this book on the life and times
and the death of the man, Ishi, I should like to name the three
people at the heart of its realization.
August Frugé, Director, now retired, of the Press of the
University of California, who first suggested and then urged
upon the editors and held to the concept and the worth of a
book such as this until it became a paper-and-print reality.
Robert F. Heizer, professor and field man, who brings
to this task, beyond his unique anthropological and archaeological
expertise, a lifetime of obsessive infatuation with the gathering
and preservation of significant source materials having to
do with all matters Indian-Californian as well
as with Ishi himself.
Ishi, the Yahi Indian, the subject of this book.
Howsoever one touches on Ishi, the touch rewards.
It illuminates the way.

Theodora Kroeber

CONTENTS

CONTENTS

INTRODUCTION

On March 25, 1916, an Indian died of tuberculosis in the hospital of the Medical School of the University of California, situated then as now on Parnassus Heights overlooking Golden Gate Park in San Francisco. His doctor and friend, Saxton Pope, a distinguished physician and surgeon on the staff of the medical school, was with him when he died, and mourned his death as did the staff of the Museum of Anthropology, next door to the hospital. As did an unknown number of people of varying ages and walks of life who had come to know the Indian over the four years and seven months he had lived at the museum.

Museum and medical records include detailed information about him during those years: recordings were made of his voice, and phonetic transcriptions of his language. The records give his cephalic index, his height, his changing weights, his hand grip on the dynamometer. There are casts of his perfectly formed feet and photographs of his equally perfect hands, and some hundreds of photographs of him in various moods and surroundings, shooting the bow, swimming, chipping arrow points; smiling and serious; ebullient, withdrawn. Dr. Pope made a death mask of his face. The record is fuller and more various than is likely to be that of most of us.

But we do not know this Indian's real name, nor is it anywhere in this book of documents, all of which relate to him. In brief résumé, his story:

On August 29, 1911, an Indian, close to death from exposure, hunger, and fright, was picked up outside a slaughterhouse near Oroville, a mining town on the Feather River in northern California.

He was taken into custody by the county sheriff, who locked him in the jail for his own protection from the forward curiosity of the local whites. The news story of this "wild man" was enhanced by the circumstance that he spoke neither English nor Spanish nor the language of any of the local Indians. The pictures and story-spread of him in the newspapers brought him to the notice of two anthropologists in the museum on Parnassus Heights, Alfred L. Kroeber and Thomas T. Waterman, who were engaged in recording the remnant languages and cultures to be gleaned from those Indians who had survived the Spanish-Mexican and Anglo-American conquests.

Waterman went to Oroville, confirmed his and Kroeber's surmise that the "wild man" was a Yahi Indian; Waterman was able to communicate with him in a limited word exchange by way of a vocabulary list he had brought from the museum, in a dialect fortunately related to the Indian's language. The Indian was, as were all Indians, a ward of the government; the Bureau of Indian Affairs in Washington would have resettled him on an Indian reservation. However, at Kroeber's request, the Bureau released him to the staff of the Museum of Art and Anthropology of the University of California. Thus it was Waterman who brought him to San Francisco and to the museum, where a room was set aside for him and other living arrangements were made.

Why was his name not the first information to be learned from him? The answer to the question lands one smack into the heart of California Indian protocol: a person was addressed or referred to by one or more identifying circumlocutionary titles or nicknames, the actual name carrying much power and magic and being altogether a most private and intimate part of one's self. Kroeber and Waterman knew this and refused to allow anyone to press the Yahi stranger to reveal his name to white strangers of whom he had known until now only that they were the murderers of his people. At Kroeber's suggestion, the Indian's nickname became "Ishi," and it is as Ishi that the world knows him—not an inappropriate name, since in Yahi it means man, a person, one of the People (the Yahi people).

Kroeber and Waterman soon determined that Ishi was in fact the last survivor of his Yahi people. A distinction between him and other last survivors of other California Indian peoples is that they were, however reluctantly, drawn early into participation with the white community. Ishi was the last California Indian—and so far as we know the last Indian in the United States, perhaps in North America—to have lived his whole life up to his capture without modification of his indigenous Stone Age culture, house, clothing, tools, food; all he did and how he did it, as well as his religion, his code, his social values, his judgments, remained within the ancestral Yahi specialization of the aboriginal pan-Californian life-pattern.

The Yahi were the southernmost of four tribelets whose village-states, as we would regard them, or worlds as the Indians regarded them, constituted the lands of the Yana people, whose individual boundaries were contiguous with one another and whose language was Yana, a subfamily of Hokan. The four shared almost but not quite identical customs, the significant variant being linguistic, each group speaking a separate dialect of Yana. A nicety of Ishi's people's speech was a subdialect spoken always by the women and by the men when speaking to or in the presence of women, but never between men alone. Yana-Yahi linguistic records do not make easy reading, but for readers who wish to consult them, the following by Edward Sapir are suggested: "The Position of Yana in the Hokan Stock," *University of California Publications in American Archaeology and Ethnology,* Vol. 13, No. 1 (1917); "Text Analyses of Three Yana Dialects," *ibid.,* Vol. 20, No. 15 (1923); and "Male and Female Forms of Speech," in St. W. J. Teeuwen, ed., *Donum Natalicum Schrijnen* (Utrecht, 1929), pp. 79-85.

Linguists and ethnographers agree that Hokan-speaking people were in all probability the earliest to have reached California, the evidence for this to be found by internal linguistic analysis (see M. Swadesh, "Time Depths in American Linguistic Groupings," *American Anthropologist,* vol. 56, pp. 361-364). Confirmatory of the linguistic evidence is the Yana arrow-release, which was unlike that of any other people in the New World, but was identical with that of the release of ancient China.

The Yana lands lay in the western foothills of Mount Lassen in interior California—rugged country, rocky and overlaid with a thick growth of chaparral. The Yahi homeland was intersected by two lively, full-flowing streams, Mill and Deer creeks, which had carved vertical canyons to a depth of more than a thousand feet. The Yahi villages of earth-covered houses were clustered along the creek banks and on the level ledges of the canyon walls, where caves offered temporary shelter and might be incorporated into a house as an extra room.

The forty-niners who approached the California border via Goose Lake and Klamath Lake crossed the border and reached the Sacramento Valley by way of the Lassen Trail, which skirted Mount Lassen to come out on the ridge between Mill and Deer creeks, thus cutting a bloody gash through the heart of the Yahi homeland. Over this trail came men on the final but unexpectedly rough and difficult lap of their crazed race to reach the "gold fields," leaving death, disruption, and disaster behind them. Whole peoples, languages, and cultures were wiped out in the wake of that first wave of the gold rush and the subsequent "settling" of California, then the Union's youngest state.

The Yana were raped, hanged, shot, scattered, sold into slavery or as indentured laborers; as a people, as a social entity, they ceased to exist. The

[2]

Yahi, whose lands were rougher and less readily accessible than those of the other Yana, fought back in a fierce, doomed effort to survive. They managed to live on, to keep to the Yahi way, but in ever-reduced numbers, until they were declared by the self-styled and locally designated and financed "Indian fighters" to have been wholly destroyed.

And so they were, except for a handful who retreated ever more deeply into their most remote caves and heaviest brush cover, where, for forty years, they maintained themselves on home ground, however shrunken in extent. Some forty of them, then thirty, then twelve or ten. Then four. And after 1908, one—Ishi the last Yahi.

The Documents

The number of documents having to do with Ishi is finite. For the reader who wishes to know something of the sources from which the story flows, there are reproduced here the principal out-of-print and most inaccessible primary materials on Ishi and the Yahi Indians.[1]

Of first importance are monographs on Ishi, his people, his languages, his medical history, whose authors are Professors Thomas T. Waterman, Alfred L. Kroeber, Edward Sapir, and Saxton T. Pope, M.D. Most of these monographs are here reprinted in full. Next in interest and importance are the books of reminiscences concerning the Yahi Indians written by white settlers in or adjacent to Yahi country in the years following closely upon the gold rush. These are usually in small editions, long out of print. Two, those written by Thankful Carson and R. A. Anderson, are reprinted in full; the others, only those parts having to do with Ishi and the Yahi. There are letters bearing on our subject, newspaper accounts, and pictures, of which we include significant examples.[2] There

are as well books and articles having to do only in part with Ishi and his people. We reprint only those parts.[3]

Beyond these essential primary materials, the editors made hard choices to keep the number of pages realistic. Readers with areas of special interest will regret some of our exclusions among the secondary but often fascinating accounts: of archaeological findings in the Yahi homeland; of linguistic quirks and grammatical technicalities—a large literature, difficult for the uninitiate; of medical history when it adds nothing to our understanding of the man Ishi.

Our order of presentation is chronological, beginning with the background materials, then going to Ishi's first entry into the outside world, then to his years at the museum, and, finally, to his death.

We have not included the occasional newspaper stories of still-living Yahi Indians supposed to have been seen or heard in the Yahi hills and caves after Ishi's departure, since none were ever substantiated. When in 1914 Ishi returned to his old home for a few weeks with Waterman, Kroeber, Pope, and Pope's son, Saxton, Jr., he found the land, the caves, and the village sites as he had left them.

But there was another sort of presence in Deer Creek canyon—or the possibility of a presence—of much concern to Ishi. You will recall the day—November 10, 1908—when a surveying party came upon and robbed the village of the four remaining

[3]

1. The material has been reset in modern type, but typographical errors and spelling idiosyncrasies have been left as they were in the original documents.

2. We have been quite selective in the number of pictures reproduced here. Illustrations within a particular document have been renumbered accordingly.

3. The documents appearing in this volume which are listed as well in the bibliography for *Ishi in Two Worlds* are from the old files and collections of monographs, articles, and pictures of the Department of Anthropology and the Bancroft Library, University of California, Berkeley. The documents not known to Theodora Kroeber at the time of her writing of the *Ishi* biography were collected by Robert F. Heizer. Max Knight, an editor with the University of California Press, tracked down and secured photocopies of the *Oroville Register* articles not drawn upon in the biography but here reproduced. Upon publication of this book, the source materials the editors have presented here go to the Bancroft Library Archives of the University of California, Berkeley, if not already on file there.

Yahi, and that two of them, the old man and the younger woman, fled over the ledge on which the village rested, into the canyon, and were never seen again. They are presumed to have met an early death, since Ishi found no least trace of them. Nor could his sick mother have long survived the fright of that day, the forced removal from her bed and her home, and the exposure, winter being upon them. Ishi could not perform the customary rites for the dead for the two lost ones, and it seems improbable that he could have done so for his mother, for crucial to these rites was prompt cremation of the body. By this act the soul was liberated, released to go directly to the trail leading westward, the Trail of the Dead, to follow it to the Land of the Dead, where family, friends, and a place at a campfire would be awaiting it. The soul of a dead person, lingering on in the Land of the Living, is in unhappy and lonely limbo and is dangerous particularly to living members of his own family. Added to the altogether fearful phantasmagoria of life for Ishi from November 10, 1908, to August 29, 1911, was the terrible uncertainty as to the fate of those three souls.

[4]

A Reminiscence

When Ishi returned to Deer Creek in 1914, he was well physically and vigorous mentally—he could now resolve the uncertainty. A reminiscence of Saxton Pope, Jr., who was twelve years old at the time of the trip, tells us that Ishi succeeded—we do not know precisely how:

The first night on Deer Creek, Saxton and Ishi spread their sleeping bags outside the circle of light from the campfire. Others of the party were close to the fire, and soon asleep. Awake, Saxton and Ishi talked, keeping their voices low. Ishi told Saxton something of his fears and that he meant not to sleep until he had searched the canyon. Saxton was to say nothing of his going—he would be back before sunrise. Barefoot, noiselessly, Ishi disappeared amongst the shadows, to return as noiselessly just before dawn. To say to Saxton, "It is good. None are lost. They found their way."[4]

Theodora Kroeber

4. Told to the author by Saxton Pope, Jr., after publication of *Ishi in Two Worlds.*

BEFORE ISHI

BEFORE ISHI

There was evidence that "wild" Indians still survived in 1911 in the unsettled and mountainous area of Tehama County. Who these people were, and what they were doing, was not an important matter to most whites, but it was of interest to a few anthropologists.

In the following accounts, recorded from 1850 to 1911, we are informed that Indians continued to occupy the Yahi area and live off the bounty of the land. Little or no effort was made to do anything for the remnants of these people, who were shunted aside in the gold rush and the following period of farming settlement and town-building. The Yahi area held little which whites really wanted, and as a result the few survivors managed to stay alive, though in decreasing numbers, well into the twentieth century.

While none of the documents for this period mention or identify the person Ishi, he was among them from about 1866 on, as a baby, a child, and a grown man. So, we read these generalized accounts of the "Mill Creeks" as records of the little Yahi nation of which Ishi was a member.

The accounts which immediately follow are variable in their credibility. We are not so much concerned here with attitudes of white residents about local Indians who were considered dangerous, or murderers, or thieves as much as we are about the cumulative effect these attitudes had on the difficulties of Indians attempting to survive in the native state. If Ishi had been shot and killed when he was fifteen years old there would be nothing known of him. His chance survival, and his rescue by anthropologists who welcomed and consulted him as a person from another and earlier world of California, is well known from the story told in *Ishi in Two Worlds*. Here was a real, alive, person of Native Californian ancestry from whom could be learned the true details of thought, culture, and language which were untouched by the influence of white culture which had dominated and influenced the native pattern since 1850. With Ishi, here was a true forest person, a man who lived by his bow and salmon spear, and who existed quite outside white civilization.

J. Goldsborough Bruff crossed the plains in 1849, leading a company of gold seekers. He was unwell, and not being able to carry his journals, notes, instruments, and collection of minerals, he decided to stay over the winter at his camp in the expectation that help would be sent from Lassen's Rancho, 32 miles away. He spent the winter and early spring months of 1849-50 near Black Rock on Mill Creek, within calling distance of one of the principal Yahi villages. Daily he saw the smoke of their fires as they of his. Despite this, he never really saw the Yahi, except for their fresh footprints and other traces. They never in any way troubled him, and the mutual discretion with which they must have kept each other in view— or just out of view—tells a good deal both about the Yahi and Bruff. He drew from the same food sources the Yahi used; he even made his many crossings and recrossings of Mill Creek using their fallen-log bridge.

Bruff is a fine reporter and artist. His is, as far as we know, the only circumstantial and straightforward journal of weather, daily activities, and the people and their behavior on the Lassen Trail of the time.

In April, 1850, barely alive from lack of food, Bruff managed to get to Lassen's, and on this last walk to help he makes a few observations about the Indians which are of interest to us because this is the first recorded mention of the Yahi.

1. Earliest Notices of the Yahi (1850)

April 8th [1850]. Thank God! 'tis day!—commences (sun rise) clear, wind light & variable, temp. 50°. Just before day-break I heard steps, on the road behind me, going up the hill, my pup barked furiously, but it was all black darkness, away from the fire, and imagining it to be only a skulking wolf, going up, on the road, I paid no attention to it. I had a good brush fire, and I knew the varmints would not approach it too close.

Last night I fixed my coffee pot under a rock, to catch water, and it was full. Put in about a gill of coffee and boiled it. Drank the fluid, and eat the solid, for breakfast. Hung my quilt to dry. The sun must have been 2 hour's high before I proceeded. On striking the road, I was astonished to see, on it, the fresh tracks of an indian. He was pidgeon-toed, and I judge small.—Ah, ha! he it was, that passed before day, whose steps I heard, and who set my dog barking!

Oh! if I can only over take him! then will I have one hearty meal! a good broil! I examined my caps, they were good. I felt relieved, it gave me additional strength; to think I might soon get a broil off an indian's leg! I could not but laugh, when I thought of it,—the expressions I have heard, how people would starve to death rather than eat human flesh! Fools! how little could they form an idea of the cravings of hunger! Let them be placed in my circumstances, and see how soon they would discard such silly ideas! My mouth fairly watered, for a piece of an indian to broil! And I continued to look out sharper for one, than for any other game. The road was slippery with mud, and full of small round stones.

From J. Goldsborough Bruff, *Gold Rush*, ed. by Georgia Willis Read and Ruth Gaines (New York: Columbia University Press, 1949), pp. 339, 342.

Having attained the summit & followed it some distance, slightly descending, but going over several slight rises in it, after which a regular descent. As I came along, was compelled to halt, and rest, at every thing on which I could also support my knapsack. Feet quite sore, shoulders very sore, and would fail altogether, but for the hope of shooting an indian, to eat. . . .

[April 9, 1850]. In a quarter mile more, I met a low square-built indian, very dark, and had slight mustache; he had just emerged from a deep gulch, on the left. He was nude, except a kind of fig-leaf, had a knife, a quiver full of arrows on his back, and a bow in his hand. He was accompanied by a small black indian dog. I spoke to him in Spanish, but he did not understand me. I then made signs that I was hungry—starving, and wanted something to eat, which he comprehended but gave me to understand he had nothing, and was on his way to Dry Creek, to shoot birds. My pup was following his dog, and I worried myself much to get her along; so glad was she to meet one of her own specie, I had to make signs to the indian to drive her back—beat her with his bow:—which he did.—While he was going off, I turned round, thought of eating him; he was then about 30 or 40 paces; but I could not shoot the poor wretch in the back: besides, he had done me a favor. So I proceeded. Could this have been a mountain indian?—the one I trailed, and wanted to eat? I dare say. I managed to get probably 2 miles farther, when I found the shrivelled carcass of an ox, on this I rested, looking to see if the indian visited my cache, but he kept lower down, crossing the road some distance this side of it. While I rested here, poor, little Nevada was gnawing and pulling about the hard withered remains I sat upon. Arose, and continued on the muddy, rough, winding road, till I at length reached and crossed 2 small branches, and a deep dry bed of another, and soon after enter[ed] the oak timber, of Deer Creek bottom. I knew now, that I was 3 miles probably, from Davis' rancho, and that it was situated down the creek, below where the ford is. I nerve myself to persevere, by constantly exclaiming, "I will soon have plenty to eat!—bread, and meat, coffee, and milk! a house to sleep in! and an end of my

[8]

sufferings!" Yes, yes, yes!—Saw a party of squaws, with large conical baskets on their backs, 2 men with them. I hailed them, the men came up, a dark wrinkled, and thin, old fellow, and a hearty-looking young man. I found they understood some Spanish; and asked for food. They pointed in two directions, telling me that Davis' was in that, and Lassen's in the other.—Hid from view by a forrest of oaks, &c. They gave me to understand, that they belonged to Lassen, had nothing to eat, and the squaws were going to dig roots. So I left them, and went on. Soon after reached the banks of Deer Creek, at the ford; now a raging flood, a perfect cataract, and deep. (The indians were armed with quivers of arrows & bows, and long knives.

From the same month, April, 1850, there is a newspaper notice of Indian-white difficulties on Deer Creek.

"We have been informed by a gentleman from Deer Creek, that one day last week, some 12 men, who had been soldiers in the Mexican War, attacked a party of Indians whom they accused of stealing animals, and killed 4 or 5 men and 1 squaw. The Indians, after running some time before their pursuers, turned round, seeing so few in chase, and the pursuer became the pursued, until they gained a stronghold in a rocky part of the mountain, where the Indians attacked them furiously, wounding, it is believed fatally, 2 of the whites, one in the shoulder and the other in the arm. The siege lasted 2 days, during which the Indians lost 17 men and 1 squaw, besides those before mentioned.

A man called Bill Ebben is the leader of the assailants. A party of 200 was organizing at Deer Creek, and were expecting to start in pursuit last Thursday morning."

The Army does not seem to have done very much about chastising the Yahi. Rock Creek, mentioned in the first two letters, actually lies

Sacramento Daily Transcript, April 5, 1850.

just south of Yahi country. Chico, mentioned in the correspondence, is also south of the Yahi area. These letters are typical of military reports of the times.

2. Army Correspondence on the Yana and Yahi (1862-1865)

State of California,
Executive Department,
Sacramento, June 27, 1862.
Brig. Gen. George Wright, U.S. Army,
*Commanding Department of the Pacific,
San Francisco, Cal.:*

General: Inclosed I send you a copy of a communication addressed to me by a committee appointed at a meeting of the citizens of Chico and vicinity, in Butte County, held on the 26th instant, in which representations are made of recent Indian outrages committed on Rock Creek, Butte Creek, and vicinity, and calling upon me for men and means, ammunition and arms, to assist them in quelling said outrages. Since receiving the communication I have learned through private sources entitled to credit that the bodies of the children referred to have been found brutally murdered. I would respectfully request that you forward to the scene of Indian depredations in Butte County one company of infantry to assist the citizens in effectually putting an end to Indian outrages. And I would also ask of you, if it is possible, to deliver to the State of California, under whatever arrangement you may think proper, 500 stand of arms, that I may enable the citizens of the different counties to protect themselves against these repeated Indian outrages, and at the same time relieve yourself from the frequent demands I am compelled to make upon you for assistance, as the State has not one stand at her command. This communication will be handed you by Dr. S. M. Sproul, a highly respectable citizen of Butte County, who will more fully explain affairs as they now exist in said county, and to whose statement I would earnestly call your attention.

From *The War of the Rebellion: Official Records of the Union and Confederate Armies*, Series 1, Vol. 50 (1897), Part I: pp. 408, 1162-1163; Part II: pp. 28, 122-123, 717, and 874-876.

[9]

I have the honor to be, very respectfully, your obedient servant,

Leland Stanford,
Governor.

[Inclosure.]
His Excellency Leland Stanford,
Governor of the State of California:

At a meeting of the citizens of Chico and vicinity, held June 26, 1862, to adopt measures for putting a stop to the depredations now being committed by the mountain Indians on Rock Creek, Butte Creek, and adjacent country, the undersigned were appointed a committee to petition Your Excellency for men and means, ammunition and arms, to assist our citizens in quelling these Indian outrages. Your petitioners would respectfully represent that said Indians have been robbing and killing our citizens, and for the protection of our lives and property we invoke Government aid. On the 25th instant one Thomas Allen, a teamster, was killed and scalped on the road from Stratton's Mill to Keefer's, his four mules shot, a valley Indian accompanying him also shot, but escaped. Three children, a boy and two girls, were gathering blackberries on Rock Creek, about six miles east of the Shasta road, where on searching for them their horses were found shot, but the children gone, leaving evidence of a struggle for escape. Portions of their dresses were found near the horses. These children are now doubtless in possession of the Indians. Parties are now in pursuit of them, but it is difficult to obtain arms and means enough to successfully pursue them. The committee has appointed Dr. S. M. Sproul to wait upon Your Excellency and more fully present our case.

J. S. Henning, *Chairman,*
E. B. Pond,
Geo. West,
S. M. Sproul,
H. H. Johnson,

Committee.

Headquarters
Department of the Pacific,
San Francisco, Cal., July 18, 1862.
Capt. H. B. Mellen,
Second Cavalry California Vols.,
Comdg. Fort Crook, Cal.:

Sir: The department commander has directed Capt. David B. Akey's company of cavalry to proceed to Red Bluffs, on the Sacramento River, for the purpose of operating against a band of Indians which has recently made incursions into the northeastern part of Tehama County, in this State. It is not known to what tribe these Indians belong, except that they are not of the tribe residing at Big Meadows, in the northwestern part of Plumas County. The latter are represented as very friendly, and in the expedition hereinafter directed the general desires you to afford them the necessary protection, not only from hostile bands of Indians, but unauthorized organizations of white men. Captain Akey will be instructed to inform you of his arrival at Red Bluffs, on the receipt of which the general desires you to proceed in the direction of the recent disturbances and act as far as possible in concert with Captain Akey against the parties who committed the outrages in Tehama County. In the interval you will inform yourself regarding the country through which you will have to pass, and gain any other information that may be useful in executing the duties assigned you. You will leave at Fort Crook one commissioned officer and five men to guard the post.

Very respectfully, your obedient servant,

Richd. C. Drum,
Assistant Adjutant-General.

Headquarters
Department of the Pacific,
San Francisco, Cal., September 15, 1862.
Capt. Henry B. Mellen,
Second Cavalry California Volunteers,
Red Bluffs, Cal.:

Sir: In reply to your letter of the 11th instant, I am instructed by the department commander to

[10]

inform you that your command will remain in the field, operating against the hostile Indians in Tehama and adjoining counties, until the objects of the expedition are accomplished, *i. e.,* the punishment of the Indians and the re-establishment of quiet and security in that quarter.

Very respectfully, your obedient servant,

R. C. Drum,
Assistant Adjutant-General.

Headquarters
Department of the Pacific,
San Francisco, Cal., January 5, 1864.
Capt. A. W. Starr,
Second Cav. California Vols.,
Comdg. Camp Bidwell, Chico, Cal.:

Sir: It is apprehended that an attack may be made by the Indians living on Mill Creek, in Tehama County, in this State, and as these are the most troublesome Indians in the country controlled by your troops, the general commanding desires you, if possible, to get hold of the leading men among them and send them to Alcatraz Island for confinement.

Very respectfully, your obedient servant,

R. C. Drum,
Assistant Adjutant-General.

Headquarters Provost Guard,
San Francisco, Cal., June 24, 1864.
Col. R. C. Drum,
Asst. Adjt. Gen., Dept. of the Pacific,
San Francisco, Cal.:

Colonel: I have the honor to report that in obedience to Special Orders, No. 132, dated headquarters Department of the Pacific, June 17, 1864, I proceeded to Chico, Butte County, Cal., and examined into the causes of the rumored and apprehended Indian troubles in that section. These apprehensions are embodied in a letter from George Wood, of the firm of Bidwell & Co., addressed to the Hon. O. C. Pratt, of San Francisco, said letter bearing date of June 11, 1864. I have conversed with many parties in relation to the

matter set forth in the letter of Mr. Wood, and from what I could learn I find that his statement is mainly correct, though perhaps somewhat exaggerated. To throw some further light upon the state of affairs at Chico and in the surrounding section of country, I add the following brief statement of facts and conclusions at which I arrived from my conversation with different parties: General Bidwell, Mr. Durham, and one or two others have for a long time past employed, subsisted, and kept under their control and charge a certain number of Indians. These Indians have always lived in that section of the country, and were upon the land, in the cultivation of which they now assist, before it came into the possession of the present owners. They are therefore in a degree civilized and somewhat domesticated, being distinguished from others of their race by the name of Valley Indians. It appears that some farmers and other persons who do not make use of the Indians in the cultivation of the land, look with more or less jealousy upon those who employ such labor, believing that it brings with it such advantages that to compete with it is impossible. This is therefore one of the causes of jealousy which exists against the Valley Indians, and one reason why some desire their removal to the reservation. Other parties may and probably do have other reasons for wishing their removal. Indeed, I may state that the removal of the Valley Indians to the reservation would give satisfaction to all parties. And again, as is always the case on the borders of civilization where Indians are found, there occurs annually to a greater or less extent Indian robberies and depredations committed by a few wandering, irresponsible, and bad Indians. Such is the case in a section of country about Chico. It is supposed by many, or at least they pretend to believe, that when these thefts and robberies are committed that the Valley Indians are cognizant of the matter, and are in some way connected with the guilty parties. This, therefore, is another cause of jealousy against the Valley Indians, and often the spirit of revenge leads to the murder of the innocent for the crimes of the guilty. It is the old repeated story, and of

[11]

necessity often yet to be repeated. Last year, as stated in the letter of Mr. Wood, an organized party of reckless white men came to Chico and killed several of the Valley Indians, supposing them connected with the parties who had committed depredations in the foot-hills some twenty or thirty miles from Chico. This year some robberies have been committed by a few Indians in the foot-hills, and it is feared that another party of white men will be organized, and that the Valley Indians will be driven off or murdered and that property at Chico may be destroyed. Those persons who employ the Valley Indians have such fears strongly impressed upon their minds, and perhaps their fears are well founded. It is for the protection of the Valley Indians and for the protection of property at Chico that troops are asked for in Mr. Wood's letter. Chico is a thriving and prosperous small country town. There is an organized volunteer company composed of its citizens now in existence. This company will appear under arms on the 4th of July. The civil law is in full force, and parties who infringe can be prosecuted and punished. It certainly seems apparent that the citizens can protect themselves and their property against any such party as was organized last year. Of what use is the civil law if the citizens do not learn to look to it for security and for protection? The U.S. soldiers in a town like Chico should be the last and only resort. It is stated in the letter of Mr. Wood that one man had been murdered by the Indians. This is by no means certain. Indeed, I am of the opinion that the majority of persons think that this man was murdered by white men for the money which he is said to have carried on his person. Taking all things into consideration, I cannot think that there is an immediate necessity for troops at Chico. It would do no harm to send troops on a short campaign through that section of country, and such a course might result in some good. I am of the opinion that no party of white men will attempt to destroy property at Chico, and that the Valley Indians can be protected, at least for a time, by those who have them in charge, should any party attempt to molest them. In my conversation with Mr. Wood I think I persuaded him

[12]

to believe that the necessity was not immediate. I think Mr. Wood and all the other parties directly interested will be perfectly satisfied if they can be assured that they can rely upon troops being sent when the necessity arises.

I have the honor to be, colonel, your obedient servant,

Jas. Van Voast,
Captain, Ninth Infantry, Provost-Marshal.

Camp Bidwell, Cal.,
April 24, 1865.

Lieut. E. D. Waite,
Actg. Asst. Adjt. Gen., District of California,
Sacramento, Cal.

Sir: I have the honor to report to the general commanding the District of California that on the 5th instant I left this camp with thirty-five men of Company I, Second Cavalry California Volunteers, en route for Pine, Deer, Mill, and Antelope Creeks for the purpose of arresting the Indians that have been committing depredations in the vicinity of those creeks. After arriving at Deer Creek I sent a detachment of fifteen men under the command of a sergeant to scout in the neighborhood of Deer and Mill Creeks, employing Mr. Hi Good (a citizen) as a guide to accompany them. At the same time I continued on to Antelope Creek with ten men, leaving ten men on Deer Creek to be sent to either party if required, and to guard the horses for the first-named party at Antelope Creek. I employed Mr. William Morgan (a citizen) as a guide to go with me on the mountains near Antelope and Dry Creeks and north of Mill Creek, some thirty-five miles north of this post. After remaining in that section, scouting the country over night and day up to the 15th instant, when I received notice of the assassination of Lieutenant Levergood, at this post, I returned to this camp, leaving the men as I had distributed them, with a sergeant in command of each detachment, until the 18th instant, when I called them in. While I was out I found a great many signs of Indians, which convinced me that the Indians were in that section gathering food of different kinds; but the country being very mountainous and covered with underbrush

I was not able to see them; at the same time they could observe every move that I made from their hiding places. I traveled several nights trying to find them by their fires without success, except once they were discovered about 8 o'clock at night by the guide and one man, who immediately returned to the detachment and gave the information, but before they got the Indians surrounded they had evacuated their position. On the 15th one of the detachment secured a horse that the Indians had left in the hurried flight and brought the same to camp, which was turned over to the quartermaster. I have no doubt but the animal was stolen from some of the settlers in that neighborhood. Becoming convinced that the Indians had scattered in different directions, I deemed it necessary to order the men to camp until the Indians would collect together, when I would send a detachment out after them again.

I have the honor to be, sir, very respectfully, your obedient servant,

J. C. Doughty,
Captain, Second California Cavalry,
Commanding Post.

The nature of Indian-white relations in Tehama County in the early 1860's can be gained from the five brief newspaper articles reprinted here from the Red Bluff Semi-weekly Independent. *Exactly what Indian tribe or tribes were involved is unclear; they may have been the northernmost Maidu, who lived immediately south of the Yahi on Rock Creek, or the Yahi themselves, or the Southern Yana.*

---

3. Newspaper Accounts of Fighting with the Yahi (1862)

July 1:

The cruel murders perpetrated at Rock Creek last week, has created a general feeling of indigna-

Red Bluff (Calif.) *Semi-weekly Independent,* July 1, July 4, August 8, and August 19, 1862.

tion among our citizens, and the general expression is, that the prowling savages must be effectually wiped out. We have received a letter from J. W. Lemons, of Deer Creek, giving the particulars of the sad affair, a portion of which has been heretofore published. From this letter we learn that the Indians, after killing and scalping Thomas Allen, and wounding the Indian boy, attacked a party of young people, out blackberrying in Rock Creek Cañon, and captured Miss Ida Heacock, aged 17 years, her sister, aged 13, and a brother aged 10. A party who went in pursuit of the Indians found the bodies of the two girls, pierced with arrows and scalped, and stripped of their clothing. The boy has not yet been found. Men all along the valley are turning out in pursuit of the murderous savages. Dr. S. M. Sproule, of Chico, has gone below for arms and ammunition, and assistance. There should be a general turnout from all sections, and every Indian exterminated that can be found in the mountains east of us. No person is safe along this valley as long as the savages are permitted to prowl around unmolested. It was only last spring that Mr. Meador was chased by Indians near Antelope, and the only way to deal with the rascals is to shoot them down upon sight.

July 4:

News came from the east side of the river, on Tuesday afternoon, that 150 Indians, painted and with heads shaved, were in the vicinity of Dye's Mill, prepared for war. The news was accompanied with the Macedonian cry, "Come over and help us!" Several citizens, this hombre among the rest, armed and equipped as the law directs, and bent upon obtaining numerous Indian scalps, responded to the call, went over to Antelope, scoured the country, but didn't get sight of an Indian, nor obtain a scalp. The alarm grew out of the breaking up of an Indian camp some 4 miles from the mill, by L. V. Loomis and 9 others, scattering the Indians, burning their camp, with all their accoutrements, and finding the clothing of the two girls that were so barbarously murdered on Rock Creek, also the boy's shoes. The red devils left in a hurry, though nearly 150 strong, on the approach of the white party, taking to the hills. . . .

[13]

August 8:

Captain Harmon Good, with his company of volunteer scouts, numbering 15 men, who have been out on the trail for some two weeks, hunting Indians, on Sunday last came upon a big Indian packing beef to the Indian camp. One of the men "drew a bead" on the red skin and shot him through. This was on Big Antelope, some 15 or 20 miles east of Red Bluff. There were supposed to be some 200 Indians in the camp, who made off, the band dividing into two companies. The scouts under Capt. Good made off in an opposite direction, for the purpose of deceiving the Indians, which ruse succeeded. Near night the party retraced their steps, found the trail of the Indians and followed it up. After reaching the vicinity, where they supposed the Indians would camp, a halt was made, and Capt. Good made a reconnoisance alone, creeping on his hands and knees, and before he was aware of it, found himself almost in the midst of the Indians, the crying of a papoose giving him the alarm. He retraced his steps as he had come, and ordered his men to surround the camp and wait for daylight before commencing the attack. At break of day several "bucks" started out to hunt for game, and coming suddenly upon Capt. Good's men, were shot. This opened the battle, and a continuous fire was poured into the Indian camp, resulting in the killing of 17, which were found dead on the fields. Six were known to be wounded, and the rest made their escape. A number of children were captured, and in the camp was found guns, ammunition, provisions and clothing. One long Kentucky rifle was found, also guns bearing the mark of the Overland Mail Company. Captain Good and company have returned for supplies, having procured which, they will again start on the trail. . . .

[14]

The Red Bluff Independent, *August 19, publishes two letters from George W. Kelley: the first, dated Deer Creek, August 15, 1862, states that on the "13th inst., 2 days after Good's command left here, the mountain Indians visited this ranch in force."*

The second letter from Kelley dated Sunday, August 17, is as follows: "Capt. Good has just arrived at our ranch with 21 Indian prisoners, captured on Mill Creek. His party will not tell how many they killed. Good's company lost 3 horses, killed in the fight, but no men. He does not know what to do with these women and children—if they were 'bucks' they would be no trouble to him. The camp was taken while the bucks were down here on their late raid."

While it is allowable to have some reservations about the glowing report of Adjutant-General Kibbe which follows, it is probably true that his expedition did kill many innocent Indians in late 1859.

Kibbe's report is remarkably undetailed about where his troops were in action, and why the expedition cost $69,000—a large sum to be charged to the state treasury in 1860, as Governor Downey pointed out. Among the areas they "cleared of Indians" was, presumably, the Mill Creek and Deer Creek zone where the Yahi lived. But the real story, if we accept Chapter VIII of Anderson's recollections, Fighting the Mill Creeks, *which appears below, may have been rather different.*

4. Adjutant-General Kibbe's Report (1860)

*Report of the Expedition
against the Indians in the
Northern Part of this State*

MESSAGE

State of California, Executive Department,
Sacramento, January 18th, 1860.
To the Honorable the Assembly of the State of California:

I herewith transmit, for the consideration of your Honorable Body, the report of the Adjutant-General Kibbe, with other documents, relating to the late expedition commanded by him, in suppressing Indian hostilities in Tehama, and ad-

---

Report of the Expedition Against the Indians in the Northern Part of This State (Sacramento: State Printer, 1860?).

joining counties, the aggregate expenses of which, according to the report, amount to the sum of sixty-nine thousand four hundred and sixty-eight dollars and forty-three cents.

While I admit the necessity which led to this expedition, and freely acknowledge the eminent services rendered by the officers and men composing the command, the expenses, so large in amount, would seem to demand a rigid scrutiny.

If it be intended to pay these expenses by direct appropriation of money, a few such will bankrupt the State Treasury. I recommend that the whole subject be referred to a committee, with power to send for persons and papers, with a view to a thorough investigation.

We have now a full treasury, and are enabled to pay all immediate demands upon it in cash. If these appropriations are continued, according to the precedent established at the last session of the Legislature, instead of being able to reduce taxation, as recommended by one of immediate predecessors, we will have to fall back on the old scrip basis, which proved so ruinous to the interests of the State.

Expenses of this nature are legally chargeable to the General Government, and it would seem advisable to issue bonds as evidence of indebtedness against the State, instead of a direct appropriation of money.

John G. Downey,
Governor

REPORT

Office Quartermaster and Adjutant-General,
Sacramento, California, January 16, 1860.
To His Excellency,
John G. Downey,
Governor of California:
Sir:—I have the honor to report, that in obedience to the orders of one of your Excellency's immediate predecessors, issued on the second of August, A.D. 1859, I proceeded to Tehama County, and on the sixteenth of the same month, organized a company of volunteers, with which I at once took the field in pursuit of those Indians, whose frequent hostilities had given rise to the necessity

for such an expedition. The depredations were chiefly confined to the white population of that tract of country extending from Butte Creek on the south, to the head of Pitt River on the north, embracing an extent of more than one hundred miles square, with rugged and lofty mountians, precipitous defiles, hidden valleys, and secure fastnesses intervening, to which they retreated for security, after having made a sudden and succesful foray; driving off the stock, destroying the improvements, and not unfrequently murdering in cold blood the defenseless inhabitants of that sparsely settled region. Indeed, in the tract of country designated, these Indians have recently had almost exclusive occupancy and control, numbering, as they did, from fifteen hundred to two thousand souls in their collected tribes or bands; they became insolent, because they believed themselves formidable, and capable of defending their strongholds against whatever force might be sent against them. This self-confidence was inspired by the inaccessible nature of the country which they inhabited, the great success which had heretofore attended their frequent depredations; the facility with which they always eluded the search of the regular troops and small parties of volunteer citizens; the latter hastily collected together from the surrounding population for mutual defense and protection, and whose limited supply of arms, munitions, and provisions, rendered it impossible for them to pursue and properly chastise an enemy as powerful as he was watchful and ingenious. On the contrary, the Indians were well-armed—after their peculiar style of warfare— seemed to be amply supplied with provisions—had a correct topographical knowledge of the country, and were exceedingly expert in the exchange of telegraphic signals, by which, communication was kept up between distant portions of the same tribe; the approach and number of an invading foe discovered; the direction of their march indicated, and such important facts ascertained as to enable them to make good their escape; and thus for a long period of time to avoid that severe punishment which their numerous outrages had richly merited. During the last four years, between

[15]

thirty and forty persons were killed by these Indians. They had set fire to, and consumed, entire fields of grain and grass, besides pillaging, and afterwards burning, the houses and cabins of the settlers.

Several expeditions, numbering respectively from fifteen to thirty men, although fitted out with an express view to take summary vengeance in their object; and even at the time when the troops under my command took the field, so bold had the Indians become, that they were extending their exploits, rapine, and murder—even into the immediate neighborhood of the camp of the regular troops—from whom, they appeared to entertain not the slightest apprehension of arrest or punishment. Knowing these facts, and having succeeded in collecting together as brave and effective a company of officers and men as any country could produce, most of them experienced mountaineers and Indian hunters, I entered at once upon the duty, heretofore found so very difficult, of penetrating to the very haunts of the savages, with a view to conquer, and if possible, rid the country forever of their presence.

The command was divided into three detachments, under charge, respectively, of Capt. Byrnes and Lieutenants Bailey and Shull. These separate detachments were directed to approach and enter the Indian country at different points. The plan of moving upon, and attacking, the rancheries of the Indians at night, I had learned by experience, was the best and only one calculated to be attended with happy results. Notwithstanding the great hazard of this mode of warfare, it was willingly and cheerfully acquiesced in by officers and men, who at once entered upon the duty assigned them—penetrating into every river valley, creek, cañon, and gulch; clambering rugged mountain sides; threading their way amid interminable forests of timber; wading through marshes; over swollen streams; encountering snows; surmounting jagged rocks—in fact, exposing themselves to all kinds of danger and fatigue, with a courage of endurance which cannot be too highly approved and commended.

It seems almost incredible that a body of ninety men, operating in different detachments, over so wide a space of broken and difficult country, could accomplish so much as those under my command have done, in so short a time. As fast as a particular locality was cleared of Indians, a detachment was left for a limited period, instructed to scout continually, with the view of discovering and preventing any attempt at return. In every instance the object designed by this precautionary measure was effectually secured. From time to time small parties of Indians were captured, until the southern portion of the country operated in contained not a warrior to offer resistance. The intermediate section was next visited, and the Indians occupying it, after several severe skirmishes, compelled to flee for safety to the country occupied by the Pitt River and Hat Creek Indians, with whom they were intimately connected, and where they doubtless felt themselves secure from further pursuit. In the meantime Callahan, McElroy, Wells, and others, had been murdered by them.

The Pitt River and Hat Creek country was regarded by the Indians as impregnable. There was a fastness here from which those who defended it had never been driven. Many attempts at dislodgment were made by bands of citizen soldiers and the regular troops. None of these proved successful. At, or near, this point I succeeded, after seven or eight days of hard scouting, in capturing two Indians. My intention being to obtain an interview with the principal chief, make known to him the object of the expedition, (which was not to kill if the Indians surrender,) to propose the terms of such surrender, and, if possible, ascertain the motive which actuated him and his people in their hostile proceedings. The desired interview was had, and resulted favorably to my expectations. The principal chief promised, with his whole tribe, to meet me the next day and proceed at once to one of the reservations. The consequences of a failure to comply with his promise were fully represented to him, notwithstanding which his pledge was broken.

Two nights afterward I attacked the Indian stronghold with forty men, completely routing those who defended it, killing several of their number and taking others prisoners; those who escaped were pursued. A number of engagements subsequently occurred with them, in which a great number were killed and captured.

After a vigorous pursuit of five weeks this chief sent in eight of his tribe, who said they had fought long enough, and that they desired to become reconciled to, and accept, the terms proposed to them. They came in to the number of four hundred and fifty, and were received in a spirit of kindness. To revert to all the different skirmishes and scouts which took place would occupy too much space for my present purpose. Although justice to the gallant volunteers might seem to demand that this data should be given; suffice it to say, that the enemy were routed from every position, whether taken to elude their pursuers or for the purpose of defense, and were finally compelled unconditionally to surrender. Out of the whole number of Indians fought about two hundred warriors were killed, and twelve hundred taken prisoners. No children were killed, and but one women, during the whole campaign. As an evidence of the intrepid bravery of these Indians I would state that on one occasion some fifteen or twenty of their warriors ensconced themselves in an almost inaccessible cañon among rocks, and dared an equal number of my command to fight them. The challenge was at once accepted, and the engagement commenced. It continued for upwards of an hour, by which time all of the enemy were killed, excepting one, who effected his escape. Not a man of the volunteers was killed, and but two wounded. During this fight, as in all the others, an interpreter was present, who called upon the Indians to surrender, with the understanding that they were to be kindly dealt with; but they refused to accept the conditions proffered.

It gives me pleasure to be able to report to your Excellency that this war has been brought to a successful termination. The tribes of Indians engaged in it, whose frequent acts of violence and atrocity had rendered them a terror to the region of country over which they roamed, are completely vanquished and subdued.

A permanent peace I hope has been secured, a peace which was conquered and which has for its tenure a much more enduring and reliable basis than the mere forms of treaty stipulations, too often misunderstood by the wily savages, and, when understood, as frequently violated to suit their own designs and convenience. Twelve hundred of these Indians were captured, and are at the present time comfortably provided for at one of the government reservations, where by good conduct and a moderate degree of industry, it is hoped the blessings of civilized life may forever be secured to them and their posterity.

There is reason for gratulation, when the immediate benefits resulting from a conclusion of this war are considered, and its remoter favorable influences should also be taken into the account. It is a salutary lesson to the tribes occupying territory contiguous to the scene of action, which they will not be likely soon to forget. It has taught them the certainty of the punishment which must sooner or later overtake them, for their hostile visitations upon the persons and property of the whites; the irrevocable nature of the destiny which awaits them in their uncivilized condition; how utterly unable they are to cope with the great nation of people who are daily taking possession of the soil, and converting it from a wilderness into vineyards and fields of waving grain; the immense superiority of this people in numbers, energy, and intelligence; the fatal and unerring precision of their improved implements of warfare; their sleepless vigilance in pursuit of a foe; their stealthy movements, both by night and day, even upon an Indian trail; their indomitable bravery in battle; their exalted magnanimity in exempting women and children from slaughter; in fine, it has taught them, that by laying down their arms and submitting to the terms proposed by the whites—who must eventually become their conquerors, if not their destroyers—their condition is greatly improved; and the alternative offered, if not precisely in accordance with their natural tastes and habits, is at least calculated to secure their comfortable nourishment and protection, with the superadded probability of elevating them in the scale of moral and intellectual greatness. I am happy in being able to bear testimony to the

[17]

prompt, skillful, and fearless manner, in which the officers and men under my command, separately and collectively, discharged the dangerous, arduous, and responsible duties devolving upon them. Captain Byrnes was an experienced and accomplished Indian fighter, with courage and discretion equal to every emergency. I was particularly fortunate in having his support at the head of one of the detachments throughout the entire campaign. I was also ably sustained by Lieuts. Bailey, Shull, McCarty, and Longley. Between these highly capable and efficient officers, it would be injustice to discriminate. There was no exposure, no peril, which each and all were not willing cheerfully to encounter—no service from which they shrank. At all hours of the day and night, with the brave men under their command, they were ready either for a march, a skirmish, or a battle, and never, for a single instant, did they falter in the hour of trial, whether on a difficult and dangerous pursuit, fording swollen streams, wading to their waist through snows, encountering chaparrel swamps, overcoming broken declivities, penetrating secret defiles, struggling among jagged and crumbling rocks, or encountering the enemy in a hand-to-hand conflict.

These gallant soldiers deserve well of the State. They volunteered in her service, not with the hope of pecuniary gain—that idea is forestalled by the paltry amount offered for their services—but because a demand was made upon their patriotism, to which they instantly and cheerfully responded, forsaking their profitable avocations, and in many instances, their comfortable homes, to undertake the trials, hardships, and hazards, of an Indian campaign. Having nobly and satisfactorily performed their duties, and ended the war in a manner which promises to be of lasting benefit to the State, it gives me pleasure to commend them to the generous consideration of the present Legislature.

In this connection of praise, the Surgeon of my command, Dr. A. W. Taliaferro, deserves to be especially noticed. Under all circumstances, and at all times, requiring the exercise of his skill, he was found to be more than equal to the delicate and responsible duties of his profession. His efforts were in every case, attended with eminent success, which is, perhaps, the highest compliment that could be paid to his acknowledged scientific talents and attainments.

The expedition was singularly fortunate in its exemption from casualties. Not a single life was lost, and the wounded all recovered.

The Commissary Department was under the management of S. D. Johns, who was found to be a very efficient officer, and who, by the practice of a rigid economy, kept down the expenses of that branch of the expedition, to the lowest possible figure, besides rendering valuable and effective service in the field.

The expenses of the expedition will be found to be exceedingly moderate, when all the circumstances are considered and compared with similar expeditions, heretofore called out on this coast, extremely low. They are therefore submitted to your Excellency and the Legislature, in the full belief that they will prove entirely satisfactory.

Every article of supply purchased, however, was procured with the understanding that the State would promptly pay the bills, which fact, it is hoped your Excellency will not fail to make known, with a view of having a sufficient appropriation passed for their liquidation.

The aggregate expenses of the expedition, exclusive of the pay of men, is fifty-eight thousand four hundred and fifty-eight dollars, from which, is to be deducted, for clothing and articles stopped against the pay of the men, the sum of eight thousand nine hundred and eighty-nine dollars and fifty-seven cents, which leaves forty-nine thousand four hundred and sixty-eight dollars and forty-three cents, ($49,468.43) as the total expense incurred, exclusive of the pay of the men. The amount of their pay, using the schedule adopted by the act making the appropriation for the expedition in Humboldt and Klamath counties, A.D. 1858-9, called into service under similar auspices, would amount in round numbers to twenty thousand dollars, ($20,000) and leave as the total expense of the expedition the sum of sixty-nine thousand four hundred and sixty-eight dollars and forty-three cents, ($69,468.43).*

It will be ascertained, upon consulting the vouchers on file in my office, and should be borne in mind, that nearly one-fourth of this whole amount of the expenses was incurred in the subsistence and transportation of Indian prisoners captured by the command. These prisoners numbered over twelve hundred, and were transported a distance of from two hundred and fifty to seven hundred miles, the cost of which was fourteen thousand and thirty dollars and forty-five cents.

This campaign has been accomplished in the brief period of four months, which, when the smallness of the force employed, the wide and difficult nature of the country explored, and the success attending the expedition are considered, must be regarded as a result which none but accomplished mountaineers and brave soldiers could accomplish.

The region traversed, is probably the roughest, and most difficult for a white man to traverse of any on the Pacific coast, and affords the best and greatest number of hiding places for the Indians. It is not only mountainous, rugged, precipitous, and broken, but is also interspersed with hundreds of valleys and lakes, in which head the numerous streams emptying into the Sacramento River, from Butte Creek to Pitt River. These valleys produce the finest qualities of grass, sufficient to sustain, annually, at least one hundred thousand head of stock, and will, I predict, be rapidly settled by our enterprising citizens.

Some twenty-five families of this year's immigration, have already taken up claims in these valleys. And this is the country which has been hitherto almost exclusively occupied by Indians, through which runs the great thoroughfare from the Sacramento Valley, to the extreme north, and over which millions of dollars worth of merchandize is annually transported; from a statement of which facts, the importance, utility, and necessity, of the expedition can, I trust, be readily comprehended by citizens of all portions of the State.

It affords me pleasure to state, also, that the citizens, generally, residing near the field of operations have co-operated with the expedition.

Respectfully submitted.
I have the honor to be,
Your ob't servant,

Wm. C. Kibbe,
Q.M. and Adj. Gen., State of Cal.,
Comd'g Expedition.

In the 1850's and '60's the Deer Creek and Mill Creek Indians, as the Yahi were then called, were repeatedly attacked. In Sauber's story, we have a participant's account of events on an Indian hunt in 1859.

The Tehama County whites were fearful of the Indians, but did not bother to think about why the latter should be aggressive. The Indians' lands had been taken from them and they were hard put to survive. That is why they robbed cabins, and after so many of them had been killed they retaliated when and where they could. A struggle that could only in the end lead to the extermination of the Indians had been set in motion.

---

5. Hi Good and the "Mill Creeks" (1859)

H. H. Sauber

In January, 1859, I was visiting at the home of my Uncle George, who lived in Tehama county, close to where the immense Stanford vineyard is now located. I had been anxious to come to California for five years past, and shall never

Overland Monthly, Vol. 30 (1897), pp. 122-127.

*A special committee appointed by the State Assembly examined Kibbe's list of claims for supplies and pay for the "Kibbe Rangers." The committee recommended a reduction of $9,000 in the amount to be paid to him. The committee members agreed that rebellious Indians had to be chastised, but protested against the large annual drains on the state treasury (*Journal of the House of Assembly of California,* 11th session [Sacramento, Calif., 1860], pp. 415-423). The recommendation for the reduction was passed by the Assembly (p. 455).—Ed.

forget with what keen delight I first beheld the grand valley of the Sacramento, bordered on the west by the blue and rugged Coast range, and on the east by that king of Western ranges, the Sierra Nevada.

The feverish, almost insane spirit which had torn asunder Eastern homes, and brought men and boys streaming over the plains and across the Isthmus, to hurl them pell mell into the mines in one blind rush for gold, had abated ere this, giving place to a more tempered spirit of speculation. General John Bidwell, the pioneer ranchman, had made the discovery that fortunes lay ready for the busy hand no less in the broad, rich valley lands, than in the gold-bearing quartz of the mountains, and had demonstrated to the world that one American at least valued a home above the fluctuating chances of attaining untold wealth. My uncle, like not a few others, had taken early advantage of General Bidwell's success, and at the time of my arrival, was living on Deer creek, farming several hundred acres of rich bottom land, and running a large band of cattle in the foothills.

[20]

I was but twenty-two, and soon fell in with the new ways and new work, and before a month had passed, had taken first lessons in plowing with an eight-mule team, harrowing, ranch blacksmithing, riding after cattle, and a dozen more vocations which one finds on a California grain and cattle ranch. It was all delightful, and my two cousins, Henry and Tom, soon became my closest friends.

But I soon found that all was not tranquillity where everyone seemed so happy and prosperous. Over those new Western homes, fast taking on the air of their Eastern progenitors, a black cloud hung which kept many hearts in constant trepidation. There was one name that drove the bloom from the cheek of matron or maid, caused little children to creep terrified into mother's arms, and sent a pallor even to the sunburnt face of the hardy father, and that was the name "Mill Creeks."

From some place, perhaps from half a dozen of the Indian bands of Northern California, parties of renegades had drifted into the dark, wild cañon of Mill creek, a cañon to this day as little known as any of equal magnitude in the United States, where they lived almost entirely secure from pursuit. From the fastnesses of this mountain gorge they made raid after raid upon the settlers of the valley, robbing, plundering, murdering.

Once they murdered three school children within ten miles of Oroville, and more than forty miles from Mill creek. Soon after, they killed a teamster and two cowboys in one afternoon, and were clear away and scudding through the hills loaded down with stolen beef, before anyone guessed that they had been out. Other victims, too numerous to mention, had fallen by their ruthless hands. In short they never robbed without murdering, even when the latter crime could aid them in no earthly way, in fact could only more inflame the whites against them.

On the face of this dark cloud of danger, which seemed never to blow entirely away, there was, especially for those living in my uncle's neighborhood, one spot of brightness, in the form of a man whose whole life seemed devoted to the destruction of the renegades and the protection of the helpless. This was Hi Good—the Boone of the Sierra. I found out nothing of his early history, whence he came, or why he erected his rude cabin in that particular spot. Suffice to know he had fought single-handed against the heartless Mill Creeks, passing unscathed through a score of desperate encounters, in which, strange to say, he was usually the aggressor. Living alone on Dry creek, within two miles of the black gorge which discharged the sullen waters of Mill creek into the broad valley, he towered like a lone, but trusty sentinel. Thrilling tales were told of his wonderful prowess, of his almost incredible success, and of the strings of black-haired scalps that adorned his house. In short the Mill Creeks were no more a terror to the whites, than was Hi Good a terror to them.

I longed to see this celebrated man, but failed to do so for several months after my arrival, although his cabin was less than six miles from my uncle's place. My desire was realized, however, before summer by reason of a startling event which set all the horrors of Indian slaughter vividly before my mind.

It was on a raw March morning, and I had set out with Cousin Tom for a deer hunt in the hills. We rode briskly up Deer creek in the biting air, manfully resisting the temptation to let drive at the bevies of quail cuddled up in the morning sun, or the wide-eyed jack rabbits that started up at our approach, only to squat stupidly among the brown rocks within easy range, as though astounded at the early interruption.

A forty minutes' ride brought us to the mouth of Deer creek's cañon. We were chilled to the bone, but soon thawed out upon reaching a long, sunny ridge, up which our mustangs toiled toward the rough ravines, belted by chaparral thickets in which we hoped to find game.

By nine o'clock we were afoot in the heart of a splendid deer country, having left our horses at the top of the first great ascent of the foothills. I was alone, Tom being below me on the hillside, when with a clip! and a chug! a spike buck sprang into view, trotted a few steps, and stopped short. My heart throbbed; for it was my first glimpse of a wild deer, and my unsteady aim would doubtless have proven of no avail. But I did not shoot. Just as my finger trembled on the trigger the lithe form bounded forward like a rubber ball, and I lowered my rifle in disappointment. Then a sharp report rang out on my left, and the bluish body disappeared. I hurried forward, wondering whether the animal was really struck, and soon found it gasping on its side, shot through the neck. Just as I reached it a deep voice spoke out close at hand:

"Saw you wasn't going to get him, young fellow, so I downed him as he made for the ridge. Spike buck ain't it?"

The bushes rattled beside me, and in an instant a tall, dark, wiry-looking man strode forward, and unceremoniously drew a keen-edged knife across the deer's throat.

"Stopping on Deer creek?" queried he without looking up, as he carefully wiped his knife on the dead animal's side.

I told him who I was, and frankly admitted that I had never killed a buck; for someway his keen eyes seemed to read me through and through, without, however, being in the least curious or

unkind. One glance at his swarthy yet handsome face called for another; and I fairly thrilled with admiration on noting his sinewy form, straight as an arrow.

"Wish he had kept on in your sight, and given you a chance at him," he went on so earnestly that it won my heart completely. "But you must take half the meat. I can't use more than half, and besides have a long tramp to make in the hills before I go home."

I thought of refusing, but there was something so impressive in his calm tones that I could not but accept. In a few minutes we had divided the carcass, whereupon he bade me a cheery good day and disappeared.

In less than an hour I was with Tom, who had killed a two point farther up the ridge. We were loading the animal on his horse, preparatory to our return, when a ragged boy of twelve or fourteen came clattering up on a vicious-looking pony. His face was freckled and dirty and pinched with cold, yet a ghostly pallor seemed to glare through the dirt and freckles.

"Better be gettin' out 'n the hills," he gasped abruptly, halting his horse by jerking on a rope looped over the animal's nose.

"What is it, kid?" asked Tom, looking up with interest.

"Mill Creeks is out," replied the boy, glancing nervously over his shoulder.

"Mill Creeks!" we cried in alarm, letting the half-raised body of the deer tumble unnoticed to the ground.

"Yep," replied our informant with chattering teeth. "Pap 'nd I jes found a dead feller down this side of Singer creek,—he lit out fer home so 's to stan by Ma 'nd the kids, 'nd tol me to tell you fellers, 'nd fer one of you to ride like h—l over to Dry creek 'nd tell Hi Good."

"Who is the dead man?" asked Tom anxiously.

"Don't know—wuz lying on his face 'nd I was afeard to turn him over, or tech him."

There was no thought in our minds now of carrying home the venison. We threw aside even the half which the stranger had given me, and mounting, hastily set off down the ridges toward

Singer creek, since it was not far out of our homeward course to where the murdered man lay. I was keenly excited and not entirely at ease, for if the renegades had slipped into the valley during the night they might still be in the hills, and the prospect of suddenly meeting them was not an alluring one. Thoughts of the tall stranger kept flitting through my mind as we spurred ahead, and a sort of presentiment seemed to tell me that he was the murdered man. My active imagination had converted this possibility into a positive fact ere we reached the scene of the tragedy. I held back aghast, while Tom overturned the lifeless form, only to start forward with a sharp exclamation as I beheld the rigid features of Dan, one of my uncle's riders, who had left the house but a few minutes ahead of us that morning.

"Three arrows, and a bullet in the neck," said Tom, bitterly, quickly examining the body. "Hasn't been dead more than three hours. Shot from behind, of course, the cowardly cusses! By gosh, Bill, they've sneaked down this morning and can't be far off now!"

"What can we do?" I asked, not a little alarmed.

"Rouse the country," cried Tom in reply, as he sprang to his horse's side. "You and the kid carry Dan down to McCartney's camp on Singer. I'm off to bring Hi Good."

And without another word he vaulted into his saddle, and galloped wildly away toward Dry creek.

The remainder of that day was a memorable one for me. I carried the murdered man to McCartney's camp, and remained with the body during the remainder of the day. The country had been alarmed, and during the afternoon nearly twenty cowboys and ranchmen gathered at the cattle camp. One man had seen a party in the hills south of Singer creek about eight o'clock, and concluded now that they must have been Indians. It was unanimously understood that no advance should be made until Hi Good arrived to take up the trail.

Hour after hour dragged along, and the sun had sunk in a bank of dark clouds which hung heavily over the crest of the distant Coast range, leaving a cold, murky twilight behind, when I was suddenly startled by the sound of a deep, familiar voice outside the cabin.

"Hi Good's come," whispered the cook as he bustled about his stove. Then the door opened, and the tall stranger whom I had met that morning in the hills, stepped quickly into the room, and to the side of the body. He examined the wounds carefully, but in perfect silence, and then walked out of the house and began questioning the man closely to ascertain just where and when he had seen the party that he supposed were Indians, having already found out where Dan had been killed from Tom.

A respectful silence pervaded the group of rough men, while Good was speaking, and as he ceased his questioning, and glanced anxiously off to the dense mass of clouds in the southern sky, I noticed them edging closer to his side, as though anxious to hear his next words. He gave another troubled glance at the scudding clouds, and said:—

"If we had one hour of daylight I could give you the direction of the trail, but this darkness is too much for human sight. If it don't rain till morning,"—and his sharp eyes once more sought the gloomy heavens,—"If it holds off till morning we are all right, but this wind is mighty discouraging."

"It'll rain afore mornin', sure as guns," said a grizzled old settler gloomily.

"Then we have but one chance of heading them before they strike Mill creek," replied Good in a thoughtful manner. "There's a slim chance that we can beat them to Grapevine, providing they went as far down as Pine creek before taking to the hills, but it'll take some hard night riding to do it."

"We're here for business, Captain, and is ready to foller when you says the word," put in a fierce-looking cattle man bluntly, and this seemed to be the general sentiment.

"Then get into your blankets, and be quick about it," said the Captain shortly. "If it should n't rain, the trail is our surest way,—for ground sign don't lie, but a very little water will spoil a good mark this time of the year, and the Mill Creeks never leave an easy trail at its best. Sleep hard, for out you come at the first drop, as our only chance then will be Grapevine pass. If the storm does hold off, the sign won't run away, and a good night's sleep will help us."

The men were not slow to follow the Captain's advice. Some lay down on the two extra bunks in the cabin; others went into the low barn; while four or five, Good among them, spread some quilts and saddle-blankets under the roof of a low woodshed which leaned against the kitchen, and sought such rest as could be found there; for all hands knew that there would be no child's play, once Hi Good struck the trail of the renegades.

I was too much excited to sleep, and therefore promised to sit by the body of Dan until the party set out, at which time I determined to accompany them at all hazards. After sitting alone for about an hour, conjuring up in my disturbed imagination all sorts of dismal pictures, I arose and stepped outside to drive away the stupor, which was beginning to overpower me, by a few draughts of cold air. All was quiet excepting the weird whistling of the wind, which seemed to be increasing, and the heavy breathing of the men in the shed. Just as I was about to turn back, a glimmer of light attracted my attention from the corner of the kitchen. Stepping forward, surprised, I stopped short on beholding the tall, erect form of Captain Good standing in the cold, night air. He was tinkering with his rifle by the light of a dim lantern, having evidently not taken a moment's sleep. Yet his black eyes were fairly dancing with impatience for action, the fierce and bloody encounters he had waged against the redskins only making him thirst for more. As I stood rooted to the spot, admiring, yet almost awed by the workings of his dark, stern visage, the first gust of the coming storm splashed against my face, and with the first pattering drops upon the shed's roof, Good turned with a gleam of pleasure shooting across his features, stepped away from the building, and took one long look at the black sky, then turning hastily, began rousing the sleeping men.

"We must move at once." I heard him say in reply to a sleepy grumble. "In five minutes the tracks will be as dead as a hammer, and there's only one chance in fifty of our beating them to Grapevine. But"—with a grim smile—"we'll give the cusses a trial."

In fifteen minutes we were mounted and off, the rain beating down in cold, steady drops that soaked and chilled us before we had ridden two miles over the dark, rocky plain. O, the gloom, the fatigue, the discomfort, of that wild night ride! Our canvas coats were soaked through and through, became stiff with cold, and were soaked again. The wind howled in our backs, as it shrouded the drenched earth in a mass of gloomy clouds, so dense that inky darkness pervaded the air, making it necessary for each rider to cling close to the dim form of the one ahead of him, in order to keep the line unbroken. In the midst of the darkness, the desolation, and the wild, cold storm, Hi Good spurred on, on, on, like a weird phantom, never stopping, never speaking, except to urge us to greater effort, plunging into cañons, through dripping thickets, across wind-swept ridges, as though possessed of supernatural sight which revealed to him every inch of the scarred and ragged wilderness.

Skirting the foot of the hills for about five miles, we plunged into Deer creek's swollen tide, crossing, not without peril, at the only ford within miles of our desired course, the Captain's unerring instinct— I know not what else to call it—leading us directly to the spot in spite of the darkness, and the heavy belt of timber which fringed the stream.

Climbing a steep pitch beyond, we traveled a short mile around the base of the hill, and stumbled, rather than climbed, down a precipitous shoulder of the mountain into Acorn hollow, at a place where one of our party at a later day met a most tragic death. Thence veering off into the hills up Dry creek, we struggled grimly through cañon and gorge, and up gigantic ridges, over which the storm whistled dismally, benumbing our stiff limbs and driving the pelting rain, now half sleet, through our sodden clothes.

I was half dead with exhaustion as we started up a long, wide ravine, its width being revealed to us by the increased fury of the storm against our right sides. My right hand comrade set his teeth hard through a plug of tobacco, and muttered with an oath.

"Twenty-mile hollow, 'nd five miles yet to Grapevine."

I could have sunk from my saddle, and been content to lie among the cold, hard rocks, letting the others ride on, and verily believe I should have done so but that my companions were ever at my elbow on either side. Any change, it seemed to me, would be a welcome relief from that constant jar, jar, jar, of my stiff and jaded mustang. I almost hated Good as I heard his calm, deep tones sweep through the blast from the darkness ahead.

"Touch 'em up, fellows! Touch 'em up! A Mill Creek travels by night the same as by day."

On and on we struggled, our poor steeds gasping frightfully and puffing great volumes of moisture from their quivering nostrils, which warmed us not a little. A long, a painful, and as it seemed to me, a final effort took us up a steep hillside, and brought us out upon the very backbone of a sharp ridge, where the storm appeared to have massed its forces in one desperate effort to hurl us over the crags and cliffs. We were in the old Lassen trail now, (though I did not know it until long afterward), and close at hand on our left yawned the black, wild, unfathomed cañon of sullen and dangerous Mill creek.

"One mile ahead and Grapevine gouges a good chunk out of this here ridge, 'nd that 's where Hi expects the Injuns to sneak inter Mill creek," said my grizzled neighbor by way of explanation.

One mile! Was it possible this horrible torture was to end? I was ready to give thanks then and there.

At last, just as the gloomy sky over the wilderness of mountains to the east began to take on the cold gray hue of dawn, I perceived those ahead of me coming to a halt. Then the stalwart form of our Captain loomed up as he returned, dismounted, toward us. A sound of low, hoarse commands followed, whereupon the tired riders threw their spurred heels over their horses' backs and came heavily to the ground. I dismounted and staggered with weariness as my feet touched the damp earth. Leaving our horses under guard in a sheltering clump of Digger pines, we plunged down a steep incline through a dense thicket of chaparral, manzanita, and scrub oak. Emerging in a moment into a small opening, we came to a halt on beholding Captain Good standing in the ghostly light, holding up a long arm for silence.

"Now look to your rifles," he whispered, when all were gathered close about him. "See that your first shot is not a snap, and for God's sake don't let off a gun too soon!"

He then gave directions as to how we would be placed in the thicket's edge, which a few hundred feet below us formed a semicircle around the head of the hollow, and told us that he would fire from about the center of the thicket as a signal for the rest of us. This of course was in case we had really beaten the Indians to the particular pass they had chosen for their retreat.

I was asleep in three minutes after sinking down on my post in the wet brush, but was soon awakened by a guarded exclamation from one of my comrades. Starting up, I perceived that it was light enough for me to make out indistinctly objects in the open ground before me.

"Injuns sure," whispered a voice at my side, and I heard the guarded click of a rifle lock. Then came a slight rattling in the brush, as another of my companions carefully altered his position. Where were Indians? I was wild with excitement; for not a living thing could I make out, although my eyes were strained nearly to bursting. Another gun lock clicked, and still I could see nothing to cause these hostile demonstrations. Turning in despair to seek an explanation from someone, I saw a man a short distance away on my right cautiously thrusting his rifle through a straggling bush, its muzzle pointing quarteringly up the ravine. Turning my head quickly, I trembled with excitement on beholding a dark form stalk out of the very head of the hollow, and advance straight for the center of the surrounding brush belt. Then came another, and another, filing into sight not more than two hundred feet away. The leader passed from sight behind a large oak. Then, Crash! a sharp rifle report roared through the hollow, followed in a second, by a wild, fierce, exultant shout from the center of the pass.

"Now, boys, let em have it," shouted some one not far away, and then Bang! Bang! Bang! the angry reports echoed around the little circle of brush, while the deadly bullets fairly screamed toward the center of the ravine.

I fired wildly into the hollow, and then with a shout sprang from my cover, and dashed pell-mell down the hill in the general charge, occasionally catching a glimpse of a swift flying figure here and there in the scattered brush before me.

Shouting, yelling, swearing, the fierce whites swept swiftly down the ravine, which deepened and widened as we advanced. I ran nearly a mile, repeatedly firing a shot at some scudding form, and was in full chase of a tall half-naked savage, who suddenly plunged into a narrow gorge and disappeared. I veered to the right and ran along the hill, expecting him to emerge into sight farther down.

"Look out, boy, he 'll double," shouted a voice behind me, and looking back, I saw Hi Good spring recklessly from a perilous height and crash out of sight into the head of the gorge.

A shriek, as of some wild beast, burst upon the air, followed by a fierce execration from Good; and then with a swish and a thud a copper-colored body shot violently through vines and shrubs and fell at full length upon the rocks above the gorge.

I sprang hastily forward, but shrank back in horror a second later, upon beholding the quivering body of the Indian, his head nearly severed from his body. In a moment the brawny victor clambered into view, coolly wiping his reeking knife on a bunch of grass, plucked from the side of the bank.

"Guess that dog 'll quit murdering," he chuckled, with a fierce laugh, glancing at his fallen foe; then turning, he started on down the ravine with long strides.

I saw no more of the fleeing renegades, and soon sat down on a rock to regain my breath. A few more shots were fired, after which a careful search through the brush and in the head of the hollow revealed twelve dead Indians, and two so badly wounded that they died within an hour. There could not have been more than four or five who escaped. Thus had the Mill Creeks once more suffered a bloody defeat through the sagacity, the perseverance, the ferocity, of Hi Good.

This is a firsthand, factual narrative of a child captured by a party of Indians believed to be Mill Creeks (Yahi), although if so they were far south of their own territory. The account gives a very real sense of the terror white settlers felt of the Yahi. Writing late in life, Thankful Carson recalls the events that occurred when she was nine years old. She was a courageous and resourceful child, but she may well have been permitted to escape by the old Indian who was guarding her. He was lame, causing him and Thankful to fall behind the others. He was also old, and his heart may not have been in this effort to kidnap a child.

6. Captured by the Mill Creek Indians (1863)

A. Thankful Carson

Chapter I

In the year 1853, December 2d, I was born at Salem, Missouri, and in the following Spring, the month of April, with my parents, Samuel and Mary Ann Lewis, and one brother James, who was then two years old, we started across the plains with ox teams for California. The late Joe Miller, the father of the late Wendell Miller, and the Williams family, together with other immigrants who crossed with us.

That same year we landed in Oroville, Butte County, then a very small settlement, consisting of but a few houses, the majority of which were mining huts. We camped on the hill just above where the town stands today, making it our temporary quarters. After looking around my father finally located in the Berry Canyon on Little Dry Creek, twelve miles north-east of Oroville, and about the same distance from Chico.

Chapter II

In those days the Indians were very hostile to the white settlers; very many and repeated depredations

A. Thankful Carson, *Captured by the Mill Creek Indians* (Chico?, Calif., 1915).

[25]

were made. I will relate a few instances: A boy about twelve years old was killed in a most barbarous way; they cut off his fingers, cut out his tongue, and were supposed to have buried him alive, but when he was found he was dead. On another occasion a man by the name of Hayes was out herding sheep. Some time during the day he went to his cabin and found it surrounded by fifteen Indians. They saw him coming; he turned and ran, but the Indians followed shooting arrows at him as he went from tree to tree. Finally they shot him with a gun through the arm. He managed to escape capture by a narrow margin.

Another incident happened about eight miles from our home. The Moody family lived in the Moody Canyon opposite the old Matthew place. One day Mrs. Moody noticed the horses in the field acting very funny. She wondered what could be the matter, so ran up stairs, to see if she could see anything. She did. Coming across the fields came a band of Indians, fifteen to twenty in number, making their way towards the house. Horrified, she ran down stairs, picked up her two children, left the house without being noticed, and fled to the valley over rocks and brush. On their return afterwards they found that the house had been robbed of all the provisions, and everything in sight broken and trampled upon. These depredations all happened about the time I was captured with my two brothers.

Chapter III

I come now to our capture by the Mill Creek Indians, in the month of July, 1863. My father was harvesting; the grain in those days was not threshed like it is today. The bundles were placed on the ground in a circle and horses driven around over them, until all the grain was out. Then it was gathered up and placed in a fanning mill to be cleaned.

My two brothers, Jimmy, aged eleven, Johnny aged six, and myself, then nine years old, went to school about three miles from home on the Cherokee road. The school-house stood about three hundred yards from Little Dry Creek in the middle of a beautiful oak grove, and my grandmother

lived just a short distance from it. Johnny did not go to school very often as he was rather young, but this particular day he wished to go with us. After school was out, about four o'clock in the afternoon, with our teacher and the Noble girls, we started for home and stopped on the way at grandmother's to get a drink of water. We then walked on together close to the Littlefield Creek where we parted from our schoolmates and went on towards our home. The Noble girls lived on the Littlefield Place, and our teacher, who was Elizabeth Swena afterwards Mrs. Wookey, now dead, was staying there at that time.

We had gone about two miles and a half talking to each other and eating what was left of our luncheon. On the way Johnny wanted a drink, so all three of us went over to Little Dry Creek about one hundred yards from the road, and stopped down at the edge of the water to drink. All was quiet, not a sound could be heard, and no one was in sight. Johnny had finished drinking and stood back a little from Jimmy and I, who were still drinking at the creek. Presently out of the quietude I heard a shot and turned to find that Jimmy was shot in the back and pitched forward into the water. Four Indians appeared and began to throw rocks and boulders at him, as he lay in the creek, to make sure that he was dead. Johnny and I stood by looking on and trembling with fear. The Indians had hidden themselves behind a tall grape vine that grew up along side of the creek bank.

Mother heard the shot that killed Jimmy, but thought it was some hunters, our home being only half a mile from the scene.

Six other Indians joined them, one of whom had one big foot and one small foot, and was called the Big Foot Indian. He had the name of being a bad Indian. Two others had their heads all tarred and were terrible to look at. The Big Foot wore Jimmy's hat. I could tell it by the string which he wore under his chin. It was made from calico and had a small red flower for the pattern. I did not notice him wearing it until we had gone on a short distance.

One Indian took me by the arm, and another lead Johnny close behind, and as we left the valley and went up the mountain side, I looked down and could see my home. I asked the Indians to let me go home, but they said "No, we are going to take you to our home, your home no more." I was barefooted and so was Johnny. We traveled up hill and down hill in a northerly direction until dusk, when we sat down and rested. The Indians asked me "if my father would follow them," to which I replied "that he would." Then one of them said "Boys we had better be going on." They could speak good English.

We traveled until late that night and over rocks and brush, they would drag us by the arms and hit us in our sides with their guns to hurry us along, until we were terribly bruised. Little Johnny would say, "Sister, I am suffering, they are hurting me." We often spoke to each other of father and mother, and wondered if we would ever see them again.

Chapter IV

We crossed the Hamlin Canyon and from there trudged on until we reached the Neal Road. John Leonard, the father of Raymond Leonard and an old friend of my parents came along the road in a wagon. At that time I did not know who it was, but it was known afterwards. It was a moonlight night, and two Indians took me and brother Johnny back in the brush from the road and placed their hands roughly over my mouth, almost smothered me to keep me from crying out. The other Indians sat under the shade of a tree close to the road as if they meant to kill Mr. Leonard, but did not harm him.

After he passed by we all crossed the Neal Road. They made me walk on my tip toes, and to force me to walk that way an Indian hit me with his gun. Johnny they carried across the dusty road. I suppose that was done so we could not be tracked. Down the hill we went to Nance Canyon, and in Nance Creek which was dry, we camped right in the bed with trees shading us. I sat flat on the rocks, Johhny lay on my lap and I covered him with my dress. One Indian lay by the side of me, and the rest slept all around. At times they would call out to me "Are you asleep?" "Go to sleep."

Mrs. A. Thankful Carson

[27]

We stayed there the rest of the night, I never closed my eyes, and not a quarter of a mile away we could hear Mr. Nance's dog barking. We left Nance Canyon early in the morning before daylight, and made our way up the hill. Johnny began to cry and could hardly walk, and when we commenced to fret, then it was that the Indians made up their minds to get rid of him. They talked together in their own tongue for a while and I knew they were plotting to do us harm. I was expecting them to kill us every minute. When we got to the ridge four Indians took Johnny back into the woods and the rest went on with me. On parting brother said "Goodbye Sister," and I answered him "Goodbye." As I went on he told me to wait and I told him that I couldn't. Then I asked the Indians if I could go back and kiss him, but they said "No" and jabbed me with their guns to go on. In a short time the four Indians again joined us and I said to them "What did you do with Johnny?" They said "He is all right. We have left him back there." I said "No, you have killed him, I know you have," but they still denied it. I was confident at the time that he was killed.

On the way through the hills we stopped at some manzanita bushes. The Indians ate some of the berries, and told me to eat some, but I refused. They offered me bread and lumps of white sugar which I could not accept for fear of being poisoned. All the time I was with them I did not eat anything, but drank a little water. While we were at the manzanita bush I saw one of the Indians with some of Johnny's clothes and one was wearing his little cap. Then I was positive that they had killed him, and I told them again that they had killed him, and still they answered "that they had not."

They said they were going to put sticks around me and burn me up; make me a living torch when they got to their camp; dance and have a good time over me. They took a stick and gagged me with it, to show me how they were going to torture me. I kept up my spirits as well as I could and when they talked of burning me up I said "No you won't burn me, what do you want to burn me for?" They tore my dress in strips from the bottom up, and set it a fire with matches, but I kept putting it out as best I could. This was early in the morning soon after Johnny was killed.

One Indian left the rest while we were at the manzanita bush, told them all "Goodbye," and came to the valley. He was not a Mill Creek Indian,

but was supposed to have been one from the Rancheria.

Chapter V

We traveled on across the hills and canyons keeping to the foothills as near as we could until we came to the Spanish Ranch. As near as I can remember we crossed it above the old mill and crossed the mill ditch just above the Groves place on Butte Creek, about five miles from Chico. My feet were so sore I could hardly wade the creek. After we crossed Butte Creek we made our way towards the hills which lie directly east of Chico, and rested for a little while under the shade of a tree. I saw a faint wagon track and asked them "to let me go for I could hear a rooster crow and it was not for to some one's house." They said "No, you can't go." I said "Let us pull straws, and if I get the longest one will you let me go?" They laughed and said "Yes." So I fixed some straws, we each chose one, and I was lucky enough to get the longest one. Then I said, "Will you let me go?" and they answered "No." I begged them, "Oh, please let me go." Then they said "All right," and they let me go about one hundred yards down the road, and then called me back. At the same time they all raised their guns to shoot me. I told them not to shoot, I would come back. So I ran back to them.

Then we went on up the hill and over towards Little Chico Creek. We stopped on the edge of a bluff overlooking the water. In the distance we saw a boy on horseback, ride into the creek and we could hear him whistling. The Indians took aim at him but did not shoot, as the horse scampered through the brush like lightning. Tom Bunnel was the boy, and is a close neighbor of mine now.

Chapter VI

We crossed Little Chico Creek and Humboldt Road making our way to the hills. Between Little and Big Chico Creeks, part of the Indians rounded up some cattle and shot a steer, while four of them rested on the hillside with me. They all took a part in skinning the beef and cut it up in quarters. They took the hide and made themselves moccasins, placed them on their feet and tied them over their toes. They wanted to make me a pair but I would not accept them, as I was afraid they would cut off my feet.

I had a pair of gold ear rings which I wore. Two Indians wanted them and caught hold of my ears to tear them out. I said "Don't, I will give them to you," so I took them out and gave one to each Indian. Then they became incensed at each other for both wanted the two ear rings and commenced to fight. One had a knife and followed me around, threatening to kill me. The Indians loaded themselves with the beef and we journeyed on until we came to Big Chico Creek just above the Thomasson old home. I sat on the bank with one Indian who was lame. We talked together and I asked him who hurt him and he told me that a white man shot him through the leg. The beef and guns were laid on the bank and the rest went in swimming, washed themselves, and had a big time in the water. After a while they came out, some on the opposite side and the others on the side where I was. We then crossed over, walked around an old brush fence and on up the hill. I was very weary and began to cry. The weather was very warm and I had walked over rocks and brush with my bare feet, up hill and down hill since before daylight, and now it was getting close to noon.

Chapter VII

Somehow or other one lone Indian was left behind with me and the others had gone on ahead. I began to lag behind. I began to beg him to let me rest, and then I would travel better with him. This Indian was heavily loaded with the meat and had two guns, and as we walked up the hill we came to a big rock. I said to him, "You take the beef and the guns up to the other Indians and let me rest on this rock, and then I will travel good with you, like I always had." He said "All right, but if you move from this rock I will kill you," and he spoke very savagely to scare me. I sat on the edge of the rock and as he moved away, I crouched down behind it. He went a short

distance and stopped to see if I was still there. I raised my head above the rock and he pointed his gun at me as if to shoot. I told him not to shoot, and slipped back to the edge of the rock. He then walked on and disappeared into the woods. I was watching him and waiting for an opportunity to escape. When I thought my way was clear I rolled over and over from the rock into a ravine then got up and ran back towards Big Chico Creek for over a mile, passed by an old cabin, and ran through thistles with my bare feet and out of the path so the Indians could not trace me. As I hurried along I heard some one talking and instantly thought it was the Indians coming after me. I made for the Creek bank and crawled under some driftwood that was hidden by bushes, and lay there trembling with fear of being recaptured. They passed along the path by me within a hundred yards from where I lay hid, but finding no trace of me they retraced their steps, again passed by me and went on their way. When I could not hear them talking and thought they were ont of sight I crawled out of my hiding place and waded the creek, which was pretty deep and swift for a little girl like I was. Footsore and weary at first I thought it impossible to cross, but would rather drown than be taken again by the Indians.

I succeeded in crossing safely, and ran for about a mile and a half across fields without a sign of a house until I came to Mrs. Thomasson's place. On the way I heard a rooster crow, and my spirits revived for I knew I was not far from some one's home. A little further on I saw two men working in a field, it was a little after noon, for there were evidences that they had eaten dinner. One was Nath Thomasson, now passed away. How joyful I felt when I saw them, and I waved my hand to them. When they saw me in the distance, one said, "There is a little Indian Squaw coming." Mr. Thomasson said "No, that is a white child and I am going to meet her."

He came on to meet me, picked me up and carried me close to the house, then set me down and went to get a melon from the garden. Mrs. Thomasson came out to the gate to meet me. I had on my old shaker bonnet, my dress was torn and my feet were both sore and bleeding. "Oh, child where have you come from?" she exclaimed. I told her that I had just got away from the Indians. She took me into the house and said "What is your name, little girl?" and I told her "Arenia Thankful Lewis." She then said "No, isn't your name Rothrock, little girl?" I told her that Lewis was my right name.

Then she took me in her arms, washed and greased my feet and picked out all the sticks and briers, and dressed me in her dead little girl's clothes. Then she gave me something to eat, and laid me down to rest, sat by me and talked to me. The men all came in to see me. The news spread all over the country that I had escaped from the Indians and all the settlers around flocked in to see me.

Chapter VIII

In the meantime father and mother were getting uneasy about us children and looked for our return from school that first evening. They thought we had stayed with grandmother, as we did not return. My parents also believed that mother's sister, our Aunt Nancy had come up from Marysville on a visit, and would be over with grandmother the next day for dinner. Mother gathered corn and prepared the dinner. No one came, and not a word from us children. Mother became very uneasy and said to father, "You had better go and see about the children." Father saddled his horse and went out to find us. As he went down the road about a mile he passed by Mr. Ackley's, a neighbor, who said, "What seems to be the matter, Sam, you are riding out in the heat of the day?" Father answered, "My children did not come home last night and I am going to see what is the matter."

He was then on his way to grandmother's. Mr. Ackley then said, "Why, your children passed here yesterday before sundown." Father cried "Oh, my God, my children are all killed by the Indians." He then rode on to grandmother's at the Littlefield place to break the news to her, also if possible to gather up a posse to trail the Indians whom they supposed had captured us.

At home mother was penning the sheep, and when she saw father riding at full gallop, with his hat in his hand, she knew something had happened to us, and went out to meet him. He said to her, "Our children are all gone, taken by the Indians." How they were overwhelmed with grief and sorrow is left for imagination.

A young man by the name of Burke, whose home was near to my parents, was teaming from Oroville to Chico, and while at the latter place got word that the little girl had gotten away from the Indians and Jimmy was lying dead in the creek in Berry Canyon just above the Berry house, and carried the news to father and mother.

Chapter IX

That evening a posse started from Mrs. Thomasson's home, and took the back track, the way I had come. In the posse were Nath Thomasson, Mrs. Thomasson's brother-in-law, John Barham, the father of Buck Barham, John Bruce, William Boness and George Winders, all of whom are now dead. There were also Sim Moak and Tom Miner and others whose names I do not remember. I rode behind Mr. Thomasson on a pillow, and he sometimes placed me on front when he thought I was tired, and we went all through the hills. We traveled back to the rock where I got away, again crossed Big Chico Creek and went on southward to where the Indians killed the beef, looked and listened, thinking little Johnny was left alive some place in the hills.

On our way we saw some Indians we supposed were the same ones we were looking for, climbing the cliffs beyond us. They had taken the back track for a short distance thinking I had gone back the way we came, and were going in a different direction altogether from what they first intended. The posse was not prepared to attack them, and I was so afraid of being taken again that I begged them to take me home, and not to bother the Indians. We searched until late that afternoon and went back to Mrs. Thomasson's home and stayed there that night.

I told them if they would go back to where Jimmy was killed in the creek I could trace the

spot to where Johnny was left. The next morning I sat behind Mr. Thomasson on a pillow, and the posse rode back to my home on Dry Creek.

My mother and grandmother had found Jimmy's body before the news reached them from Chico, and we met my parents and neighbors bringing him to be buried over in Clear Creek graveyard over five miles from our home.

What a rejoicing there was when I saw father and mother, and how glad they were to have me back alive. We all turned back and went with them to the funeral. After it was over the crowd went back as far as grandmother's house which was about two miles from the grave yard, and stayed there that night.

Mother never went back to our old home in the canyon, but lived afterwards not far from my grandmother's, which was nearer to the valley.

The next morning the posse, my father with them and I behind Mr. Thomasson, who would not listen at any time to any plans made by the men, but to my directions, for he thought I was the one to know, took the trail back to Little Dry Creek where Jimmy was shot. When we saw a sign Mr. Thomasson would call out, "Here are the tracks, my little girl is right." Back again we went, over the Berry Hills to Hamlin Canyon, on across to Nance Canyon, and up to the Ridge. "Now," I said, "you may look for Johnny, for he is not far from here." The men all scattered in different directions, and soon found him. He was stripped naked, thrown into a manzanita bush and killed with rocks. His skull was broken, and his body was black and swollen from being exposed to the hot sun for two days and a half. Father sat down and cried bitterly. Some of the men guarded the corpse while the rest went back to Mr. Nance's place in the canyon. They took the best boards from the barn, planed them and made a very neat little coffin. Mrs. Nance gave them sheets and they wrapped him carefully in them, and laid him in the coffin as well as they could.

It was night; he was placed in a buggy and my father and I drove back with him along the Cherokee Road to grandmother's home, ate supper and rested there that night.

[31]

This picture of Mrs. Thomasson and I was taken on the very spot where I came to after my escape from the Indians in 1863, fifty-one years ago. It is calculated that I traveled from eighteen to twenty miles going back and forth that day from school and then on through the hills to Mrs. Thomasson's home the next day.

The next morning the neighbors all joined us and went on to where Jimmy was buried and there laid little Johnny.

For a long time afterwards I was deathly afraid of Indians, much more so than when I was with them. If dogs barked in the night I would quake in fear of them coming.

All the time I was with them I told them I would not run away. I would stay with them and mind them, but I was always on the watch for an opportunity to get away. I did not appear to be much afraid of them. I would run down hills with them, and even took a pin and pinned up the shirt sleeve of one of them which was badly torn, and did many little acts that gave them confidence in me. Some people think that was why they did not kill me.

It is claimed that I am the only living person ever captured by Indians and got away, in the State of California.

Chapter X

[32]

In conclusion may I state that I am now living on the corner of Wisconsin and Davis streets, Chapmantown, Chico, and my age is sixty-one years. I was married three times. My first husband was John Bidsworth, the father of William Bidsworth, who died many years ago. My second husband, Jerome Winders, the father of Emma E. and George W. Winders, also died. George H. Carson is my present husband.

People have often asked me if Thankful was given to me after I got away from the Indians. That was not so. It was given to me at my birth.

Mrs. Thomasson who cared for me is now living on Humboldt Avenue. She and I together had our pictures taken on November 9th, 1914, at her old home on the very spot where I came to her fifty-one years ago. She came across the plains to California in the month of March, 1854, one month before my parents came.

Great numbers of Indians, among them Big Foot, were captured and killed not long afterwards. My father, with a posse, came to Chico and killed two who were known to be bad ones, right in front of the present Salem Street School House. near the large oak tree still standing there. It was claimed one was a Mill Creek Indian, and the other one was from the Rancheria. As my father raised his gun to shoot, several shot at the same time.

After our capture by the Indians, the farmers and ranchers became more vigilant and were better organized for the suppression of these acts of cruelty by Indians.

This, the only true account and the first ever written by me.

Robert A. Anderson, author of Fighting the Mill Creeks, *came as a very young man to the Oroville area in 1857. His friend Sim Moak's description of Anderson (below) sufficiently indicates, when stripped of its adulatory excess, that Anderson was indeed a hero of his time and place—the Indian Fighter par excellence. He became sheriff and was the principal figure in the final extermination of the Yahi peoples. His own account, presumably written when he was seventy or thereabouts, is firsthand, candid, clear. It is reprinted in full here.*

Adjutant-General Kibbe's campaign of 1859, whose goal was the same as Anderson's, is contained also in this volume. The reader may be interested to compare the two accounts.

7. Fighting the Mill Creeks (1857-1865)

R. A. Anderson

Chapter I

Crossing the plains in '57, I tried mining for a short time on the North Fork of Feather River, but soon continued my journey to the Sacramento Valley and settled on Deer Creek. With broad plains to the north and south fit only for grazing purposes, the fertile land along the creek bottom seemed doubly attractive, and for several years I engaged in gardening. By way of quick delivery, I possessed an ox team, while my market lay wherever buyers were to be found. I made one trip with

R. A. Anderson, *Fighting the Mill Creeks: Being a Personal Account of Campaigns Against Indians of the Northern Sierras* (Chico, Calif.: Chico Record Press, 1909).

Captain Anderson, from a photograph taken in 1866

my vegetables as far away as the mountains of Trinity.

Later I sold out and went into the cattle business. In 1861, snow fell in the valley to the depth of six inches and lay on for two weeks. That snow put me out of the cattle business.

During these years Indians were numerous. Those who infested the region where I lived were called Mill Creeks or Deer Creeks, the rough canyons of these two streams offering thousands of hiding places to these wild bands. During the winter of 1857 they caused much uneasiness among the settlers. Many raids were made into the valley, followed always by swift retreats into the hills. People were killed, dwellings burned, and stock driven off. These depredations occurred usually along the edge of the valley, but extended on some occasions as far as the Sacramento River.

This state of things could not continue. The Indians, with the accustomed stealth of savages, always made their attacks unexpectedly. Since the settler could not guard against surprise, it was decided to retaliate by carrying the war into the Indians' own territory.

Jack Spaulding, who claimed to have had experience in fighting the reds, organized a party of fifteen men for the purpose of following the marauders into the hills. Hi Good and myself were members of this party. Good, whose acquaintance with the hills was extensive, was elected Lieutenant, while Spaulding acted as Captain.

We knew that to beat the savages we must outplay them at their own game; therefore, we traveled by night, lying over in the daytime. Passing northeasterly over the foothills we kept to the broad ridge between Deer Creek and Mill Creek, this being the ridge along which the Lassen Trail leads.

After two night of travel we reached old Bluff Camp, which was one of the stopping places of the early emigrant trains. It lies in the midst of a vast forest just over the ridge on the Mill Creek slope.

Here we found considerable snow still lying on the cool floor of the pinery, and signs of the Indians were numerous. They had been about the spring in considerable numbers, and the greenest scout in our party could easily discover their trails leading through the forest.

We were taken into a steep, sheltered ravine, where it was thought we would be hidden; then Good and Spaulding set out on a still hunt to try and locate the Indians' camp.

Our leaders had been gone but a short time when the mountains on both sides of us suddenly began to blaze with rifle shots, the reports booming heavily through the dense forest. The Indians had taken the first trick. To say that we were a startled lot of man-hunters would be to put it mildly. I frankly admit that I was ready to run four ways at once. Our retreat was a scramble for first place. I had another man's rifle and someone else had mine. A companion and I were streaking it up the hill, slipping on the pine needles and making, it seemed to us, about as much progress backward as forward. The bullets of the Indians were playing lively tunes about our ears. Suddenly a small pine limb, clipped off by a piece of lead, fell just over the other man's head, and at the same instant he fell flat and

[33]

lay limp. I sprang toward him, reached down and clasped his body in my arms, determined to do my best to rescue his body; but I felt his sides shaking convulsively in my hands and in a second he had rolled over, laughing heartily, and asked:

"What's the rush? What the devil are you running for?"

His fall was due to the pine needles and not to a bullet.

When we had finally gathered together at the head of the hollow and had taken a hasty inventory of our numbers, our excitement was in no wise allayed. One man was gone! The Indians had got a scalp!

There was nothing to do but to return to the scene of the ambush and make a search for the body. The Indians had stopped firing now and, of course, were nowhere to be seen. Slowly and cautiously we crept back down the ravine, peering and peeping, and ready to shoot at the first thing that moved, or to run at the first sound, we hardly knew which. But, behold! at last we found our missing comrade, sitting placidly upon a rock and wondering where the profanely qualified nation we had been! He was extremely deaf and swore that he had not heard a single shot nor seen an Indian.

Good and Spaulding soon came running up, as ready for retreat as the rest of us. As soon as we got into something like order, the Indians melted away, but the surprise had taken all the hunt out of us for the time.

The next morning we started for the valley, the Indians hanging on our flanks and rear, clear to the edge of the hills. Many times, as we topped a ridge and looked back, we could see our dusky pursuers peering over the last ridge behind us and keeping tab upon our movements. It was useless to attempt to lead them into an ambush, for they knew our exact number, and as we wound up the slope ahead of them they would make their count, and if our full number was not in sight would make a detour around the intervening ravine.

We were gone on this expedition four days, and on our return had to draw pretty freely upon our imaginations for stories that would satisfy our friends.

After this, I became better acquainted with Hi Good. He lived near me on Deer Creek, and we were together on several of the subsequent Indian hunts. We both thought that the savages would be encouraged by our failure to beat them, and warned our neighbors to be on the alert.

Our surmises were correct. In a short time a neighbor's barn was visited in the night and four very valuable mules spirited away. The Indians had a habit of stealing all horses and mules that they could lay their hands on, driving them into the hills and butchering them. Perhaps they preferred them to cattle, because with them they could beat a more hasty retreat; but it always seemed to me as if they liked horseflesh better than beef and mule-flesh better than either.

Upon receiving word of this last robbery, Good and I enlisted as helpers a young man named Jones and another named George Carter, and started for the hills. These young men seemed to have plenty of nerve, especially Jones, who had been with us on the former hunt and who, I believe, was the coolest man of the party when the surprise came.

We advanced swiftly into the hills, picked up the Indians' trail, and, the second day out, located their camp. They were snuggled away near the bed of Dry Creek, well up toward the head of that stream, but still several miles below the pinery.

We promptly made an attack. We were sheltered behind bowlders, while the Mill Creeks were partially protected by a cave. However, we had obtained a position from which we could shoot directly into the cave and it was not long until we had them moving.

We got no Indians, but recaptured considerable stolen plunder. They had killed the mules. On this and subsequent hunts we learned that the crafty fellows made a practice of secreting their supply of "jerked" mule-meat or other provisions in some spot at a distance from where they camped, so that if their camp were surprised their food would still be safe, and in all the years that I followed them I never but once found their hidden meat-house.

We returned home much elated with our success. Indeed, it put quite a bunch of feathers in our caps when compared with our previous attempt.

Chapter II

The "Boys in the Hills," as the Indians were frequently called, were not at all satisfied with such an ending of their raid, so soon left another midnight mark upon the whites. Our only chance to reach them was through a surprise, so we permitted several small raids to go by unnoticed, in order that our chances of springing a surprise would be strengthened.

In fact, the depredations continued all through the winter of '57 and '58, and finally complaints were made to General Kibbey, who was then stationed at Sacramento, and a company of troopers was sent up the river by steamboat. They disembarked at Tehama and caused quite a ripple of excitement in that thriving river town by the glitter of their arms and uniforms.

Hi Good and I went to see them after they had made camp, and both of us came to the conclusion that they might be successful in an open country, but that there was little chance of their capturing any Indians in the hills.

Our conclusions proved to be well-founded. The troops, well-mounted, marched gallantly out across the plains and swept up the slope of the hills in fine military array. Their first search seemed to be directed to finding a good camping place, but before they found it the Mill Creeks found them, and back to the valley they marched, making rather better time than on the upward march.

As a matter of course, this encouraged the "Boys in the Hills." Again the troops made an advance and again they were surprised and forced to retreat. This occurred several times, and the soldiers finally gave it up as a bad job and quit the game.

From this time onward it seemed as though the Indians never let a chance slip to do the whites damage. Affairs went on in this way until the spring of 1859, when the raids became so frequent that the valley was thoroughly roused. It was decided to raise a subscription among the settlers in order to get means to carry on an exhaustive campaign against the renegades, a number of atrocious murders having by this time been added to the list of the Indians' misdeeds.

A fund of three thousand dollars was secured and placed, I think, in the hands of a man named Cohen. Cohen was a merchant who conducted a store at the Mayhew stage station on Deer Creek. Hi Good, John Breckenridge and myself, together with William Simmons, John Martin, John McCord, one Cartin and a man whom we called "Slim," were selected and engaged to hunt the red men for two months. This gave us a company of six to press the chase, with two to care for our pack animals and attend camp. We had two mules and a horse to carry our supplies, but no animals to ride, for we knew that the trail we were about to follow would lead us into the wildest and most rugged gorges of the Northern Sierras.

Learning of our intended expedition, General Kibbey sent Captain Burns of the army to take command of our party. He arrived in good time and we started on June the 15th. It was, I think, the hottest day I ever experienced in the Sacramento Valley. Many of the old settlers will remember the time, as it was the day that old Tehama burned.

We marched across the dreary, lava-capped foothills on the south side of Deer Creek, and the first day's march proved Captain Burns' unfitness for the task before us. He became completely exhausted, and was sent back to the valley from Deer Creek Flats, where we had made our first camp, and that ended his participation in the two months' hunt.

Left to our own resources, we elected Breckenridge captain and pressed forward. The Indians were evidently well posted as to our movements and intentions, for they secreted their squaws and papooses in the most hidden recesses of the mountains and then proceeded to lead us a merry chase through the dark forests and rugged canyons.

McCord was well acquainted with the hills, and with one companion he usually moved camp, often taking roundabout ways to reach points which the balance of us gained by following the routes taken by the Indians.

Our first separation from our train occurred at the Flats. McCord and companion went by way of the ridge up which the Campbell Trail now leads, crossed Deer Creek at about the point now known as the Polk place, and thence moved northward to Bluff Camp. The rest of us, with provisions enough to last two days, crossed Deer Creek near the mouth of Sulphur Creek, climbed the north wall of the canyon, and so on across Digger Pine Flat and to the pinery about in the region of the Moak Trail.

At Bluff Camp we rejoined McCord. After holding a council, Breckenridge decided that it was best to send a scouting party up the Lassen Trail as far as Deer Creek Meadows, in hopes of picking up the Indians' trail. Our entire party moved up the ridge past Lost Camp and on over what is called the Summit, although it is no real water divide, and down into the cold valley of Onion Creek. This stream is named from the patches of wild onions that are found here and there along its course.

Here we left our camp, while Breckenridge, Hi Good and myself, with the two mules, pushed on to Deer Creek Meadows. We found no Indian signs, but as we approached the level, grassy floor of the meadow we spied five grizzly bears busy among some rotten logs that lay near a cluster of tamaracks. At once we proposed a bear hunt. Breckenridge consented, providing that he could engineer the sport. Hi and I agreed to this, as our acqaintance with grizzlies was very limited.

Accordingly the captain led the pack animals back into the heavy timber which covered the surrounding mountains and grew to the very edge of the meadow. Tying them securely he returned and directed us each to pick out a convenient tree that we were sure we could climb in case of necessity. After providing ourselves, like prudent soldiers, with our means of retreat, we slipped forward a short distance, keeping out of sight of the bears behind a big log. Breckenridge was to take the first shot, and he told us to hammer away at the bear he should shoot until it was done for. The affair had to be handled quite differently to what it would today, as we had none but muzzle-loading rifles and six-shooters.

When all were ready, Breckenridge threw a shot into a huge grizzly and it ripped at its side with

its teeth and sent up a terrific bellow. Hi and I let go at the wounded beast and we soon had it down and out. Then on to the next. For a time we were kept mighty busy loading and firing, but the bears never seemed to know where the shots were coming from, and so our trees were not put to use. We killed four and sent the fifth one off badly crippled.

They were huge creatures, weighing, I should judge, a thousand pounds each. We carefully removed their galls, which we knew we could sell to Chinamen. The Chinese use them in preparing some kind of medicine and in those days often paid as high as fifteen dollars apiece for them. The feet we also lopped off. They were to serve as food. After being roasted in hot ashes they make a most toothsome dish. The sixteen feet made a considerable pack in themselves. The carcasses and skins we left.

Chapter III

Finishing our bear hunt, we returned to Onion Creek and our entire party then moved back to Bluff Camp. Having failed to strike Indian signs up-country, we decided to swing down into Mill Creek Canyon and cross toward Black Butte on the north side of that stream.

On that day's march, Williams and I had charge of the pack animals. While making our way along the steep side of the canyon we came to a slide full of loose shale. To climb above or below it seemed a hopeless task, so we quickly decided to attempt to hustle our animals across it. We made a brisk start, but in a moment packs and animals, men and guns were tumbling and bouncing and rolling toward Mill Creek at a rate that would have established a record, I am sure, if there had been a stop-watch present to time our speed. Our pack animals got out of the scrape with nothing worse than a few bruises, but I was less fortunate, as I wrenched my ankle badly and for a time was in great pain.

We crossed to the north side of the creek and made camp. Being unfit for scouting duty, I was left with McCord to tend camp, while the balance of the party separated, three going up and three down the canyon to look for sign. They remained away all night.

We were camped on a point some distance up from the creek, the stream forming a bend around the foot of the point. As is usual in this rough canyon, the point ended in a series of cliffs. During the evening we heard chopping, and after a time a tree fell. We were speculating about the matter, and in the meantime keeping outside the circle of light cast by our little fire, when a rifle shot suddenly rang out and a bullet spat into our camp. We seized our rifles and prepared for a brush, but our stealthy foes kept out of sight, though they continued to throw lead in the direction of our camp until well into the night. However, no damage was done except to interfere with a good night's sleep.

Next morning we made an investigation and found that a large party of Indians had been camped under the cliffs only a few hundred yards below us, and that a tree had been thrown across the creek to afford them a bridge to the south side. The camp had evidently been occupied by the women and children, with only a few men, but of course the entire party was now gone.

When Breckenridge returned, we made our report and took him down to the deserted camp. As soon as he found that the runaways were women and children, he said:

"Let them go; we must find the warriors."

Again scouting parties were sent out. Although my ankle was still somewhat stiff and swollen, I was able to make pretty fair headway along the rough and rocky hillsides. I went down the canyon and after traveling a mile or more discovered a fresh trail leading northward toward the head of Paynes Creek. It had been made by warriors, fully a dozen in number.

I reported to our captain and our plans were quickly made. The pack animals were sent around by a devious course to meet us again at Battle Creek Meadows, while we followed the trail.

We were beginning by this time to get an understanding of the signs by means of which the Indians regulated their movements, and this knowledge later became of great use to us. For instance, they were traveling toward the north. On top of the first ridge that the trail crossed would be found three stones piled one upon another on some rock. This meant that the party was to come together for camp or other purposes in the third canyon beyond. On the next ridge would be two stones placed in the same way upon a wayside bowlder, and on the next one. Thus, a party, finding a monument of stones, had but to count the stones in order to know where the meeting place was to be, and immediately, if there were a number together, they would scatter, each man to himself, only to congregate later at the appointed place. After we once learned to read these signs, much tedious trailing was saved us, for we had but to count the intervening ridges, as the Indians did, and devote our close work to the final hollow.

We made the advance to Battle Creek Meadows without mishap. The beautiful little valley was at this time a perfect sea of tall grass, in the midst of which, along the winding streams, were magnificent beds of wild strawberries; yet the forest surrounding the meadows was still streaked with drifts of snow.

In the edge of the meadow we found where the Indians had camped. As well as we could read the signs, they were two nights ahead of us. They had left a couple of green bear skins lying beside their extinguished fire.

It was near the end of the day when we discovered the abandoned camp, and, as our pack train had not yet arrived, we decided to try to get some venison and at the same time endeavor to discover which way the Indians had taken on departing.

Good and Simmons went up the creek, while Williams and I went down. Simmons shot at and wounded a bear. It chased him and he yelled for Hi to shoot it. Before the latter could come up, however, Simmons was so closely pressed that he concluded his time had come. He had not been able to reload his rifle and there was no tree close by that he could climb. Finally, when the bear was close upon him, he stopped and the beast, instead of closing in on him, immediately began to circle around him, growling savagely. Hi came up, and afterwards declared that it was equal to a one-ringed circus to see Simmons turning cautiously around so as to keep his face to the circling beast. After enjoying the show for a while, Hi threw a shot into the bear, and it made for the timber, badly crippled.

Meanwhile, Williams and I had been having our share of the fun. We were traveling along close to the willows that fringed the creek, when a large, barren doe sprang up. We both shot at her and one of our bullets broke her hip. I followed the deer into the willows, without stopping to reload my rifle, and, soon catching sight of her, finished her with a shot from my six-shooter. As I was threshing through the brush to where she lay, Williams suddenly shouted:

"Look out for that bear!"

I whirled about and beheld a huge grizzly stalking deliberately through the willows, not fifty feet away. Without stopping to consider what I was doing, I cut loose with my revolver, and down the big beast went, slashing the ground with his teeth. In a second he was up, and I fired again and down he went a second time. So a third and a fourth bullet I threw into him, and then it abruptly dawned upon me that I had but one bullet lift in my six-shooter and none in my rifle. Luckily, the bear paid no attention whatever to me. In fact, it appeared not to have seen me. Williams now gave it a shot from his rifle and it put off through the willows. The next morning we found it lying dead not far away.

[38]

The pack animals joined us that night, but our provisions were too low to warrant us in starting on a long chase, so four of us were sent over toward Hot Spring Valley to hunt for deer. We got five, and, returning to camp, were busily "jerking" the meat, when some of our scouts discovered the Indians' trail leading out toward the Lassen Buttes.

Chapter IV

Six of us promptly set out upon the trail, carrying each four days' rations, and a hard run we had of it. Up through the heavy forest to the lofty backbone west of what is now called the Morgan Springs Valley, along this high ridge until we had reached the upper timber line, and still onward and upward until we found ourselves upon Lassen's snow-capped peak. The trail led directly past the Buttes, west of the dreary lava of the Cinder Cone region and on toward the unmapped canyon of Pitt River.

On the border of that turbulent stream the redskins doubled on us, and once more we were headed toward the south. Our camp had been ordered to return to Black Buttes on Mill Creek, and to await us there. Coming back on a course much farther west than that followed on the outward trip, we came upon a sawmill out in the region northeast of Red Bluff. There great excitement prevailed. The skulking Indians, preceding us by a day, had run upon one of the bull-punchers near the mill, had killed him and chased his team over a cliff.

Some of the lumber-jacks were trying to find the Indians, while others seemed to be afraid that the Indians would find them. Our provisions were gone, so we went to the cook-house and demanded food. We got what we asked for and hurried onward, the trail still leading us toward the south.

During these severe days our rations consisted principally of sugar. Each man could carry enough to last him several days, and, eked out with manzanita berries, this ration really kept us in good strength. The time ordinarily spent in cooking was saved and gave us that much more time for the business of following the trail. We soon got in the habit of keeping our hunger appeased by frequently dipping into our little sugar sacks, and not infrequently followed the trail for ten or even twelve hours at a stretch without a single stop of more than a few minutes' duration. When it grew too dark for us to read the ground sign, we had but to scrape together a pile of leaves or pine needles and sleep until daylight should come again, and then proceed on our way.

We crossed Mill Creek and Deer Creek and followed the trail as far as the Keefer ridge, between Rock Creek and Chico Creek. Our provisions were by this time completely exhausted, so we returned to the valley for more.

While in the valley a message reached us from the Butte Creek country, warning us to follow the Indians no farther, and stating that a company of fifteen miners would be waiting for us if we persisted in the pursuit. We had always felt certain that the Mill Creeks procured arms and ammunition through friendly relations with whites. This note of warning seemed to settle the matter, and to indicate where the whites in question were to be found.

We thought it best to secure reinforcements before making another advance. My brother, Jack, who lived with me on Deer Creek, and a man named Bates joined our force. We returned to the hills and made camp at a little spring near the present site of the Cole place on the Cohasset ridge.

Believing that the Indians were reinforced, not only by the fifteen miners, but by some of the Butte Creek Indians as well, we now used every precaution in trailing them. Hi Good and I did most of the scouting. One of us would follow the ground sign, while the other acted as lookout to avoid running into an ambush. We had to do most of our work by daylight, but the balance of the party moved only at night.

Crossing Chico Creek Canyon, we reached the ridge beyond, and finally discovered what seemed to be a large camp at or near the present site of the Forest Ranch. After a careful study of the ground, we returned to our camp. On this return trip we ran upon an Indian scout, and after a long, hard chase, killed him. We carried his scalp to camp with us, this being the first trophy we had taken in the campaign.

Upon receiving our report, Captain Breckenridge at once gave orders for an advance. Of course, we had to move in the night. It was a weary climb out of Chico Creek Canyon in the darkness, but we made it and succeeded in surrounding the hostile camp before daylight. Our number being limited and having a pretty large circle to form, it left us separated, man from man, by spaces of about seventy-five yards.

I had been assigned to a position eastward of the camp and very close, as I afterward learned, to the trail which led toward the mining village at the forks of Butte Creek. The forest trees afforded us ample hiding places and we had been ordered to hold our fire until it was perfectly light. Hi Good was on my right and Brother Jack upon my left.

As the gray dawn melted into daylight, the outlines of the camp became clearer. It was evidently a permanent meeting place, as there were signs of its having been frequently occupied. Directly in front of me and standing something like a hundred yards apart were two lofty pine trees, trimmed of branches except for small tufts of foliage on their tops, and, what was my surprise, as the heavens grew brighter, to behold a large American flag depending from the top of each tree.

The Indians, as we afterward learned, had been enjoying a celebration in company with their friends from Butte Creek, and did not prove to be early risers. The sun had crept up to the tops of the pines on the hill east of us before there was any stir in the camp. Then a man emerged from a cluster of little firs and came shuffling up the trail directly toward where I lay. Captain Breckenridge had not yet given the signal to commence firing, so I slipped around my tree in order to remain hidden. As the man approached and passed me, I perceived that he was not an Indian, but a Spaniard. However, birds flocking together on this occasion were to be considered birds of a feather. The man had got but a few paces past me when Hi Good spied him. In a moment Good's rifle spoke, and the Spaniard, wounded, sprang back toward the camp. As he ran another rifle over on the other side of our circle cracked, and he fell dead.

The camp was roused. In a twinkling, up the Indians sprang, men, women and children, and as if with one impulse they swarmed up the slope directly toward where I lay. In a moment I was enveloped in the wild stampede. I shot and then clubbed my rifle and struggled against the rush. Good and Jack came to my assistance, and together we turned them back. The balance of our party were pouring shots into them and they soon began to seek shelter amid the logs and thickets of small forest trees.

Our orders from Breckenridge had been to allow no one to break through the circle, but to spare the women and children. This was a most difficult program to carry out. The bucks were armed and were returning our fire. The squaws soon perceived that we were seeking to spare their lives, and so they clung to the bucks. This made it difficult to get a bead upon the one without endangering the other. Seeing that this state of affairs would not do, we sent word from man to man around to the captain and asked him for new orders. Soon the word came back: "Let the squaws and children pass out."

Good, who could speak the Indian dialect, promptly shouted the order to the Indians. They eagerly seized upon the suggestion, but we were soon to learn that the order was a serious mistake. A warrior would wrap himself in a blanket, throw another blanket or a basket over his head, with a rifle concealed next to his body, seize a child by the hand, or hoist one upon his back, and go shuffling past us.

Soon we came in possession of the camp. There was not a bad Indian to be found, but about forty good ones lay scattered about.

[40]   While rejoicing over our victory, shots began to ring out and bullets to sing about our ears, and we suddenly found ourselves where so lately we had had the Indians. They were shooting at us from all sides. I heard Hi Good cursing like a wagon-master and saw him trying to get a bead on an Indian. He was behind a tree, from both sides of which pieces of bark were flying as from a woodman's ax. However, our luck had not deserted us. Not one of our party was hit. We charged and scattered the Indians, then kept out guards while we prepared and ate our breakfasts.

Two barrels, partly filled with whiskey, were in the camp, as well as other evidences which pointed to the fact that whites had joined with the redskins in the recent celebration. We soon took our departure for our own camp across Chico Creek, each man well burdened with plunder from the captured camp. I had found three good six-shooters, which I thrust under my belt, thinking these to be about as useful as anything to be had.

Chapter V

We were filing down the hill into Chico Creek Canyon, and were perhaps a little careless of our advance, when we ran suddenly into an ambush. Six or seven of the Mill Creeks, undoubtedly part of those who had escaped from the camp, had hidden along the trail and, suddenly rising above the birch brush, let us have it. We were strung along in single file. Six of our party were ahead of me, and I suddenly saw them all go down. However, not one was hurt. The Indians disappeared in an instant. In the one glimpse I caught of them I threw up my rifle and fired. I saw one fall with a broken thigh, and sprang after him. Just as I leaped the man behind me fired and the powder from his rifle blackened my right ear. Sliding and crawling down the steep hillside, the wounded Indian could travel nearly as fast as I could. I chased him nearly to the bottom of the canyon before I finished him. The chase cost me my three new six-shooters, all of which were pulled from my belt by the clinging brush.

I rejoined the balance of the party and we had pushed on well down to the creek, when we discovered five of the Indians far above us upon a cliff on the north wall of the canyon. For a few minutes we discussed the probabilities of their being the same party which had ambushed us. Some of our party believed that they were not Indians at all.

During the discussion, I was standing looking upward, the left side of my head touching an oak tree. All at once I saw a puff of smoke arise from the distant cliff, and in a moment I was down and out. A bullet had cut in between my head and the oak, driven my scalp full of bark, and left me senseless for twenty minutes. The scar from that shot forms a very considerable bald spot on my head today.

We returned to our camp on the Keefer ridge. A man by the name of King at that time had a sawmill a few miles farther up the ridge. Just after we reached camp, two teamsters drove up the old road toward this mill. One of them was my old friend, Perry McIntosh, the other a man named Lindsay. I told Breckenridge that some of us ought to overtake the teamsters and guard them to the mill, as the Indians were likely to overhaul them. The captain thought that the trip to the mill could be made in safety.

However, it was not. The Indians, sure enough, spied the teamsters, waylaid them, and shot Lindsay. McIntosh escaped, reached the mill, and later rescued Lindsay, who subsequently recovered.

News of the fight at Forest Ranch quickly reached the valley, and for a time exaggerated stories were in circulation to the effect that our entire party had been killed. Coon Garner raised a party of fifteen and hastened into the hills to look us up. If I remember correctly, P. M. Guynn and Dan Sutherland are the only surviving members of that party.

We had moved back across Chico Creek, and Garner's party found us encamped near the site of the Doe Mill. We had revisited the battle-ground at Forest Ranch, only to find that the surviving Indians had returned and burned the bodies of their slain.

We were not yet satisfied with the state of affairs at the forks of Butte Creek. Scouting through that canyon we jumped some Indians, who promptly ran for the bottom of the canyon. Our enlarged party at once swarmed down the hillside toward the mining town. Breckenridge had ordered us to kill any Indian found even in the streets of the village, but to shoot none who had sought shelter within the houses.

Some of the fleeing Indians headed straight for the village. Knowing a short course to a footbridge where I believed they would cross the stream, I called to Williams and together we raced to that point. We succeeded in tumbling several Indians off the bridge into the creek as they sought to cross.

Then we entered the village. The Indians were there in considerable numbers, but all had prudently disappeared within the houses. A man named Wallace conducted a store. He resented our appearance, and, stepping outside his store, shouted to us that if a single Indian were killed he would follow us up and kill six white men. As soon as Breckenridge entered the town, I reported Wallace's remark.

"Point out that man to me!" said he, abruptly.

"He is standing back of that counter, and has two six-shooters beside him," replied I.

"Can you cover him from where you stand?"

I answered that I could, and at once threw my gun on the man. Breckenridge entered the store, strode up to Wallace, and told him very plainly why we had followed the Indians to Butte Creek. He declared that we had long suspected and now had proof that the Mill Creeks received support from either the Butte Creek Indians or the miners, or both, and that the arms and ammunition secured in this way were used to murder white people of the country farther north. Breckenridge was not a pleasant man to have for an enemy, and Wallace had departed very far from his boastful, threatening manner before the former was through with him.

We learned later that the store-keeper's squaw had received a wound in the Forest Ranch fight, which fact probably accounted for the stand Wallace took. In the course of the controversy, he remarked that if we had been a day earlier at Forest Ranch we would have found him at the camp, to which he received the comforting reply that if such had been the case he would surely have met with exactly the same treatment as that accorded the Indians.

All this time a group of Indians was stationed in back part of the store. After Breckenridge had freed his mind to Wallace, I told some of the boys to keep an eye on the store-keeper, as I wished to take a look at an Indian whom I had seen in the back room. This Indian was seated upon a keg. I had recognized him as a young fellow whom I had shot down during the Forest Ranch fight, thinking him dead, only to find him missing after the battle.

I approached him now and asked him how he felt, to which he made no reply. I was curious to learn just how much an Indian could endure in the way of a gun-shot wound. I pulled his shirt up over his head and there were the wounds, indicating that my bullet had entered his right breast and passed out under his left shoulder-blade. The bullet must have been deflected in some way, since a straight line drawn from one wound to the other would have pierced his heart; yet here he sat, apparently in good health, three days after the battle!

We moved camp to a ridge some miles below the forks and spent several days trying to straighten

[41]

out affairs with the Indians of Butte Creek. We captured a chief called "The Old Captain," and, as soon as he found himself within our power, he professed to be very friendly and assured us that if we would but lie low for a time he and his men would capture the remainder of the Mill Creeks for us.

I had no faith whatever in the old fellow, or in his protestations of friendship; but Breckenridge seemed to think that he could be trusted, or at least that it was our duty to give him a trial. As a sort of hostage, we kept "The Old Captain" in our camp while a young Indian of his clan, called "Tony," was sent out to muster the warriors. He returned with about fifteen of them, and they spent several days in our midst. They declared that the proper way to get the Mill Creeks was to slip up on them and fight in the old style of Indian warfare,—that is, with bows and arrows. During several days they made much ado of practicing with these ancient weapons, and I must do them the credit of saying that some of them shot extremely well. Finally a war party set out, under the leadership of "Tony," "The Old Captain" still being held as hostage.

The chief's squaw was allowed to visit him, and she came and went at will, thus, of course, keeping him in communication with the rest of his people, those who pretended to be on the warpath included. During the day he was allowed to roam about our camp, but at night he was lodged in a vacant cabin that stood near, one man being detailed to guard him.

One night, after Tony's party had been several days gone, the old rascal pretended to be very sick, and finally prevailed upon his guard to lead him some distance from the cabin. They had barely got beyond the bounds of the sleeping encampment when the Indian made a sudden break for liberty. The guard gave chase, and after a hundred-yard dash overhauled him and brought him back. Thereafter he was secured by ropes.

This action of the chief convinced Breckenridge of my way of thinking regarding the trickery of the Butte Creeks, so it was decided to hunt up the pretended war party and see what they were up to.

The following morning we split up into scouting parties and set out. Ad Williams and I made a search of the canyon in the direction of Hell Town. We were advancing along the ridge, from which we could keep a sharp lookout into the ravines below and upon the opposite wall of the canyon. I finally spied some figures far below us, and on the opposite side of the creek. They soon disappeared within a dense thicket, and, not long afterward, we were able to make out a faint ribbon of smoke curling up above the brush.

We decided to investigate, so slid cautiously down the hillside, crossed the creek, and, creeping into the thicket, found seven of our Butte Creek "allies" lounging idly about a tiny fire. Tony was among the number. We lost no time in making them our prisoners and starting with them back to camp.

While we were toiling up the hill, within perhaps a mile of our destination, we suddenly heard a fusillade of shots coming from the direction of our camp. The shooting continued for some time, those engaged seeming to be moving toward the breaks of the canyon, the last shot or two being fired over the slope of the ridge.

We soon reached camp and learned the cause of the disturbance. Those of our party who were in camp had been scattered carelessly about, paying no heed to "The Old Captain," who suddenly jumped free from his ropes, gave a triumphant whoop, and started like a deer toward the canyon. He had secured a knife in some way, cut his bonds beneath his blanket, and then made his second break for liberty.

None of the Whites had their rifles at hand, but most of them promptly drew their six-shooters and opened on the scudding red man. His rush was so sudden, however, that he escaped the first scattering volley and outstripped all his pursuers excepting Hi Good, who was swift of foot and had great powers of endurance.

Good continued to run and shoot without bringing the Indian down, until he had emptied his revolver. Not being able to reload on the run, he swept onward with his weapon empty, and, getting close enough soon after crossing the brow of the hill, he threw his revolver and knocked the Indian down. Before the latter could recover, Good overhauled him and soon after returned with him to camp. The chief had been shot twice in the chase and was so badly wounded that when we moved away we left him to the care of his squaw. I think that he subsequently recovered.

Chapter VI

Another incident that occurred while we were encamped at this place might be worthy of mention. Two of our party, Bates and a man named Wash Cox, the latter being of Garner's party, returned one day from a hunting trip and said that they had killed two bears and left them hanging in a tree. They wished someone else to go after the carcasses. I agreed to bring in the meat, and set out at once.

On reaching the spot to which they had directed me, however, I was surprised and disgusted to find two fat hogs awaiting me. After debating the situation in my own mind for a time, I finally decided to carry the meat to camp, as I had promised. Immediately on reaching camp, however, I reported the affair to Breckenridge, and told him that it looked like a slippery trick, to get someone else besides the real culprits involved.

The captain looked at the matter in the same light as myself, and he lost no time in calling Bates and Cox before him. He told them that he would not countenance any such thievery and ordered them to hunt up a man named Harris, to whom it was found the hogs belonged, pay him for the animals, and that then they would be drummed out of camp as unfit members of our party.

The two men left camp and stayed away for some time. When they returned they asserted that they had found Harris and offered him pay for the hogs, which he refused. This may have been true, but it did not lessen the offense of having killed the animals.

The second part of the men's sentence had yet to be carried out, Garner having agreed with Breckenridge in the matter. Hi Good, as our second in command, was left to carry the order out. He commanded Bates and Cox to move, and

ordered the rest of us to provide all the music that could be coaxed out of the pots and pans of our camping outfit. The rest of us were ready for our parts, but now a halt came in the proceedings, for Bates entered a strong protest. He swore that he would not be driven out of camp in this way and that there were not enough of us to force him to go. He stepped up to Good and struck him and in a moment the two were fighting desperately. Bates was a powerful man and for a time it looked as though he would master his man, but Good's endurance was the greater and he at length knocked Bates down and was beating him cruelly when I stopped him. Then the two men were drummed out of camp, according to orders.

The recaptured Butte Creeks tried to explain their failure to do as promised by pretending that they had overtaken the Mill Creeks and been whipped. They now promised to go with us and lead us to the hiding places of the renegades. I considered this promise as little likely to be fulfilled as the former one, but it was decided to give the Indians another trial.

Accordingly, it was arranged that the balance of the party were to march through the hills to the Sidoros place on Rock Creek, while Hi Good and I should bring the seven captive Indians directly to the valley, thence move northward along the edge of the valley to the same point. We traveled as rapidly as we could, but night overtook us when we were but a short distance north of Chico Creek. We decided to lie over till morning. We halted beneath a large oak and I said to Hi:

"You guard the Indians the first half of the night and I'll take the last half; or turn it about, just as you like."

"Guard be d——d!" said Good. "I'm going to sleep."

And he proceeded to snuggle down on the ground. I told him that the Indians would knock us on the head and skip out to join the Mill Creeks as sure as we both slept, but he declared that they wouldn't lay a finger upon us. Say what I could he would take no hand in the guarding, so I sat awake all night while he slept. The Indians made no break, either to escape or to harm us, but I

[43]

have always felt satisfied that the white scalps that they most longed to handle would have been dangling at their belts in short order had I relaxed my vigilance.

Next day we reached the Sidoros place, where the entire party was reunited. After dinner, someone remarked that there was a fine swimming hole up the creek a mile or so. Old man McCord wanted to take a swim. Immediately, Tony, the Indian, asked Breckenridge if he and his party could not go along and shoot some fish with their arrows. Breckenridge consented, and I volunteered to go along, saying that a bath would not hurt me in the least. I was satisfied that the Indians would try to escape.

We reached the swimming hole in due time, and McCord took his bath, while I sat on the bank, the Indians meantime being very intent on their fishing. They got several pike and suckers and appeared to be very much interested in the sport.

After McCord left the water, I stripped and plunged in. I had no sooner struck the water than a whoop rang out, and, like a flash, every Indian leaped into the brush and started to run up the creek. McCord was too slow to stop them. I sprang up the bank, seized my six-shooter and put after them. I chased them for a mile and got only one flying shot, but did no damage. In the course of the chase I suddenly found myself running full tilt past a house that stood amid some trees not far from the creek. There were some members of the household standing in the doorway, doubtless attracted by the scudding Indians. I tortured my naked feet frightfully in the course of that run; nevertheless, I managed to make a wide detour around that house on my return to camp. The last I saw of the Butte Creeks they were streaking it like quails up the hill toward where a section of the Richardson rock-wall now stands.

It was about this time that word came to me that the Indians had visited my place on Deer Creek, burned my house and barn, killed five head of cattle and practically cleaned me out. My brother, Jack, was then living with me. Shortly before this, during a trip to Marysville, he had pur-

chased a seventy-five-dollar suit of clothes. Some time later, up Deer Creek Canyon, I killed an Indian who had on the vest and trousers of that suit.

Chapter VII

It was decided to give the Mill Creeks another blow. We felt satisfied that those who had escaped from Forest Ranch had joined with another party in Deer Creek. The main party, including Garner's force, was to march back across the foothills and into the pinery as far as Cold Springs, which lies on top of the mountain south of Deer Creek, while scouting parties were looking for fresh Indian sign in the surrounding country.

Ad Williams and I pushed north to Deer Creek and then advanced up the rugged canyon of that stream. On the second day out we struck a fresh trail and that evening located the Indians' camp in the bottom of the canyon, perhaps two miles above where Tom Polk's cabin now stands.

We swung back to Cold Springs and made our report. The main party at once dropped over the ridge into the big canyon and began its slow, cautious march toward the camp. When night fell again we were not more than a mile below the camp. The Indians gave no indications of being alarmed. Our plans were accordingly made for the attack. During the hours of darkness we would creep forward through the steep, tangled ravines, surround the sleeping Indians, and strike as soon as it became light enough to draw bead.

The Indians were strung out for some distance along the south side of the stream. It was broad daylight before we were opposite the lower ones. I was advancing with a number of others as rapidly as possible along the steep hillside, in order to get on the up-stream side, and was probably midway of the scattered camp, when a rifle suddenly rang out from somewhere in the rear of our line. Simmons had spied a dusky form rising above a bowlder and, thinking that we were discovered, had fired.

The alarmed Indians at once fled up-stream. We killed a number, but many escaped up that brushy, bowlder-strewn canyon. In the course of the running fight, I noticed several Indians springing down a steep bank into the creek. I watched for them to climb up the farther bank, but none appeared. Other searchers up and down the stream failed to discover them, so I decided that the best way to find what had become of them would be to follow them. I accordingly leaped down the bank into the stream. The moment I struck the water a gun snapped close behind me, and, glancing back, I beheld a group of the Indians huddled together in water nearly waist deep within a cavern that led back under the bank. A young man called "Billy" was in their midst, and it was he who had snapped his gun at me. The water had probably dampened his powder.

I at once called to the men on the bank above that I had found the runaways, and, throwing my gun on this Billy, ordered him to march out and surrender. He did so, and all the others, about a dozen in number, followed. They were mostly squaws and children.

Several of our party knew this Billy to be a dangerous and troublesome customer. I kept hold of his wrist after I got up the bank, not intending that he should try any of his slippery tricks upon me. I asked him if he knew who had shot Lindsay, and he gruffly replied:

"I shoot him."

After the ball was over I led Billy up to Brecken-ridge and said that he had confessed to shooting Lindsay. The captain was a peculiar man. He was usually very deliberate in his movements, but was possessed of great strength. He put the question to the Indian himself, as calmly as a teacher might ask a pupil his name:

"Do you know who shot Lindsay?"

"I shoot him."

And the captain replied, very calmly, "Then I will shoot you," and he proceeded to pull his revolver from its scabbard as leisurely as though he were about to indulge in target practice. As he was raising the weapon, and while its muzzle was still pointing downward, it was discharged. Imme-diately I let go of the Indian's wrist and slapped my hand to my side. The bullet had struck a stone, glanced upward, bored through the two thicknesses of my heavy belt, and, flattened like a coin, lay burning under my skin. The way I flung off that belt and tore at that hot lead was certainly not slow, and afforded some of the boys much merriment.

Meanwhile, the Indian, freed from my grip, had grappled with Breckenridge and the two were in the midst of a desperate struggle. Thinking the captain hard pressed, some of the boys were for rushing to his assistance, but I waved them back and told them that any man who was so many kinds of a fool as to let off his gun accidentally deserved no better treatment than to be killed by a thieving Mill Creek. However, Breckenridge soon overpowered his foe and killed him.

After this young Indian was finished, we collected our prisoners and started down the canyon, but soon found that there was another member of the tribe who was bent on making us trouble. This was an Indian who was called "The Doctor." He was really a chief. His squaw was in our possession and the chief certainly put up a game fight against odds.

We had gone but a short distance when he raised up from behind a rock a short distance ahead and fired, but his bullet went wild. We gave chase, but he disappeared, only to repeat his ambush act several times, always, for some reason, failing to get his man.

Finally we came to a halt in a plum thicket not far above the present site of the Polk barn. Most of the boys were helping themselves to plums, the rest of us guarding the prisoners. Suddenly the old chief arose in the very center of that plum thicket and tried another flying shot. He sank down again immediately, and, in the confusion of the moment, escaped from the thicket, slipped down to the creek, and crossed. Then from the opposite side of the stream he continued to shoot at us. We had a pretty good chance at him now and soon sent him to shelter in a pile of rocks. It would be a difficult matter for him to get to another shelter from where he was, so we kept him in play while Hi Good slipped across the creek and made a detour to get above him. Soon Good's rifle cracked and in a moment the Indian's body came rolling down the steep hillside. His squaw gave one glance at the

[45]

lifeless form, then withdrew her gaze with no sign whatever of excitement or grief. Some of the other squaws, however, sent up a dismal wail, which was probably the death-song of their tribe.

Many stories have been circulated regarding a bear-skin full of watches and coin which this old "Doctor" is believed to have left within the cave under the creek bank where the Indians had taken shelter. There may have been some small foundation in fact for these reports, but I have never believed that there was wealth enough hidden in that cave to pay a man for the hardships of a trip into the canyon to get it.

Chapter VIII

Returning to the valley, we again made camp on Rock Creek. It was decided that the prisoners should be taken to the Yumalacca Reservation, which lay on the western side of the Sacramento Valley, in the southern part of what is now Tehama county. Hi Good and I made the journey, having hired a team and wagon for the purpose.

Upon our return, our party broke up, the two months for which we had enlisted having expired some time before. Those of us who lived in the Deer Creek country started afoot across the plans toward our homes. We had gone but a couple of miles when we spied an infantry company marching toward the hills. The two parties came together at a point on the plains about one and one-half miles east of my present residence.

We found the soldiers to be under the command of Kibbey. He had learned of our campaign against the Indians, and had come up in person to wind up the affair. He listened attentively to a verbal report of our experiences, and then took down the names of the six of us who had been so long upon the Indian's trail. He said that we would be enrolled in the regular service and should share in all government awards for the duty done. However, that is the last I have ever heard of the matter. Four of our party were prevailed upon to go with the soldiers as guides, but Breckenridge and Hi Good and I went on home.

The history of Kibbey's campaign can be quickly summed up. He roamed through the mountains for several weeks, going as far east as the Big Meadows, where he seized a number of perfectly harmless Indians as prisoners. He returned by way of Butte Creek, where he got more prisoners, and, proceeding to Chico, "captured" the Bidwell Indians and transported the entire lot to the Reservation. He did not get a single Mill Creek, or any other Indian who had ever caused the whites any trouble.

General Bidwell promptly went to Sacramento and gave bonds for the good behavior of his Indians, whereupon the Government authorities released them, and they returned to Chico.

The other Indians jumped the Reservation, singly or in small squads, and drifted back to their former haunts. Some perhaps became contented with the life there and remained. However, taken as a movement to rid the foothills of the bad Indians, Kibbey's campaign was an absolute failure. In one way, it resulted in making matters worse in our part of the country, for the more dangerous of the Indians, on returning from the Reservation, were apt to bring others of like character with them, and, in this way, undoubtedly, a number of tough redskins were added to the bands in the hills.

During the winter of '59 and '60 the raids of the Indians followed one another with startling swiftness and regularity. Scarcely a week passed that some rancher or stockman did not suffer the loss of cattle, horses or mules, and every precaution taken to guard against the slippery red-men proved futile. Finally, they grew so bold as to pay a visit to Hi Good's rock corral on Deer Creek and to drive off some work cattle that belonged to Good and me.

At this time, a young man named Bowman, but whom we always called "Bully," was living with Hi. "Bully" had had no experience in fighting Indians, but he seemed a bold young fellow and we had confidence in him.

The three of us at once set out after the cattle thieves. We had no difficulty in following their trail, the Indians having become arrogant through their recent successes. We trailed them up Dry Creek and located their temporary camp near the head of that stream, some distance below the pine timber.

When discovered, the Indians were engaged in butchering a part of the stolen cattle. We were on the opposite side of the ravine from them, and, having a good view of their position, opened fire upon them. They seized their rifles and

Robert A. Anderson, early-day Indian fighter and former sheriff of Butte County, California.

returned our fire. We noticed immediately that they had our range perfectly, and were dropping their bullets very close to us. In fact, it was but a few moments until I heard Good cursing savagely.

"What's the matter?" I called.

"They've plugged me!" he replied, then, between a groan and an oath, added: "I believe my leg's busted."

I made my way to his side and found that he had been shot through the thigh. The wound was very painful and left him for a time almost helpless.

A shout of triumph from the Indians told us that they were aware of their success. The bullets were falling thicker and closer each moment, and I felt certain that we would soon all be picked off unless we could make a speedy change in the course of the battle.

I told Hi to drop down behind a big bowlder, while "Bully" and I should try to force the Indians out of their present position. Good did as I requested, and "Bully" and I made a sudden charge forward. We dashed down the slope, thus placing ourselves on the hillside closer to and below the Indians, and then began our advance toward them by leaping from one shelter to another. Immediately, as I expected, their bullets began to fly high. For a time it was give and take at a lively rate, and I noticed that "Bully" was behaving like a veteran. Since our every rush was toward the front, however, the Indians soon began to give way, and then we hustled them the harder.

As they passed up the hill in retreat, we began to hear Hi's rifle cracking from across the ravine. Soon he set up a shout. We thought that he might be hard pressed, so hurried to him, but found that he only wanted us to assist him to his feet. He was not suffering so badly now, but was unable to walk. We did not carry him, but placed him between us and then had him thrown his arms over our shoulders.

In this manner we made our way over the twenty rough miles of the foothills to the valley. Not only did we support our wounded comrade, but we drove before us four of the oxen that we recovered.

Good's hurt was only a flesh wound, and we were in no particular hurry to reach our homes, as

[47]

we did not think it necessary to procure the services of a doctor. In a few weeks Good was fully recovered.

Many of the Mill Creeks at this time were good shots. I have frequently found where they have indulged in target practice, and, considering the distances and size of the targets, am convinced that they could shoot as accurately as the average white man. But they possessed two weaknesses that are common to many whites,—once get them rattled, and the danger of their hitting you became lessened by many degrees; and they could not shoot accurately down hill. It was for the first of these reasons, largely, that we always planned to give them a surprise. They invariably outnumbered us and it became necessary to even up matters as much as possible by rattling them in the start.

During these times Hi and I, sometimes with "Bully" and sometimes by ourselves, made many scouting trips into the hills and managed to reduce the number of bad Indians on almost every trip. Still, their numbers remained undiminished as far as we could judge by the damage done, and we became convinced that they were being constantly re-inforced.

I often told Hi that it was a mistake to leave the squaws in the hills, since it was but natural for the bucks to find them, and as fast as the latter were put out of the way, others from the Reservation, or from more distant parts of the mountains, would take their places.

Chapter IX

About the middle of the winter (1859), Hi Good, Carter and I indulged in a sort of wild-goose chase which netted us next to nothing in the way of success, but which brought me nearer death than many close-range gun-fights have since done. Hi had become convinced that we could unearth a winter camp of the Indians by a careful search up Deer Creek Canyon.

At first I opposed his plans, but at last consented to accompany him and Carter. We set out afoot, each carrying his rifle, six-shooter and rations, besides a generous roll of blankets, for the mid-winter season, even in California, does not permit

of a bed of dried leaves. I was not yet twenty years of age, and so, of course, was buoyed up by the elasticity of youth. My companions were only a few years older. If I am not mistaken, I was the youngest member of our party in all our principal campaigns against the Indians.

We moved up Deer Creek under threatening skies. For two days we pushed deeper into the canyon, reaching a point rather higher than the Jackson Mine, but found no fresh signs of Indians. The third day out we swung over by Bluff Camp and then, as the inevitable Christmas storm shrouded the gloomy forests and dreary foothills, we tuerned our faces toward the valley.

A bad day we had of it, especially after leaving the shelter of the pines. Rain soaked our clothing, and then came a fine drizzle, half snow, half rain, to chill us to the marrow. A few miles below the timber belt, with the night rapidly drawing on, we halted beside a gnarled digger pine and built a fire. And beside that fire we spent the night,—not sleeping, mind you, nor even lying down, but revolving slowly so that the soaking and roasting processes, going on at the same time on different surfaces of our bodies, might be equally distributed.

Our search so far having proved fruitless, we had ample time during the night to discuss plans for the future. Good argued that the Indians must have moved over into Mill Creek, but along about this time my memory began to inform me very persistently that I had promised to accompany two young ladies on the following night to a dance at Oak Grove, that being the name then applied to the Phillips place on Pine Creek.

Hi finally announced that at break of day we would start for Mill Creek. I told him that he could count me out, as I was going to the dance. He laughed at me, and told me that I would never get there. That made me the more determined that I would, so at daybreak we split, Good and Carter making toward the big canyon to the north, while I started straight for the valley.

It was still raining in torrents. I passed down the ridge that divides the two principal branches of Dry Creek, keeping a little over the backbone so as to be sheltered from the wind. I was striding along, thinking very little of Indians and very much of more agreeable objects, when suddenly I shot out into open view of a large party of the redskins, snuggled under a drooping cave not sixty yards away.

They saw me as soon as I them. There was a general scramble among them for their weapons, but while they scrambled I slid around the point and beat a swift retreat up the next ravine. I saw that I had no business at close range tackling that Christmas party. I did not fire a short, nor did the Indians. Later, when I had gained a loftier position on the next ridge to the south, I paused long enough to spy them out once more in the cave, but there was no evidence to show that they were attempting a pursuit.

I kept on my course down the slope of the hills and reached the footlog opposite Good's cabin about the middle of the afternoon. This log was one that had been felled as a bridge and then flattened along the upper surface so as to afford safer footing. I had crossed it many times and felt no hesitation in stepping upon it now, although the creek was flowing, a turbulent flood, beneath it.

I had reached the middle of the passage and was directly over the wickedest part of the current, when that treacherous log snapped beneath me and in a second I was being tumbled down a crazy reach of the stream like a chip,—and not floating, either, for I was under as much as I was above the surface and felt, at times, as though my head were scraping the bottom. I tried to swim, but I might as well have tried to walk on the surface. In fact, in a very short time it dawned upon me that I was drowning. I made a frantic effort to seize something for support, and then, without a touch of real pain, I lost consciousness.

An old man named Dean was at this time living with Good. He had been seated at the cabin gazing out toward the rapidly rising water in the creek. In the course of their journeys up or down the banks his eyes had detected the footbridge, staunch and safe. When next his sight fell upon the same spot, the bridge was gone. This interested him. After musing upon the matter for a time, it slowly dawned upon him that someone might have gone

down with the log. He promptly ran to the bank, followed it down-stream for two hundred and fifty yards, and there, in an eddy, spied my body lying next the bank.

He rushed to where I lay, nearly submerged and apparently dead, seized me by the feet and dragged me up the bank. My blankets and six-shooter were still strapped to me, while I grasped my rifle in one hand and a clump of willow bushes in the other. It was perhaps a lucky chance that he drew me out of the water and up the bank feet first, for that caused the water to run from my stomach and lungs and doubtless saved my life.

I soon revived, but felt far from gay. By means of strong draughts of whiskey and of vigorous rubbing I was soon put upon my feet, when I walked home. I accompanied my girl friends to the dance that night, but I did not dance.

It was at this gathering that I first met Mr. Ira Wetherby, who has since become so well and so favorably known to me.

Good and Carter did not get home until the following day, having failed to locate any Indians in the canyon of Mill Creek.

Chapter X

In June of 1862, the whites of the upper valley were roused as they had never been before by the atrocities of the Mill Creeks. A skulking band swept through the foothills, killing stock, burning cabins, and injuring the whites in every way possible, until they reached the Keefer ridge. There they lay in wait for a teamster, who was hauling for Keefer, and shot him to death beside his team.

Thirsting for more blood, they dropped down into Rock Creek Canyon and slipped toward the valley where a number of settlers lived. Unfortunately, three of the Hickok children were gathering blackberries along the creek side, some distance above their home, which was on the place now known as the Burch ranch. The oldest of the three was a graceful girl of sixteen, the second a girl of fourteen, and the third a boy some years younger.

The two girls were shot to death with arrows, and their bodies left in the bushes beside the stream, while the little boy was dragged away into the hills.

The Indians knew that these murders could not go long unnoticed, as there was considerable travel up and down the Keefer road. In fact, the bodies of the murdered girls were found late in the afternoon of the day on which they were killed, and then indeed were the whites aroused to the danger that so constantly hovered over their homes.

Many parties were raised and hurried into the hills. In fact, the feeling against the Indians was so bitter that it was proposed to make a general clean-up, even of the friendly Indians, of which there were camps at Bidwell's, at Keefer's, and at the Phillips place on Pine Creek; but Mr. Hickok, the bereaved father, forbade this being done on his behalf, and, of course, at such a time, his wishes were respected.

I was asked to take up the chase, but there was sickness in my family at the time and I could not leave home. However, Hi Good and "Bully" responded to the call, and Sandy Young, boss vaquero on the Bidwell Rancho, was of Hi's party. This, I think, was the first occasion on which these two men worked together on an Indian trail.

They traced the Indians northward past Deer Creek, Dry Creek, and Mill Creek, and finally overhauled them, I think, in the head of Antelope Creek east of Red Bluff. They found the mangled remains of the captured white boy amid signs which indicated that he had been made to move around in a circle, probably being tied, while he was stoned to death by the children of the savages.

The whites made a pretty good clean-up on this occasion. A day or two later I was sitting on my porch when Hi and Sandy rode past on their way home. Hi showed me eight fresh scalps that he had tied to his saddle.

And still the Mill Creeks remained in sufficient numbers to leave their terrible mark upon the white man's home. Somewhat later, as I recall it, than the killing of the Hickok children, the Indians floated through the hills still farther south, and this time the blow fell upon the Lewis family, who lived in the Clear Creek country, about midway between Chico and Oroville.

As on the former occasion, the blood-thirsty wretches slipped down to the very edge of the valley, and made their attack by stealth upon those who were helpless to defend themselves. The story as it came to me was like this: The three Lewis children, a girl and two boys, were on their road home from school. They had reached a brook and the oldest boy was stooping over to drink, when the hidden Indians shot him through the head, killing him instantly. The girl and younger boy, the latter a little fellow just starting to school, were seized and hustled into the hills. The little boy soon became leg-weary and his brains were dashed out against a rock. The girl was hurried forward until night came on.

The party was then well up on a hillside above a stream. For some reason, a portion of the Indians pushed forward and left the captive in charge of one of their number as guard. This guard seemed especially anxious to be permitted to follow his fellows. He placed the girl upon a large rock, motioned for her to remain there, and then set out a short distance in the direction taken by the other Indians.

The moment his back was turned, the plucky little girl slid down from the rock, but her keeper was stealthily watching her. He ran back to her, seized her and shook her, and, drawing his knife, made motions as though about to cut her throat. She cowered and slunk away as if in abject fear, and, thinking that he had her completely intimidated, he placed her once more upon the rock and moved away.

However, the girl's wit had not deserted her. The Indian had no sooner moved away than she slipped down from the rock and darted into a little ravine that creased the hillside. The darkness favored her. She made her way to the bottom of the canyon, discovered which way the water was flowing, and, in spite of the anxious search of the whole party of Indians, escaped and made her way to the valley.

I think that it was on this same raid that the Indians robbed the home of one "Portugee Al," who lived in the head of Little Chico Creek, taking, among other articles, his wife's hat. They also, on their return toward Mill Creek, robbed a man named Bolivar, who lived near the present site of the Richardson Springs.

A party was promptly mustered, of which I was a member. Sim and Jake Moak of Chico were also of the party. We struck through the hills and picked up the Indians' trail south of Deer Creek. It led down into the deep canyon, crossed Deer Creek just above the mouth of Sulphur Creek, and headed directly up toward the towering cliff that walls the gorge on the north.

Just east of the principal cliff is a steep, wedge-like defile, up which it is possible for one to climb to the top. Up this narrow pass we crept single file. Why the Indians did not turn on us and annihilate our entire party has always been a mystery to me, for we found them on the flat just beyond the crest.

They spied us before we were fairly upon them, and away they went, dodging and ducking through the thickets like frightened deer. I brought down one with a short from my double-barrel, but he was up and streaking it through the brush before I could lay hands upon him. Several of us followed him for a half-mile or more down the slope toward Little Dry Creek before we finished him.

We had but one horse with us on this trip, and this animal we left at Sulphur Creek. In the course of the attack and chase, I lost my hat, but among the plunder recaptured from the Indians was found the gaily-beribboned headgear which had been stolen from "Portugee Al's" wife. On the home-ward trip, the boys insisted that I should wear the recovered hat, in place of the one I had lost, and that I should ride the horse. I did so, but it can be imagined the figure I presented, wearing that absurd hat and with an Indian scalp tied to my saddle.

Chapter XI

In August of this year the Indians paid me a friendly call. It was a Sunday morning. Upon arising and stepping out of doors, my attention was at once drawn to a column of smoke curling up from my barn. My neighbors, the Carters, were gone at this time, and the three boys of the family, fearful of a night attack at the hands of the Mill Creeks, had come to my place to sleep.

I immediately shouted to them that the barn was afire and started on a run for the building. One glance convinced me that the fire had but recently been started and could be easily stopped. Some loose hay had been flung down in the shed where my horses had been stabled, and fired, but the blaze had not yet reached the mow or taken hold of the building. The glance that told me this informed me likewise that my two horses, that had been left stabled the evening before, were gone.

The bank of the creek was but a couple of rods away. I seized a bucket and sprang toward it. As I dipped up a bucket of water, I perceived Indian tracks leading into the stream. Rocks near the bank were still wet from the wash caused by the hurry-ing men or beasts. In fact, glancing farther, I saw one of the horses returning toward the stream on the north side.

I returned with the bucket of water and soon had the fire extinguished. By this time the boys were out, so while I secured my rifle and six-shooter, I had one of them run and get up a saddle horse that was loose in the pasture. But on going to the barn to saddle up, I found myself balked, as the two saddles that I had left hanging in the barn were both gone.

I knew that it would be useless to try to ride the animal bareback, as I had tried it several times before, always to meet with defeat; and yet I was not in a humor to neglect the polite attention paid me by the Indians. There was nothing to be done but to take it afoot, and so I started.

Instead of crossing the creek and attempting to overhaul the renegades by means of a stern chase, I ran at top speed up the stream, along the south bank. I reached Hi Good's cabin, after a run of a mile and a half, and hailed him, telling him in as few words as possible what had occurred.

Good snatched up his weapons and joined me. I had run many a half-mile race with Hi, and must admit that I usually took second money, but on this day I was to see him reach the limit of his powers of endurance.

We crossed the creek at the mouth of the canyon, and, still running, pressed up the long slope direct-ly toward the north. We knew that the Indians should be down nearer the plains on our left.

On reaching the crest that overlooked a sharp-sided ravine called Acorn Hollow, we very soon spied the Indians a half-mile down the hollow, and perhaps a quarter of a mile north of us. They had

[51]

evidently already discovered us, for they remained but a moment beside the stolen horse, which we found later they were in the act of repacking, and then they broke into a hasty retreat, leaving the animal behind.

They did not attempt to swing up into the hills, but instead pushed out across the high, open plain that extends northward toward Dry Creek. There were seven of them, Billy Sill being of the number. He was carrying a pair of my buckskin leggings across his arm.

Taking in the situation at a glance, Good remarked that he believed he could run down the hollow, follow the Indians out onto the open plain and overhaul them before they reached the shelter of Dry Creek, but I told him that I was going to hold my present position and try to head them from finally getting into Mill Creek.

Away then we went on our respective courses. I could see the Indians much of the time and could see Good many hundred yards behind them. His turning down the hollow added a half mile or more to his course, and the lead this gave the Indians was too much for him to overcome.

When the Indians scuttled into the brushy bottom of Dry Creek, he was still far out on the open plain. After leaving this depression, the redskins swerved to the right and sped up the long slope toward the breaks of Mill Creek. The many miles of the chase had left me by this time nearly blown. I saw that I was not going to be able to beat the Indians to the protecting belt of timber that lay on the crest of the slope. However, the courses we were now pursuing were bringing us gradually nearer together. I could see a dusky form now and then gliding upward through the trees and brush that sprinkled the hillside.

Putting forth a mighty effort, I increased my pace a trifle, and keeping this up for an eighth of a mile or so reached a spot from which I believed the scudding Indians must come into view. Almost immediately I saw the leader swing across the very space I had picked upon. He was considerably over two hundred yards away, but I knew that I was not going to get closer, so I threw up my rifle and fired at him. I missed, and he swiftly whirled about and

[52]

returned the compliment. This gave me time for my second barrel, and he fell at the crack of my gun. The balance of the party glided like lightning behind covers and began pouring in a hot fire toward my place of concealment. Most of their bullets flew high, as was invariably the case when the redskins were aiming downward. In fact, it was only now and then that a shot struck close to me. On the other hand, Good, who was far below me on the hillside, had a perfect shower of bullets dropping about him during the entire engagement. He was so completely exhausted by the long run across the plains that he did not get into the fight at all.

I kept pounding away as long as the Indians returned my fire, but so closely did they cling to their cover that I was not able to score a second time. After a time they worked back toward the top of the ridge, and, carrying off their wounded comrade, made good their escape into that everlasting haven of refuge,—the wilds of Mill Creek's Canyon.

Then I returned to Hi and we proceeded to help each other home. The tramp back across the plains was one of the hardest jobs I have ever undertaken. Words cannot express the relief we both felt when we at length reached the spot where the abandoned horse was awaiting us. One of my saddles had been cut to pieces to provide straps and strings for tying the stolen plunder onto the horse. This plunder consisted principally of corn and other vegetables which the Indians had collected from the gardens of Deer Creek.

We reached Hi's cabin late in the afternoon and were quite ready for our Sunday breakfasts. At the Carter place we found quite a party of neighbors collected. They had heard the firing and were just on the point of starting to our assistance.

A few weeks later a squaw coming from the hills reported that the wounded Indian had succumbed to his injuries, after a few days.

Chapter XII

One day in June, 1863, Solomon Gore, who lived on Rock Creek, hurried to my house and reported that the Mill Creeks had stolen two horses from him. He asked me if I could get the animals back. I replied that I thought I could if I had someone to accompany me to the hills. Accordingly, Tom Gore and Jack Howser agreed to go with me.

We struck off northeasterly through the hills and were not long in finding the Indians' trail. I had no difficulty in following it, and we pushed forward rapidly. Shortly before night we met one of the stolen horses. It was a young animal, and had evidently escaped from the Indians in some way and was returning to its master.

We had started so late in the day that night overtook us before we had covered many miles. We made our beds by simply selecting convenient places to stretch our frames among the bowlders, where I, for one, slept tranquilly until morning.

With the break of day we were up and once more on the trail. We passed through the Singer Creek country and in a couple of hours came to the borders of the Deer Creek Flats.

As we approached the level land of the Flats, we spied five bears busily digging on an open space ahead. I knew that the Indians were many miles ahead of us, so I suggested to the boys that we have some fun with the bears.

"You may have all the fun you like," said Tom Gore, "but please wait until I get up a tree before you begin."

Jack Howser was of the same way of thinking. I laughed at them and told them to shin up their trees, but to leave a convenient one for me in case I should need it. They were not long in getting up into a couple of oaks, and then I moved cautiously out toward a large tree which enabled me, unseen, to approach within one hundred and fifty yards of the feeding bears. This tree was too large to be easily climbed, which was the reason I had selected a smaller one farther back.

The bears were totally unaware of our presence. I waited until the largest one turned full side toward me, when I raised my rifle and let her have it. She slashed at her ribs with her teeth and sent up a fierce bellow, but after a moment seemed to recover in a measure. At the very least, I had roused her curiosity, for she reared up and sat upon her haunches, looking extremely vicious. She was

directly facing me, so I threw a second ball into her. Then she caught sight of me and charged. I ran for my tree and swung myself up into its branches. When I thought that I was out of the bear's reach, I looked back and was just in time to see her turn end for end as she ran. She did not rise and I afterward found that my second bullet had bitten off the end of her heart.

However, the other bears were yet to be reckoned with. They seemed to consist of two two-year-olds and two yearlings, probably all offspring of the old one. I reloaded my rifle, then dropped to the ground, Tom and Jack yelling at me as though they thought I was as good as eaten alive. One of the bears came a short distance toward me, and I sank on one knee, waited until it was within forty feet, then dropped it dead at one shot. The others were at a loss what to do. While they continued to sniff at the old one and to toddle about in perplexity, I killed two more of them and crippled the fifth one, which got away.

We secured the gall-bladders from the four dead animals, and then took up once more the trail of the Indians. I had little hopes of being able to overtake them short of Mill Creek Canyon, but, of course, I had to follow the trail in order to make sure.

We dropped down into Deer Creek and crossed this stream, as we had on several previous occasions, near the mouth of Sulphur Creek. Again the trail led us up that frightful ascent toward the wedge-like defile in the upper cliff, and, incredible as it may see, we found that the Indians had taken the stolen horse up that way. Tom and Jack declared that they could see scars upon the small trees where the animal had hung on by his teeth.

We crossed through the broad canyons of Little and Big Dry Creeks, and so at length reached the breaks of Mill Creek. From here we could see for miles over the wild regions of that great canyon, and I told the boys that we would take a good look before going farther, as there were ten chances to one that the Indians were snuggled away somewhere under our feet.

After a careful observation, I at length discovered some human figures moving about a hillside, fully two miles below us. We scrutinized them

[53]

closely and came to the conclusion that it was a number of squaws, gathering grass-seed. Their camp was nowhere in sight, but I knew that we could find the camp by watching the squaws.

Bidding the boys to avoid being seen, as they would avoid a pestilence, I led them down the long slope, keeping as deeply as possible within the shelter of ravines and thickets. In this way we were enabled to approach within three hundred yards of the squaws.

We were lying under a jutting pile of rocks, peering out at them and picking out our next line of advance, when suddenly a signal shout was heard, coming from some point above us. I knew at once that we were discovered by a lookout. The squaws, however, paid no heed, evidently not having heard the cry; but in a moment it was repeated, and this time they heard it. In a moment they were scurrying down the hill.

"Our only show is to follow them!" I cried, and springing up I bounded down the hill in pursuit. I proved to be a swifter runner than my two comrades and soon left them behind. As I ran I heard one of them shoot, but I kept on, for I wanted to find the Indians' camp.

The fleeing squaws disappeared over a brow of the ridge, but I kept on down the point which led toward the creek, and all at once I came within full sight of the camp. It lay about two hundred yards below me and seemed to be in a state of confusion. I saw Indians flying about, trying to pile articles upon the single horse that stood in their midst. I could see that there were many bucks present, so waited a few moments for Tom and Jack to join me. They failed to put in an appearance, however, and I knew that I must act quickly or let the entire party escape. I watched for a good chance and soon, drawing down on a big fellow, added one more good Indian to the list with the first shot.

The other warriors immediately sprang to their guns and, locating me by the smoke from my rifle, began sending bullets whining and whistling about me. With the first volley they disappeared, dropping behind the rocks and bushes, but they continued to find the way to my position. For some time we exchanged shots. I was behind a tree which was not more than eight inches in diameter,

though there were moments when I warmly wished that it were eight feet. However, having my double-barrel, I was able to fool them. They perceived that I was alone, and frequently, after I fired, some of them would expose themselves for a moment in seeking to secure better cover, and each time they made this mistake I dropped one in his tracks with my second barrel.

At length Jack and Tom came down to where I lay, and a more helpless pair of Indian fighters I never saw! One had the lock wrenched off his rifle, while the other had his ramrod broken off in his gun-barrel. Neither could fire a shot. At that time I had my last bullet in my rifle, but luckily Tom's bullets were the same calibre as mine. I quickly deprived him of all he had, and just at that moment the Mill Creeks turned loose a most vicious volley. The bullets plowed and hissed among the rocks beside us, and in a second the two of them were trying to hide with me behind my little eight-inch tree.

I told them that our only show was to charge and put the Indians on the run. They agreed to follow my lead, so we sprang out and rushed down the hill. The Indians broke and fled and we gained their camp in safety.

"Now hustle," said I, "or they will slip back and make it hot for us from that brush!"

We soon had the recovered horse loaded with such articles as we could hastily pick up. There was a pile of new quilts lying beneath a tree, probably having been snatched from some foothill cabin, and as I picked one of them up a lank Indian boy sprang up and stood watching us in blank surprise. He had slept peacefully through the entire battle.

"There's your chance!" said I to Tom and Jack. "If you want to kill an Indian on this trip, bag that fellow."

But neither of them would raise a hand against him, and we went away and left him staring stupidly after us.

When we reached the top of the ridge, we sat down for a breathing spell.

"Well, Bob," said Jack, "how many of those fellows do you think you got? I saw two."

"I counted three" said Tom.

I told them that I thought there were six or seven scattered along the hillside.

We struck off down the slope of the foothills and reached the valley without mishap. We went by way of Hi Good's cabin, and stopped there for lunch. Hi was at home and listened with great interest to an account of our experiences. He remarked, when we had finished:

"You fellows can consider that you got off very lucky. I came down through that country the other day, and took a peep at that camp, and there were at least thirty bucks there. I guess if the whole party had been at home that you three would have been left in the hills."

I told him that it looked to me like there were just about thirty warriors there when I opened fire upon them.

About two weeks later, Hi came one day to my place. He said that a squaw had come to his place from Mill Creek, a few days after we had paid our visit to the Indians' camp, and had told him that there were seven killed and two badly wounded in that battle, which proved that my estimate had not been far wrong.

Chapter XIII

The final conflict with the Mill Creeks occurred in 1865. I was then living at my present home, eight miles north of Chico. About the middle of August, business took me to the old grist mill that stood at the mouth of Butte Creek Canyon. I made the trip on horseback.

As I was riding up Edgar Slough, I noticed a group of some half a dozen men break from the woods at about the point where the Schwein slaughter-house now stands. On nearer approach, I perceived that they were all strangers. I also discovered that they were all armed and seemed to be in a state of great excitement.

"Have you seen a party of men anywhere on the road between here and Chico?" asked one, eagerly.

"How many?" I asked.

"Six."

"No. What's up?"

"We're after Bidwell's Indians!"

Then they told me how the Indians had made a raid into the Concow country, had killed a man and two women, horribly mutilating the latter, had slaughtered hogs and cattle out of pure cruelty, and had then melted away.

"Why do you think it the work of the Bidwell Indians?" I asked.

"We KNOW it is! Their trail leads straight out through the hills in this direction. We followed it to the Johnson place, and it points for Chico. Listen to that shooting, boys!"—for at that instant a shot or two and some cries were heard from toward Chico Creek. "Hurry up! let's don't miss it all!" and they were about to rush away.

"Gentlemen," said I, "you are barking up the wrong tree!"

They paused.

"What do you know about it?" asked one.

"Simply this: That trail you've been following is a blind. Bidwell's Indians haven't been near Concow, and Bidwell's Indians haven't killed anyone."

"Then what Indians did it?"

"The Mill Creeks."

They had all heard of the Mill Creeks, but some were still in doubt.

"Who are you?" asked one.

I told him my name, and they seemed more willing to listen to me. I assured them that the Bidwell Indians were perfectly quiet and well-behaved, and that the Mill Creeks had more than once attempted to saddle some of their own crimes upon them. I added that if they wished to find the real culprits they had better strike for the canyon of Deer Creek or of Mill Creek.

While we were talking, I saw a group of men leave the woods a mile or so east of us.

"There is the rest of your outfit," I said, and on approaching and joining them we found that this was true.

With this new party was one Bill Matthews; also a young man named Frank Curtis, who was a brother, I think, of Henry Curtis, who then conducted a tannery on Rock Creek, and with whom I was well acquainted.

I repeated what I had told the first-comers, and told them that they would surely breed trouble for themselves if they bothered Bidwell's Indians; and, besides, would be wasting their time and allowing the real culprits to escape.

A short consultation was held among their leaders, and then I was asked if I would lead them into the Mill Creek country. I replied that I had business at the grist mill, but that I would ride there and return as soon as possible, and would join them on Rock Creek. I assured them that there was not one chance in a hundred of our overtaking the Indians short of Mill Creek, and that there would be many miles of rough country to travel over before reaching that point.

I finished my mission at the mill, and, hurrying home, moved my family over to the Gore place on Rock Creek. The Concow men were awaiting me there, and we started next morning. Henry Curtis had joined the party and was practically leader of the Concow force.

I told Curtis that we would probably strike the trail on Deer Creek Flats, so we headed for that region. On Deer Creek we found Hi Good, who promptly jioned us. We reached the Flats late in the afternoon, and there, sure enough, we found a fresh Indian trail leading toward the north.

We made camp beside the spring, on the Flats, and while gathered about the camp-fire before retiring it was suggested that we organize by electing a captain. I was elected and Good was chosen second in command.

Next morning we were up and away almost with the break of day. In order to make sure that the Indians had not dodged to right or left, I followed the trail, keeping usually about two hundred yards ahead of the main party, with Hi beside me as my lookout. In this way we filed down through the wild gorge of Deer Creek, across that stream, and on across the less rugged slopes of the two Dry Creeks, and so by the middle of the afternoon reached the top of the ridge which overlooks the broad canyon of Mill Creek.

Climbing to a point from which we had a good outlook, Good and I made a close inspection of the region below us. At length the glint as of some bright object caught my eye far down in the very bottom of the canyon. It was fully three miles distant. I believed it to be the sun flashing from a rifle-barrel and pointed it out to Hi. Soon we saw a tiny white object move down the side of a little rounded knoll close to the creek, and both recognized it as a human figure.

"That's their lookout," I said, "and I believe it's Billy Sill. He had on a white shirt when he ran away. They are camped beside those three little knolls just the other side of the creek."

"Just this side, you mean," said Hi.

"No. The north side."

We both remembered the three knobs, but could not agree as to which side of the stream they occupied, and the water could not be seen from where we were to decide the matter. We argued for some time and at length Hi said:

"Well, you're the doctor. What shall we do?"

I replied that we would swing back around a high point on the summit of the ridge, march down to the bottom of the canyon, cross the creek a half mile or more below the three knolls, and then make our advance by moving up-stream.

This plan I communicated to the main party. We slipped into a hidden ravine and filed slowly and cautiously downward toward the bottom of the canyon, exercising the utmost care to keep from falling under the eye of the hawk-like lookouts that we knew were stationed on lofty points here and there. The ravine was very brushy and strewn with bowlders, yet at times we had to crawl on our hands and knees to remain hidden.

At last we accomplished the descent successfully, and waded through the foaming waters of Mill Creek to the north side. We were still a good, safe distance below where I knew the camp must be, so I ordered that the entire party advance slowly up-stream. We moved up some distance from the creek and kept under the coves that headed the glades.

A little before actual sunset,—the sun being gone long since from the bottom of that deep canyon, —a number of moving objects on the hillside below us caught my eye. I gave the signal to lie low, and the entire party sank down among the rocks.

Soon four squaws came filing along a dim trail, wending their way up the creek. We were not discovered, and the squaws passed on around a bend a few hundred yards above us and disappeared. This made Hi and I feel more certain than ever that the Indians were camped about in the region of the three knolls.

Chapter XIV

I moved the party a short distance farther up-stream, then grouped them beneath the spreading branches of an oak and ordered them to lie down and to remain absolutely quiet, until I should return.

Selecting Good as my companion, we made plans to find out, if possible, the exact location of the camp. We removed our boots, laid aside our rifles, and, with only our revolvers as weapons, slipped into the water and started to make our way up-stream. Our progress was extremely slow. The night was very dark, and the stream was turbulent and filled with bowlders. We tried to keep under the bank as much as possible, for fear of brushing into some sentinel above it, but at times found the water too deep for us, when we were compelled to crawl like snakes through the bordering fringe of trees and brush.

Just below the three round-topped knolls the stream broadened into a natural ford. The knolls stood on the north side of the stream, and between them and the ford lay a flat sand-bar. At length we approached this broader stretch of water. The bank broke off straight to the water. It was not over three feet high and was clear of trees and brush.

Suddenly a dog broke forth into wild barking close in front of us, and, springing toward the bank, bayed furiously in our very faces. We could feel his hot breath and could have struck him with our six-shooters had we wished. Instead of turning about or making any attempt to beat a retreat, we crouched still for a minute or more, while the dog made the echoes of that deep canyon resound with his cries of defiance.

Peering over the bank in the midst of this uproar, we plainly perceived several forms rise up to sitting postures on the bar in front of us. We were almost abreast of the camp. The Indians probably thought that the dog was baying some wild beast, for none of them arose to investigate, and Good and I pain-stakingly made our way back down-stream, the dog following us to within one hundred yards of where the main party lay.

Just before we reached the point where we had entered the stream, Good, in some way, loosened a heavy stone from the bank, which rolled into the water, struck his bare foot and crushed off a toe-nail. I helped him bandage the injured member with a poultice of tobacco, after which we joined the rest of the party and made our plans for the attack upon the Indians.

We decided to move forward just in time to get the camp surrounded before the break of day. Hi, with six men, was left to advance upon the camp in the same manner that he and I had already adopted, while I took the balance of the force for a detour which would bring us against the Indians from the up-stream side.

We had a difficult climb, for we were compelled to swing some distance up the rough hillside in order to avoid springing an alarm, but made it successfully. As day began to peep over the high walls of the canyon, I found myself lying about thirty feet above one of the three little knolls that had served us so well as land-marks. I had left orders for Hi's party to lie quiet and let us make the attack. This would throw the Indians onto the bar next the open ford, where they would be completely at the mercy of both our forces.

It grew lighter and still no sound disturbed the morning excepting the incessant roar of the near-by stream. Henry Curtis was close to my right. Suddenly he chirped like a bird. I glanced toward him and saw him pointing toward the top of the knoll. Turning my eyes thither I was just in time to see the half-breed, Billy Sill, lowering his rifle in a line with my head. I rolled behind a tree, and the half-breed, knowing that he was seen, sank out of sight behind a rock. I had ample time, in the glimpse I caught of him, to see that he still wore a white shirt.

Almost on the instant that he disappeared, Good's rifle cracked, and the fight was on. We crowded forward and poured a hot fire into the Indians from up-stream, while Good's men ham-mered them from below. Into the stream they leaped, but few got out alive. Instead, many dead bodies floated down the rapid current.

[57]

Billy Sill made a break to escape by leaping straight up the mountain-side. Several shot at him, but missed. I swung my rifle on him and cut him down just as he was about to spring into a thicket. As he rolled toward the creek he cursed me venomously with his last breath. He was known to many of us, having lived from childhood with Uncle Dan Sill. He had been herding sheep for Sill a short time before this, when one day he left the band and joined the Mill Creeks.

This battle practically ended the scourge of the Mill Creeks. I had often argued with Good regarding the disposition of the Indians. He believed in killing every man or well-grown boy, but in leaving the women unmolested in their mountain retreats. It was plain to me that we must also get rid of the women. On this occasion the Concow people were intensely wrought up over the horrible atrocities practiced by the Indians on the white women whom they killed, and I had told them that they were at liberty to deal with the Indians as they saw fit.

[58]

While ransacking the camp after the battle was over, a little child possessing six toes on each foot was found. Hi Good at once took a notion to the child and said that he wished to take it home with him. Knowing that he had odd tastes about such things, I consented, whereupon he declared that he must take along a squaw to carry the child. I asked Curtis what his pleasure was in the matter, and, after consulting with some of his own party, he grudgingly agreed.

The woman selected for the purpose was slightly wounded in the heel. She packed the youngster in stolid silence up the long hill, and over its crest into Twenty-Mile Hollow. Here, however, she became sullen and refused to go a step farther. I gave her over to the Concow people and they left her to swell the number of the dead.

If I remember correctly, one of the women murdered by the Indians at Concow had recently come over from England and had in her posession several hundred dollars in English sovereigns. This money was taken by the murderers, but we failed to find any of it.

However, at this time Sandy Young was stopping at Big Meadows, in charge of the Bidwell stock.

The marauding Mill Creeks, in the course of their raid, had swung around by the Meadows, where they had killed a number of the Indians of that region and carried away a number of squaws.

The Big Meadows red-men were afraid of their desperate enemies, and would not take the field against them except under Young's leadership. Consequently, the latter got a force together and came down through Deer Creek Meadows and Onion Creek and so along the Lassen Trail to Bluff Camp, where they swung into Mill Creek Canyon.

They reached the old camp at the three knolls just three days after we had been there. Sandy said that it looked as though a cyclone had struck that spot. In making a search over the battle-ground he found where something had been buried in the sand and a fire made above it to hide the spot. Examiinng it closely, he unearthed an English sovereign. The balance of the money had evidently been dug up and carried away by the survivors among the Indians, and probably today lies hidden away in some one of the many caverns of that mighty canyon.

Chapter XV

It was well known that several bucks and a number of squaws and children escaped during that last fight at the three knolls. They remained hidden away in the depth of the canyons, sallying out occasionally to plunder foothill cabins, but dealing no more death to the white man. Their reign of mischief-making seemed to be at an end, and yet were they to be heard from, at least indirectly, once more.

After many months a number of squaws humbly presented themselves to Hi Good and told him that the entire remnant of the tribe would surrender if assured of his protection. Hi was then living on Dry Creek. Negotiations were carried on for some time, and at length two bucks and three squaws, with a number of children, moved down to Good's place and told him that they were ready to be taken to the Reservation.

However, reduced as they were to this pitiful handful, their innate treachery had not been beaten out of them. Living with Good was an Indian boy whom he had raised from childhood. This boy was now about sixteen, and I have never had a doubt that he was influenced by the older Indians to turn traitor against the man who had given him a home.

With genuine Indian patience he watched and waited for his opportunity. It came one day when Good rode over to the Carter place on Deer Creek for vegetables. After he was gone, the Indian boy took Hi's rifle and slipped after him. He met Good returning near Acorn Hollow, a brush-sided ravine that puts out from the hills less than a mile north of Deer Creek.

Hi was walking and leading his horse by means of the bridle-rein, the animal carrying a sack of garden stuff. The Indian permitted his victim to get within easy range, when, from his hidden lair, he took deliberate aim and fired. Good fell, but rose again and started toward his assailant. The Indian, being uninjured, easily kept out of his grasp, and a second and a third bullet he drove into the white man's body before the latter sank down dead.

The murderer then tried to dispose of the body. He placed a rope around the dead man, and, looping it to the saddle-horn, dragged the body some distance up the hollow, rolled it over a step bank, then, climbing down, piled stones upon it.

The older Indians at once fled to the hills, but the boy, if he went with them, soon returned to Dry Creek. Inquiries for Good were soon made and the conduct of the Indian boy excited suspicion. He had an unusual amount of money in his possession, and was found to be wearing a large silver ring of Hi's upon his finger. Furthermore, he boastfully carried Hi's rifle about with him.

Friends instituted a search and the body was soon found. The Indian boy was taken to Acorn Hollow by Sandy Young and a number of others. When shown the dead body, he at first denied all knowledge of the crime; but soon his manner altered and he calmly made a full confession, and even led the whites to the spot where the fatal shots had been fired, and explained every step of the tragedy.

After all had been told, Sandy significantly picked up his rifle, and his companions slipped away, knowing that an act of retributive justice was about to be enacted. Soon the sharp crack of

the rifle rang out above the chaparral and the last chapter in the tragic death of Hi Good had been written.

A word as to the other members of our party who trailed and fought the Indians through so many hard days. Breckenridge went to the lower country, where he met his death in a campaign against the Indians of Arizona. Simmons, Martin and Williams drifted to other regions, where I lost all trace of them. "Bully" went to Nevada, where he secured employment as hunter for a force of soldiers. While so employed, he one day met a group of Piute Indians. They exchanged cordial greetings as they rode past, but after riding a few rods they suddenly whirled and shot him in the back, killing him instantly.

Sandy Young lived in Chico for a number of years after most of the others had passed away. Finally, in company with Dan Sutherland, he went to the Klamath River and engaged in mining. There he mysteriously disappeared. His body was never found, but it is generally believed that he was treacherously murdered and his body disposed of in some remote portion of that wild country.

It is but just that I should mention, in closing, the circumstances which raised the hand of the Mill Creek forever against the white. As in almost every similar instance in American history, the first act of injustice, the first spilling of blood, must be laid at the white man's door.

A party of the Indians were encamped at the Carter place on Deer Creek, being employed as workmen by the Carter brothers. Some among them killed a cow brute belonging to the white men. The Carters got a small party together, followed the Indians up to a foothill camp, and attacked them without giving the latter a chance to explain their action, or make good the loss of the slaughtered animal. Several Indians and one white man were killed, and the fires of hatred kindled in the heart of the savage were such as could be quenched only in the one way.

A remnant of the Indians who caused so much uneasiness in those early days still remains hidden away in the dark caverns of the hills. They haunt that stretch of country from Deer Creek to Mill Creek, making stealthy descents upon the cabin of the white man, but committing no serious crimes. The have developed the art of hiding to a perfection greater than that of the beasts of the woods, and, while in no wise dangerous, they are probably today the wildest people in America.

Sim Moak was born in 1845 near Albany, New York. He came to California in 1863 and settled in Chico. Apparently the most exciting experiences Moak had in the '60's and '70's were the Indian-hunting expeditions he engaged in. The incidents he describes are also covered in R. A. Anderson's Fighting the Mill Creeks, *reprinted above. The killing of the Lewis children in 1863 is independently described by Thankful Carson, a survivor, and by Anderson in Chapter X of his narrative (both above).*

---

8. The Last of the Mill Creeks (1862-1870)

Sim Moak

[60]

The Massacre of the Hickok Children

In the settlement of Butte, Tehama and Shasta counties in the early sixties the people living in and along the foot hills were in danger of being slain by a band of Indians, known as the Mill Creeks as their main camp was at Black Rock on Mill Creek. They were a cruel, blood-thirsty band. The chief was called Big Foot, as he had six toes on his right foot.

The killing of the Hickok children was in June, 1862. The Hickok children, two girls and a boy were gathering black berries on Rock Creek about three-quarters of a mile from their home when they were surrounded by a number of Indians. They first shot the oldest girl, she was seventeen years old. When found she was entirely nude. They then shot the younger girl, fifteen years old, but she ran to Rock Creek and fell with her face in the water. They did not take her clothing as she was

Sim Moak, *The Last of the Mill Creeks and Early Life in Northern California* (Chico, Calif., 1923). Extracts here are from pp. 11-14, 18-27, 30-34.

in full dress when found. Just then Tom Allen came upon the scene. He was hauling lumber for a man by the name of Keefer. They immediately attacked Allen. He was found scalped with his throat cut. Seventeen arrows had been shot in him and seven had gone partly through so that they had to be pulled out the opposite side.

The little boy of twelve years, they captured and took with them. A company of about thirty men started after the Indians. They did not know anything about tracking the Indians and went in the hills without provisions and had to come back. This Mr. Keefer had a rancheria on his ranch, a sawmill in the mountains and a grist mill a short distance below the Hickok home. Mr. Keefer sent for Hi. Good, who was known to be a great Indian trailer, and Indian fighter. When Good arrived Mr. Keefer said, "Mr. Good, I want you to get the Hickok boy, you can have all the money you want." He then emptied his purse of seventy-five dollars and gave it to Good. Good had a man living with him by the name of Bowman, so he and Bowman, William Sublet and Obe Fields went to the Indian camp at Black Rock, which they found deserted. The finally found the trail going north out of the canyon. This they followed up a long ridge and near the top they found the boy by the odor. They made a litter of their clothing and packed the little fellow out to Good's place in the valley, thirty-five miles. It was a trip that none but heroic men could endure. The little boy was buried by the side of his sisters in the Chico cemetery.

My wife went to school with the baby sister of the Hickok children. She used to cry and tell about the massacre.

The first person buried in the Chico cemetery was a man by the name of Fry, he was killed by the Mill Creek Indians. T. F. Rinehart provided in his will for a monument to be put at Fry's grave.

The Massacre of the Lewis Children

The killing of the Lewis children by the Mill Creek Indians was in the Summer of 1863 on the fifth or sixth of July. Sam Lewis lived on Dry Creek, seventeen miles southeast of Chico on Cherokee road. His children were going to school

Left to right: Sim Moak, Captain R. A. Anderson, and Jake Moak

about two miles from their home. The elder boy, Jimmy, eleven years old, the girl, Thankful, nine, and Little Johnny, six. The little fellow did not go to school regularly but on this particular day asked to go and his mother let him go. As they were returning home in the evening the little boy wanted a drink. They left the road and went to the creek and lay down to drink. The oldest boy was drinking, the little boy and sister were standing waiting for him. The first thing they knew they heard a shot and Jimmy was shot in the back and pitched forward in the water. Four Indians appeared and began throwing rocks and boulders on him to make sure he was dead. The little boy and girl stood looking on, trembling with fear. Six other Indians then joined them, one of them had one big foot and one small one. This was Big Foot, the Chief of the Mill Creeks. They then started for the hills. They forced the children along until way in the night, until they came to Nance Canyon, where they camped. The little girl held the little boy on her lap and did not sleep. They left camp before daylight. Johnny began to cry. He and the little girl were barefooted. When the little boy began to weaken four of the Indians

took him back out of sight of the girl. She said, "You are going to kill little brother, let me go and kiss him."

They said, "No, he is all right." She said she knew they had killed him when they came back, as Big Foot had the little boy's hat on his head and one had his clothes.

They then crossed Butte Creek and then Little Chico Creek and between Little and Big Chico Creeks they rounded up some cattle and shot a steer of General Bidwell's. They skinned it and made mocassins, which they tied on their feet. They cut strips of meat and ate it raw, the blood running over their chins. They wanted the little girl to eat it, but she would not. They cut a lot of meat to take with them. They were heavily loaded. The girl had a pair of gold ear rings in her ears. Two Indians attempted to tear them out. She told them she would give the ear rings to them. They began to fight as they both wanted them. She stopped the fight by giving one to each of the Indians.

The Indian who had her in charge was lame and when they crossed the Big Chico Creek he and the girl were some distance behind the others. She

[61]

told him she wanted to rest and for him to go and get some of them to help him with his load of meat as they could not keep up. He said, "You can rest if you want, run, if you do, I shoot." She sat down behind a large boulder. The Indian went up the hill until he was out of sight. She then rolled down the hill until she came to the creek, she jumped in and ran down it until the water got too deep. She then ran up the bank and down the creek until she saw a drift pile and she crawled under it and lay very still. Soon she heard them talking as they were looking for her. Finally all was still. She crawled out and ran down the bank of the creek to the Thomasson home and was met at the door by Mrs. Thomasson, in whose outstretched arms she fell.

She told them how the Indians had had her and she got away. Mrs. Thomasson gave her dinner and washed her feet and greased them and made her as comfortable as possible. Just then, Nath. Thomasson came on horseback. He asked if she could go back the way the Indians came. She said she could, so Mrs. Thomasson put a pillow on the horse behind the saddle and put her on it. They went to the butchered steer and when they got to Little Chico Creek the horse could not get up the bluff, so he took the road and took her home. When they got there Mr. Lewis and his neighbors had found the elder boy and had just buried him.

In the meantime when the children did not come home Mr. Lewis thought they had stayed with their grandmother, who lived near the schoolhouse, but he could not rest. The next morning he saddled his horse and went to see where they were and as he was paassing Mr. Ackley's house, Ackley said, "Where are you going, Sam?" He said that he was going to see why the children did not come home. Mr. Ackley said, "They passed here before sundown."

Mr. Lewis said, "My children are killed by the Indians." He then rode back and saw the Indian's tracks in the road and rode home and told Mrs. Lewis. He then notified his neighbors and they soon found Jimmy, the murdered boy.

When Mr. Thomasson came with the little girl she said she could take them to the place where she last saw Johnny. So she directed them and

when they got to the place she told them to hunt for him. They soon found him where he had been thrown in a large manzanita bush. He had been beaten with clubs and rocks and stripped naked. He was so bruised and beaten they could not dress him to bury him. They wrapped him in a sheet and laid him in the coffin.

In the morning when they left the camp in Nance Canyon one of the Indians left the others and went to the valley. The little girl did not know if he went to the Neal Rancheria or to the Bidwell Rancheria.

This brutal murder aroused the whole country, so there was a mass meeting held at the Pentz Ranch about two miles from the Lewis home. People came from all over the county, about five hundred in number. Some wanted to kill all the Indians in the valley and in the hills. General Bidwell was there and plead for his Indians, saying he knew them to be innocent, and I believe they were.

All the Indians in the hills were notified to be at the Bidwell Rancheria by a certain date or if caught in the hills after that date they would be shot on sight. A great many came and one day was set for Mr. Lewis and the little girl to come and investigate. They took the little girl and led her by the row of Indians. She finally stopped and took a good look at one of the Indians and said: "He looks just like the one that left the others the morning they killed Johnny." There was another Indian who had the name of being a bad one. It did not take more than suspicion to shoot an Indian in those days. They quickly tied their hands behind them and took them just to the outskirts of the town and there Mr. Lewis and six or seven or his neighbors tied the Indians to two small trees and Mr. Lewis and the others all shot at once and two Indians went to the Happy Hunting Ground. . . .

The Massacre at the Workman Home

The massacre at the Workman Home in Concow Valley was in August, 1865. The Workman family consisted at the time of which I write of Mrs. Workman, her sister, Miss Smith, who had just come from Australia, and an old man, who went by the name of English John. Mr. Workman was a miner; his claim was some distance from his home, and he would be at the mine for several days at a time before coming home.

On the 26th day of August, Mrs. Workman and Miss Smith were making dresses of fine silk, that Miss Smith had brought her. Miss Smith looked up the road and saw nine Indians coming. She said, "See those Indians? How savage they look and they have guns." As the Indians started to come in the front gate she quickly locked the front door and ran out the back door. One of the Indians ran around the house and as she came out shot her, she ran to the barn, where she fell. Mrs. Workman ran screaming, and as she came out the Indian struck her on the head with his gun knocking her down; he then threw a large rock on her chest. The old man was working in the garden under the hill when he heard the shot and Mrs. Workman's scream, started for the house and as he came to the garden gate, one of the Indians shot him through the heart. The Indians then robbed the house. They cut Miss Smith's throat, scalped her and mutilated her body in such a shocking manner it is unprintable. They then cut the old man's throat and scalped him. They seemed to have forgotten Mrs. Workman at the back door as they did not molest her.

Sometime after the Indians had gone Mrs. Workman regained consciousness. She could not walk, so she crawled down the road to Mr. Mullen's place. Mullen went to a quartz mill nearby and gave the alarm. The miners all turned out, but it was after dark before they reached the Workman home and they did not find Miss Smith's body until the next morning. Mrs. Workman lingered for some time before she died.

The Indians, after taking all in the house, including sixteen hundred dollars in English sovereigns belonging to Miss Smith, Workman's gold watch and gold dust, they started down the road. As they came around a bend they met Joe Miller, father of Wendell Miller, President of the First National Bank of Chico. They immediately fired on him. He was riding a mule which took fright and ran away. One bullet struck the saddle horn and one struck Mr. Miller in the right side, just below the ribs, followed around the abdomen, just tearing the skin and came out on the left side. Miller had a leather bound account book in his right side pocket, the bullet struck it and it was all that saved his life. He said he did not think a mule could run as fast as that one did. He took around through the brush and got to his home in Cherokee. When they came to dress the wound they found he was not as badly wounded as they thought at first.

At that time I was working for a man by the name of Tood, about one mile north of Durham. On the 27th of August about eleven o'clock the thresher broke down and as there was no foundry nearer than Marysville it would take four or five days before the thresher would be in running order, so Mr. Tood paid off the hands and asked them in to dinner and asked all to come back and help him out with his crop. At the dinner table came the news of the Workman family at Concow.

I had my saddle horse and I started home. We lived at that time in Little Chico Canyon. On my way I saw nine or ten men coming along the foot of the hill. I rode over to them and asked where they were going, they said that they were trailing the Indians. I told them R. A. Anderson had sent word that if the Indians committed any depredations about here we should come north to Rock Creek and head them off. I then turned and started for Rock Creek and got there just at dark. Jack Houser had a tannery there. Henry and Frank Curtis and Tom Gore were there and the five of use went to the Gore barn and stayed until it began to get light. The next morning we went up the road to the old Hickok cabin where we found the tracks of the Indians. They had gone to the cabin and looked in. It was the place where the Hickok children lived when they were murdered by this same band of Indians.

We went back to Mr. Gore's. Mrs. Gore gave me breakfast and I then started for R. A. Anderson's and met Mr. Anderson, his wife and children going to Gore's place to spend the day. Mrs. Gore was Mrs. Anderson's mother. Anderson had his old long rifle with him.

Houser and the Curtises' wanted to go direct to Deer Creek, but I told them it would not be right as the Concow men had come so far. I came back along the foothills looking for them and found them at Mud Creek. Hardy Thomasson, my neighbor, was with them. I told them to come with me to Gore's, that Anderson and several others were there waiting for them. When we arrived Mrs. Gore gave us our dinner, then we started for Deer Creek. Thomasson and I had our saddle horses. We gave them to the men from Concow who had come so far and they would change off riding when we got to Good's place on Deer Creek. The sheep herder said Good had gone to Tehama and that he would be back before night.

When Good came and was told about the murder he said, "All right, we will go for them in the morning. How are you fixed for grub? We told him we had raw bacon and crackers. He said, "Save it, no telling how long we will be out." He then jumped over the fence and caught a large fat wether and cut his throat and said for us to make our supper and breakfast on mutton. We got some salt and cut strips of mutton and roasted it and made supper and breakfast of it the next morning.

We started very early. There were sixteen of us. We went up in the hills on the south side of Deer Creek until we came to Deer Creek flats. Good and Anderson told us to wait and they would go ahead and look for the Indians' trail. They found it at the upper spring. They then called us from there. We went down a long ridge until we came to Deer Creek. We saw the tracks in the sand. The Chief, Old Big Foot, and his son, Young Big Foot, were both in the party; both had six toes on the right foot. We took our clothes off and forded the creek and followed the trail up the north side of the creek until we came to the foot of Iron Mountain. Here we lost the trial as there were so many tracks going in every way.

As we were looking to see which way they had gone William Merathew went in a thicket and the first thing we knew he came running. We thought to see an Indian at his heels and instantly a half dozen guns were in readiness to stop Mr. Red Skin, when we saw him grab his hat and fight the yellow

jackets. He had got in their nest. One of the men went to the creek and called us, he had found a large tree that had floated down and made a fine crossing. We crossed over and found the Indian camp deserted. It had been occupied by the squaws and papooses while the Indians were away. They had left in the morning, we knew, as there was still coals in their fires. We slicked off strips of raw bacon and put it between two crackers and this was our supper. When we were after the Indians no one was allowed to build a fire or fire a gun, for we never knew how near we were to them. The next morning we had breakfast of raw bacon and crackers. At break of day we were climbing out of Deer Creek. On the north side of this canyon is a spring named by the emigrants who came by the Lassen Trail route as Grape Vine Spring. Here the Indians had stopped and undone some of their packages. I found a spool of silk thread and showed it to Good. He said, "All right, boys, we will get them." We went to the top of the hill and came to the Lassen Trail. Here one of the men left us, saying that he was sick. This left fifteen of us. The next canyon to cross was Boat Gunnell Hollow, it was very brushy and we were always on the lookout for fear of being ambushed.

Good and Anderson said they were sure we would find the Indians at Black Rock on Mill Creek. After crossing Boat Gunnell we went down a long barren ridge into Mill Creek with Anderson in the lead. He dropped suddenly to his knees and said, "Keep low, boys." I crawled up and asked him what he had seen. On the north side of Mill Creek is a long and very high bluff, at the foot of which is a number of springs; they make a green sward of the hillside. Anderson said, "Look about the center of that green place, and as he turned we could see his gun barrel glisten when the sun shone on it. It was so far we could just see a small object, so we swung off to the left and went down the water way of the ravine. It was very rough. When we got about half way down we came to a place of very steep slick lava; at the foot of it, it broke in a bluff about eight feet high. We could not go around it for the brush. Good said, "Uncap your guns and straddle a stick just like you did when you were boys." We did and when we started we sure went, it was like going on ice. When we got to the bottom we had to jump about eight feet. We all got down all right.

When we got to Mill Creek we lay down in a patch of tall rushes growing there. Good and Anderson left their guns with us and crawled up the creek with their revolvers to see if they could locate the camp. They came back about dark and said they saw two squaws gathering something on the hillside and watched to see where they went. They came to the creek. We lay there until ten o'clock at night, then we took our clothes off and crossed the creek and lay down on the rocks on the hillside.

At daybreak Anderson took half the men and formed a half circle to the left and Good took the other half and formed a half circle to the right with Good and Anderson in the center. Anderson told Curtis and I to go down the creek through the thicket and said he would let us know if anything turned up. Where we had come down the creek was a chaparral thicket. Sometimes we would have to crawl to get through. William Merithew was on the extreme right and I was on the extreme left.

The creek had formed a sand bar on which the Indians were camped. Back of the sand bar the creek had washed and made a bank eigth or ten feet high which hid them from us. Merithew had traveled fast and had gotten to the creek some distance below the sand bar when we looked up the creek and saw an Indian coming off the sand bar with a gun. He was too far to chance a shot, then we saw Anderson coming down the hill toward the creek and motioned to him. Anderson ran but the Indian had seen him and ducked under the bank and ran to the ford and started to cross. The Indian had not seen Good, who by this time had got to about twenty yards of the ford. When the Indian got in the creek, he could not run, as it was too swift and Good shot him. The bullet struck him below the right shoulder and came out at the left breast, he crossed the creek and ran down about twenty steps along the bank and fell.

As soon as Good shot, Anderson shouted, "Down the creek, boys, down the creek." We ran down the creek to the Indian camp where all was confusion. It came like a thunder bolt out of a clear sky. The plan had been carried out with such discretion that they did not dream of a white man being within miles of them, nor did they think they had seen their last day on earth, or scalped the last white woman or murdered the last little child. The fight was fast and furious for about twenty minutes. Hi Good and Hardy Thomasson ran across the creek and as I looked down the creek I saw an Indian running down along it. I called to Good and Thomasson to look out down the creek. The Concow men said, "We will get him." They fired revolvers and shot guns, but the Indian kept on running, so I said, "You will get nothing." "So I yelled and they both heard me and both ran, Thomasson got to the creek just as the squaw was crossing and said, "Come back or I will shoot." She came out to him. She had a little Indian girl strapped on her back. We could not tell from where we were whether it was a buck or squaw. By this time the fight was all over, except one Indian, who had gotten on a high bluff east of us. He kept loading and firing as fast as he could. We could hear the bullets whistle, but they aimed too high and struck in the hill back of us. Anderson said, "I will stop him." He raised his gun and elevated it so he thought it would reach him and fired. The bullet struck between the Indian's feet and scattered the lava all over him. He was so scared he fell down and then jumped up, grabbed a small bundle and his gun and run in the brush and that was the last we saw of him. While he was shooting at us he yelled terrible oaths at us.

The next thing was what to do with the squaw and pappoose. One of the buck shot had struck her on the right ankle bone and glanced down the thick skin of her heel. One of the men took his knife and cut it out, then we filled the cut with pine pitch. We concluded to bring her to Chico and turn her over to Bidwell and his Indians and tell them to have her forthcoming at any time we would ask to see her.

The first Indian shot by Good had Workman's stove pipe hat on his head and one of Workman's white shirts on. This was all in the way of clothing.

I saw him lying with the rifle in his hand so I went to get it, but Good got to him first and was scalping him. I saw he had in his belt a very nice ivory-handled revolver and the muzzle loading pistol I have and two large knives. As I was taking the belt, Good said, "Give me the revolver, won't you?

"Sure," I replied, and laid it by his feet. The Indian had a death grip on the rifle and Good and I had to pry his hand open to get it. The summer before they had robbed the Dargy home on Big Chico Creek of everything, they even emptied the feather beds of the feathers and took the ticks and had taken the rifle. We knew it to be the Dargy rifle, so Thomasson and I carried it out to Good's place on Deer Creek, 35 miles, besides our own guns. It was a task never to be forgotten. He told Dargy he could get it at Good's place, which he did.

We gathered all the Indian plunder we did not want and burned it. I got some very nice keepsakes and took some of them East with me and gave them to my sister and mother.

The Concow men who had seen how horrible Miss Smith had been mutilated could not get enough revenge, it seemed. I saw one of them after an Indian was killed and scalped, cut his throat and twist his head half off and he said, "You will not kill any more women and children." After Good had taken all the scalps, which he did in this way—he took a buckskin string and sack needle and tied a knot in the end and salted the scalp and run the needle through it down to the knot, then tied another knot about two inches above the scalp and it was ready for the next one. The string was fastened to his belt and you can imagine a great tall man with a string of scalps from his belt to his ankle. When this was finished we had breakfast, it consisted of one soda cracker and a small piece of raw bacon.

In coming to this country Miss Smith had brought some very fine silks and shawls, these the squaws had torn in strips and had them pinned over their shoulders.

About eight o'clock we started for home. It was thirty-five miles to Good's place, the nearest white habitation. We had water three times. The Emigrant Spring on the Lassen Trail had gone dry, so we cut sticks and dug until we got water. We all drank and gave the squaw a drink, then we were ready to come on but the squaw would not come. We tried every way to persuade her; cut a cane and took hold of her arms, to help her and did all we could, but she was determined she would not come. Good told us to give the baby to him, and set it on the knapsack, it had to hold fast or fall off so it put its arms around Good's neck and he went down the hill out of sight. We though she would follow the child but she would not. Curtis told her to go back. She went back fifty or sixty yards to where the trail passed between two big rocks. Here she lay down and pulled the shawl over her head. Curtis went back. We heard the revolver shot and we knew what had happened.

We got to Good's place after dark and we were so tired we lay down without any supper. The Indians had a large white dog that had disappeared in the fight. Just as we lay down the shepherd dogs began to fight so I struck a light and here was that Indian dog. Good got a chain and captured him and gave him to Mrs. Lewis on Deer Creek. The Mill Creeks were so thoroughly punished that they never committed any more murders.

The next morning Thomasson and I saddled our horses and came to Pine Creek to the Oak Grove Hotel and Stage Station. It was owned by a Mr. Phillips and rented to Mr. Hickok, the father of the children that had been murdered by the Mill Creeks. We stopped and asked if we could get breakfast. Mrs. Hickok gave us a good breakfast and when we asked Mr. Hickok what the bill was he said half a dollar a piece. We paid it willingly as we had had nothing to eat since the morning before at Black Rock, when our breakfast had consisted of one soda cracker and a small slice of raw bacon. I always thought if it had been me when asked what the price was for breakfast and it had been my children that had been murdered by those Indians, I would have said, "Nothing at all, there is nothing too good in this place for you men." We then started for Chico twelve miles farther on. When we got to Bidwell's we told of the good luck we had in surrounding the Indian camp and sending a good many Indians to the happy hunting ground.

Bidwell immediately ordered two four-horse teams hitched to two coaches and ordered them to go as fast as possible and meet the Concow men and bring them to Chico. He then went to the Chico Hotel and told Mr. Wetherby, the proprietor, to give them the best dinner the market afforded and charge it to him. After dinner he ordered his drivers to take the men home to Concow valley.

Good kept the little Indian girl. The next spring when I was at Good's place, I asked Good where she was. He said that she was out gathering flowers. Presently she came and stood between his knees, he patted her head and she went to sleep. Good put her in a little bed and said, "When she wakes up I will show you something." Good had a partner by the name of Barrington, a Frenchman. Mrs. Barrington was Spanish. When the little girl awoke and came out Good spoke to Barrington and his wife and they all three talked to her. Barrington spoke French, Mrs. Barrington Spanish and Good English, and the little girl could speak all three languages. Good at that time was running a pack train to Idaho. Mrs. Barrington wanted to go to her people in Mexico as Good bought Barrington out and told them when they left to take the little girl up the canyon to the old sheep herder who had a squaw for his wife and while Good was gone the little girl took sick and died.

The Robbing of the Silva Home

The robbing of the Silva home by the Mill Creek Indians, was on April 24th, 1866. Mr. Silva was away, Mrs. Silva and the hired man were at the ranch. About noon they saw a swarm of bees go by and light down the canyon. They took a box and went to hive them. When this was done they started for the house and saw the Indians packing the bedding out. Just then the Indians saw them and fired, but they were too far away and did not get hit. They immediately started for our home, about a mile down the canyon. The hired man got there first and all he could say was, "Indians." Immediately after came Mrs. Silva. When she got

there she fell in a faint. My brother's wife restored her. I was away. My brother told his wife to run some bullets for the big rifle, while he caught a horse. (In those days we had muzzle loading fire arms.) He took the gun and rode up the canyon as fast as he could but when he got there the Indians were gone. He went on up the canyon to Boness' place; here he found Boness, Jack Reed and Dutch Charley; the three came to our house with him.

Just then I got home. They told me. I got my gun and we started. We got to Chico and it being Sunday, the two stores were closed, so we found one of the clerks and got two sacks of crackers and two sides of bacon and away we went.

We rode to the Phillbrook place on Mud Creek and slept in a barn. Mr. Phillbrook gave us breakfast and we started for R. A. Anderson's place on Rock Creek. Mr. Anderson, Perry McIntosh, Tom Gore, Rich Goe and Boliver made the party. We then went to Good's place on Deer Creek. Good said it was impossible for him to go. He was running a pack train to Idaho and his forty pack animals and men and merchandise were there and all ready to start next morning. He said that, if the Indians had committed murder he would go, but as it was just robbery we would have to let him off, and as Anderson could track the Indians we started on.

We found their trail on Deer Creek Flats. These flats are not on the creek, but on the bluff. We then went down the Indian trail to the creek, where we found the Indians had crossed. There were two large lava boulders in the creek. The Indians had made a crossing by putting poles from the bank to the rock and from rock to rock. After they had crossed they pulled the last span and let it go down the creek. When we saw what they had done we were up against it as the creek was very high. Jack Reed was one of those men, who at all time had a way of getting out of difficulties, he said, "I will go on the bridge to the farthest rock and you go and get long poles and shove in the creek; slant them so they will drift toward the opposite side." We did as he said and he caught two and rolled them on the bank. Then he took and put the end he had in notches in the rock. We then crossed, all but McIntosh. He would come across to the further rock and then go back. It was a dangerous crossing. If a man fell in he would have drowned as the creek was a roaring torrent. We coaxed and pleaded and finally were going to leave him when he came over.

We traveled up the creek and came to a very high bluff. Here we found a trail going up the bluff. It was very steep, but the only way. We had to go Indian file one behind the other. When we got to the top, my brother, Jake, was in the lead, Anderson next and I next. I heard Jake say, "There they are, Bob." From the top of the bluff the ground sloped to a ravine about fifty or sixty yards and there they were camped.

We ran down among them. It was a great surprise to the Indians, and also to us as we did not think of finding them there. But then the thing was on in earnest, every one loading and firing as fast as he could and Indians dropping or trying to get away. Some were badly wounded.

Mrs. Silva some time before had gone to Chico and bought a wide brimmed spring hat and had had the milliner put flowers all over it; one young Indian had the hat tied on his head and when they broke to run Anderson started after him. They had a muddy flat to cross, and I believe that Indian could out-run anyone in the United States if Anderson was after him. I ran across the ravine and had got on the bank and as I looked down I saw an Indian running down the ravine. I started after him. He was bothered in running as it was very rocky and I had good ground and as I gained on him I thought I would chance a shot. I did not know where brother Jake was until I heard him say, "See those two running through the buck brush." I heard him shoot. He said, "I have got one." The one I was after kept running as my shot had not stopped him. I continued running after him, loading as I ran. The water at the foot of the ravine ran over a bluff, about seven feet high, in sheets about six feet wide. On the south there was a thicket under the bluff and when the Indian jumped off the bluff I lost sight of him. Jake came up and said, "What became of your Indian." I said, "He is in that thicket." Jake went around and got down the

bluff and went through the thicket. Then Anderson came; I told him the Indian must be in the thicket. He told Jake to be careful, but he made a thorough search and said, "He is not there." I was beaten, as the hillside was all open country, and if he had gone in any direction I would have seen him.

When Jake got in front of the waterfall he said, "There is a great hole in the rock under that water." He cocked his gun, sprang through the waterfall and instantly we heard the shot, he hollered, "He is here. I got him." He came backing out through the waterfall, dragging the Indian out by his long hair.

Jake and I went to find the Indian Jake shot. He had a red bandana handkerchief; this, Jake said he threw up when the bullet hit him. We found the handkerchief, it had files, shoemaker's thread and wax, sack twine and needles and was full of such things, but we could not find the Indian. Anderson called us and said, "They are just like ground squirrels, hard to kill." The Indian was found in '70 by Drennans.

The Indian Anderson took after lost the flowered bonnet. Anderson had it and in the chase lost his hat. We went back to their camp and got almost all they had stolen. There was a man in our party by the name of Boliver. The Indians, after robbing the Silva home, went by Boliver's place and robbed it. Jake was prowling around the camp and directly he came back with a new pair of boots. Boliver said that they looked just like a pair of boots he had bought Saturday. He was a large man and the boots just fit him. He had on a pair of old shoes that were worn out, so he threw them away and wore the boots.

When they robbed the Boliver home his saddle horse was in the corral; the Indians caught and hamstrung it and when found, was sitting with its forefeet on the ground. Boliver had to shoot him.

Mr. Silva had taken his pack horse. We left all our horses at Good's place, so we all took a load of plunder and packed it out to the valley. Anderson was riding a very small white mule and as we were coming down the stage road one of the party said that Anderson must wear the flowered hat. We untied it from the top of the pack and Anderson

Sandy Young, Hi Good, Jay Salisbury and Indian Ned. Ned later killed Good, and Young then killed Ned.

being such a large man we had to tie it on his head. We then took a scalp and fastened it on the mule's rump. We met several emigrant wagons going to Oregon. When we met them the drivers would stop and the canvas would part, and the women and children's heads would poke out. It was a sight to see that large man riding such a small mule, the long rifle across in front of him and the flowered bonnet and the long haired scalp. This was the last time we had to punish those Indians. . . .

The Murder of Hi Good

When I first met Hi. Good and R. A. Anderson, they were in the prime of life. Good at that time was twenty-nine years old and as handsome a man as I ever saw. I often heard it said that the Indians killed the girl he was going to marry while crossing the plains. Anderson was twenty-five years old and as fine a specimen of manhood as one would wish to see. They were large men, shrewd and fearless. They were leaders of men. Anderson was elected sheriff of Butte county, two terms and if Good had lived he could have had any office in Tehama county he wanted. If it had not been for them, more white people living in Butte and Tehama counties would have been murdered by the barbarous Mill Creeks. Their business was never so urgent or time so precious they could not leave all to go forth to avenge the wrongs of the white settlers, committed by the red men. When a party of us settlers would start to clean up the Indians, we would elect a captain and it would always be Good or Anderson. The captain always was entitled to the scalps. At one time Good had forty hanging in the poplar tree by his house.

In the early history of this state, when the law of the land was just at the stage where the right belonged to the strongest, and the Mill Creek Indians were a thorn in the side of the settlers, on account of their depredations, which at times amounted to murder, Hi. Good was one of the active leaders of the white men in their raids upon the Indians' strongholds. A great deal of interesting local history clings to this early day character, a strong fearless man and a leader of men.

Good was born in Ohio. His age I did not know, but when I first knew him he seemed to be about thirty-one or thirty-two years of age. He was a tall, athletic fellow and very handsome, straight as an arrow and brave as a lion. It was to him and R. A. Anderson that the people living in Butte and Tehama counties confided in when they wished their wrongs avenged, wrongs that had been committed by the Mill Creek Indians. Good was one of the best Indian trailers in Northern California, and a dead shot.

Good's dramatic death and events which led up to it were as follows:

Good was in the sheep business and in need of a herder at the time I speak of. Dan Sill, a friend of Good's had an Indian boy living with him in Tehama. Good asked for the boy but Sill told him he had

better not employ the Indian because he was a bad one and as sure as fate some day he would kill him. Good laughed and said that he and the Indian would get along all right.

All went well until the spring of 1870. Good sold a portion of his sheep for seven thousand dollars. He had borrowed three thousand from Sam Gyle of Tehama. This sum he paid after the sale and buried the four thousand dollars. On the 27th of April Good and his boon companions, Sandy Young and Obe Fields, left on a prospecting trip. They left with the purpose in view of finding the Mill Creeks and getting their booty as it was generally known that they had two or three thousand dollars. When they started, Good told the Indian that he did not need to herd the sheep as Jack Brennan, the other herder could do all the work in caring for the sheep and for him to stay about the camp and do the cooking.

The Indian knew Good had money buried and as soon as Good was gone he began hunting for it. In his efforts to find it he tore up the cobble stone hearth in front of the fireplace and dug several places where he thought it might be. He tore up some of the wood floor. When Good returned on the 29th of April, he determined immediately from the condition of the house what had been going on. The Indian had taken the ashes from the fireplace and given the hearth and floor a good scrubbing. "What has been going on here, Ned?" asked Good.

"The place got so dirty I though I would clean it up a bit," said the Indian. Good lived in Acorn Hollow at this time and had a fine ranch and garden on Deer Creek about one mile and a half south. "I will go to the garden and get some vegetables," said Good.

Young came to Chico as soon as Good left. The Indian said to Obe, "I will take his gun and see if I can kill some squirrels." Obe being an elderly man sought the comfort of one of the beds and went to sleep. He said he did not hear the Indian shoot and if he did he would not have remembered it as the Indian boy was always doing more or less shooting about the place. Soon after the Indian came back and got supper. Good, however, did not come. After breakfast the next morning, Obe said,

"I will saddle Bally (his horse) and see why he did not come home." Instead of going the trail that led out of the hollow he led the horse up the steep hill back of the house to the rocky plain. If he had gone the trail he would have probably found Good. On reaching the garden, Obe inquired for Good and was told that he had left before sundown. Obe returned the same way he had gone. When he got back the Indian was on hand and had Good's horse, saying he found it back up the hollow tied to a tree. Obe said that he would go to the picnic being held on Deer Creek. Here he found Dan Delany and George Carter and a number of Good's best friends and they all started back. In crossing the rocky plain, one of the party said, "Hold on, something has been dragged here." Obe looked and said, "That is Buck's track." They followed the direction of the shoe marks indicated and in a desolate ravine against a small tree they found the body of the stalwart, athletic Good, practically covered with rocks.

After leaving Good there the Indian went down to the Widow Lewis' place on Deer Creek. Mrs. Lewis and her daughter were in the yard. The Indian rode up and took a twenty dollar piece out of his pocket and said, "I will give this to see Hi. Good's boots." Mrs. Lewis said, "What is the matter with Hi Good?"

The Indian said, "He is missing." In showing the money they noticed Good's gold ring on his finger. He had robbed Good of his money and taken the ring; but had not taken his gold watch.

As soon as Good's body was found, one of the party went to Tehama to notify the coroner, while another came to Chico to notify Sandy Young. Some of the party went to the camp and some stayed with the corps. Finally the Indian came to camp. They askd him about Hi. He said he did not know anything about him and went outside and sat down on a bench and placed his head in his hands. Obe went out and sat down alongside of the Indian. Finally Obe asked the Indian where the first shot hit Hi. The Indian said, "Through the hips," and then jumped up and caught Obe around the neck and said, "Don't tell them, or they will kill me." Obe then went to the cabin door, where

he met Young, who had arrived from Chico. He said, "Ned killed Hi."

"How do you know?" asked Young.

"He told me," was the answer.

"Tell him to come in. The Indian was asked by Sandy why he killed Hi. The Indian replied that he didn't know, but he guessed to see how he would act. Thereupon, Sandy began to cry. Then the Indian told how he had hid behind the big oak tree and as Hi. came down the trail leading his horse by the long bridle reins and singing, he shot him and as he staggered down the hill he shot him twice, all three bullets going true, as the Indian was a good shot. Then Sandy said, "Take the Indian up the trail and we will see how he will act." They tied the Indian's hands behind him, took him up the trail and tied him to the limb of an oak tree. Sandy went about sixty feet away and turned and fired, the bullet struck the Indian in the back of the neck, he fell and quivered. They cut him loose and he died. His bones lay there for two years. Brother Jake and I used to drive the cattle by them. Two young students from Colusa came and took the skeleton away.

Good is buried in the Tehama cemetery. Sandy sent Good's gold watch to his father in Ohio. Good always buried his money, as there were no banks in Northern California. There are, I think, five hundreds holes dug around the cabin and corral by different parties, searching for the money. It may have been found, but not that I know of.

My brother and I could not find out if there was a monument at Good's grave, so we went to Tehama three years ago. We found the grave and a marble slab stating that he died, May 4th, 1870, aged 34 years. This closes the chapter of one of California's Grand Men.

Other Depredations by Mill Creek Indians

In 1862 they robbed the George Senedeker home, taking his rifle and three hundred dollars in cash.

They robbed the Alpaugh place of seven head of fine horses, drove them to Mill Creek and cut their throats.

In August, 1862 they waylaid and killed two miners on the North Fork of the Feather River.

[71]

They stole two of Bob Anderson's horses and set his barn on fire. After a long chase the horses were recovered and one of the Indians wounded. It was learned later that the wounded Indian died of his injuries in June of that year, 1863.

Later a band of these same Indians made a raid on Mr. Gore's ranch and stole all his horses. R. A. Anderson, Tom Gore and Jack Powers started in pursuit. They succeeded in recovering the horses and Anderson, single handed, killed seven of the Indians and wounded two.

On the thirteenth of April, 1865, a band of this same tribe descended on the Moore home on Mud Creek, which they robbed of over a thousand dollars, after having killed old Grandma Moore. Before leaving they set the house on fire and burned the body of Mrs. Moore up in her own home.

Jeremiah Curtin, a linguist and author of Creation Myths of Primitive America, *was in northern California twenty years after the 1864 completion of the extermination of the Yana as a people was accomplished. He learned many details of the events of twenty years before from white settlers whom he came to know. His reporting is scholarly, restrained, and as accurate as his source material allows. The information he received concerning Ishi's people, the Yahi, was vague and hearsay. His valuable collection of Yana myths was made by him from surviving Yana individuals—or part-Yana, who were employed on the ranches of white settlers who were Curtin's hosts during his stay.*

9. The Yanas (1864)

Jeremiah Curtin

As a preface to the few myths of the Yanas which have survived, I beg to offer the following words touching this ill-fated people:

Previous to August, 1864, the Yanas numbered about three thousand, as I have been informed on

From Jeremiah Curtin, *Creation Myths of Primitive America* (Boston, 1898), pp. 517-520.

the sound authority of reliable white men. Taking the names and population of villages given me by surviving Indians, I should say that this estimate is not too large.

During the second half of August, 1864, the Yanas were massacred, with the exception of a small remnant.

The Indians of California, and especially those of Sacramento Valley, were among the most harmless of human beings. Instead of being dangerous to settlers, they worked for them in return for fair wages. The Yanas were distinguished beyond others for readiness to earn money. White men occupied in tilling land knew their value, and employed them every season in haymaking and harvesting.

At the present day the Wintus, and the few Yanas that are left, go down the valley and labor during the season in hop-fields and vineyards.

Why were the Yanas killed?

The answer is as follows: Certain Indians lived, or rather lurked, around Mill Creek, in wild places somewhat east of Tehama and north of Chico. These Mill Creek Indians were fugitives; outlaws from various tribes, among others from the Yanas. To injure the latter, they went to the Yana country about the middle of August, 1864, and killed two white women, Mrs. Allen and Mrs. Jones. Four children also were left for dead by them, but the children recovered. After the murders the Mill Creeks returned home unnoticed, carrying various plundered articles with them.

Two parties of white men were formed at once to avenge the women and four children. Without trying in any way to learn who the guilty were, they fell upon the Yanas immediately, sparing neither sex nor age. They had resolved to exterminate the whole nation. The following few details will show the character of their work:—

At Millville, twelve miles east of Redding, white men seized two Yana girls and a man. These they shot about fifty yards from the village hotel. At another place they came to the house of a white woman who had a Yana girl, seven or eight years of age. They seized this child, in spite of the woman, and shot her through the head. "We must kill them, big and little," said the leader; "nits will be lice."

A few miles north of Millville lived a Yana girl named Eliza, industrious and much liked by those who knew her. She was working for a farmer at the time. The party stopped before this house, and three of the men entered it. "Eliza, come out," said one of them; "we are going to kill you." She begged for her life. To the spokesman, who had worked for her employer some time before, she said: "Don't kill me; when you were here I cooked for you, I washed for you, I was kind to you; I never asked pay of you; don't kill me now."

Her prayers were vain. They took Eliza, with her aunt and uncle, a short distance from the house and shot the three. My informant counted eleven bullets in Eliza's breast.

After this murder the party took a drink and started; but the leader, in killing Eliza, said, "I don't think that little squaw is dead yet." So he turned back and smashed in her skull with his musket. The man who counted the bullet holes in her bosom, himself a white man, saw her after the skull was broken. He knew the girl well, and gave me these details.

Another party went to a farm on Little Cow Creek where they found three Yana men threshing hayseed in a barn. The farmer was not at home. They killed the three Indians, and went to the house. The three wives of the men killed in the barn were there and began to scream. The farmer's wife hurried out with a quilt, threw it around the three women, and stood in front of them, holding the ends of the quilt. "If you kill them you will kill me," said she, facing the party. The woman was undaunted, and, as it happened, was big with child. To kill, or attempt to kill, under those conditions, would be a deed too ghastly for even such heroes; so they went away, swearing that they would kill the "squaws" later. These three Indian women were saved and taken beyond the reach of danger by two white men.

And so the "avengers" of Mrs. Allen and Mrs. Jones continued. At one place they killed an Indian woman and her infant, at another three women. In the town of Cottonwood they killed twenty Yanas of both sexes. The most terrible slaughter in any place was near the head of Oak Run, where three hundred Yanas had met at a religious dance. These were attacked in force, and not a soul escaped. The slaughter went on day after day till the entire land of the Yanas was cleared. The few who escaped were those who happened to be away from home, outside their country, and about twelve who were saved by Mr. Oliver and Mr. Disselhorst, both of Redding. The whole number of surviving Yanas of pure and mixed blood was not far from fifty.

Some time after the bloody work was done it was discovered that the Mill Creek outlaws had killed Mrs. Allen and Mrs. Jones, and that the Yanas were innocent. The Mill Creeks were left unpunished.

My inquiries as to how civilized men could commit such atrocities found the following answers:—

In 1864 there was a large floating and mining population in Northern California, which "had no use for Indians," and was ready to kill them on slight provocation. In distinction to these people was a small number of settlers who lived among the Yanas in friendship, and hired them to work on land. The killing was done by men who did not know the Yanas. Those settlers who did know the Yanas were overawed, and were unable to save them, except secretly, as in the case of the two men who rescued the three women on Little Cow Creek by conveying them beyond danger. Oliver and Disselhorst, who saved twelve, were at the edge of Redding, where support was possible. At first the rage of the killing parties was boundless; they swore that white women would not be murdered again in that country, and that not an Indian should be left alive in it. An intense feeling of indignation at the murder, coupled with an unspeakable contempt for Indians, was the motive in the breasts of most of the white men. Had they looked on the Yanas with ordinary feelings of justice, they would have tried to find the guilty instead of slaughtering a whole nation. There was another element among the slayers of the Indians,— a vile one, an element which strives to attach itself to every movement, good or bad in all places—a plundering element. That year the Yanas had worked a good deal, and it was not uncommon for single persons of them to have from $40 to

[73]

$60. One informant told me that a man showed a friend of his $400 which he had taken from murdered Indians. Money and everything of value that the Yanas had was snatched up by these robbers.

Nearly all the men who killed the Yanas have gone out of the country or are dead. A few are in Northern California yet, and the children of some of the dead ones are living there now. Though one's indignation at the deeds of 1864 be great, there is no use in mentioning names at this hour. All that is left is to do for the poor remnant of an interesting people that which we have done for Indians in other parts: give them land properly surveyed and the means to begin life on it.

Stephen Powers, who can be called the first scientific ethnologist of California, published the following selection first in the Overland Monthly, *Vol. 12 (1874), pp. 412-424. It was printed in slightly amended form in his* Tribes of California *(1877). The Koḿ-bo were the Yahi, and were understood, correctly, by Powers to be part of the Yana nation whom he labeled as Nozi. In 1874 there were, according to Powers, only five of this tribe known; actually there must have been more.*

---

10. The Koḿ-bo [Yahi] (1874)

Stephen Powers

In writing of this tribe, I am compelled for once to forego the name employed by themselves. It is not known to any man living save themselves, and probably it will not be until the grave gives up its dead. The above is the name given to them by their neighbors of Indian Valley, a tribe of the Maidu Nation.

If the Nozi are a peculiar people, these are extraordinary; if the Nozi appear to be foreign to California, these are doubly foreign. They seem likely to present a spectacle which is without a parallel in human history—that of a barbaric race

From Stephen Powers, *Tribes of California*, Contributions to North American Ethnology (Washington, D.C.: U.S. Department of Interior), Vol. III (1877), pp. 277-281.

resisting civilization with arms in their hands, to the last man, and the last squaw, and the last pappoose. They were once a numerous and thrifty tribe. Now there are only five of them left—two men, two women, and a child. No human eye ever beholds them, except now and then some lonely hunter, perhaps, prowling and crouching for days over the volcanic wastes and scraggy forests which they inhabit. Just at nightfall he may catch a glimpse of a faint camp-fire, with figures flitting about it; but before he can creep within rifle-range of it the figures have disappeared, the flame wastes slowly out, and he arrives only to find that the objects of his search have indeed been there before him, but are gone. They cooked there their hasty evening repast, but they will sleep somewhere else, with no camp-fire to guide a lurking enemy within reach. For days and weeks together they never touch the earth, stepping always from one volcanic stone to another. They never leave a broken twig or a disturbed leaf behind them. Probably no day of the year ever passes over their heads but some one of this doomed nation of five sits crouching on a hillock or in a tree-top, within easy eye-shot of his fellows; and not a hare can move upon the earth beneath without its motions being heeded and recorded by the watcher's eye. There are men in and around Chico who have sworn a great oath of vengeance that these five Indians shall die a bloody death; but weeks, months, and years have passed away, and brought for their oaths no fulfillment. There is now wanting only a month of four years since they have ever been seen together so that their number could be certainly known. In February, 1870, some hunters had succeeded in capturing the two remaining squaws, whereupon they opened communication with the men, and promised them a safe-conduct and the release of their squaws if they would come in and promise to abandon hostilities. The two men came in, bringing the child. It was the intention of the hunters, as one of them candidly avowed to me, to have seized them and secretly put the whole five out of existence. While they were in camp, one of the hunters conceived an absurd whim to weigh himself, and threw a

THE KOM-BO

rope over a limb for that purpose, at which the
wily savages took fright, and they all bounded
away like frightened deer and escaped. But they
had remained long enough for an American, as
eagle-eyed as themselves, to observe that one of
the two warriors had a gunshot wound in one hand,
and many others on his arm, forming an almost
unbroken cicatrix from hand to elbow. Probably
no white man's eyes will ever again behold them
all together alive.

When they were more numerous than now, they
occupied both Mill Creek and Deer Creek; but
nowadays they live wholly in the great volcanic
terraces and low mountains west of Mill Creek
Meadows. Down to 1858 they lived at peace with
the whites, but since that time they have waged
unrelenting and ceaseless war—ceaseless except for
a casual truce like that above described. Their
hostilities have been characterized by so many and
such awful atrocities that there are men, as above-
mentioned, who have sworn an oath that they
shall die. All these seventeen years they have warred
against the world and against fate. Expelled from
the rich and teeming meadows which were their
chosen home; hemmed in on these great, hot,
volcanic table-lands where nothing can live but
a few stunted trees, and so destitute of water that
this forms at once a security against civilized foes
and their own constant menace of death—a region
accursed of Heaven and spewed out even by the
earth—they have seen one after another of the
craven tribes bow the knee and make terms with
the enemy; but still their voice has been stern and
steady for war; still they have crouched and hovered in their almost disembodied life over these
arid plains until all are gone but five. Despite all
their bloody and hellish treacheries, there is something sublime in this.

So far as their customs have been observed,
they have some which are Californian, but more
which are decidedly foreign. They burn the dead,
and are remarkably fond of bathing.

On the other hand, the customs which are foreign to California are numerous and significant.
First, they have no assembly chamber and consequently no indoor dances, but only circular

dances in the open air. The assembly chamber is
the one capital shibboleth of the California Indian.
Second, they did not erect the warm and heavily-
earthed lodges which the Indians of this State are
so fond of, but mere brush-wood shelters, and
often they had no refuge but caves and dens. Third,
they inflicted cruel and awful tortures on their
captives, like the Algonkin races. Whatever abomi-
nations the indigenous races may have perpetrated
on the dead, the torture of the living was essentially foreign to California. Fourth, they had a
mode of capturing deer which no other California
tribe employed, as far as known. Taking the antlers of a buck when they were green and velvety,
they split them open on the under side and removed the pith, which rendered them so light that
an Indian could carry them on his head. Then he
would dress himself in the skin and go to meet
the herd, or rather thrust his head out from the
bushes, taking care not to expose himself too
much, and imitate the peculiar habit which a
buck has of constantly groping about with his
head, lifting it up and down, nibbling a little
here and a little there. At a proper time he
would shoot an arrow into one of them, and
the stupid things would stare and step softly
about, in their peering and inquisitive way, until
a number of them were knocked over. Fifth,
their unconquerable and undying determination
to fight it out to the bitter end is not a California Indian trait. Sixth, their aboriginal habit of
singeing or cropping off their hair within an inch
of their heads contrasts strongly with the long
locks of the Californians.

Several years ago this tribe committed a massacre
near Chico, and Sandy Young, a renowned hunter
of that country, with a companion, captured two
squaws, a mother and a daughter, who promised
to guide them to the camp of the murderers. They
set out at nightfall in the dead of winter. It was
sleeting, raining, and blowing that night as if "the
de'il had business on his hands". But they passed
rapidly on without halt or hesitation, for the
squaws led the way boldly. From nightfall until
long after midnight they held on their dreary
trail, stumbling and floundering occasionally, but

[75]

speaking scarcely a word; nor was there a moment's cessation in the execrable, bitter sleet and rain. At length they came to a creek which was swollen and booming. In the pitchy darkness it was manifestly impassable. They sounded it in various places, and could find no crossing. While the hunters were groping hither and thither, and shouting to each other above the raging of the torrent, the squaws disappeared. No hallooing could elicit a response from them. The two men considered themselves betrayed, and prepared for treachery. Suddenly there came floating out on the storm and the roaring a thin young squeal. The party had been re-enforced by one. The hunters then grasped the situation, and, laughing, set about collecting some dry stuff and making a fire. They were benumbed and half-frozen themselves, and supposed of course the women would come in as soon as they observed the fire. But no, they wanted no fire, or, if they did, their aboriginal modesty would not allow them to resort to it under these circumstances. The grandmother took the new-born babe, amid the almost palpable blackness of darkness, the sleeting, and the yelling winds, and dipped it in the ice-cold creek. Again and again she dipped it, while now and then the hunters could hear its stout-lunged protest above the roaring. Not only did the infant survive this unparalleled treatment, but it grew excellently well. In memory of the extraordinary circumstances under which it was ushered into this world, Young named it "Snowflake," and it is living to this day, a wild-eyed lad in Tehama.

[76]

This brief newspaper article of March 19, 1911, is the first public notice of the expedition made by T. T. Waterman of the University of California and two companions to locate the reported survivors of the Mill Creek and Deer Creek Indians, four of whom had been surprised by a surveying party some months earlier. Further details are given by A. L. Kroeber in "The Elusive Mill Creeks," below, and by T. T. Waterman in "The Yana Indians" in Chapter IV, below.

11. Lost Indian Tribe in Tehama Wilds

*State University Expedition Discovers
Descendants of 1870 Massacre*

Berkeley, March 18.—Living in the impenetrable crags and canyons of Mill and Deer creeks less than 20 miles from the cities of the upper Sacramento valley, a tribe of the Mill creek Indians, long thought extinct, has been discovered by the anthropologists of the University of California under Prof. A. L. Kroeber.

A troop of United States cavalry has been asked by the university to run the tribe to earth with the hope of preserving the aborigines, their language and customs in the interest of science.

Though the Indians have set up an independent government almost in sight of Pullman trains few settlers of the region know of the existence of this tribe, which numbers less than a score. Other Indians in the vicinity have scoffed at the stories of settlers that their sheep have come home with arrows in their flanks. These Indians denied that any of the primitive people were alive.

Residents of Tehama and Red Bluff, the nearest cities, are least inclined to believe that this tribe survived a massacre in early days when the settlers arose en masse and slew all the Indians in the region.

The evidence of the arrow heads and the rifling of a ranch cabins and cabins in remote parts of Mill creek canyon started an investigation by the University of California scientists, who took the trail heavily armed under the direction of T. T. Waterman.

They returned yesterday without having held communication with the tribe, who fled at their approach, but they obtained photographs of their abandoned huts and a large number of baskets and other utensils.

After the massacre of 1870, when the settlers of northern California arose against the Indians, five of the aborigines, remnants of the Kombo, an offshoot of the Nozi tribes escaped. In 40 years

"Lost Indian Tribe in Tehama Wilds," *San Francisco Call,* March 19, 1911.

these five have grown into a tribe eking out an existence by spearing salmon and eating acorns.

Shunned by white man, they themselves fled at the approach of strangers. Two men, a woman and a crone have been seen.

J. R. Gleeson's account includes his opinion that the Mill Creek and Deer Creek Indians survived in small numbers. Gleeson was probably stimulated to write this because of the announcement a week before in the San Francisco Call *of the University of California expedition to the Yabi country to try to locate survivors of the small group encountered by the surveyors in 1908.*

---

12. "Lost Indians" Easily Traced

Butte County Band Remnants of Old-Time Diggers Who Fought the Settlers and Stole Their Stock

John Rodney Gleeson

On account of the fuss lately being made by the learned scientific gentlemen of the University of California over lost Indians on Mill Creek and Deer Creek, in Northern California, the writer will try to tell, as briefly as possible, what he knows about the Bidwell Indians on Rancho Chico and incidentally what he does not know concerning the lost Mill and Deer Creeks.

During a 20 years sojourn in Chico I had two most remarkable men for employers. First Charles V. Hobart, who never had a dollar of his own, but who nevertheless had the handling of millions in the English export grain trade and spent that money like a prince; second, General John Bidwell, who had over a million dollars tied up in his 23,000 acre Rancho Chico and its splendid equipment, and never had a real ready dollar to spend. When he and his good wife executed the last mortgage on Rancho Chico before me to the James Lick Trust for $350,000, Bidwell felt poorer than the poorest Indian on his great estate. I only mention these facts to prove that my position as trusted employe

From *Stockton Daily Record,* March 26, 1911.

of these two men gave me advantages to meet and study the people and affairs of that period. Amongst the things that greatly interested me were the Rancho Chico Indians, with whom I had almost daily contact for seven years, as cashier and paymaster for Bidwell.

A Trusted Indian

On Rancho Chico were no less than 300 gates, many of which were kept closed and locked. Riding or driving over the ranch it was most important to have along a nimble companion to open and shut these gates. For this purpose I had Billy Simpson, an Indian for whom I formed a great attachment. After the death of my wife I would often take my two infant girls for a day's outing in Iron Canyon, with Billy Simpson to open gates, hold the horses and do other stunts.

On these trips Billy took particular delight in amusing the babies with real Indian stories, doing Indian tricks, calling wild birds, chipmunks and catching snakes and frogs for their amusement. I trusted Billy and Billy trusted me, and on our return to town would drop me at the Bidwell office and take the children home and I never had him betray an important trust.

In this exchange of confidence I was enabled to get sketches of Indian history not obtainable in any other way. In this way I learned much of the early Indian troubles and something about the renegade Indians supposed to then be living in the wilds of Deer and Mill creeks. These stories I could later establish by intercourse with the older and more silent Indians of the Bidwell tribe.

Old-Time Indians

The notable Indian characters that I now recall of that time were Nopanny, a sort of squaw high priestess; Pullissa, her husband, who could drive the straightest farrow that I ever saw put across a field. Billy Preacher, Pullissa's brother; Billy Conway, a clever ventriloquist; Mike, the lineal chief whom dissipation robbed of his birthright; Lafonso the chief, who took Mike's unfulfilled place; Maggie Lafonso, the chief's little daughter; Lady Mary and Sarah, her constant companion,

[77]

two barefooted crones whose ages were supposed to be over 100 years; Austin, the totally blind fiddler, who could find his way unassisted over miles of Rancho Chico; old Ko-Ko-Mo, the only Indian permitted to have a gun, with which he killed yellowhammers, for which I had orders to pay him five cents a scalp.

From all these I got fragments of stories about the bad Mill and Deer Creek Indians. On great Indian days visits were exchanged with Boggs' Ranch Indians, Tehamas, Red Bluffs, Stony Creeks and with the Kanakas from the mouth of the Feather River, but never a Mill or Deer Creek was known to come.

The Wild Mill Creeks

I have reason to believe that the Mill and Deer Creeks were clandestinely helped by J. L. Keefer, a rich farmer and sawmill owner of North Butte county, but of this I have no confirmation. Keefer was a quaint Pennsylvania Dutchman, and a most estimable man. On his death, some years ago, I think these poor ostracized wild men lost a noble and generous friend.

In his book published in 1909, my old and esteemed friend Bob Anderson, ex-Sheriff of Butte county and noted Indian fighter, expressed a belief that the Mill Creeks were at that time still existing in small numbers and he calls them the wildest people in America.

The building of the Humboldt wagon road before the days of railroads in California, took all the freight and travel to Idaho and Montana via Chico, entirely away from the Lassen trail and Deer Creek pass and left that section an abandoned wilderness, which it is to this day.

I have been told by Jim Montgomery, Joe Haughton, Charlie Pond and Bob Anderson that along the Lassen trail were strewn old wagons, ox yokes, cook stoves, early mining machines and all sorts of things abandoned by emigrant trains on their way to the gold rush of '49 across the Sierra Nevada mountains. No enterprising junk man has ever had the courage to penetrate this wilderness in search of spoils.

Your late esteemed townsman, James M. Welsh, had his first job in California as miller at the Bidwell mill on the banks of Chico Creek. This was in the days of the Indian wars with the settlers along the creeks north and south of Chico. Mr. Welsh told me a short time before his death that he knew personally Sandy Young who was at one time Bidwell's head stock man, and a noted Indian fighter, who disappeared and was never found or accounted for. Mr. Welsh told me that he believed the Indians got Sandy and burned his body.

Killed Settlers and Stole Stock

Deer Creek empties into the Sacramento river through the great Stanford Ranch at Vina and no gold was ever found on this creek, which accounts for the wide berth given it by early miners.

Mill Creek empties into the Sacramento river near the town of Tehama and was likewise barren of gold diggings.

From the stories told me by Indian fighters of the early days I am convinced that the lost Indians were remnants of the bands of "diggers" that came out from Deer Creek and Mill Creek to forage on the country and make raids on the stock owned by the settlers. These renegades kept out of sight much of the time, but they were known to be men killers and whites who had the nerve frequently followed them to their haunts and shot them as they appeared in openings where guns could be leveled at them.

The settlers had to corral their stock nights to prevent loss by Indian raiders who were after meat rather than horses. After a raid into the valley the Indians retreated always into the dense brush covered haunts where they are still believed to be living, but it is certain that not many of them are alive now for they have always been marked as renegades who respect no law of white men and needed killing. The so-called Bidwell Indians became useful helpers in ranch work, but the elusive Mill Creeks never sought friendship with white people.

Historically of No Value

There are men of pluck in Butte county who would be willing to chase these "lost Indians" into their recesses if it was worth while, but it would be a difficult undertaking for the country is as wild today as it was in the days of gold seeking and it would be necessary to crawl through dense brush and chapparel thickets that would tear off the skin of white men for useless results. . . .

Presumably Waterman's expedition in search of the Yahi in October, 1910, was done with the knowledge of the Lassen National Forest Supervisor, L. A. Kling. The following note is reprinted from a mimeographed newsletter issued by the Supervisor for the information of foresters in his district. (The area is now a national park.)

---

13. Indians in the Forest (1911)

The Lassen Forest has the unique distinction of having a wild band of real live Indians roaming around on it within sight of the smoke of the engines pulling Pullmans up and down the Sacramento Valley. Strange as it may seem, it is now an undisputed fact that such is the case, as evidenced by the camps of our red neighbors that have recently been found on Deer Creek in District 1.

In the fall of 1908 a surveyor ran across an old Indian fishing in Deer Creek. He told some nearby stockmen and they by trailing him found the camp, in which were about six or seven adults. The camp was on top of a lava rim on the south side of the Deer Creek Canyon, which is a brushy, barren bluff, strewn with immense boulders, that was impassable to horses, and almost impenetrable by men, even by crawling on all fours. The Indians were startled by the unexpected intrusion and all ran and escaped with the exception of an old "mahala," who was rolled out of a quilt much to the surprise of one of the party of surveyors. This old woman was apparently as old as the hills around there and spoke a few words about a "papoose" and seemed much frightened. The rest of them ran away, but returned later and took her away with them. They found in the camp a large pot of acorns cooking, and provisions that had been stolen from different cow camps; enough, it is said, to have lasted a year or two. The discoverers

From *Lassen Magazine* (Lassen National Forest, Calif., May 1911).

took away with them as relics arrows and quivers, tanned hides of different animals, and moccasins, which I have seen myself on a ranch near Vina.

Hearing all the recent reports of the wild band of Indians up in the Mill and Deer Creek country, on the Lassen Forest, we decided to do a little investigating, to convince ourselves, if possible, whether or not there were actually any aboriginal savages having their abode on the National Forest. It is indeed strange, and hard to believe, that in this progressive age, within 30 miles of street cars and moving picture shows, there should be human beings so wild and savage that they have been able to hide away from the sight of white men for such a length of time, without being seen, or leaving any signs of their habitations.

On April 13, 1911, H. H. Hume, surveyor, discovered an Indian cache which was seen by myself and Deputy Supervisor LaPlant on April 23. This cache was hanging up high in the top of a live oak, consisting of several barley sacks and pieces of canvass, wrapped around soft tanned deer hides with the hair on, moccasins, bundles of Digger pine pitch wrapped up in pine needles, and very neatly done up in strips of blue overalls that they had found and probably had been discarded by campers. All the pine needles were from the Digger pine and were arranged with their sheathed ends all pointing in the same direction. Among the things was a bar of ordinary washing soap that had not been used, and probably was kept by them as a curiosity, or may be was mistaken for a gold brick. We found also a black substance, cylindrical in shape, about three inches long and one inch in diameter, that resembled and tasted like sweetened charcoal. This, and the pitch pine needles, we presumed to have been kept for medicinal purposes. We also found a few nails and screws tied up in a rag, evidently by a woman, judging by the knots. There was also a sharp piece of steel with an eye at the large end, which was probably used as a needle to sew skins for moccasins and robes with sinews. This tribe, it is said, are the sole survivors of the *Kombo,* an offshoot of the *Nozi Digger Indians,* and are all that is left of the vast number that once roamed the Sacramento Valley and in 1870 killed several white men, women, and

[79]

children, and were soon afterwards almost exterminated by the settlers.

It has been doubted that they still exist at the present time as none had been seen, but it is not remarkable that no one had seen them until they were found by the cattlemen, as they were always careful to hide all their tracks by burying all their refuse and ashes from their fires, cutting all the necessary trees that they made their arrows from close to the ground so as to cover up the stumps, and never using any trails, always going to and from their camps by a circuitous route, so as not to make any trails, and by leaving twigs and brush behind them exactly as they found them as they crawled around in the undergrowth.

How many lions have been seen by stockmen in their lives? Not many. So is it to be wondered at, if an Indian having the cunning of a wild animal, combined with the intelligence of a human being, could not keep hidden from view of the white men. Some one has suggested that a U.S. Cavalry run the tribe to earth with the hope of preserving the aborigines, their languages and customs, in the interest of science; which is absurd, as it would be far easier to corral a bunch of Native-Son Jack-Rabbits. . . .

[80]

Alfred Kroeber's history of the Yahi and the story of their being sighted by the party of surveyors is the stage-setting for the actual appearance of the last survivor, Ishi, in late August, 1911. This article, however, was written and in print before Ishi "surrendered" to the whites at Oroville. Waterman's expedition in search of the little Yahi band seen by the surveying party is best described here by Kroeber.

---

14. The Elusive Mill Creeks (1911)

A. L. Kroeber

A totally wild and independent tribe of Indians, without firearms, fleeing at the approach of the

First printed in *Travel Magazine*, August, 1911. Reprinted in *The Mill Creek Indians and Ishi* (Berkeley: University of California Printing Department, 1972), with a Preface by A. B. Elsasser.

white man, hidden away for more than forty years in the heart of one of the longest settled and most densely populated States of the West, and living today under absolutely aboriginal conditions, is so startling a statement that its first announcement has usually been met with a smile instead of credence, and yet has been proved to be an incontrovertible fact.

These strange and elusive people are the remnant of a band in California formerly known to the Americans as the Mill Creek tribe and to their Indian neighbors as the Kombo. They have secreted themselves these many years, in which they were long believed extinct, in an inaccessible tract in the range of their old haunts on Mill Creek and Deer Creek, in Tehama County in the northern part of the Golden State. Here, less than 150 miles from San Francisco, and within fifteen miles of prosperous agricultural towns in the rich Sacramento valley, they have remained undisturbed and unseen by the intrusive white man until the announcement of their discovery just made by the Anthropological Department of the University of California.

To understand how a handful of savages could have accomplished this baffling and astounding feat, it is necessary to go back to the beginning of their history—a short story, for many men are still living who saw and took part in the occupation of California by the enterprising American pioneer and miner.

Less than a hundred years ago there lived in that part of California which is comprised within the angle formed by the Sacramento River and its greatest tributary the Pit, in Shasta and Tehama counties, a tribe of Indians utterly distinct from all their neighbors. These came to be generally called the Nozi, though their own name for themselves is Yana, a word meaning "people" in the native dialect, and accepted by ethnologists and historians as the correct designation of the group. The Yana were a small tribe, limited in territory and never populous. They were, however, more warlike than their neighbors, who partook of the sluggish and apathetic character so marked among the Indians of California and who were, therefore, ill able to withstand the sudden and fierce attacks of the unique but dreaded mountaineers.

The language spoken by these people has been found to be entirely unrelated to all the other native idioms of the Pacific coast, in fact of the American continent. This in itself is not so surprising as it might seem, for the dialects of the native Californians were broken up into many distinct groups or families, each unconnected with all the others. But in this babel and multiplicity of tongues the Yana stood out through the peculiarity of possessing two languages, one spoken by the men and the other by the women. Nearly every word differed in its termination, or in some other way, according as it was uttered by males or females. A father conversing with his daughter, or a husband talking to his wife, had need, therefore, of speaking one language and having at least an understanding of another.

This strange and apparently unwieldy dualism is almost unparalleled. It recurs again among the Caribs, who were found in West Indies by the successors of Columbus. Here, however, the women of the tribe were mainly captives from other islands. They retained their native speech and taught it to their daughters, while their sons grew up learning to speak the proper Carib dialect of their fathers. In the case of the Yana we know of no such wholesale captures; in fact the men's language and the women's language are not radically distinct as among the Caribs, but are merely modifications of the same fundamental form of speech. It would thus seem that the double tongue is a development that arose within the tribe. It is probably an outgrowth of some peculiar set of social institutions, though to conjecture the precise nature of these customs would be purely speculative.

The Yana lived in two main divisions, and in accord with the hostile character of the group these were frequently at war with each other. The northern division was the larger and may originally have numbered a thousand souls. The southern band, who are our long-lost and now rediscovered Mill Creeks, were always less numerous, but made up for this deficiency by an even greater pugnacity and irreconcilability than their northern brethren. They were literally the terror of all the surrounding tribes, who could never succeed in patching up amicable relations with them for even a short space.

All the Indians of California have decreased greatly in numbers since the coming of the Spaniard and then of the American. This has been due chiefly to newly imported diseases, against which their constitutions offered no resistance, and to the change of mode of life enforced by contact with civilization. In the case of the northern Yana, war was an added factor, until to-day only some fifteen or twenty of the tribe remain. The University of California some years ago carried on an ethnological investigation of this fragment, with the purpose of preserving for record their language, their beliefs, and such of their old customs as they still practised or remembered, as well as with the hope of thereby throwing some light on their origin. The latter expectation was not fulfilled, as the Yanas' own traditions and their speech give no indication of the country whence they came nor the manner of their migration. So far as their origin is concerned they are still a people of mystery. A rich store of other information, including a valuable collection of mythological traditions and a thorough grammar of the language, were, however, obtained and are in preparation for publication; in fact, in part have already been issued, for the information of scholars and the curious.

[81]

The southern Yana, or Mill Creeks, met with a much more romantic fate than their kinsmen. When the American came on the scene, took up their lands for farming or cattle raising, and at the point of the rifle drove them off if they interfered, as happened before ten years had elapsed after the first gold rush, the Mill Creeks, like so many of their brethren, resisted. They did not, however, after the first disastrous conflict taught them the overwhelming superiority of the white man's firearms and his organization, tamely desist and accept the inevitable. Instead, they only hardened their undying spirit of tenacity and love of independence and began a series of vigorous reprisals. For nearly ten years they maintained unflagging warfare, destructive mainly to themselves, but nevertheless of unparalleled stubbornness, with the settlers of Tehama and Butte counties. Hardly recovered from one blow, the survivors would raid in another direction, and in such cases they spared neither sex nor age. Atrocities committed on white women and children roused the settlers' resentment to the highest pitch, and every Indian outrage was more than requited, but still the diminishing band kept up the unequal struggle.

In this constant guerilla warfare, which the Indians were enabled to continue as long as they did largely on account of the difficult nature of the country which they inhabited, there remained to them but little opportunity and time to gather the wild foods and to pursue the fishing and hunting on which they had been wont to depend for their subsistence. Driven by hunger, they were incited to fresh raids, the prime purpose of which was the slaughter of cattle or horses that should appease their appetites; but once the lust of conflict was kindled, it did not stop short until cabins had gone up in flames, victims had been mutilated, and captives tortured.

About 1862 these troubles had assumed such proportions that an organized party of Americans ran down the main body of Mill Creeks and made short work of them. All the men that were encountered were killed, but the women and children, provided they offered no resistance, were spared. This crushing blow was thought to have ended all further hostilities, but within a year or two the reduced survivers were back at their old trade. In 1865 they brought vengeance on themselves once more by murdering two American women. The party which set out in pursuit located the Indians in camp on Deer Creek, a stream a few miles to the south of Mill Creek and flowing through a country of the same character. They divided into two bodies, which at daybreak attacked the Indians from above and below. By this time the settlers were wrought up to such a point that they made no exceptions and killed women and children. In justification of this act it can only be said that they were convinced that as long as any members of this implacable tribe remained alive they would with the ensuing years breed fresh enemies. After the battle, or rather the slaughter, had ceased, a little Indian boy was found hidden in one of the cabins. One of the men of the party, taking a fancy to him, wished to preserve his life and decided to take the child home with him. To make this possible

and properly care for him, the party agreed to spare one of the women. She accordingly set out with the victors on their homeward march, stolidly and silently carrying the boy. After some miles, however, she became sullen, and no threats could induce her to continue. The party, therefore, moved on with the boy, leaving one or two of their number behind to carry out the sinister instructions given them.

The leader of the settlers in most of their excursions against the Indians was a young man named Hiram Good, known throughout the vicinity as a dead shot. He was, however, actuated by humane motives, and while he remained in command women and children were never wantonly killed. In spite of this kindness of heart he met with a tragic fate, which may almost be looked upon as retribution for the cold-bloodedness with which his fellow countrymen carried out the last act in the conflict. He also had adopted a little Indian captive. As the boy grew up toward manhood, he continued to live with his protector and benefactor. Although repeatedly warned by his neighbors, Good retained implicit confidence in the stripling. At last, however, the boy during his master's absence secured the latter's gun, waylaid him on his return to his cabin, and shot him. He was quickly apprehended by friends of Good, made a full and unreserved confession, and was promptly executed without reference to sheriff, judge, or district attorney.

The last defeat of the Mill Creeks ended all conflict. It was at first thought that the entire tribe had been exterminated. It soon proved that this was not the case, but as the survivors were less than half a dozen and without firearms, all danger for them was past. For a few years they were occasionally seen skulking in the hills, but always kept out of reach. In 1870 two hunters ran across their camp and surprised the two surviving women before they could escape. By maintaining guard over these they were soon enabled to open communication with the two men who now constituted the only remaining warriors of the band. On being promised safety and the release of their women, the men joined the party, bringing with them a child. These five persons were all that were then left of this once proud nation.

The hunters, however, remembered the conditions of a few years before, and waited only for an opportunity, as they subsequently avowed, or at least alleged, for dispatching the whole party of their captives. For some reason they considered it best to defer this act, and before they could carry it out one of them had occasion to unwind a coil of rope. The Indians at once scented the hangman's noose and with one accord made a sudden dash for liberty. Before the white men could point their rifles at them they had made their escape through the brush.

Since that time they were never seen again until their recent rediscovery. For many years, for a whole generation in fact, they were believed dead. Starvation or exposure was supposed to have accomplished what little the guns of the settlers had left incomplete. During all the forty years from 1870 to 1910, this devoted band of five remained completely hidden away, but preserving an absolute independence. Over them the Government of these United States had no more jurisdiction than over the remotest tribe in central Africa. They were without question the smallest free people in the world.

As one after another of their number died, their places were taken by the children that grew up, their number remaining always small but fairly constant.

A few years ago the first rumors regarding the resurrection of the Mill Creeks began to drift in. They met at first with no confidence whatever. Newspaper dispatches reported that cattle men in nearby Shasta county were suffering loss of stock from marauding Indians, and representations were even alleged to have been made to Washington, but the feeling of the few who heard of the matter was that the acts complained of were the deeds of occasional civilized Indians who had turned to cattle stealing, or even perhaps of Americans who would be only too anxious to have the blame laid at the door or these peaceful people. The incident was soon forgotten, and while an occasional report of wild Indians in the fastnesses surrounding Lassen Peak might still circulate in the vicinity, it was believed by no one but a few remote ranchers who now and then had before their eyes more tangible evidence in the form of arrowpoints sticking in the flanks of sheep or cows.

Until to-day the inhabitants of the neighboring towns of Tehama and Vina, distant less than fifteen miles in an air line from the home of the tribe, have been the most skeptical regarding its existence, and shake their heads at the "yarns" which they allege are spun by the isolated dwellers in the hills, who "have more wealth of time than topics of conversation, and therefore are wont to give their imagination full play."

Just before the close of the year 1909* a party of surveyors working in Deer Creek Cañon suddenly stumbled across an Indian camp, from which two half-naked Indian men and a woman, as nearly as they could observe, made a hurried exit to disappear into the surrounding thick brush. The surveyors and their companions advanced cautiously and explored the habitation. Baskets, blankets of skins, points of harpoons for spearing salmon, bows and arrows and other implements of native manufacture were scattered about, mixed with jute and flour bags, and knives, saws, files, and tools stolen from neighboring cabins. Some of these articles were subsequently identified by their owners.

When a pile of skins and rags was thrown aside, an old crone was found cowering in a corner of the hut. She was dragged into daylight, and when she saw that her captors meant no evil so far as her safety was concerned, became partly reassured and tried to open communication with them. As she spoke only Indian, this attempt was not very successful. She knew one word of Spanish, the term *malo,* bad, which she uttered repeatedly in pointing to her legs, which were covered with sores and encased in tight wrappings of strips of buckskin. The old woman, perhaps on account of her age or because of this affliction, had been unable to escape with the others. The party soon left the camp, and the woman no doubt was carried off by her kinsmen. When the surveyors a few

[83]

* T. T. Waterman in "The Yana Indians" (in Chapter 4, below), gives the date as November 10, 1908; the *Lassen Magazine* (above) also says that the sighting by the surveyors was in the fall of 1908.—Ed.

days later came back to the camp they found it entirely deserted.

The report of this occurrence had some little publicity by word of mouth, but like all those that preceded it was met mainly with skepticism or scorn. But the rumor carried as far as the University of California, to whose anthropological department it was communicated by Dr. David P. Barrows, late Director of Education in the Philippine Islands, and by Mr. A. H. Allen, both members of the faculty of the institution.

While these reports seemed inherently incredible, they were accompanied by such circumstantial detail that it seemed important to the writer of this account to investigate the matter further. The description of the Indians also tallied so perfectly with what was last reported of the Mill Creeks more than a generation before, and with what was known of their character and habits, that the coincidence of an alleged group of wild people living in precisely the old habitat of this tribe could scarcely be fortuitous, unless the stories received were made up out of whole cloth on the basis of ancient actual events. It was clear that if these people existed they were the Kombo branch of the Yana; the only difficulty was in understanding how they could have kept themselves alive and remained entirely unknown for the many years that had elapsed.

Inquiry in the vicinity, and a visit to the mouth of Deer Creek Cañon, resulted in additional confirmation, with the consequence that it was decided to fit out an expedition which would thoroughly search the tract haunted by the Indians and if possible find them and open communication with them. A large party was determined to be of no avail, for a number of men could not hope to keep their presence unknown to the Indians and would therefore minimize the chances of success. The best season for instituting the search seemed to be in late fall, after the first rains of the mild California winter.

The party as organized was in charge of T. T. Waterman, instructor in anthropology in the University and an ethnologist of training and field experience among several of the California tribes. Accompanying him were J. W. Hunt, an engineer,

and Merle Apperson, the son of one of the members of the party of surveyors, and thoroughly acquainted with the territory.

Outfitting at Vina the three adventurers sallied forth on a quest which, while it never brought them in sight of any of the people, led them for a month over every square rod of the tract in which the Indians made their home, and resulted in the acquisition of incontrovertible evidence of their existence in a wild state.

Why the Indians escaped is not hard to understand. Knowing the country more intimately than anyone else, and imbued by a lifetime of precautions with eternal vigilance, they undoubtedly heard or caught sight of the party of searchers from a distance, retreated before them, and subsequently by a circuitous route slipped back to a place of comparative security which had already been examined. Two trailing dogs were taken along in the hope that they might be of service in locating the aborigines, but the rains that fell seemed to have effaced the Indians' trails. At any rate the dogs never picked up a fresh scent, so that the Indians had ample opportunity to keep changing their location at night.

Their territory was found to be surprisingly small. It consists of two closely adjacent tracts, each about three miles long and a little more than half a mile wide, in the cañon of Deer Creek on the south side of the stream. As soon as these stretches began to be penetrated by the Waterman party, it was discovered why the Indians had so long eluded communication. The entire ground is one mass of disintegrated rock, the fragments ranging from the size of a head to that of a house. Every foot of ground and every cranny between the stones is covered with an impenetrably dense growth of oak and other scrub. It was only occasionally that the party could see ten yards ahead. Going up on the bluff that overshadowed the cañon did not help matters, for there the eye encountered only a heaving waste of boulders and tree tops, between and below which a thousand people could have securely kept out of sight.

The Indians in traveling from one point to another either leap from rock to rock leaving no tracks behind them, or if they make their way through the brush, construct their trails under the vegetation instead of through it. They must, therefore, often make progress on hands and knees. Where branches must be cut out for such a trail, they are never chopped with an ax, the sound of which might attract an occasional rancher riding after his cattle, or a stray wayfarer. They are invariably broken or bent by hand, or silently sawed away with an old saw or file obtained in the course of a depredation.

By thus following close to the ground the Indians render their trails invisible even as one passes through the country. What is more, the cattle that may now and then wander into the territory do not have a chance to follow and beat out and make visible the paths, as they might if these were open to the sky. Every evidence of the Indians' work shows the same perpetual elusiveness and unceasingly painstaking care to avoid detection. They have evidently learned to prize their isolation and liberty above everything else and balk at no hardship and no labor to maintain their lifelong condition undisturbed.

Three huts or camps were found, all of them, however, showing no signs of occupation for at least some months past. All of these were constructed of limbs of trees and poles. The covering had mostly fallen away, but what remained consisted of boughs and grass or old skins and pilfered rags.

The weapons used by these strange people are the aboriginal bow and arrow. The arrow is feathered and painted as of old. As flint became scarce, the Indians learned to chip points of the identical shape from bottles and fragments of glass which they picked up in their nocturnal wanderings.

Among other products of civilization the Mill Creeks had obtained at different times possession of a number of guns. At the present time they never attempt to use these, but whether from superstition or from lack of ammunition must be left to conjecture. Probably the more prosaic explanation is the true one. Every gun that falls into their hands is dismounted and taken apart. A number of triggers, cocks, and barrels were found. These are probably of service to them as tools of various kinds.

The principal food of the band seems still to be the aboriginal staple of the California Indians, the acorn, which they can secure in comparative abundance. Acorns, while known as an excellent mast for hogs, are so saturated with tannic acid, the same substance that renders the bark of the oak the favorite material of the tanner, that they are absolutely unpalatable in the raw state, and most civilized people have never even suspected that they can be utilized as a most nourishing food. The Indians grind the meat of the acorn into a fine flour and then pour hot water over the mass until the bitter principle has been entirely eliminated and carried away in solution. The resulting product much resembles wheat flour in appearance and taste, differing from it principally in containing a greater proportion of starch and in being slightly oily when prepared from certain species of acorns. It is cooked with water into a sort of mush or thick soup, in baskets of aboriginal manufacture, stones which have been heated in the fire being dropped into the mass until it is brought up to the boiling point. Among the objects brought back by the expedition is an old basket found in one of the abandoned huts with traces of acorn meal still adhering to it, clear evidence that the Mill Creeks still follow this method of obtaining their daily bread.

Salmon are abundant in Deer Creek at a certain season of the year and are both speared and netted, as implements for both purposes show. Deer are hunted by an ingenious device. As the death dealing range of an arrow is much more limited than that of a rifle, the great problem of the aboriginal hunter is to come close enough to his quarry before it takes alarm and bounds away. These Indians accordingly construct a mask or headdress out of the stuffed skin of the head of a deer. To this they fasten if necessary real or imitation antlers. Provided with this and with a deerskin blanket thrown over his back, the hunter drops on hands and knees and begins to approach one of the animals. He raises himself sufficiently so that the false head appears above the brush. The deer, seeing what appears to be a companion, takes no alarm, provided he is approached from the leeward side; and may even be led by his curiosity to approach.

[85]

Once within range, the hunter, without rising, dispatches his arrow, and if his aim is true brings home both food and future clothing.

The garments are still of the aboriginal type, of skins. Wildcat and deer hides are both employed, but the favorite is a blanket woven of strips of rabbit fur. Many cottontails or jackrabbits go into the making of one of these articles, which when it is complete resembles in its structure a piece of coarsely woven cloth, but to the eye has the appearance of a continuous stretch of fur on both the front and back. It is the warmest sort of blanket that can be imagined and equally useful as a wrapper around the body in the daytime and as bedding at night.

After nearly four weeks of the hardest kind of traveling, in the course of which progress of two miles or even one mile a day was sometimes thought lucky, the University party returned to civilization minus the sought-for Indians but with photographs and specimens which definitely established their existence.

It is to be hoped that the Office of Indian Affairs may be able to take some action in regard to these interesting and unfortunate beings. If they continue their present mode of life, the settlers in the vicinity are likely to suffer further loss of property and livestock. If the Indians are ever caught in the act of marauding it may go hard with them, for the rancher in these districts rarely has his rifle far from his hand, and can scarcely be blamed for resorting to violence when his belongings have repeatedly been seized and are again in danger.

If the band can be captured, or even located, it should not be hard to provide for them. There are several Indian reservations in California, and the Government has lately done most praiseworthy though long delayed work in acquiring small tracts for the survivors of the numerous landless tribes that have lived for many years as scattered outcasts on the fringes of civilization. The number of these people is so insignificant that they could readily be incorporated with any other group. More feasible still would be to grant them a few square miles in the inaccessible and worthless cañon of Deer Creek where they now live. They could then be assured of a home and a refuge of protection, and there is little doubt that if once they could rely on security under the law they would be glad to lay aside their inherited fear and hostility and settle down to a more prosaic but comfortable mode of life. They have long since learned the folly of opposing the white man by force, and however habit may have dulled the edge of their hardships, there is little doubt that once they had tasted the routine of three regular meals a day and of a roof over their heads to keep the rain out, they would welcome the change. Nothing would be more fitting than to secure them at least part of the ancestral territory which they have so long maintained and there allow them to work out their salvation in their own way under the fostering and restraining guidance of the Government.

How they can be captured and brought in is, however, another and more difficult problem. It is the unanimous opinion of those acquainted with them that a troop of cavalry might scour the region of Deer Creek and Mill Creek for months without laying hands on them. Possibly a gradually narrowing circle of men might enclose them and finally drive them to the center. Literally an army would, however, be requisite to work out such a plan, for there are innumerable places where if the gap between two sentries measured only a few yards the Indians could safely slip out between them in the dark of night. The chances of success are greatest for a small party operating along the same lines as that from the University, but with longer time at command. It is not at all improbable that if the Indians were led to think that they were not being pursued they might venture into communication, for there must be many needs that they would be glad to satisfy by trade, and curiosity cannot be entirely extinct in the breasts of even these people. Once communication had been opened, and the savages assured of pacific intentions particularly if they were allowed to depart unmolested and enriched by a little tobacco or trinkets, they would soon return. Once their confidence was gained, everything else would almost certainly follow as a matter of course, provided they were dealt with in a tactful manner.

To the ethnologist and the historian, as well as to the philanthropist, nothing could be more desirable than such a termination. These people must preserve, besides their language, many entirely aboriginal beliefs and innumerable native customs and practises. Their former history, while in open conflict with civilization, as well as their successful concealment from it for so long a time, arouses an interest in the breast of everyone. A record of their wanderings, their vigilance, their traits and habits, would appeal to the historian, while a knowledge of their ancient institutions and traditions, preserved from purely aboriginal times into the Twentieth Century, would be a rich mine to the ethnologist and anthropologist of the future.

Such is the history to date of this smallest and most remarkable people, the last free survivors of the American red man, who by an unexampled fortitude and stubbornness of character have succeeded in holding out against the overwhelming tide of civilization twenty-five years longer even than Geronimo's famous band of Apaches. What the future may bring no one can tell, but it is certain that before their record is finally closed at least one other chapter of entrancing interest will be added.

[87]

ISHI ENTERS CIVILIZATION

ISHI ENTERS CIVILIZATION

The first notices of Ishi appeared in newspapers. Reprinted here are eleven such articles, ten of them printed within a month of Ishi's appearance at the Oroville slaughterhouse, when there was a great deal of public interest in the event.

The local daily newspaper, the *Oroville Register*, was—expectedly—the first paper to print the story of Ishi's capture at the slaughterhouse only a few miles outside Oroville. He was lodged in the Oroville jail within the hour, as it were, of his capture. The story was picked up and by the next day was front-page news in San Francisco and across the country. The early stories in the other papers do little more than repeat the original *Register* account, or they add details that are flamboyant and made up. That the fact of the capture should be accurate, and the elaborations largely inaccurate, is not surprising, the inaccuracies showing themselves up as more facts regarding Ishi were gradually accumulated.

[91]

1. Newspaper Accounts of Ishi's Capture (1911)

August 29

An aboriginal Indian, clad in a rough canvas shirt which reached to his knees, beneath which was a frayed undershirt that had been picked up somewhere in his wanderings, was taken into custody last evening by Sheriff Webber and Constable Toland at the Ward slaughter-house on the Quincy road. He had evidently been driven by hunger to the slaughter-house, as he was almost in a starving condition, and at the Sheriff's office ate ravenously of the food that was set before him.

Not a single word of English does he know, nor a single syllable of the language of the Digger Indians, the tribe which lived around here. Where he came from is a mystery. The most plausible explanation seems to be that he is probably the surviving member of the little group of uncivilized Deer Creek Indians who were driven from their hiding place two years ago.

News of the presence of the Indian was telephoned to the Sheriff's office by the employees at the slaughter-house. They informed Sheriff Webber that they had "something out there," and they did not know what it was.

Sheriff Webber and Constable Toland immediately left for the slaughter-house. Upon their arrival they found the men standing guard over the Indian, who was sitting crouched up in a corner. He offered no resistance when the Sheriff motioned to him to come with him, but for safety's sake handcuffs were clasped upon him.

Untouched by Civilization

In the Sheriff's office he was surrounded by a curious throng. He made a pathetic figure crouched upon the floor. He is evidently about 60 years of age. The canvas from which his outer shirt was made had been roughly sewed together. His undershirt had evidently been stolen in a raid upon some cabin. His feet were almost as wide as they were

Oroville Register, August 29, 1911.

long, showing plainly that he had never worn either moccasins or shoes. In his ears were rings made of buckskin thongs.

Over his shoulder a rough canvas bag was carried. In it a few manzanita berries were found and some sinews of deer meat. By motions, the Indian explained that he had been eating these.

Not a Digger Indian

The appearance of the Indian shows that he does not belong to the Digger tribe. Supporting the theory that he may be the last surviving member of the Deer Creek tribe is the fact that he resembles the Modoc Indians, to which tribe the Deer Creek Indians belonged.

Ravenous With Hunger

On his arrival in the office Under-Sheriff Will White immediately placed a meal before him. The menu included beans served piping hot, bread and butter, and doughnuts. The Indian ate ravenously, tearing the bread apart bit by bit. An amusing incident occurred while he was eating the beans. Under-Sheriff White interrupted him to press a doughnut upon him. The Indian took it in one hand gingerly, still holding the bowl of beans in the other. He examined the doughnut suspiciously. Then in an experimental fashion he tasted a small piece. No sooner had the doughnut touched the palate than he dropped the beans, seized the doughnut in both hands, and there was nothing more doing for the beans until the doughnut had been finished.

Not Acquainted With Firearms

After Sheriff Webber had removed the cartridges from his revolver he gave the weapon to the Indian. The aborigine showed no evidence that he knew anything regarding its use. A cigarette was offered to him, and while it was very evident that he knew what tobacco was, he had never smoked it in that form, and had to be taught the art. His curiosity, however, was chiefly aroused at writing. This seemed to amuse him greatly, and as the operation was shown him he watched the marks with the greatest amazement.

Apparently the Indian has never come in contact with civilization, except as he has assisted in robbing some lonely cabin near his hiding places.

In an attempt to ascertain something about him, Charles Gramps was found. He conversed with the aborigine in the tongue of the Digger Indians. The latter comprehended nothing of what he said, nor could Gramps understand a word that the aborigine uttered.

Last of the Deer Creeks

The attire of the Indian, his general appearance, and his presence here, are strongly indicative of the fact that he belongs to the Deer Creek tribe of wild and uncivilized Indians. These Indians were originally proud and warlike, and their frequent depredations upon the white settlers led to an organized war against them. Robert A. Anderson, the father of R.N. Anderson, of this city, later Sheriff of the county, was the leader of the band that attacked the Indians, after repeated forays upon the white settlers had been made. The band was practically exterminated, but as Mr. Anderson states in the book he has written upon these Indian wars, "a remnant of the Indians who caused so much uneasiness in those early days still remains hidden away in the dark caverns of the hills. They haunt that stretch of country from Deer Creek to Mill Creek, making stealthy descents upon the cabin of the white man, but committing no serious crimes. They have developed the art of hiding to a perfection greater than that of the beasts of the woods, and, while in no wise dangerous, they are probably today the wildest people in America."

Two years ago a surveying party drove the Indians from their last hiding place. As far as could be ascertained, the remnant of the once proud tribe at that time consisted of four bucks and one squaw. Apparently they again disappeared. It is believed that the aborigine who was captured last evening is either the last surviving member of the party, or that he was one delegated by the others to make a foray upon the slaughter-house. Had the men not been working there later than usual, and had the dogs not detected the wild man, the foray would have been successful.

August 30

In the weird pantomime, which has in all ages been the medium through which people of different tongues converse, the Indian found on Monday on the Quincy road yesterday told as best he could the story of his wanderings. The tale more firmly confirms the belief that the Indian is the last surviving member of the uncivilized Deer Creek Indians. Sweeping his hands north and east, he indicated from where he had come. Enumerating on his fingers, he informed the officers who had him in charge that originally there had been four in the band. By the same pantomime he conveyed to the officers that two of the band had been drowned; that he and a mahala had come on alone; that the mahala had died and been partially devoured by coyotes; that he had come to the slaughter-house alone; and that there were no more of his people to be found. In view of the fact that the surveying party which drove the remnant of the tribe from their Deer Creek fastnesses stated that they encountered four of these wild Indians, three bucks and a squaw, it would seem almost conclusive that the last surviving member of the tribe was the Indian whose appearance here has aroused the curiosity of the whole city and country side.

Taken to Place Where Found

With the idea that if taken to the place where he was found he might lead the officers to his hiding place, the man was taken to the slaughter-house on the Quincy road yesterday by Under-Sheriff White and Deputy Sheriff McKee. By signs they managed to convey to him what was desired. The idea grasped, he in his turn proceeded in pantomime and by signs to tell the story of his wanderings.

Came From Northeast

Sweeping his hand toward the north and east he indicated that he had started far away. Couuting on his hands and pointing to himself, he conveyed

Oroville Register, August 30, 1911.

[93]

the information that at first there had been four in the party. He indicated how step by step they had wandered on throughout the mountains.

Two Are Drowned

At some point in the journey two were drowned. The Indian indicated that they had attempted to cross a stream and that the water had poured over them, drowning two. He then showed how he had dug graves and buried the two companions, and over this imaginary grave he chanted a mournful incantation for the dead.

Mahala Devoured By Wild Beasts

He again indicated that two had wandered on. Here the auditors could understand the first word, "mahala." His mahala had become sick. He indicated that he had left her lying down and that he had gone for water. When he returned, the mahala had died, and already coyotes had started to devour her body. He imitated the barking of coyotes, and showed where the beasts had eaten the arms and the breast. Again he indicated that he had dug a shallow grave, had placed the mahala there, and again he paused for a moment to chant his weird and mournful incantation for the dead.

Proceeded Here Alone

From there, raising one finger and pointing at himself, he showed that he had proceeded alone; that there were no others for whom the officers could look, nor was there any place to which he could lead them. Convinced of this fact, he was again placed in the buggy and the officers returned with him to the County Jail.

Hundreds View Man

The Register was no more than off the press yesterday morning than the Sheriff's office began to be besieged with people who desired to see the savage. All day long there was a continual stream of people passing upstairs to the cell in which the Indian was kept. It is estimated that there were fully 1,000 people who viewed the Indian yesterday.

Proves Absolutely Unresponsive

Some of those who viewed him would name the various Indian tribes, in the hope of awakening a response from him. "Modoc," "Piute," "Nevada," and other names were given, but there was no apparent evidence that the Indian understood any of the words.

Will Call on University

Professor Kroeber, of the University of California, who has made a special study of native Indian tribes and their languages, will be apprised regarding the Indian, in order that he may come here, if he so desires. The Bureau of Indian Affairs will at the same time be informed that the Indian is in custody here, and that the county desires to turn him over to the Federal Government, of whom he is properly the ward.

August 31

The developments of yesterday in the case of the aboriginal Indian now a captive at the County Jail tended more and more to confirm the opinion that he is of local origin. The news of his capture has been disseminated among the Indians of the county, and many of them wandered into town to see him. He was addressed in the tongues of the various Indian tribes, but the efforts of those seeking to learn anything of him proved almost wholly barren. He does not understand the language of the Digger Indians or of the Yuba or Bidwell Indians. Neither could he understand Chickasaw, Choctaw, Chinook, or Cherokee. Nor on his part was it possible for him to make his auditors acquainted with his language.

Knew Word "Chico"

The single exception, that tends strongly to support the theory that he is of local origin, occurred when Mrs. C. F. Belding, who speaks four Indian languages, spoke to him, and when Will Conway, an Indian from the Bidwell Indian village, addressed him. In a sentence addressed to Mrs. Belding he distinctly said the word "chico." To

Oroville Register, **August 31, 1911.**

what he referred is not known. The word "chico" is itself an Indian word, and his ignorance of all things civilized precludes the idea that he could have intended it for the city that bears that name. It was apparently rather used in its original Indian sense. Will Conway at one time seemed to make himself intelligible by an Indian sign, but the Indian in his turn could not make himself intelligible to Conway, nor could Conway again make himself understood by the aborigine.

Indians Completely Mystified

The Indians who gathered to see him were as much mystified as were the whites. He had never been seen by any of them, nor had any of them heard of or about him. He was as strange to them as a visitor from another world.

Thinks He Is in Happy Hunting Grounds

Again yesterday there was a continual stream of the curious at the County Jail to see the strange captive. While he cannot express himself, it is a safe bet that the Indian half believes he has reached the Happy Hunting Grounds. With all he wants to eat, an audience watching his every movement, he is thoroughly enjoying himself. Moreover the humor of the situation is not lost upon him. When a party including three ladies was taken to his cell last evening he broke into a loud guffaw. When he rose from his bed in his tattered one-garment canvas shirt to greet his visitors the situation seemed to appeal to all as deliciously funny, and Indian, white people and all laughed until the very jail rang.

Likes Civilized Food

The Indian is also receiving his first introduction to civilized food, and he appears to enjoy it. Bananas, oranges, apples and other fruits have been sent to him. He knows how to eat none of them. The banana he started to eat skin and all, with an evident lack of relish. When he was instructed how to peel the fruit he gave evidence of enjoying it hugely. A tomato was next given him, and he immediately started to peel it as he had done the banana, but there he bumped against some of the inconsistencies of civilization, and was instructed that he must eat it without peeling it. An orange was entirely new to him, and he also had to be instructed that it was to be peeled before taking.

Territory of Deer Creek Indians

Among the visitors at the County Jail yesterday afternoon was County Surveyor M. C. Polk. According to Mr. Polk, who is well versed in the matter, the Deer Creek Indians had as their zone a territory reaching from Mill Creek in Tehama County on the north to Concow in Butte County on the south. They would pass from one part of the territory to the other, going through the Cohasset district, where, years ago, in cold blood, they killed a settler. Driven out of the Deer Creek country, it is believed that the band of four wandered to the south over the ground that members of their tribe before them had passed, and that, as related in the Register of yesterday, death took three of their number and starvation compelled the other to forego the hiding habits of years and to seek civilization for food.

[95]

Will Be Shown Implements of Tribe

Mr. Polk has in his possession some of the arrows, blankets, and other implements of the Deer Creek Indians. He will bring these to the County Jail and exhibit them to the aborigine. It is thought that their recognition by him would be proof positive of his origin.

Indian Says He Understood

Upon his return to Chico yesterday William Conway, the Bidwell Indian, gave out a statement to the effect that he had conversed with the aborigine and that he had been told a number of things by the Indian. He states that he gave the Indian the high sign of the tribe, and that the aborigine immediately responded. The officials state that an Indian sign given by Conway was understood, but beyond that it was plain that neither could make himself intelligible to the other.

Conway states that the jargon of the Indian closely resembles that of the Tehama tribe of

Indians. He states that the aborigine told him that he had traveled for ten days without food, and that when he was first taken captive he thought the white people intended to fatten him and kill him. He further states that the aborigine told him his papoose had died, but that his squaw was still in the mountains.

His statement contains a number of other matters so improbable that little credence is given to the whole tale.

Keeps Hair Short By Burning

Much curiosity has been expressed relative to the manner in which the Indian keeps his hair short. The officials of the jail managed to convey to him this idea, and by lighting a stick he showed how he singed his hair, according to a custom not uncommon among Indians.

---

[96] *This is one of the earliest metropolitan newspaper reports on Ishi. The first local notice was in the* Oroville Register, *August 29, 1911, reprinted above. Much of the phraseology of the San Francisco story is that of the Oroville paper.*

---

2. Tribe's Dirge Chanted by Savage

Last of 'Deers' Wails a Requiem

Oroville. August 30. In the weird pantomime which in all ages has been the medium which peoples of different tongues converse, an Indian found on Monday in the mountain wilderness near Oroville told to-day the story of his wanderings.

That he is the last surviving member of the Deer Creek tribe, long believed to be extinct, at one time regarded as the most savage aborigines in America, there remains no doubt.

He is a savage of the most primitive type. He speaks no dialect that can be recognized. He understands no word spoken to him.

But with gestures more eloquent and expressive than could have been the spoken word, he laid

San Francisco Examiner, **August 31, 1911.**

bare the tragedy of his people in a silence broken only by his mournful incantations chanted to the Great Spirit when his story dealt with death.

Tribe Lives Like Beasts

Wilder than other tribes, the Deer Creek Indians fled before the white man's approach—fled into mountain fastnesses where they lived as the beasts.

They suffered and starved. Their number dwindled till only four remained, three braves and a squaw.

The wild waters of a mountain torrent carried to death two of the braves.

The Indian just found and his "mahala" had wandered on and on until she, too, was called by death and coyotes feasted off her body.

With the idea that he might lead the authorities to his hiding place, the man was taken to the place where he was captured. By signs they managed to conveyed to him what was desired. The idea grasped, he proceeded in pantomime and by signs to tell the story of his wanderings.

Sweeping his hands toward the north and the east, he indicated that he had started far away. Counting on his hands and pointing to himself, he conveyed the information that at first there had been four in the party.

He indicated how, step by step, they had wandered on through the mountains. The drowning of two was told in graphic, though silent, manual. The Indian indicated that the party had attempted to cross a stream, and that the water had swept half of the band to death.

Dirge Chanted for Dead

He then showed how he had dug graves and buried the two companions. Over this imaginary grave he chanted a mournful incantation for the dead.

He again indicated that the remaining two had wandered on. Here the auditors could understand the first word, "mahala."

His mahala had become sick. He indicated that he had left her lying down, and that he had gone for water. When he returned the mahala had died, and already coyotes had started to devour her body.

He imitated the barking of coyotes, and showed where the beasts had eaten her arms and breast.

Again he indicated that he had dug a shallow grave and had placed the mahala there. Again he paused for a moment to chant his weird incantation for the dead.

From there, raising one finger and pointing to himself, he showed that he had proceeded alone— that there were no others for whom to look nor was there any place to which he could lead them.

Puzzle to Indians

Indians from the whole contryside have been brought to talk with him, and white men acquainted with many Indian languages have also been here. To all he is an enigma. None of them can understand him, nor can he understand any of them.

The Deer Creek Indians were originally proud and war-like. Their frequent depredations upon the white settlers led to an organized war against them.

Robert A. Anderson was the leader of the band that attacked the Indians after repeated forays upon the white settlers. The band was practically exterminated, but, as Anderson tells in a book he wrote three years ago concerning these Indian wars, a remnant of the Indians still remained hidden away in the caverns of the hills.

Hiding Becomes an Art

They haunt that stretch of country from Deer Creek to Mill Creek. They have developed the art of hiding to a perfection greater than that of the beasts of the woods.

Though in no wise dangerous they are probably to-day the wildest people in America.

Two years ago a surveying party drove the Indians from their last hiding place. As far as could be ascertained the remnant of the once proud tribe at that time consisted of four bucks and one squaw.

It is believed that the Indian captured is the only survivor of this band, and hence the least civilized man in America.

Mary Ashe Miller was a good observer and good reporter. Her description of Ishi, written about *a week after he walked out of the wilds, alone and afraid, is excellent. From it we can learn how little time was required for Ishi to begin his adjustment to a second, and wholly new, world, friends, and way of life.*

3. Indian Enigma Is Study for Scientists

Mary Ashe Miller

Deciphering a human document, with the key to most of the hieroglyphics lost, is the baffling but absorbingly delightful task which Dr. A. L. Kroeber and T. T. Waterman of the University of California have set for themselves. The document is the Deer Creek Indian captured recently near Oroville, who should by every rule and reckoning be the loneliest man on earth. He is the last of his tribe; when he dies his language becomes dead also; he has feared people, both whites and Indians to such an extent that he has wandered, alone, like a hunted animal, since the death of his tribal brothers and sisters.

The man is as aboriginal in his mode of life as though he inhabited the heart of an African jungle, all of his methods are those of primitive peoples. Hunting has been his only means of living and that has been done with a bow and arrow of his own manufacture, and with snares. Probably no more interesting individual could be found today than this nameless Indian.

Frightens his Discoverers

He was captured at the slaughter house about three miles out of Oroville, where he was trying to steal some meat. The dogs barked so ferociously one night that the men employed there went out to discover the cause of the trouble. They found the Indian, wearing a single shirt like garment made of a piece of canvas, crouched in a corner, frightened half to death.

His discoverers were as badly frightened as he was and telephoned to the sheriff in Oroville to come and get what they had found. The Indian was taken to town and lodged in the jail and a

From *San Francisco Call,* September 6, 1911.

[97]

search for an interpreter began. Hundreds of Indians from all the surrounding country came and every Indian tongue was tried, but to no avail.

Finally Waterman, instructor in the anthropological department at the University of California, went to see him. He had a list of words of the North Yana speech and found that the unknown one recognized some of them with greatest delight. Sam Batwee, one of the oldest of the remaining score of Indians of the North Yana tribe was sent for from Redding. Batwee frightened the Indian more at first than did the white men, but now they have become very friendly.

Lived in Dense Jungle

The unknown is a South Yana, it is said, and Doctor Kroeber said the two languages were related probably as closely as Spanish and Portuguese, so that communication, while possible, is by no means easy.

It has been proved that the Indian is one of four who lived for some years in a patch of thickest brush in the heart of Tehama county. Practically on the great Stanford ranch, within two miles of a ranch house, these Indians lived without being discovered. The wooded bit was between a high cliff and a stream, Deer creek, and was about three miles long by one mile wide.

So dense was this jungle that not even cattle penetrated it, but in it was the Indians' camp. Two years ago a party of surveyors ran a line which passed through the camp and after the manner of surveyors they proceeded to chop their way through the brush primeval.

This frightened the Indians away; they fled to the mountains, and this man, the sole survivor, has probably lived by hunting, creeping up to ranch houses and stealing bits of food, finding deserted camps and foraging there and eating berries and roots. When he was captured he had a few manzanita berries and on those he had lived for some time, he said.

It is difficult to realize that he is absolutely aboriginal, yet seeing must be believing. He is without trace or taint of civilization, but he is learning fast and seems to enjoy the process.

[98]

Is Likable Old Indian

If he may be considered as a sample, man has not been invariably improved by the march of time. The Indian is wonderfully quick and intelligent, he has a delightful sense of humor, he is docile, cheerful and amiable, friendly, courageous, self controlled and reserved, and a great many other things that make him a very likable sort of a person. Waterman says he has learned to sincerely admire and like the old fellow during their intercourse. Although he is probably about 60 or 65 years old, he doesn't look it by 15 or 20 years. In appearance he is far superior to the average California Indian. He is nearly six feet tall, well muscled and not thin. His face is rather the pointed type, with a long chin and upper lip and a straight nose. His eyes are large, very black, of course, and exceedingly bright and wideawake. His eyelashes are the variety that bring to mind the idea that he bought them by the yard and was rather extravagant about it. His thick hair is jet black and short, he having burned it off after the death of his family. His hands are long and narrow, with very long fingers. The palms show that he has never done manual labor of any kind, as they are as soft as a woman's.

His ears and inner cartilage of his nose are pierced, and this, Sam Batwee explains, is "what he b'lieve." It is "medicine" or religious faith that by this means he is saved from going to "bad place" and will certainly go to "good place" after death. Little knotted strings, apparently sinews of animals, are in the holes, which are of considerable size.

Coming down on the train from Oroville was a great ordeal for the Indian, but he showed his fear only in the tenseness of attitude maintained and by his closely clenched hands.

"Much To See Here"

Crossing the bay was a wonderful experience, and yesterday morning as he stood in front of the Affiliated colleges he asked Batwee as to the direction of where he crossed the big water. Batwee said: "First, yesterday, he frightened very much, now today he think all very funny. He like it, tickle him. He like this place here. Much to see, big water off there" and he waved his hand toward the ocean, "plenty houses, many things to see."

The first time that the unknown refused to obey orders was yesterday. He was to be photographed in a garment of skins, and when the dressing for the aboriginal part began he refused to remove his overalls.

"He say he not see any other people go without them," said Batwee, "and he say he never take them off no more."

Nor would he, so the overalls had to be rolled to the knees and the skins draped over them as best they might be. He was taken to the west end of the museum building and on the edge of the Sutro forest he was posed. The battery of half a dozen cameras focused upon him was a new experience and evidently a somewhat terrifying one. He stood with his head back and a half smile on his face, but his compressed lips and dilated nostrils showed that he was far from happy.

"Tell him, Batwee, white man just play," said Waterman, and the explanation seemed to reassure him.

After the camera men left he squatted in the sand and seemed happier than when in a chair under a roof. He was given a couple of sticks used by some tribe for fire making, taken from the museum, and he was delighted, showing at once that he knew what they were for. After a few seconds of twirling the sticks and making them smoke, he gave up and told Batwee that it was the wrong kind of wood.

Then he did some most delightful pantomime bits. Folding a leaf between his lips he sucked on it so strongly that a wailing sound, closely resembling the bleating of a fawn resulted. This was an illustration of his mode of deer hunting. When he hid himself and bleated the deer were sure to come. He was like a child "showing off" yesterday. Smiling delightedly he showed how, after he had called the deer, he drew back his bow to the farthest limit and let the arrow fly. Then he galloped away with his hands, indicating that the deer had escaped, making tracks in the sand with his two fingers.

He Has No Name

Then he bleated again and showed another deer approaching from the other side. Again he drew his bow, and that time the deer was his. Rabbits he hunted with a queer sound, resembling more the popping of gigantic corks than anything else. Queer tracks were made in the sand and strange gestures—all of which indicated rabbits. Bear he described by growls, more tracks in the sand, and finally by raising his arms high and lowering his head, bringing to mind by his mimicry the terrible "Truce of the Bear." He did not shoot the bear, but ran away and climbed a tree. Salmon fishing he illustrates, too, with prayers and the tossing of roots into the stream.

He talked to Batwee freely, but would tell little that was personal.

His name, if he knows it, he keeps to himself. It is considered bad form among aboriginal tribes, I am told, to ask any one's name, and it is seldom divulged until a firm basis of friendship is established. The unknown, however, declares he has no name. In reply to Batwee's questions, he shows by a wandering forefinger that he has been all alone. There was no one, he says, to tell him his name and he has none.

He is so desirous of "doing as the Romans do" since he arrived in civilization that it was thought he might be induced to tell his name when he knew that all white men had them. Batwee told him it was customary in the best circles, or words to that effect, and in response he declared his entire willingness to have a name. He had none, he reiterated, but if any one had one to give him he would gladly receive it.

Batwee calls him John, but Doctor Kroeber declared that lacking in individuality.

"We must have a name for him, though," said Waterman. "We can't go on calling him 'Hay, there.'"

For the present his christening will be deferred, in the hope that some name may develop later.

All questions as to his wife he evades. He has a word, "maeela," which was at first mistaken for "mahala," which the Indians use for "wife," but that is not the meaning, Waterman says.

[99]

When he is asked anything about his wife, he begins to tell Indian myths or legends; how the cöyotes stole the fire; bits of stories of women's work; imitations of a woman cooking mush, with bubbling sounds of boiling. This is perhaps because aboriginal tribes will never speak of the dead.

Waterman said yesterday: "It's as though you asked a man when he got his divorce and he began to tell you the story of 'Cinderella.'"

He will eat anything that is given him without much apparent preference. Sweets, however, he seems fond of, and doughnuts delight him. He knew nothing, of course, of eating with knives or forks, but he was taught in the Oroville jail to eat with a spoon. This habit he has adopted, and when given a peach proceeded to eat it with his spoon.

He has likewise learned to smoke cigarettes, and already his fingers are badly stained. When he was given chewing tobacco he ate it. Batwee remonstrated with him and asked if it did not make him sick. This unknown denied, and said that it made him strong, did him good. When he was wandering, he used some sort of Indian wild tobacco, but his first taste of plug cut or its equivalent he received from the jailer at Oroville.

He told Batwee that this man, big man, all the same as chief, had given him tobacco and also the blue shirt and overalls which he was wearing.

Charles L. Davis of Washington, D.C., who is an Indian inspector, happened to be in San Francisco, and went out to see the Indian yesterday.

In parting, he presented the unknown with his knife, saying that he wanted him to remember him in case they ever met again. The Indian accepted it and seemed to know its use, opening the blades and finally putting it in his pocket. His newly acquired pockets, by the way, are as keen a delight to him as are those of a small boy, and he has a great collection of odds and ends in them already.

I thought I would give him a present, too, but found I had nothing either amusing or instructive with me save a white bone police whistle. This I blew for him, which seemed to please him greatly; then I gave it to him. He tried to blow it, but was afraid to put it between his lips at first. When he

[100]

understood the method of manipulating it and found he must blow it hard, he blew a mighty blast. Nothing that he has had since he left the wilds has pleased him more, Waterman said. He would blow it with all his might, and then laugh heartily. Finally he fairly got the giggles, laughing out loud. Doctor Kroeber was away when he first whistled, and when the former returned the Indian became suddenly shy and wouldn't blow. At the noon hour a siren whistle, some place off across the city, sounded. He looked at me and smiled, and I nodded at the whistle in his hand. He laughed again and, with a sly look at Doctor Kroeber, blew with all his might and main.

All of this sounds as though the absolutely primitive state of the man's mind and life might be exaggerated. No one who sees him can doubt the statement of the anthropologists that he is the find of a lifetime on account of his lack of up-to-dateness.

What he can tell will be of the greatest value to them. . . .

Philip H. Kinsley's article in the San Francisco Examiner *of the same date (September 6, 1911) gives us further impressions of Ishi, now living in San Francisco, having been transported there two days before from Oroville.*

4. Untainted Life Revealed by Aborigine

Philip H. Kinsley

> In "Ishi," as we have decided to call the Indian captured near Oroville, I can safely say that we have the most uncivilized and uncontaminated man in the world to-day—Prof. A. L. Kroeber of the department of Anthropology, University of California.

On the heights back of the Affiliated Colleges yesterday afternoon a newspaper photographer put his new felt hat on a stick, set the stick in the

San Francisco Examiner, September 6, 1911.

ground and put an ancient bow and arrow from the museum in the hands of Ishi, the "wild man," who was captured last week near Oroville and brought here Monday night.

Ishi was told by sign language to shoot the owner of the hat, thinking it was a joke and that the headpiece was safe enough.

The Indian laughed gleefully as he fingered the bow. It was the first thing he had seen in days that he understood. He squinted along the arrow and felt the tip and shook his head to say that it was not sharp enough. Then he laughed again and fitted the arrow to the bow, and before you could say Jack Robinson he had sent the arrow ripping through the center of the new felt hat 100 feet away. He capered in glee while the photographer sadly picked up his hat.

Accuracy Meant Food

That was not play with Ishi. For many years, hidden in the wilds of the Sacramento Valley, it had meant meat to him. This and fishing and trapping. His hands are as soft as a woman's. He has taken his game as his fathers took it for hundreds of years.

Ishi is no fairy story—no dream of the dime museum press agent. He is a man "unspotted by the world."

He looks like many other Indians, but he is unlike any other. His chin is a little sharper and his profile is delicate. His hair is short, for he is in mourning for his "mahala" or wife. When she died and the coyotes fought over her body he singed his long hair with a redhot coal and pulled the whiskers from his chin one by one. That is the way this Indian mourns.

They have put Ishi—"the Man"—under the microscope out at the Affiliated Colleges. The professors are gloating, for he opens a new world to them. He is the greatest anthropological treasure they have ever captured.

Man of Age Now Dead

In him you may see the same manner of man that the Fathers of the Order of St. Francis found in California when they pushed north on their missionary journey to San Francisco bay 150 years ago. He speaks an unknown tongue. He has a conception of his own of the creation of the world and the signs of nature.

He propitiates the gods of storm and lightning and sings incantations to the fish of the rivers. He wears a piece of thong in this nose and ears to take him to the Indian heaven when he dies.

He is absolutely [innocent] of all modern life. The greatest thing that he ever saw in the way of civilization, before he was captured in a corral, while trying to steal meat last week, was the railroad trains thundering through the Sacramento valley.

Hat Merely an Ornament

He was naked save for a sack when they found him. They clothed him in a blue shirt and a pair of overalls and gave him a straw hat, which is constantly falling off or tipping over one ear. Shoes he could not wear. They had to dress him as they would dress a child and he wore his clothes with all the grace of a lay figure in a second hand shop on the water front. They just hung there and he felt of them wonderingly, especially the brown silk tie that was fastened to the shirt.

They gave him a little whistle and he clung to it with all the joy of a five-year-old, blowing it at intervals and laughing.

It was with the greatest difficulty that he was persuaded to undress and get into a bed last night. He made it understood that as everyone else wore clothes he also would wear them and that he would never take them off again.

Though he had gone practically naked all his life, he refused yesterday to undress and put on skins to have his picture taken. Something new has been born within him the last two days.

There is something simple and pathetic about Ishi. He is a child with all a child's wonder over new things—not a murderous savage. He had never seen the ocean until yesterday and yet he looked at the great blue stretch of water from the heights with no more change of expression than a two-year-old baby when shown the same splendor.

[101]

He laughs a great deal. The smallest things amuse him. The wonderful things that men and women wear and the wonderful houses in which they live please him greatly. He saw a gardener picking flowers in the lawn in front of the college and he laughed and made a motion of eating. He thought the man was picking things to eat.

Accepts Lot Trustfully

He eats anything that is set before him with great and simple trust that the wonderful beings who have taken him into captivity mean well by him.

He is afraid and tries hard not to show it. He was frightened badly at the engine in the Oroville railroad station Monday night. When he got into the train, however, he looked at passing sights with enjoyment. When he sees anything that he does not understand and that frightens him he grows rigid and his hands grip something. Very little expression ever crosses his face.

When he stepped into the ferryboat Monday night he was frightened again, walking gingerly as though he thought the floor would not hold him. When the whistle blew he trembled and grew rigid, displaying the same fear again that the baby shows.

A camera was a source of infinite pleasure to him and when he looked into the reflector, and saw his friend, T. T. Waterman, instructor in the college who brought him from Oroville, he chuckled. A watch held further wonders for him and he held it to his ear to hear the tick with the intent interest of a child.

Money Only Pretty Toy

Money is as rare to him as a bird of paradise. He recognizes the eagle on a silver dollar and strokes the silver for its brightness, but that is all it means to him. It has been as useless during all his life— which is supposed to be about 50 years—as it was to Robinson Crusoe.

Ishi learned to smoke in the Oroville jail and he sat contentedly puffing at a cigarette as the scientists and reporters gathered round him yesterday afternoon. He was a little afraid of every new person and showed plainly that all he wanted was to have something to eat and to be unmolested, yet he was docile and showed his soft hands and hard feet when asked.

He was studied as a new species of insect by the scientists. They carried note books and jotted down everything he did. A telephone was put to his ear to see how he would take it. Waterman talked a little Indian language at him, but Ishi would not respond. He was dismayed and afraid of the wonderful instrument. After he is a little more accustomed to things they will show him a phonograph.

Ishi does not sit down in ordinary fashion. He squats on his ankles by the hour, his little brown eyes under the shock of black hair going in wonder from one thing to another.

Reticence Principal Trait

The professors have not been able to get much out of Ishi yet. With true Indian reticence he refuses to talk about himself. They have not been able to get his real name, for it is not etiquette for an Indian to tell any one his own name.

They have not been able to tell whether he has left any other members of his tribe in the wilderness of the Deer Creek canyon, where the northern of the Yanas, to which he belongs, were massacred by white settlers forty years ago. Since that time the Ishi has dodged all signs of the terrible whites. When he was caught he was crouching in terror of his life in a dark corner of a corral.

Waterman thinks that he is the last member of his tribe, but Professor Kroeber thinks that there may be others hidden away in the bush. The story of the last wanderings of Ishi, as given in Oroville, may be all a misunderstanding, according to Kroeber. The only reason he thinks it may be true is that the Indian has singed hair.

Makes Offering to Gods

Just what Ishi thinks of God he has not told yet. He has several gods, evidently. During a storm he scatters offerings in four spots around the tree which shelters him. This is to bribe the god of lightning not to strike the tree.

His observation of small things is remarkable. When he was in jail Waterman asked him what the cot he was sitting on was made of.

"Wood?" asked Waterman, in the dialect.

The Indian made it understood that it was sugar pine. He had noticed this with the same naturalness that you would notice whether it was a Masonic or Turk street car coming.

He has eaten with his fingers all his life, but in five days he has learned to use the knife, fork and spoon. Before that he ate thin soup with three fingers crooked, and thick soup with two fingers.

About 300 words of his language have been noted by the scientists. There is no word that is like any other Indian language. Even Sam Batwee, a Southern Yana Indian, who has been brought to the Affiliated Colleges to help in the investigation, cannot understood much.

Has Language of Own

These are some of the words as discovered by Waterman:

Tullale - throat.

Manqu - ear.

Kitcauna - teeth.

Quyolla - hair.

Tolla - hand.

Lolla - foot.

The plural of all his words is the "wi" ending. For instance feet is "llola-wi". White man is "saltu." The sun is "tuihi." The white men's houses is "saltu wawi."

Thus, by slow and painful stages a form of communication somewhat better than the sign language is being built up between these representatives of modern learning and the most ignorant man in the world.

He has told the scientists that he thinks this is a great country. He says he is not cold and that he would like to do and live differently and be as other men.

He has not shown any signs of being homesick and laughs whenever "marimi" or woman is mentioned.

A woman came to see him yesterday and he hardly dared look at her. She had a "Votes for Women" button on, and he saw that it was bright and colored and laughed, but he was plainly afraid of her, which may not, after all, show such a high degree of savagery.

Tones High and Musical

When he speaks his tones are throaty, high keyed and musical, something of the plaintiveness of a child in it. He is not very strong. His muscles are not developed, and his grip on the testing machine is of low record.

"The capture of this man is of the utmost importance," said Professor Kroeber. "He represents a new and supposedly extinct dialect. He says he is of the Yahi tribe. He is more of an aborigine than any of the Indians we have been working with for ten years. He knows nothing of the whites.

"He has a theory of creation all his own that we may be able to get out of him when he has grown to be less afraid of us. He is exactly the kind of man who was in California 100 years ago."

[103]

These two San Francisco newspaper articles of September 7, 1911, were written by reporters who were permitted to sit in on the interviewing of Ishi. They are factual and perceptive. In them we see Ishi becoming increasingly accustomed to his new surroundings, and telling the first part of a Yahi folktale to Waterman, with Sam Batwi as interpreter.

The first account was probably written by Mary Ashe Miller, who wrote the previous Call *story (reprinted above).*

5. Tribe Survivor Counts to Five, But That's All

He Tells Them the Love Story of Wood Duck, Who Couldn't Get a Wife

That the aboriginal man, the Deer creek Indian, "Ishi," meaning "man," as he is called for want of the better name, can count only up to five is the most important discovery made yesterday by T. T.

San Francisco Call, September 7, 1911.

Waterman of the anthropological department of the state university.

Most of Waterman's time is spent delving into the hidden treasures of the Indian's mind, but progress is of necessity slow, as there is no means of communication save through the interpretation of Sam Batwee's imperfect English and dissimilar Yana speech.

Both the Indians are deeply interested in Waterman's efforts to evolve a vocabulary for the unknown and will talk by the hour. Yesterday while they were at work and Waterman was writing down the words as rapidly as he could gain them he was called to the telephone. The unknown began a lengthy harangue, pointing to the book and pencil used for the list, and apparently complaining.

Sam Batwee said, when questioned, that the Indian thought if they were going to work it should be steadily done.

How Wood Duck Loved

"He say better work all time, no leave, go away, stop," said Sam.

All afternoon nearly was consumed with the recital of a wonderful Indian tale, which, like a Chinese tragedy, wound its way with deliberation. It was all about the wood duck, U-Tut-Ne, who said he wanted to get married, but who never, so long as the tale extended yesterday, found a woman to his liking.

Batwee said finally that he could not understand the conduct of the wood duck as related by Ishi. It seemed to him that the wood duck didn't want a wife at all.

"I don't think he want any one at all, but I don't blame him. All those women got no business come there at all. Well, I take the first one come, maybe take all," said Batwee, large-heartedly.

The wood duck lived with his two sisters, and because he wanted a wife he sang a song—which was warranted to make all women love him. As illustrated by Ishi yesterday, It could hardly be successful along those lines now. "Wino-tay," it ran, and that was all. Over and over, with rising or falling inflection and an occasional quaver, he chanted "Wino-tay, Wino-tay."

Sam Batwee evidently takes a pride in his friend's performances, for he urged the unknown to sit up straight when he sang. U-Tut-Ne was visited first of all by the little striped skunk-woman, Ke-Tip-Ku, who came out of the east in a hurry to marry him. He sent her away because she did not smell right.

Wherein They Failed

The wood duck had a way of sniffing the air after he sang and he could by this means tell when a woman was beginning to talk or think of him and to start to come to him, even though she were 100 miles away. He would then order his sisters up, some times in the middle of the night, to prepare food, for, to all the women who came to marry him, he presented a large basket of food, after he had refused them.

He was singularly correct in his treatment of those who came to marry him, and even though he had sniffed the air and knew they were coming, he always sent his sisters out to greet them on their arrival and pretended he didn't know who they were. After the little striped skunk woman came the flint woman, Kaka-Kina, who was dismissed because she had no eyes; the crane woman, Giri-Giri, who met with no favor becuase she spoke the language of another tribe, her talk being Wintun; the water bug woman, Hop-Yu-Mu-Ku; the turtle woman, dressed up in an elk skin; the beaver woman, the fishhawk woman, the abalone woman, the bat woman and last of all on his list, the rain-crow woman, came also and none met with anything cheering in their reception except the basket of food. When it is finally finished the results will be announced. *

Stories Just a Pastime

All of this took some hours, but it was explained that Indians tell stories merely to pass the time,

* The next day's issue of the *Call* had the sequel: Mary Ashe Miller reported that early the following morning Ishi finished the tale: Wood Duck falls in love with a beautiful young girl, but she is won by a rival, Kalchauna the Lizard. Kalchauna cuts Wood Duck in two, but he is restored to life after someone—perhaps his sisters—puts his eyebrows in a basket of water. However, Lizard has meanwhile married the young girl, and so Wood Duck is left alone.—Ed.

and see no necessity to hurry. Night is the usual time for story telling, and Ishi said yesterday that it was no time to be telling stories, it was not dark enough.

Yesterday morning Ishi was taken upstairs to the museum at the Affiliated colleges and shown specimens of the Indian tribes of California, most of them from the Maidu and Wintun Indians of the Sacramento valley. From him yesterday the names of some 300 objects were gained by Waterman. Ishi was greatly delighted with the collection and recognized most of the exhibits, frequently giving interesting bits of information regarding them.

Magnesite, or guid-ji, as he called it, is a mineral substance which when baked in the fire for many hours becomes red. He began to describe, as soon as he saw it, the method of digging it out of the ground and of making it into beads.

It was shown yesterday that Ishi has yet another of the cardinal virtues. He is very orderly. Articles are never left lying around. Everything must be put away, and he never throws matches, cigarette ashes or ends on the floor.

He was given some candy yesterday, which he thought was "medicine," but ate with great enjoyment. As soon as he had eaten a few pieces he closed the bag and put it away on a shelf in the room.

Squawker is the Best Yet

Another present he had was a "squawker," one of the "Balloon whistles" which when blown up collapse with dying wails. It was evidently one of the surprises of his new life, and he watched the red tissue shrink noisily with wide-eyed wonder. It pleased him, though, and he laughed merrily over it.

He is very polite and thoughtful, offering a match to a fellow smoker after lighting his own cigarette. He is also observing the English speech and has gained one or two words already. Money is the first of these, sad to relate, and water is the other, both of which he tried on Sam Batwee night before last. He was shown pictures of his deserted camp in the Deer Creek canyon, taken by Waterman when on a visit there about a year

ago. These he recognized at once and some of his possessions brought to the Museum were seized upon and claimed for his own at once.

One of the interesting possessions in his camp was a deer's head, dried, stuffed with grasses and used as a decoy for hunting.

6. Ishi Tells Tale of Wood Duck for 6 Hours

Aborigine Has 19 Forest Maids Apply for Squaw Job, but Bride Is Still Mystery

Ishi, the aboriginal Indian who was captured in the mountain wilds near Oroville and brought to this city last Monday, started telling a story yesterday of the loves of U-Tut-Ne, the Wood Duck.

With occasional interruptions while T. T. Waterman, the Indian expert of the University of California, who has become Ishi's guardian, refused vaudeville, circus, and theatrical offers for his ward, the wild man, who is no longer wild, related three hours' worth of U-Tut-Ne's experiences.

At night Ishi went on with the story for three hours and though no less than nineteen of the maidens of the wood had offered themselves as squaws, U-Tut-Ne still remained a bachelor.

Today the story will go on. Waterman hopes before night to learn the name and identity of the bride.

Sings Wood Duck Song

Ishi sang U-Tut-Ne's love song and Waterman recorded the aboriginal strains on a phonograph record for preservation. The song contains three words. Ishi used three tones in singing it. He sang it for hours with dignity and sweetness. Whenever he sang he rose to his feet. While he told U-Tut-Ne's story he sat in a chair or squatted on the floor.

The aborigine had an eye-opening day yesterday. He has come to regard Waterman with a child-like trust, but yesterday he found fault with the Indian expert for what Ishi regarded as a breach of etiquette.

When the university man left several times in the telling of U-Tut-Ne's loves to answer telephone

San Francisco Examiner, September 7, 1911.

[105]

calls or see visitors, Ishi told Sam Batwee, an Indian of the North Yana tribe who is trying to interpret Ishi's talk, that the head man Waterman would better stay and listen if he wanted to hear the rest of the story.

Bed Is New Luxury

Ishi awoke, after a night in a bed, a new luxury, at 5 in the morning. He got up at once and was shown where he could wash his face. Then he breakfasted, eating whatever was given him without question. The morning was spent in the identification of more than 300 Indian relics at the Affiliated Colleges Museum, Waterman obtaining the Indian names of each.

Early in the afternoon the whole building in which Ishi was sitting suddenly quivered. There was a terrific report. Ishi jumped to his feet and stood for a moment with fear in every feature.

"What fall down? A great stone?" he asked Sam Batwee. A twelve-inch gun had been discharged over at Fort Barry. The thing was not explained. When a second report came Ishi sat with hands demurely clasped in his lap and said nothing.

Many Theatrical Offers

In the meantime, theatrical offers poured in upon Waterman. A Sacramento man offered Waterman $2,000 spot cash to show Ishi for two weeks in Sacramento. There was a fabulous vaudeville offer, though what Ishi could do on the stage is not clear. Possibly he might use his deadly bow and arrow shooting hats from the heads of women who neglect to remove them in the theatres.

Then came the story of U-Tut-Ne. Evidently it is to be a serial story, for seven hours seem to have got the story only well started. Here is the story:

U-Tut-Ne, the Wood Duck, grew up and wanted a wife. So, early one morning he began to sing a love song. He sat up in bed and sang: "Wen o tay, wen o tay, wen o tay."

Ishi droned on with this song for five minutes.

Nineteen Damsels Seek Hand

Then U-Tut-Ne stood up and turned to the four corners of the earth. As he turned he looked far

away. When he had turned until he looked into the north he stopped and called in his two sisters. Their names were U-Tut-Na and U-Tut-Ni.

Nineteen times Ishi repeated this story, always in ths same words, about nineteen damsels who came to wed the singer, and each time he intoned the love song and each time the sisters provided baskets filled plentifully with meal for the disappointed ones. Each day U-Tut-Ne killed game in the woods and his sisters cooked it.

It was with difficulty that Ishi was induced to tell the story yesterday. "Too early," said he, looking at the sun. "To-night."

Dexterous With "Makings"

Mystery surrounds Ishi's dexterity in rolling brown-paper cigarettes. This is supposed to have come down to him from his ancestors. He smoked a native tobacco, it is declared, in the Tehama county hills, rolling cigarettes in bark and smoking a rude stone pipe.

He was supplied with papers in the Oroville jail, when first captured, and seems to have aptly learned the trick of fashioning the "paisano" smoke.

To-day an attempt will be made to get Ishi to talk into a stenographer's phonograph. His voice is so low that the success of this experiment is doubtful.

Waterman will further gain the Indian's confidence before bringing in the phonograph, as, if Ishi comes to the conclusion that there is witchery in it, there may be no records, and they, Waterman says, would be unparalleled in the history of anthropology.

Here is another newspaperman's report, to which is appended a commentary by A. L. Kroeber which may be the most direct psychological analysis of Ishi which exists. Elsewhere Kroeber (in the first selection of Chapter IV) refers to this incident of the theater and says that the reporter got the story "out of his imagination," and reaffirms that the show was "absolutely meaningless to him [Ishi]." We can accept Kroeber's evaluation as that of a trained psychologist and ethnographer.

7. Ishi, the Last Aboriginal Savage in America, Finds Enchantment in a Vaudeville Show

Grant Wallace

With broad shoulders squared, head bravely thrown back and eyes somber with fear and wonder he pussyfooted down the aisle of rich plush and into his private box above the glittering splendors of the Orpheum stage—Ishi, the primordial man, the only really wild Indian in existence, and the last of his tribe.

With an assumption of stern dignity, yet trembling from burntoff hair to bare feet, the last of the cavemen took his seat among the crimson plush draperies and the glittering electric lights of the large box. At his side were learned pundits, professors of anthropology and ethnology. Almost touching elbows with the saddle-colored primordial man were gentlewomen of the conquering people, soft-voiced and beautiful, their white shoulders agleam with flashing jewels: When they gave the wild man a friendly nod and a smile, the wild man removed the cigar from his lips, dug the broad red toes of his bare feet deeper into the plush carpets and smiled back at these splendid beings of another world. He smiled and nodded bravely and benignantly, unashamed and outwardly serene. Yet inwardly quaking with so great a fear that a cold perspiration beaded his forehead. And when he glanced from the twinkling goddesses on the Orpheum stage to the thousand strange beings banked below and around and above him, his long tapering fingers that might well have belonged to an artist and a thinker, clutched the leathern arms of his chair in repressed terror, till the blood was driven from the slender nails.

Cold terror sat upon him at first, but terror bravely mastered and hidden under a mask of stoicism such as only a son of the wilderness may wear. It was as if you or I had been plucked suddenly out of the middle of a black nightmare and flung neck and crop into a mob of madcap

San Francisco Sunday Call, October 8, 1911.

revelers in some weird valley of the moon, our minds still obfuscated with a lingering doubt as to whether we had landed in heaven or in hell.

Never before had he seen white people, excepting in small groups. He could not believe there were so many people in the world, and knowing nothing of paleface custom, save what he had seen once, 40 years ago, when the gold seekers had slaughtered practically all of his tribe before his eyes, it is small wonder that he misjudged the spirit of vaudeville. To him the stage was the mystery room of the gods, the singers were priests, the dancers were medicine men and women, and the orchestra was designed to drive the devils out of the sick people, whose grinning and hand-clapping puzzled him sorely. Later he asked Sam Batwee, the interpreter, whether the applause helped to drive the demons away, as he had observed that everybody ran off the stage when the people spatted their hands together.

That trail which led down the aisles of the white man's house of frivolous medicine was the strangest trail ever followed by the bare feet of this most amazing of living men. For two generations this barbarian had lived a life of terror, prowling and hiding in the shin oak thickets, caves and canyons of Tehama county. Forty years ago he had seen almost the last remnants of his proud and warlike people slain by the "thunder sticks" of the white settlers. For forty years he, with the three or four of his tribe who escaped the heavy hand of civilization, led the life of Crusoe—surrounded on all sides by a sea of white people, yet never once seen by human eyes in all those years. Great must have been the terror that could make them choose solitude and cold and starvation for near a lifetime rather than brave the eye and the gun of the paleface.

Believing himself to be hunted by the White Terror all these years, Ishi has lived the life of the hunted, the life of the deer and the rabbit. He has subsisted on acorns, weed seeds, soaproot and such game as his arrows could slay. Without clothing save the skins of wild beasts, bare of leg and of head as of foot, for he had no moccasins, he was able to produce occasional fire by rubbing two sticks together, yet he denied himself even this poor luxury, excepting in the dense woods or on dark nights, lest the smoke betray him. Forty years of solitude, of hiding, of fear, he lived; and back of that perhaps 40,000 years of similar tribal life of solitude, of prowling, or terror. Of a verity, if any man in the world can be said to have qualified as the abysmal brute the caveman of the type that lived 50,000 years ago, the primordial savage of the stone age, with a mind unspoiled by contact with civilization, Ishi is the man.

And yet "Ishi" is not his name. It is not stone-age etiquette to tell your name to strangers, for any enemy who learns your name may use it to put a jinx on you—so reasons the man of the wilderness. The professors therefore named him Ishi, which he says means "full-grown man." They had to take his word for it, because he is the only being alive who speaks the language of the tribe of the South Yanas. That is the reason the scientists regard him as such an amazingly interesting human document. When Ishi dies the language and traditions and history of his once powerful tribe will die, too. For that reason they are keeping him secluded in the hall of Egyptian mummies at the museum of anthropology, studying his amazingly quick "mental reactions" and persuading him to inscribe the myths and traditions of the Yana people on enduring plates of rubberoid by talking into the tin funnel of a phonograph. Already Professor Waterman, by the aid of Batwee, an interpreter who belongs to the North Yana tribe, distantly related, has secured a list of about 2,000 words of the hitherto unknown language, which soon will be deader than sanskrit.

"It is almost unbelievable," said Professor Kroeber. "Here is a man, the last remnant of a once proud and warlike tribe, who, through terror of the white man, has successfully hidden himself away from human sight for 40 years. Surrounded on all sides by white men and civilized Indians of other tribes, he has lived like a hunted beast, more completely alone than Robinson Crusoe on his remote island, never exchanging a word with them, permitting no human eye to see him. We find that he has perceptive powers far keener than those of highly educated white men. He reasons

well, grasps an idea quickly, has a keen sense of humor, is gentle, thoughtful, and courteous and has a higher type of mentality than most Indians."

Professor Waterman went further, summing up the results of his psychological tests with the statement that "this wild man has a better head on him than a good many college men."

The university professors, who have added Ishi to their museum of antiquities and curiosities and who are conducting this series of scientific experiments on him, justly regard him as a unique specimen of the genus homo, the like of which does not exist in all the world. They call him the "uncontaminated man," the one man who (possibly from lack of opportunity to talk) has never told a lie; the one man with no redeeming vices and no upsetting sins. This conclusion was decided doubtless from the fact that Ishi had never been brought into contact with the contaminating influences of civilization; therefore to permit the barbarian to mingle with our unsettled civilization is to expose him to contamination.

If all these things be true, then I am responsible, I doubt not, for the beginning of the undoing of the last, lone spotless man, for I may as well own up that it was I who inveigled him into the tinselled ambush of the temple of music and folly, gave him the first joy ride between the cliff-like skyscrapers and through dense mobs of his ancient enemies, and prevailed on him not to kneel in adoration at the feet of the first white goddess he had ever seen, as he was about to do, but to shake hands with her instead. The paleface goddess, it is true, was the silvery voiced and fascinating Orpheum headliner, Lily Lena of the London music halls; but even after she had exchanged the last of her half dozen Paris gowns of iridescent hues for a quiet street dress and had tripped into Ishi's box and sat at his side, patting his scarred brown hand, the cave man clung to his delusion that Miss Lena was the great medicine goddess of the palefaces.

But this is getting ahead of the story. As the evening wore on his courage rose by degrees, and he was able to withdraw the eye of apprehension from the sea of faces around him and to focus his attention on the glitter and melody and horseplay back of the footlights. When the Brazilian dancing men in their spangles and gay colors began whirling their bodies over their heads in the mad abandon of the new society dance, the wild man leaned far forward and fixed an unblinking gaze upon the graceful figures below him. Suddenly the red lights were snapped on and the red lights were a bloody moon of the stage setting. Ishi blinked rapidly, gasped, and gripped the arm of Professor Kroeber, looking around into our faces to read what "sign" might be writ there, of fear or of fortitude. We nodded and smiled encouragement. Hope and confidence returned to him. Rosner's music makers struck up a merrier tune, and the dancers whirled and clung and vaulted with a speed and abandon seldom equaled in any aboriginal medicine dance.

Ishi half rose and hung over the edge of the box in his excitement. He was breathing hard and his eyes were glittering through their long, sweeping lashes. Sam Batwee, the one-eyed old interpreter, plucked him back to propriety and to his seat. Ishi knew all about that dance. He explained that it illustrated an ancient tradition of his people—the story of the Lying Coyote, whose suit had been scorned by the wonderful dancing maiden.

"Wait," said the wily coyote. "A great chief will come. You will know him by his oiled and painted face. If you dance well before him you may win his love."

The coyote then retired, painted and greased his own face, and when he returned the maiden danced with him. Just as in this Brazilian dance. Thus the adolescent dancing maiden was taken to wife by the lying coyote.

This is one of the legends which Ishi already had spoken into the phonograph. And it is identical, by the way, with the coyote legend recorded by the early fathers at the old mission of San Juan Capistrano 135 years ago.

When the Australian wood choppers began throwing their heavy axes across the stage, tomahawk fashion, sinking the flung blades deep into an opposite tree, or cutting off limbs with unerring accuracy at a distance of 40 feet, Ishi sat up and chortled with shrill glee. Here was something he could understand—a man could kill a bear that way. Batwee nudged him and asked him how he

liked it. "Good work!" said Ishi. "I don't think I could do it."

Strangely enough the ruder horseplay of the succeeding comedians got few laughs from the primitive man. It was the subtle wit of Edwin Stevens and the vocal nonsense of Harry Breen that made him smile. Apparently through some subtle telepathic connection, the Indian was able to come in with his laugh at the right second, often just a little ahead of the rest of the audience, though, of course, he had not understood a word. Possibly his extraordinarily acute perceptive powers aided him in this, for not the slightest motion or intonation escaped him. The only bad break he made was at the conclusion of Stevens' tragic colloquy over the telephone with an imaginary wife who was supposed to be burning to death in a hotel fire. As the actor flung down the phone in horror Ishi looked around at me and laughed gleefully, as much as to say:

"He can't fool me. That was a joke." So perhaps, it wasn't such a bad break, after all.

The beer-drinking act of Sam Mann amused him hugely. When Mann drained a large stein holding apparently a gallon, Ishi's sharp eyes detected the false bottom which took up most of the interior of the stein and pointed to it, laughing in shrill falsetto tones. He saw the joke that was being played on the audience.

By the time Harry Breen began improvising his rapid fire songs containing impromptu jokes on individuals in the audience, Ishi was in his element. No longer afraid, he was ready to laugh with the most frivolous of the pale faces. But when Breen introduced Ishi himself into his topical song, he failed to score a hit with the aborigine. Breen had caught sight of the wild man, and without pausing to take a breath he incorporated this stanza into his song:

The Indian cave man next I see
With the professors from the universitee;
He smokes a bad cigar and he hasn't any socks,
And he's laughing, although he's sure in a box.

That got a laugh from all the rest of the house and everybody stood up to see. Instantly the Indian collapsed into the inscrutable, suspicious

[109]

barbarian. Fear again sat upon him. That battery of 2,000 eyes turned upon him was too much even for his stoicism. The professors patted his back and endeavored to convince him that he was not chosen for immediate slaughter, but it was a long while before his trepidation gave way to smiles again.

Then came the stunt wherein Lily Lena, in half a dozen changes of spangled and glittering raiment, did things which convinced the Indian Crusoe that he had blundered into the abode of the gods. I had been watching Ishi's face while the "goddess" did her turn in the spotlight. The look of pleased curiosity and the broad smiles with which he had evinced his appreciation of the humor of Edwin Stevens and of the red-headed college kid, who was able to play two tunes at once on the piano while standing on his head, slowly gave place to an expression of profound awe and reverence as Lily Lena appeared and went through her kaleidoscopic changes of costumes and of up-to-date songs. Slowly Ishi rose to his feet. He fixed on the lady an unwinking gaze of such intensity as to draw her attention away from a row of Johnnies to whom she had been warbling. Her eyes met those of the wild man. She faced him bravely and with dazzling white arms held out toward the thunderstruck worshiper, sang to him the words of "Have You Ever Loved Another Little Girl?"

The cold sweat was standing out on Ishi's forehead. His face was drawn. His fingers, grasping the crimson hangings, trembled visibly and his first cigar, which he had been puffing with pretended sangfroid, now slowly grew cold and dropped from his teeth. Professors Kroeber and Waterman, studying these unusual emotions in the interests of psychology, now leaned toward him, ready to grab the wild man before he could leap to the stage.

The little song bird from London was no longer the leading attraction. A thousand people were craning their necks, not toward the stage, but toward the broad-shouldered Indian, who was leaning out of the box above it, half crouching, as if for a spring. It was clear that Ishi, for the moment, was the headline attraction.

The tense situation was broken by the actress herself. She finished her melodious admonition to the fascinated wild man to "Take it Nice and Easy," and skipped blithely away behind the scenes. Ishi awoke from the spell, looked furtively about, found every eye in the house again fixed upon him and subsided hastily into his seat. He was so evidently laboring under strong excitement that I asked Batwee, the interpreter, to question him.

"He says," explained Batwee, "that this must be the great medicine woman, the dancing goddess of the other world. His people had a tradition about her. Now he sees her. He thinks maybe this is the heaven of the white folks."

Poor, simple-minded wild man! He could not know that the heaven of the white people is never likely to be so crowded as their vaudeville houses, nor that so far there never has been half the scramble to get through the pearly gates that there is every night to get a front seat in the Orpheum's top gallery.

After all, this man, the most lonesome man in the world, inasmuch as he has never told a lie, was excusable for suspecting that he had been suddenly transported into a section of the happy hunting grounds surpassing his most ecstatic dreams of music and glitter and glory. The only wonder is that he was not driven mad, yet he held himself in check like a Spartan hero. Doubtless as he sat facing the strange creatures, the blazing colored lights and the weird music, he felt like a toad that had fallen into fairyland. Yet for the most part this savage, who for 40 years had crept on hands and knees under the chaparral, fearing to make a trail lest the white people follow and slay him, sat like a dignified trust magnate at an investigation, only quaking, but with head erect and smiling in the face of possible destruction. There was courage for you—and fortitude and self-control. As Professor Kroeber put it:

"This is the most wonderful thing Ishi has ever seen. It is as much of a voyage into the unknown, which to a primitive man is always full of pitfalls and terrors, as would be the coming to earth of a man from Mars. He has never seen a crowd before, never saw a theater, and he is not yet fully assured that his life is not to be sacrificed at any moment. When he entered the theater and faced the crowd and the calcium lights he shook with terror, but in a few minutes he had perfect control of his motions and sat through the ordeal with as much composure and smiled and smoked as complacently as any blase theater goer. It was heroic. And his belief that Miss Lena was the sacred medicine woman was the most interesting development of this experiment."

As for Miss Lena, she did what she could to reassure her humble adorer as to her strictly human origin, but with indifferent success. When I informed her that the last man of his race desired to prostrate himself at her feet she promptly entered the box and sat down by him.

He made a sort of obeisance. What other expression he might have given to his reverence will never be known, for with the words, "God help him—God help the poor man!" she seized his hand, shook it and patted him reassuringly on the shoulder. He tried to smile back at her, but succeeded only in convulsing his features into a painful expression of awe and wonder. After the song woman had spoken many gentle words of sympathy to the wild man a look of intense happiness spread over his face. If there had been any lingering doubt in his mind as to her place in the pantheon of the gods the talisman which she gave him dispelled it. Now he was sure she was the goddess. He rolled the little gift into a small wad and placed it reverently in his shirt pocket over his heart, explaining to Batwee that it was the great medicine ball that would ward off all evil. And yet what the little singer from London had given the wild man of Tehama was only a stick of chewing gum.

8. It's All Too Much for Ishi, Says the Scientist

A. L. Kroeber
Professor of Anthropology,
University of California

That which made the first impression upon Ishi at the vaudeville performance in the Orpheum theater was the crowd. The performance itself I am sure he did not appreciate. He laughed when

San Francisco Call, October 8, 1911.

the crowd laughed, but not because he understood the humor of any of the acts. It was the greatest crowd, 1,500 or 2,000 people packed into one place, which excited and impressed him most and for some time he did not even seem conscious of the stage or the players. If a similar gathering had cried and shrieked he would have done the same; as it was he laughed. It was simply the physiological effect of the crowd upon him. His high unnatural giggle is like that of a young girl and does not necessarily signify that any appeal is made to his sense of humor. He laughs when he is embarrassed, as a great many people do, and it is a simple matter to make him blush.

Even the woodchoppers' act meant little to him. He had probably used some form of hatchet in his time, but that the Australians were doing anything better, or anything requiring greater skill than his own I do not think he realized.

Yet there is nothing undeveloped about him; he has the mind of a man and is a man in every sense. With the exception of the habits which he has acquired by his manner of living he is thoroughly normal. He imitates readily and seems to adapt himself to the usages of civilization very quickly, but he has not the least initiative.

[111]

Nine-tenths of that which goes on around him he does not understand, for all the conditions of his new manner of living are so totally different that he accepts everything at its face value and never thinks of questioning anything. He is no longer bewildered, he just accepts. It is as though we were to visit the moon. We would get used to the novelty of it in a short time and then when the surprise had worn off, while we understood nothing of what was going on about us we should learn to take it all for granted.

I have tried to teach him English, but he will not learn it. He repeats the words after me readily enough, but when he is told to use them, he refuses. It is embarrassment, self-consciousness or timidity, but it is not inaptitude. I try to teach him to count and he understands the meaning of the words, but he refuses to use them. I thought at first that if he were thrown upon his own resources he would learn to take care of himself, but he has been alone so long that it does not seem to matter to him whether any one understands him or not. When he talks to me, although Sam Batwee may not be present, he uses his own tongue and appears to be just as happy although he knows I can not understand, as though I understood it all.

It is probable, too, that if he were turned out to shift for himself he would attach himself to the first person who came along. He does not consider himself a part of the civilization about him, and makes no effort to become a part of it. While he has learned to wear clothes, to wash his face and seems perfectly happy in his surroundings, he is no more fit to go out into the world now than he was a month ago. His attitude toward everything about him is just like that of a puppy. He is interested in everything, but he never questions orders. He comes running when you call him, and if you were to tell him to stand in the corner or stand on his head, if he were able he would do it without hesitation.

For a time I believed that he was unhappy, but when Batwee asked him if he would rather live with the white men or the Indians he said he preferred to stay where he was.

[112]

Dr. A. L. Kroeber with Ishi in 1911.

This article, written by Kroeber, is one of the earliest pieces of the ethnographic record which was elicited from Ishi. There was much more to come, as the next chapter demonstrates.

9. The Only Man in America Who Knows No Christmas — Ishi

Dr. A. L. Kroeber
University of California Museum
of Anthropology, Affiliated Colleges

In all America there is perhaps only one sane, intelligent man to whose pulse the coming of Christmas will bring no quickening. He is the one man to whom the very name of Christmas carries no significance whatever. He is Ishi, a California Indian, the least civilized man in the world, who is being cared for by Dr. Kroeber at the Affiliated colleges. Though communication can now be had to a limited extent with Ishi by use of the vocabulary of the Yana tongue that has been compiled, it will be practically impossible to convey to the aborigine any conception of the meaning of the great Christian celebration. He knows no Christ, no Christmas tree; the turkey dinner he will eat on the holiday will seem to him merely some special dispensation of his woodland gods.—Editor.

When Ishi, the last "uncontaminated" aboriginal American Indian in the United States, left the Oroville jail, which had been the first home civilization was able to offer him, for his new abiding place at the University of California Museum of Anthropology at the Affiliated colleges in San Francisco he brought with him much primeval and tribal lore of the most ancient of arts which will prove as romantic to the student of the future as it is fascinating to the twentieth-century American of today.

San Francisco Call, December 17, 1911.

The world old industries which this living survival of an extinct civilization practices within sight of trolley cars and sound of the telephone bell are not the sole invention of his own peculiar people, the Southern Yana. Most of the ingenious devices demonstrated by Ishi have been observed among other races of rudimentary culture, and some of them have been carefully studied by delvers into the past. But when archaeologists and antiquaries first turned to such inquiries the arts themselves were already moribund, if not extinct. There are not a few old American Indians that can still chip an arrow point, and many even of the middle aged in the various tribes have heard of the skill of their ancestors, and though without experience themselves possess more or less vague ideas of the process.

But all other aborigines that retain such knowledge have grown up amid the influences of a higher civilization than their own. They have shot rifles in place of arrows, struck the ever ready match instead of the fire drill, and their nets, even if of ancient pattern, are woven of cotton twine, where their grandfathers used native fibers. Such men live in houses and wear overalls; they know what school and church are. In the remotest places, in the very fringes and outskirts of civilization, the force of modernity has entered with a penetration that is hard to realize.

From all these near savages, Ishi stands out like a drop of oil in a tank of water. He has been all his lifetime surrounded by civilization, yet never a part of it; in fact, absolutely unaware of its meaning. He has heard trains thunder by, but their purpose remained a mystery; from his hiding place he has seen the whites shooting, but how the guns "broke" and "broke" again was as unexplained to him as to the warriors of Montezuma when they first resisted the little army of Cortez. Only to him and his little band of now dead tribal kinsmen were the old crafts and practices still daily habits, the only means of subsistence and shelter. To other so-called savages the flaking of a stone tool is only a memory; to Ishi it was, until yesterday, a reality and a necessity.

Two of the ancient crafts stand out above all others as essential, and both are among the most primeval inventions of mankind. Fire is needed by all men for warmth and cooking; and in the absence of metals, stone tools for cutting and weapons are indispensable. There is no people on earth, no matter how degraded its mode of life, that did not possess a knowledge of these fundamental arts. And as far back in time as science can trace human existence both crafts reveal their existence. Charcoal and chipped flints have been discovered in all the oldest deposits, 250,000, perhaps 500,000 or more years in age. In fact, flint flakes far antedate the remains of man's bones. Through these rude but enduring works of his hands, man's existence is proved for ages before the appearance of the first evidence of his body in the shape of fossile finds.

Why are chipped flint implements the earliest relics of the race? Skins and fabrics and wooden tools of course can not survive more than a few thousand years; but bone and shell, which are easily worked, and soft stone capable of being rubbed, and porous rock that is readily ground into shape will endure forever, and yet are not represented in the most primitive discoveries.

The final answer is perhaps to be sought in psychology, in some revelation of the inherent nature of the human mind; but science supplies at least a partial explanation in more concrete facts. The character of the material is the key to the problem. Flint, which is at once one of the hardest of natural products and one requiring the greatest skill to manipulate successfully, is also the substance that from its constitution and properties lends itself so readily to working as almost to force on the half brute, half human mind the idea of a tool.

A piece of granite, when struck, cracks; if rubbed, it will grind away, a mass of flint splits. Here in a nutshell is the secret that the stone age men discovered, and that civilization, weighted down with products of forged steel, open-hearth processes, and laboratory tests, forgot until the patient searching of archaeologists rediscovered it. Flint and the allied substances break clean under a blow, with a resulting sharp edge. Fine grained, almost structureless, hard and brittle, it does not crumble, but, as the impact is delivered by a skilled hand, splits with a regularity that can be almost absolutely

[113]

predicted. Ordinary stone is tougher, but yields gradually and irregularly to repeated impressions. Flint alone fractures as the workman directs. It is almost like another substance, softer and clearer, more familiar to us civilized moderns, and now largely manufactured artificially, but with many of same properties—ice.

We have all seen a 250 pound slab of ice severed more smoothly than a saw could perform the process by a few deft strikes of the tool guided by the hand of the experienced worker. Cutting, grinding, careful picking only delay or spoil the desired result. A few swift blows in the right direction and delivered in the proper place and the work is done.

The whole art of working flint is a trick—simple as the planting of the egg of Columbus—requiring practice, but once mastered, practically infallible. And it is more that interesting to the student of the development of the human mind, it is supremely important as the first device of general practical utility perfected by the dawning mentality of the human species. When flint was first chipped, spear, dagger, knife, ax, plane and scraper—weapon, household implement and tool—were invented. It was indeed a nameless and inglorious but a greater Columbus that struck the first half-conscious blows on this remarkable material that for a quarter of a million years was to determine and reflect the progress of civilization.

But the broken flint, however great the advancement it marked over the toolless age, was but a rough and ready implement, lacking in detail and refinement. The first period of man's development, the Chellean, was superseded 150,000 years ago—some say it was 250,000—by the second or Mousterian, when the cavemen of western Europe made a new discovery of the manifold forces of physical nature and entered on a more advanced stage of progress. This was the fact that flint will not only split under a blow, but that it will flake or chip in small pieces under pressure applied at one point. The hewn implements of the preceding age were then made as before, but instead of being left as they came from the first workshop were subjected to another and finishing process. That this was indeed a higher stage of development is shown by the fact that it involved a manufacturing implement.

[114]

The arrow flaker is the first tool-making tool. It is therefore in one sense the original ancestor of all manufacturing machinery, and for this reason the simple horn-pointed stick that Ishi guides with his elbow and fingers is of extraordinary interest to us.

When a piece of flint is pressed near the fractured edge with a point, even though this be somewhat softer, a fragment of the stone—a flake—at last flies off, leaving the edge thinner and sharper. It is also likely to be slightly notched, but the very serration gives a better cutting effect. If now the pressure is reapplied at adjacent points, flake after flake is dislodged, until the edge, heretofore smooth but comparatively blunt, is composed of a series of fine saw teeth. This was the implement of man of the second period, a combination knife and saw.

The next step was perhaps not reached for 50,000 years more. Instead of the retouched edge being confined to one side of the implement, both edges were flaked, and drawn together toward a point. First came the hewn point tool; second the flaked-edged implement; third the flaked pointed object—spear point, harpoon head, perhaps even arrow point. All this was practiced before the last ice left the northern hemisphere, while the mammoth and wild horse still roamed Europe and men lived in caves; before reindeer were chased by the savage hunters, and earlier than man reached America. And here is where Ishi stands today. He embodies and illustrates this most venerable of arts, neglected and all but forgotten today, but still the deep-sunken basis on which our own civilization rests.

Ishi's tool is as simple as its knowledge is ancient. A stick about 18 inches long, so as to reach from his elbows to just beyond his fingers, a tip of deer antler tied to the end of the wood, its point neither quite sharp nor yet blunt—in the left hand a scrap of skin to serve as a pad or cushion for the prospective arrowhead—and his outfit is complete.

The butt of the stick is held to his ribs by his elbow, to give steadiness and a fulcrum. The hand grasps the other end. The horn point bears down with an almost imperceptible motion on the flint. For a moment nothing happens. Then, almost in silence, with a barely audible click, a minute fragment of stone detaches itself and drops off. The point moves along an eighth or perhaps a quarter of an inch; a couple of seconds, and the operation is repeated. The edge is gone over again and again of necessity; the point of the arrow becomes sharper and sharper, and in 15 minutes the implement that controlled the destiny of nations until the discovery of metals is perfect. Nothing is simpler when once mastered, and yet months, if not years, of patient practice are needed to acquire dexterity.

Ishi's people possessed one great advantage that nature did not furnish to his remote ancestors of the cave period of Europe; the occurrence in California of natural or volcanic glass, obsidian, as the minerologists term it. A true glass, though made in the interior of the earth and black and nearly opaque, it is harder, more brittle, but also sharper than flint, and being of homogeneous structure it flakes even more regularly. It is found in Shasta, Lake, Napa, and Mono counties and was so much appreciated by all the aborigines of California that even Indians far removed from these districts acquired it by trade, and no tribe in the state was without it. It was obsidian that Ishi used by preference in his wild state, and it was in obsidian that he demonstrated his skill one Sunday afternoon to more than 1,000 marveling visitors to the museum of anthropology at the affiliated colleges.

By a strange irony, however, most of the arrows with which Ishi killed deer, bear, and wildcats during his life, were tipped with points made by him out of an undisputed product of civilization— glass from windows or bottles. When his few surviving people took to the brush in deadly fear of the supposedly murderous Americans, trade with the obsidian-gathering tribes to the north and south was cut off. On Deer creek and the vicinity the material does not occur. In his timid nightly prowlings Ishi therefore carefully picked up and hoarded the discarded beer bottles and silimar [similar] refuse of glass that the dusty teamster or cattle man had thrown away. Such a prize was of more value than a rich pocket of gold, for from the fragments he shaped at his leisure his all important "ammunition."

The ancient fire drill, that of our "pre-Adamite" ancestors, the cave men and their predecessors, is not positively known. Being presumably of wood,

all specimens have no doubt perished countless ages ago. But that these early people, some of them certainly only half men—the "missing link" of popular fancy—had and used fire, and could produce and control it, is rendered certain by the discovery of abundant deposits of charcoal and pockets of ashes in the most primeval strata in which flint tools or human bones have been found.

Hasty travelers every now and then have reported encountering in the jungle a naked people so utterly savage and untutored that while they cooked with fire they could not make it; and if once it went out it was necessary to replenish the embers from a friendly tribe that was more fortunate, or to wait for lightning to set alight some tree. Some even more reckless voyagers speak of people so primitive or degraded that they did not understand the use of fire for cooking and warmth. More careful inquiry has in every case found such statements to be erroneous. All students of the science of man now are certain not only that all living people can produce fire at will, but that this ability was one of the earliest achievements of the race—this and the flint industry, in fact, marking the first twin accomplishments of the human species.

Before phosporous matches, flint and steel were used to strike a light. Earlier still, flint on flint, or two pieces of quartz, were employed for the purpose. Earliest and most primitive of all were two sticks, the "fire drill," such as Ishi uses, one of the simplest of implements and in the hands of the expert savage, one of the most effective.

The fire drill apparatus consists of two pieces, a lower and an upper. Scientists speak of them as the "hearth" and the "drill." The hearth is a flattened little slab with one or more holes, which serve as sockets in which the drill is rotated. This drill is nothing but an ordinary round stick of suitable wood.

In the story books one reads of the hero "rubbing" two sticks together until a spark "leapt" forth. No man on earth could produce fire in such a way. He could rub until doomsday and accomplish nothing but to make his arms and back ache. The effort must be concentrated in one small spot before the human body can convert the friction of the moving wood into heat. This is the purpose of the socket in the "hearth."

It has sometimes been thought that the secret of the art lies in the mysterious qualities of certain special kinds of wood, which alone are fit for the purpose. Ishi insists on a buckeye stick for his drill, but only because he has always been used to this material. Poison oak, sage brush, and many other fairly hard woods answer equally well, in fact, admirably.

The lower piece must be softer, but an equal variety of trees and brush will serve. Willow and cedar are usually convenient and readily shaped. It is only necessary that both pieces are seasoned and dry and yet not too old and brittle.

When about to drill Ishi squats in characteristic pose, holding the ends of the hearth steady against the ground with his toes. At other times he kneels on the board to clamp it down. The drill is stood upright in the little hole in the hearth, grasped between the palms of the open hands as these are pressed together, and then rubbed back and forth in opposite directions.

With each motion the drill is forced to rotate, first to right, then to left. The hands at the same time bear downward, pressing the revolving stick into the socket, in which it scrapes and rubs rapidly. By this motion small particles of wood are ground off and forced out of the hole. In a few seconds they become brown; a little smoke begins to arise from the point of contact, and with each succeeding turn of the drill the wood dust turns darker and darker, until at last it issues pure charcoal and a cloud of smoke emerges from the twirling apparatus. Ishi works harder and harder as he approaches his goal, the drill whirls faster and finally a tiny spark suddenly is glowing in the little pile of powder. The end is achieved and it only remains to pile on tinder—a little shredded inner bark of the willow, thistledown, or dried moss— to blow the spark into flame, and soon a blaze sparkles merrily.

Considerable strength and much skill are, however, required for this simple process. The drill must be firmly and continually pressed down into the hearth or sufficient friction to engender fire heat will not be produced. A weakling need not attempt the task. On the other hand, too heavy pressure at the outset exhausts the operator's strength, so that when the crucial moment comes and the spark is nearly at hand his vigor fails him. Then, too, as the hands bear down on the drill they gradually slip downward along it until, just before the hearth is touched by them, the palms must be quickly raised to the upper end of the stick and there reapplied to their task. While this is being done, the drill stands still, and too long an interval allows the heated points of contact to cool. Often the hands must be shifted just as the spark is about to appear, and during the transfer all the progress already made is lost.

The whole process in fact requires manual tact of a kind that only long experience can teach. The fire must be literally coached, firmly and steadily, out of the unwilling wood. It is a matter of nursing the operation along. Brute violence and hastiness accomplish nothing, but indifference, lassitude or a moment's cessation of the continuous pressure and rotation are equally fatal. Ishi's patience, perseverance, and delicate control of strength are exactly the requisite qualities.

Could Ishi, overtaken away from his hut by a heavy rain, make a fire to shelter himself? Without his drill it is hardly possible. Wet trees and dripping branches will not twirl into fire any more than soaked matches will strike. Under the shelter of an overhanging rock he might succeed in whittling dry suitable pieces of the heart of a tree. But as he actually lived in the wilderness, this was probably not often necessary, for as the careful hunter rolls his match safe in a strip of oilskin, Ishi, if traveling in stormy weather, would carry his drill protected from the elements in a covering of buckskin, dry and ready for use the moment shelter was reached.

Many other arts of this strange living survival of aboriginal pre-civilization are of interest—his nets, woven like those of the American fishermen, but of strange materials; his baskets, in which he cooked, his admirably ingenious salmon spear, and many others. But the flint arrow point and the fire drill stand out as the two features which this belated stone age man, the last person in the United States to come into contact with civilization, has absolutely in common with the pre-historic cave dwellers who lived even before America was "discovered" by its aboriginal inhabitants.

ISHI AMONG THE ANTHROPOLOGISTS

ISHI AMONG THE ANTHROPOLOGISTS

This is the longest piece written about Ishi by Kroeber. It is important in the history of Ishi. Here the report of five still-living Yahi mentioned by Stephen Powers in 1870 (see Chapter 10, above) is associated with Ishi—he seems to have been the child mentioned. In 1908 or 1909, nearly forty years later, there were still four or five survivors. Ishi, though not seen, was one of that group, and the "old, decrepit, and sick crone" might have been one of the women seen in 1870, almost certainly Ishi's mother.

The value of this article is in sketching Ishi's personality.

1. Ishi, the Last Aborigine (1912)

A. L. Kroeber

At Eleven o'clock in the evening on Labor Day, 1911, there stepped off the ferry boat into the glare of electric lights, into the shouting of hotel runners, and the clanging of trolley cars on Market Street, San Francisco, Ishi, the last wild Indian in the United States.

Ishi belongs to the lost Southern Yana tribe that formerly lived in Tehama County, in northern California. This tribe, after years of guerilla warfare, was practically exterminated by the whites by massacre, in 1865. The five survivors took refuge in the utterly wild cañon of Deer Creek in Tehama

First printed in *The World's Work*, July, 1912, pp. 304-308. Reprinted in *The Mill Creek Indians and Ishi* (Berkeley: University of California Printing Department, 1972), with a Preface by A. B. Elsasser.

County, and the last recorded time that any one saw them was in 1870. There were two men, two women, and a child—probably Ishi, for he has told how, when he was a small boy, "so high," the white men came at sunrise and killed his people in their camp.

In November, 1909,* a party of waterright surveyors working laboriously down the cañon, came on a hut, from which dashed two or three men or women, leaving one old, decrepit, and sick crone behind. Unable to converse with her, the surveyors left her undisturbed; but all attempts to open negotiations with the other Indians failed, so great was their fear.

Within a year, news of this adventure reached the University of California, where the Indians in question were at once identified, by their condition and location, as the long lost Southern Yana, the relatives of the almost extinct Northern Yana, whose dialect and customs had been investigated by the University ethnologists only a year or two before. After some confirming inquiries in the vicinity, a party was organized in the fall of 1910 to hunt for the Indians. A month in the cañon, in which practically every foot of their territory was gone over, revealed no Indians, but ample evidence of their recent existence—huts, smoke houses, baskets, nets, pestles, flint chips, and so forth. It was concluded that they had seen the expedition first and had kept consistently out of its way.

* Concerning this date, see editor's footnote to Kroeber's "The Elusive Mill Creeks" (above).—Ed.

Then, at the end of August, 1911, came despatches announcing the capture, near Oroville, some forty miles to the south of Deer Creek, and in a well-settled district, of a lone wild Indian. He had been trying to break into a slaughterhouse, and had been placed in jail, where neither Indians nor whites could converse with him. A member of the staff of the anthropological department of the University of California arrived, armed with a Northern Yana vocabulary and the first communication with the aborigine began, much to the amazement of the local Indians. The next day Sam Batwi, a North Yana interpreter, arrived in response to a telegraphic call, and while finding the dialect different from his own and difficult to manage, was able to make more headway. No formal charge had been placed against the wild man, and in a few days the Sheriff of Butte County obligingly released him to the University authorities— an arrangement sanctioned by the United States Indian Office.

In justice to Ishi, his own version of his "capture" should be given. His people were all dead, he said. A woman and a child had been drowned in crossing a stream. The old woman found by the surveyors was dead. For some time he had been entirely alone—poor, often hungry, with nothing to live for. This, by the way, was no doubt the reason for his drifting, perhaps aimlessly, so far southward of his old home. One day he made up his mind to "come in." He expected to be killed, he said, but that no longer mattered. So he walked westward all day, without meeting any one, and at dusk came to a house where meat was hung up. Tired, hungry, and thirsty, he sat down. Soon a boy came out with a lantern, saw him, recoiled, and called a man, who ran up. In response to Ishi's signs, they gave him a pair of overalls—for he was naked except for a rude homemade garment, half shirt, half cape—ordered him into their wagon, and drove him to town, where he was put into a large and fine house—the jail—and very kindly treated and well fed by a big chief— the deputy sheriff.

Etiquette of the Proper Name

Ishi's name is not genuine. When the reporters swarmed out to the University Museum of Anthropology in San Francisco the morning after he arrived, their second inquiry was for his age, their first for his name. Sam Batwi asked him, but to all inquiries he shook his head and said that he had been alone so long that he had no one to name him. This was pure fiction, but polite fiction, for the strongest Indian etiquette, in Ishi's part of the world, demands that a person shall never tell his own name, at least not in reply to a direct request. To this day Ishi has never disclosed his real name; and so strong does his sense of propriety on this point remain, that he will not yet pronounce the word Ishi, though he answers readily to the appellation. The name is singularly appropriate, being the Yana word for "man."

He was a curious and pathetic figure in those days. Timid, gentle, an ever-pervading and only too obvious fear held down and concealed to the best of his ability, he nevertheless started and leaped at the slightest sudden sound. A new sight, or the crowding around of half a dozen people, made his limbs rigid. If his hand had been held and was released, his arm remained frozen in the air for several minutes. The first boom from a cannon fired in artillery practice at the Presidio several miles away, raised him a foot from his chair. And yet, with it all, he displayed keen observation, much interest, and sometimes delight. Only it was the little things that woke responses in him. The first penny whistle given him roused more expression and spontaneity that the thousands of houses spread out before him as he stood on the high terrace of the Museum and looked over the city.

One curious, patient gesture, which has never quite left him, was characteristic of him in those days—a raising high up of his mobile arched eyebrows. It was an expression of wonder, but also of ignorance, of incomprehension, like our shrugging of the shoulders. It was his one sign, for he seemed afraid to use his limbs freely at that time, and even since, when he feels perfectly at home, has been given but little to gestures. He sometimes uses them effectively when he wishes to explain, but never profusely nor with any exceptional or instinctive ability to make them plain to every one.

Afraid of Crowds

His one great dread, which he overcame but slowly, was of crowds. It is not hard to understand this in view of his lonely life in a tribe of five. A lone American had always been a signal of imminent danger to him; no wonder that a hundred literally paralyzed him. A week after his arrival in San Francisco he was taken for an automobile ride, through Golden Gate Park, and to the ocean beach. The one thing above all others that drew his attention was the Sunday crowds. He had never been at the ocean and until that week had never even seen it from a distance. It was therefore anticipated that the surf, which as a phenomenon of nature he could understand, would interest him more that the works of civilization. But when the car reached the bluff looking down on the breakers, with a long, sandy beach studded with thousands of holiday-seekers stretching miles away, everything else was forgotten and the exclamation *"hansi saltu!"* "many white people," burst involuntarily from him.

The shock of this effect over, his mind became more receptive for smaller things. As the machine wound around the drives in the park, the elevated group of University buildings, of which the Museum is one, occasionally came into view, and each time a smile would break over his features as he pointed with a nod of his head and said *wowi* (home). As one drive turned into another that had previously been traversed in the opposite direction, or only crossed it, his keen sense of locality asserted itself, and again and again he told the interpreter that the party had passed there before. The car followed one of the less frequented by-roads and disturbed a flock of the quail that roam the park in a half wild state as the squirrels do in Eastern cities; instantly he stood up, following their every movement with the hunter's instinct and no doubt with a feeling of home and kinship. Next to the undreamed-of crowd of people, the familiar birds stirred his emotions more than anything else during the ride.

Stone Age Vaudeville

A week later he was invited to a vaudeville performance by an enterprising newspaper man in search of a story. Sam explained to him as best he might; and Ishi answered that he was willing if I, or one of the people from the Museum, whom he had learned to know, went with him. The reporter got his story. But he got it out of his imagination. For two acts Ishi sat in his box seat and looked at the audience. So many people crowded together so closely were more remarkable than the mysterious capers that a couple of actors might be cutting on the stage. Gradually he followed the other members of the party and the more sophisticated interpreter, and turned his eyes forward. When the audience laughed, he giggled with them, out of a pure automatic response or suggestion, for they might be laughing at a pun, a joke conveyed in words that were totally incomprehensible to him. Horse-play and acrobatics had no more effect; in the midst of an act of purely physical appeal, his attention was apt to wander. When a character or event on the stage was called to his notice, he smiled politely but embarrassedly, or watched the motions of the suggestor instead of the thing pointed out. It was all absolutely meaningless to him.

By this time Ishi had come to look upon the Museum as his home—not only for the time being, but forever. The Bureau of Indian Affairs sent its Special Agent for California to see him and form plans for his future. Ishi was told that he was free to go back where he came from, or to go where other Indians lived under the care of the American Government; but he promptly shook his head. "I will live like the white people from now on," he said to the interpreter. "I want to stay where I am. I will grow old here, and die in this house." He has never swerved from this first declaration.

Quick with Cravat, Slow with Shoes

His intelligence and quick perception showed themselves from the first. Getting in and out of his coat made some little difficulty for a time, but

[121]

everything else about his clothes seemed to come as natural, once he had them on, as to a civilized person. One demonstration taught him to tie a four-in-hand cravat. His pockets quickly contained an assortment of junk worthy of a small boy. In fact, three days in clothing brought him to a condition where he refused to strip for the photographer—absolutely the only occasion when he balked at obeying orders. He saw everyone else wearing clothes and would never take them off again, he said with metaphorical emphasis.

Shoes alone had no attraction for him. It was thought that they might incommode him, so he was not pressed, but asked if he wished them. "I see the ground is stone here," he said. "Walking on that all the time, I would wear out shoes; but my feet will never wear out"—an answer perhaps partly dictated by inborn politeness, but as ingenuous as logical. It was not until the rainy season set in and he underwent an unexpected attack of pneumonia, that he was provided with shoes, and then seemed content.

[122]

There were other instances where he reasoned more consistently than our civilization. He learned very quickly that meat, potato, vegetables, and soup are not eaten with the tools that nature provides; and he was so anxious to conform with good manners that he tried to use a teaspoon to eat the first peach that was handed to him.

He picked up with equal facility the daily duties which were assigned him to provide exercise in compensation for the unwonted indoor and sedentary life that the city was imposing. A few days' practice, and he was bustling about the Museum in early morning hours handling the broom, the mop, and the duster with the skill of an experienced janitor, probably with greater care, and certainly with the same willing gentleness that marked all his actions. In this or some similar direction seems to lie the avenue of his future adaptation to the material problems of livelihood and civilization.

Dislike of the English Language

One remarkable fact so far has stood out against his progress toward real civilization: a reluctance to learn English. In several months of association only with people of English speech (Sam, the half-satisfactory interpreter, remained only a few weeks) one would expect a tolerable proficiency in the new language, an ability of expression at least lively and fluent if not correct. But a few dozen names of objects and persons are all that have crossed his lips. It is not inability that is at fault, for his pronunciation, when called upon to repeat what is spoken to him, is excellent, and some words, such as "water," "money," and "chicken," blossomed from him in a very few days. Strange to say, a certain bashfulness seems to lie at the bottom of this backwardness; and this shamefacedness is no doubt accentuated by the tremendous difference that civilization must have impressed on him as existing between all white people on the one hand and himself on the other. He feels himself so distinct from his new world, that such a thing as deliberately imitating civilized people and making himself one of them has apparently never dawned upon him. He is one and they are others; that is in the inevitable nature of things, he thinks; and so he does not dream of revolting, of attempting to bridge the gulf by acquiring a new means of communication. Everything in his behavior, his constant and gentle obedience at the slightest suggestion, his readiness to leave the determination of the most trivial and intimate personal details to those about him, points in the same direction. It would seem that such a position of separation and aloofness would depress to dejection, but Ishi's demeanor is cheerful, and the only time he has not smiled on seeing an acquaintance was when he was sick in bed.

An Indian's Blush

But even stronger than this sense of distinctness, which operates only negatively, is a violent bashfulness. When, on urging, he repeats a name that is being taught him, he blushes; when he slips out for the first time a new English word or phrase, he blushes and smiles like a girl. And Ishi's blush is real. His face mantles and clouds with a frequency and intensity never approached by any other Indian that I have seen.

What interests him most is the names of people. *"Achi djeyauna"* (what is his name?), is his first and often repeated question, until he has mastered the appellation of a newcomer. Next after individuals come nationalities and conspicuous professions. "Dutchman" and "Chinaman" were early favorites; but mounted police officers impressed his imagination even more, as being great chiefs, and he tried repeatedly until he could say "bahleeceman." The first Chinaman that he saw, by the way, happened to be an editor in American clothes and among Americans, but Ishi declared at once that he was no American but an Indian—no "ghost" but a "person," to translate his native Yana literally. Soon he began to note distinguishing racial characteristics, and to push up with his fingers the outer corners of his eyes when he said "Chinaman." And then would follow another giggle and blush.

An Aboriginal Shave

Ishi put on weight rapidly after coming within reach of the fleshpots of civilization and their three times a day recurrence. In a couple of months he had gained between forty and fifty pounds. His face is as clean of beard as when he was discovered, and has not been touched by a razor. This is not a racial characteristic but the result of his substitute for shaving. He pulls out his beard hairs one by one as soon as they emerge—a habit formerly universal among all tribes on the continent, but less frequently practised to-day. In this connection he manifests a peculiar personal refinement: he never follows the habit when in company. It was only after three months of constant association that I actually saw him for the first time at what must be a daily pursuit.

What Ishi's future will be is hard to predict. He himself does not worry about it in the least. He is safe in friendly hands, with no cares, and is content to let it go at that. Until he learns English he can only remain the ward of some one, as now he is the ward of the United States and in charge of the University of California.

The strange history of this survivor from the past seems to show that intelligence is not the monopoly of civilization, and that lack of civilization is perhaps due not so much to want of sense and ability as to lack of knowledge and precedent. Ishi has as good a head as the average American; but he is unspeakably ignorant. He knows nothing,

or knew nothing, six months ago, of hours and years, of money and labor and pay, of government and authority, of newspapers and business, of the other thousands of things that make up our life. In short, he has really lived in the stone age, as has so often been said. That this does not involve a semi-animal, brutal, merely instinctive, and inferior mental capacity, is clear in his case, and may perhaps be inferred for other uncultured people. What it does involve, is an almost inconceivable difference in education, in opportunity, in a past of many centuries of achievement on which the present can build. Ishi himself is no nearer the "missing link" or any antecedent form of human life than we are; but in what his environment, his associates, and his puny native civilization have made him, he represents a stage through which our ancestors passed thousands of years ago.

Waterman wrote more about Ishi than any of the several other anthropologists who worked at recording his stock of knowledge. The present article is mainly the historical background of the Yahi from about 1850 on. Material from the writings Waterman cites—the War of the Rebellion, Fighting the Mill Creeks, and Tribes of California— is reprinted in the present volume.

The long extract on Ishi himself at the end of this article is taken from another article by Waterman, "Ishi, the Last Yahi Indian," Southern Workman, *Vol. 46, No. 10 (1917), pp. 528-537.*

---

2. The Last Wild Tribe of California (1915)

T. T. Waterman

In the fall of 1908 some attention was aroused in the press by a story to the effect that hunters had encountered in the state of California a tribe of Indians who were still in the stone age. The idea of a "wild" tribe in a thickly settled region like California was so novel that it served to awaken a very wide interest. The Indians themselves, however, had meanwhile vanished. Some three years

Popular Science Monthly, March, 1915, pp. 233-244.

later an individual who had all the appearance of belonging to this group was apprehended in northern California. He was put in jail, and a few days later turned over to the university. Since then he has been received everywhere as the last survivor of his tribe. The whole series of incidents deserves some explanation. I think it ought to be said at the outset that the story as given in the papers of that period is quite true. The individual captured in 1911 was a surviving member of a stone-age tribe. He is still alive and well at the university; and he has given from time to time extremely interesting accounts of the history of his people.

I should like to explain first of all the rather unusual career of this tribe, and how they happened to remain "wild." The occupation of California by the whites is usually pictured as a peaceful transaction. We hear little of Indian wars in connection with this state. The California tribes pursued, as it happened, a more or less settled mode of life. Being non-migratory, they were peculiarly open to attack and reprisal for any resistance they could have offered to the white invasion. The influx of whites moreover was on the whole so sudden and overwhelming that those Indian disturbances which did occur were soon forgotten. It is quite possible that if California had been settled one family at a time as New England was, "massacres" and "wars" would have occurred that would have rung down the ages like the wars waged by the Indians on the Colonies. If there had been a long course of conflicts, our California tribes might have developed a name for ferocity like that enjoyed by the Mohawk, or the Apache. As a matter of fact, the white occupation here was accomplished by violence and bloodshed, and through armed conflict with the natives far and wide. The U.S. Army records show almost as many movements of troops against the Indians as occurred in any other area of the same extent. The whole period of "occupation" was so short, however, that Indian troubles for the most part were soon things of the past.

So much for the general situation in California. In the wild and rugged part of the state, Indian resistance lasted for a long time. One such area was west of the Sacramento in the Siskiyou region,

along the upper waters of the Trinity and Eel rivers. "Bad" Indians used to frequent the wilds in this part of the state long after the tribal organizations had broken down. Such Indians caused some little trouble to enterprising settlers in the hills. A region where the Indian opposition was still more spirited and where Indian disturbances dragged out still longer was in northeastern California. Here the Pitt River Indians, and later the Modocs, put up a number of very spirited contests before knuckling under. The whites, on the whole, were very bitter towards "wild" Indians, even when harmless, and blamed them for everything, from the occurrence of freshets to the presence of potato-bugs.

It must of course be recognized that the occupation of California by the whites was inevitable. The Indians had to be dispossessed to make room for the new order. The white occupation, however, was not only inevitable, it was relentless. The methods used are not a thing of which we can be proud. The whites, for example, introduced into California, where it was unknown prior to their coming, the practise of scalping. It was very much the fashion in the early days for white settlers and miners to carry on Indian wars individually and informally. The line between their actions and plain murder is rather hard to draw. Many of the white loafers and irresponsibles that "bummed" around the frontier settlements used to preach openly a doctrine of "exterminating" the Indians. A very considerable proportion of our "Indian fighters" in this state deserved, in strict justice, to be hung. It may throw some light in general on the nature and methods of these "wars" to state that there existed in California, long after the close of the civil war, a lively traffic in Indian slaves. White administration of Indian affairs in the more easterly states impresses one most by its hopeless stupidity. The history of whites and Indians in California impresses one rather with a sense of the white man's ruthlessness.

The Yahi Tribe

In the northeastern part of the Sacramento valley there lived a nation of Indians who were early driven into a vigorous hostility to the whites. They had already, from their friction with other tribes, developed some adeptness in raiding and thieving, and in a sort of guerilla warfare. Their northern branch, the so-called Nozi, after a time capitulated, and became hangers-on of civilization. The southern branch of the stock, calling themselves simply Yahi, or "people," and inhabiting a stretch of country immediately east of the Sacramento, kept the whites in a state of uncertainty for a considerably longer time. There is one relatively small region in particular which came to be specially identified with this small group of Indians. That is the country immediately about Mill Creek. East of the Sacramento, along the waters of Antelope Creek, Mill Creek, Dry Creek, Deer Creek and Butte Creek, the country is covered with a cap of lava. The original source of this lava was, I believe, the mountain which has recently been attracting so much attention to itself—Lassen Butte.* The elevation of the region frequented by hostile Indians is not great (it all lies below the level of the pine forest) but the streams have cut in the lava a large number of rough cañons and gullies. Near as it is to the level valley, the country is extremely rugged. Cliffs, crags, and sudden promontories are frequent, and there are great numbers of caves. While the settlement and cultivation of the valley has gone forward very rapidly, this region in the foothills has remained almost untouched. To-day this "lava" country is the resort of animals (and to a certain extent, of plants) which are becoming extinct elsewhere. In this small region in north central California the Yahi made a determined stand against civilization.

In the course of their life in these cañons they developed an intense hatred and fear of the whites. They came to be hunted very much like wild animals. Accordingly they developed peculiar habits of visiting the valley in sudden forays, escaping instantly to the hills afterwards. These sudden visitations, often resulting in the loss of life as well as property, were a genuine bugbear to homesteaders. On the other hand, the Indians were on their

*Lassen Peak erupted in 1914 and was intermittently active until 1921.—Ed.

part often harried by famine. Pressure from the whites prevented them from making full use of the natural foods the country afforded. Even acorn-gathering was for them a dangerous pursuit, since it gave opportunity for white attack. Their natural means of subsistence therefore seem to have been almost entirely cut off. An idea of their desperation may be gathered from the fact that on at least one occasion when they attacked the whites and were chased, their plunder consisted of a mule-load of vegetables. In other words, they took the field and risked their lives for the sake of a few squashes and some ears of corn.

It has always been supposed that remnants of several tribes made up these Mill Creek renegades. From what we have recently learned, it seems very unlikely that there was more than one tribe involved. In the first place, the only member of this hostile group who has ever been questioned, expresses the liveliest dislike of all other tribes. He seems, and always has seemed, more ready to make friends with the whites themselves, than with the neighboring groups of Indians. In the second place, all the other Indian tribes of the region profess the liveliest horror of the Yahi. This awe extends even to the country to-day which the Yahi frequented. Even the Yahi and the Nozi, though they spoke dialects of one language (the so-called Yana) express the most unrelenting hostility for each other. In other words, the Indians who lurked about in the Mill Creek hills for several decades after the settlement of the valley, were probably the remnant of a comparatively pure group, since there was little likelihood of intermixture.

The Mill Creek "War"

Between the years 1850 and 1865 this group was more or less under observation by the government. Rumors of battle, murder and sudden death came frequently from this region to the central authorities in San Francisco and Sacramento. On one or two occasions attempts were made by the War Department to apply the universal remedy for Indian troubles—removal to a reservation. Details concerning the movement of troops and some very heated correspondence relative to this tribe may be found in the government records (War Records, Volume 50). The names of some very distinguished Californians appear in this connection. I recall especially Governor Stanford, and General Albert Sydney Johnston. The only book I know of which deals exclusively with events in the Yahi region is a small but vivid volume written by R. A. Anderson, an actor in the events, and sometime sheriff of Butte County ("Fighting the Mill Creeks," Chico, Cal., 1909). This little work checks up with the records of the War Department. The "war" with this small tribe seems to be quite overlooked in the histories of California. There is no mention of it in either Bancroft or Hittell. The reason probably is that it was very much like what had happened, or was happening, on a larger scale elsewhere. The War Department correspondence is quite full for the period covered.

The end of the Mill Creek "war" was unusual and to some extent tragic. A party of armed whites, acting without other authority than resentment and an inborn savagery, surprised the tribe on the upper waters of Mill Creek in 1865. Their effort apparently was to wipe out this Indian group on the spot. On the admission of men who took part in the action, fire was opened on the defenceless Indians in the early morning, and an uncertain number of them, men, women and children, shot down. A few, not more than three or four, perhaps, escaped into the brush and got clear. The Mill Creek tribe as a tribe disappeared from history at this time. With one or two possible exceptions, nothing was seen of it again for over thirty-five years.

Hidden Life of the Survivors

The survivors who escaped these executive measures of 1865 were too few in number to resume their old mode of life. They were, on the other hand, so small a party that they succeeded in hiding away. Little by little they emerged from their hiding places and took up again the procuring of food by hunting and fishing. They did not, however, allow themselves to be seen. They undoubtedly expected annihilation to follow on discovery, and probably there was sound judgment behind

this belief. The almost entire absence of information concerning them proves that they took to the wildest places, and stayed there. All that we positively know about them is that they disappeared in 1865, but were still alive in 1908. Under the circumstances, they must have remained "primitive." Only the primitive mode of life was open to them. They were primitive when they went into retirement, and it was their salvation. When seen again in 1908 they still used the bow and arrow and other aboriginal appliances, and were absolutely unfamiliar with the usages of civilization. Their avoidance of observation of any kind left them as isolated as if they had been literally on another continent.

Our information concerning them during this period is very scanty. The existence of "wild" Indians in this part of the world was known, or at least believed in, in many quarters, in spite of definite information. Thus Stephen Powers in his classical "Tribes of California" (U.S. Department of the Interior, Contributions to North American Ethnology, Vol. 3) says, without giving names, that five of this tribe, two men, two women, and a boy, were seen in 1870. This group gave from time to time

Deer Creek Cañon. The last refuge of the "Yahi" tribe.

further proof of their existence by their habit of secretly taking food from distant and lonely mountain cabins. It is a settled fact, that this fugitive remnant of a tribe did fairly well with their primitive mode of life, except in the late winter and early spring. By that time their stores were usually exhausted and the salmon had not yet begun to run in the streams. Their fear of the whites forbade any change of home or habitation in search of food. The only course possible, aside from quiet starvation, was to seek out some white man's cabin somewhere in the hills, help themselves to food as quickly as possible, and carry it back to their lurking places. This they seem to have done on several occasions almost every year. To this we probably owe the fact that the group managed to remain alive. This robbing of cabins could not, of course, pass unnoticed. Such cabins as exist in these hills are mere temporary shelters, utilized by wandering hunters and stockmen. Any passer-by, according to the custom of the country, is at liberty to invite himself into a cabin if he happens to find one that is in use at all, and is supposed to give himself full rights and privileges, including the use of all solids and liquids. This is a sort of informal hospitality which prevails universally. The Indians, when compelled to risk discovery in visiting a cabin, took as much food as they possibly could, to lessen the chances of having to make another trip, and ran away. They usually made a systematic collection of everything eatable, down to the last scrap, and carried it off. While the mountaineer has liberal notions of hospitality, they do not extend to this. The visits of the Indians were bitterly resented. They left their unwilling host in most cases, on his return, no resource but to walk back to civilization, empty within and without.

Such food-gathering expeditions were conducted with true Indian slyness. In spite of the fact that such "robberies" were fairly frequent, and extended over a period of thirty years, the Indians were never seen. Not only that, but no one ever found so much as a track or footprint. Often the only trace the Indians left of their presence was a total disappearance of everything edible. On one occasion a white mother returned to her homestead from

Watching for salmon.

berry-picking with two small children, to find nothing in her larder but two cold boiled potatoes. On another occasion, two mountaineers, who left in their camp two months' provisions, found on their return only part of a sack of barley. On other occasions the Indians took from camps even the barley that was intended for horse feed. Many of these robberies might have been blamed to white men, except for the fact that stuff was taken which a white man would not bother with; for example, the barley just mentioned. While useless to a white, it was readily usable by starving Indians who were accustomed to making food our of acorns and grass seeds, and had at hand their primitive devices for milling such things. On the other hand, the small quantities of canned stuff found in the cabins and camps were never touched. The Indians seemed to have a peculiar fear of it, perhaps from one or two unfortunate experiences, with canned goods that had spoiled. On at least one occasion there was taken from a cabin a small quantity of flour conspicuously labelled *poisoned.* No white man would have taken chances with this flour, however hungry.

More than once on such expeditions the Indians were perilously near exposure. Once an excited white man, with a repeating rifle and dogs, trailed them so closely that in crossing a stream they dropped a piece of headgear in their hurry. This headdress, fearfully and wonderfully wrought out of scraps of a dozen different fabrics, is now in our Museum. At the time of this escape the Indians were not seen, though where they had forded the stream the rocks were still wet.

Mere chance on several occasions nearly resulted in discovery for them. A hunter one time, passing along in the winter, noticed a low smoke rising out of a snow-covered thicket across a stream where he knew that no white man would have been. Later on, after the final emergence of the tribe from their obscurity, we found the remains of one of their encampments in this very thicket.

Such is the only actual evidence we have of the life of this tribe for over a generation. The most important change within that period is a shift in their habitat. After the massacre of '65 they lived at various places up and down the stream known as Mill Creek, robbing cabins when driven by famine. After 1885 however no more cabins were robbed along this stream. The Indians were evidently driven out by the increasing degree of settlement. The next stream to the south is known as Deer Creek. The gorge through which this stream passes is rugged and wild in the extreme. It is in fact one of the most picturesque cañons in California. The wildest part of the cañon of Deer Creek was their last home.

Below the mouth of a side branch known as Sulphur Creek, the cliffs which hem in the main stream open out into a fairly wide valley. Between the base of the cliffs on the south side and the stream itself, is a long slope composed of lava detritus. This slope consists of rocks piled up in tremendous confusion, traversed with deep gullies, and overgrown with a perfect mat of scrub oak. The brush is so thick that it is practically impenetrable. Even sheep and cattle avoid the place. I doubt if such animals could make their way through it. Two or three miles through this thicket is a good day's work for a man. Here the Yahi tribe, or its remnant, found a final refuge. In one edge of this jungle, on a shoulder overlooking the stream, under some pepperwoods or laurel, they built some tiny lodges. To this locality and little village they gave the name of Bear's Hiding Place. * The mountains and plateaus hereabout are useless for cultivation. The lava cliffs contain no metals. The country is quite unfrequented except for cattlemen and cowboys, who come at certain times of the year and "round up" their stock. Since the live stock never penetrated the jungle where the Indians lived, the stockmen also avoided it. Here for over twenty years the Indians lurked in peace.

They do not seem to have lived here exclusively. As far as we can gather at the present time, they ranged in the summer as far east as Mount Lassen. On the upper slopes of this tremendous peak they found plenty of game, and no one to disturb them. When it grew cold they returned to the foothills and passed the winter at Bear's Hiding Place. Near the lodges there is to be found a circular pit some three or four feet deep. This pit they were accustomed to pack full of snow. The melting of this snow gave them a supply of water and saved them the trouble and risk of going down to the creek, some five hundred feet below.

The village site has now been visited by a number of people, scientific and otherwise. I think they will all agree that the placing of the lodges was the work of people who were not only desperately anxious to hide themselves, but who knew thoroughly well how to do it. The houses were built

---

* As Waterman explains later in this article, he is writing after Ishi's return visit to his old home in May, 1914, accompanied by Kroeber, Waterman, Pope, and Pope's young son.—Ed.

where they were invisible from the cliffs on either side. The Indians passed down to the creek, which was very important to them on account of the fish in it, under the shelter of a growth of laurel. Thus they could move about and still remain hidden. Moreover, they avoided making visible trails, especially near the water. The little path that leads down from the lodges under and through the thicket, ramifies and disappears as it approaches the stream. In other words, they went down by different ways, to avoid making one conspicuous pathway. In making the needful paths through the brush, they bent aside the necessary twigs. Cutting or breaking them would have made the path much more conspicuous. I doubt if an observer on the cliff would ever have seen the Indians if he had been looking directly down upon them. Altogether, the place and its selection showed considerable evidence of craft, and to the wandering hunter or rider on the mountains round about, the locality would

Making a salmon-spear. Two foreshafts, which are to carry toggles, are being fastened in place with cord.

have looked always like a genuine bear's hiding place, for all the evndence of human habitation to be seen.

The Breaking Up of the Hidden Village

Such was the life of this group until the year 1908. At that time a party of surveyors, on engineering business, happened by mere luck to encounter them. One evening a naked savage was suddenly observed, standing on a rock by the stream side, armed with a long spear. This resulted, from all accounts, in the equal alarm of all parties. The next morning, those members of the party who had not run all the way to camp, went down to the place, cast about in the brush, and finally came upon the Indian lodges. Two Indians, running for their lives, were actually seen—one of them an old man, helped along by a middle-aged woman. This fleeting glimpse is all that we know of these individuals. They have never been seen again. Their actual fate is still unknown. In camp was found, under some blankets, a partially paralyzed old woman, frightened nearly to death, unable to move. The whites did what they could for this old person, then helped themselves, mainly in a spirit of curiosity, to the contents of the camp—bows, arrows, skin blankets—and after prying about, went back to camp for dinner. When they returned next day the old woman was gone.

Such was the tragic end of the last remnant of the Yahi tribe. Except for one individual, our account closes here. The members of the tribe who were seen at this time seem to have perished from cold, hunger, and exposure, without ever returning to their camp.

Nearly three years later, in August, 1911, at a slaughter-house four miles from Oroville, eighty miles away, one morning there suddenly appeared from nowhere a naked Indian. His only garment was an old castoff undershirt. He was thin, hungry, greatly worn, and of most unusual appearance. The people in charge of the premises telephoned to the sheriff and reported with some excitement the presence of a "wild man." No one, Indian or white, could make him understand a word. The sheriff of Butte County came out, took the wild

[129]

man in charge and gave him, as the most available lodging, the insane cell of the jail. When the news reached the university, the appearance of this strange Indian was at once connected with the Yahi tribe of Deer Creek, in which the department of anthropology had long been interested. It fell to the lot of the present writer to journey to Oroville to identify him. Our only resource was to "try him out" with a vocabulary in the Nozi dialect, since there was no material in existence in what was thought to be his own proper language. The first impression received of the wild Indian was the sight of him, draped in a canvas apron they had hurriedly put on him at the slaughter-house, sitting on the edge of a cot in his cell, still uncertain of his fate, and answering *ulisi* ("[I don't] understand") to all the questions that were being fired at him in English, Spanish and half a dozen Indian languages, by visitors. The present writer's amateur attempts at Yana were equally unintelligible to him for a long time. An agreement was finally reached, however, on the word for the material of which his cot was made, *si'win'i*, or yellow pine. His face lightened up at this word, though he evidently could hardly trust his senses. These were probably the first intelligible sounds he had heard from a human being in three years.

Since those days he has become a regular member of the Museum staff. He has revisited Deer Creek cañon in our company, and there is not a foot of the country he does not know. There is not the slightest doubt that it has been his home. He led the party to the old lodges in the jungle at Bear's Hiding Place, he communicated scores of place-names up and down the stream for miles, and even led the way over to his old lurking places on Mill Creek, some distance to the north. In other words, he has told us all he could, in a general way, about the tribe. He has, however, been curiously backward in telling the intimate history of his own immediate group. He has gone so far as to say that the middle-aged woman who was seen was his sister, that the very old woman was his mother, that the old man, however, was not his father. In general he speaks of them with reluctance. His reasons for this are not at all mysterious. These

people are dead, and to the Indian that is ample cause for avoiding all mention of them. In the first place, if, in the world of spirits, they hear their names being mentioned, they may take it (horror of horrors!) for a summons. Hence to taboo their names or any conversation about them is mere commonplace caution. Moreover, to speak of them and their life makes the survivor sad. At worst, to mention the dead is dreadful; at best, it is a serious disrespect. For all of these reasons our surviving tribesman avoids talking of his own personal history. It is all mixed up with that of these other, deceased persons. It is impossible to discuss recent events without bringing in their names, so he usually prefers to talk of other things. He is always ready to talk at length about the general mode of life of his people—anything in fact that does not have personal details in it. He is anxious and enthusiastic in explaining his religious and mythical ideas. As a general thing, the more ancient the lore, the more volubly he discourses. We expect some day to insinuate ourselves behind his reserve, and learn the real history of his movements during the last three or four years before his "capture." His particular secretiveness in certain matters may be illustrated by the fact that he has never told us his own name. We address him usually in his own tongue as "Ishi," which means simply "man." His actual personal name is still unknown, and possibly always will be.

Two pictures are reproduced which were taken on the visit that he made in our company to his old haunts on Deer Creek. He was in familiar surroundings, thoroughly at home, told us details concerning the mode of life and enlarged in many directions on hunting and other tribal pursuits. Thus he named for us several hundred species of plants, and described in detail the uses to which his people put them. He is a very remarkable man, aside from his extraordinary personal history, and after all his hard life, very communicative and lovable. He is quite possibly, of all the Indians of North America to-day, the one who has most nearly the primitive viewpoint. His impressions of our civilization when we finally understand them will probably bring out many curious and interesting points. He will be able, moreover, to give us, from the primitive standpoint, information about a little-known chapter of history.

From time to time reports come in of evidence pointing to Indians who are still hiding away in the mountains east of the Sacramento. It is very hard in many cases to say just what the basis of these reports is. It is not absolutely impossible that there are one or more members of the Yahi group still wandering about in the wilderness. Let us hope that if there are any others of this group still alive we may ultimately succeed in bringing all of them together.

This is the first of two detailed accounts of the culture of the Yana Indians, of whom the Yahi were the southernmost group. The other study (not reprinted here) is by Edward Sapir and Leslie Spier, "Notes on the Culture of the Yana," University of California Anthropological Records, Vol. 3, No. 3 (1943). In Waterman's study Yana-Yahi history and culture are skillfully blended.

---

3. The Yana Indians (1918)

T. T. Waterman

The present paper is an attempt to summarize the history of a small group of Indians in northeastern California. They are usually referred to as a "stock" for lack of a better term. "Yana" applies really to the natives speaking a certain group of dialects; and hence such a word as tribe, though in common use when referring to Indians, seems hardly appropriate here. The people concerned had apparently no political unity. The characteristic thing for the group as a whole is the linguistic bond, for in other matters, such as culture and physical make-up, these people exhibit relatively few differences from their neighbors. The stock is an important one, however, not solely for its own sake, but also because, for certain rather extra-

University of California Publications in American Archaeology and Ethnology, Vol. 13, No. 2 (1918), pp. 35-102.

ordinary reasons, a few members of it remained conservative much longer than the other Indians in California, retaining their primitive mode of life in a very unusual degree until 1908. I should like to recount the career of these Indians, from the date of the white occupation to the present, with special reference to the one division which eventually became dissociated from the rest, and preserved what might be called its independence, for so long. The story is one that has a good deal of human interest. At the present time the whole linguistic stock is practically extinct, not more than a few dozen scattered individuals surviving.

The Yana territory lay in Tehama County, east of the Sacramento River, its southern margin some one hundred and fifty miles north of San Francisco. It was a rather compact area adjacent to the eastern border of the Sacramento Valley, but, on the whole, outside of it. Their original domain was a region some thirty miles in width, between the edge of the great valley and the Sierra crest. From north to south it extended about seventy miles. The Yana seem to have been somewhat crowded by numerically stronger stocks on every side, and to have been always more or less on the defensive. While occasionally referred to by various writers, they remained until recent years relatively little known. In their general mode of existence, their material culture, and their mythology, they may be considered a typical Californian people.

[131]

Literature

The published materials used in the present study are listed in a terminal bibliography. Of these papers I should like to mention certain ones as especially important. The classical work on the Californian Indians is by Stephen Powers, *Tribes of California.* This monograph devotes several pages to the Indians we are dealing with, though under different names. His "Nozi" and "Kombo" tribes belong to the stock now recognized as Yana. What he has to say is highly colored and brief, but rather useful. Jeremiah Curtin, a famous author and linguist, who for a time was associated with the Bureau of American Ethnology, worked with the Yana and developed a good deal of sentimental interest in them, busying himself in their behalf in the east. In his *Creation Myths of Primitive America* there are thirteen Yana myths (the last in his series) and some information in the form of notes. By far the most important investigations however, are those of Dr. Edward Sapir, in recent years director of ethnological work in the Canadian Geological Survey. An early paper, *Yana Texts*, containing twenty-seven myths and a good deal of ethnography in the form of texts and notes, has recently been supplemented by a second paper on the relation of the Yanan dialects with the dialects of other areas. A brief but highly important paper by Kroeber and Dixon, *New Linguistic Families in California*, deals among other matters with the general relation of Yanan with other languages.

Some of the information embodied in the present paper was obtained directly from informants who were personally familiar with the episodes discussed. The native geographical information especially was obtained in large part from Ishi, the last survivor of that group of Yana who remained in a primitive state. This informant died at the University of California in March, 1916.

Geography and Habitat

No effort has been made in the present paper to go systematically into the matter of ethnography, although there is considerable information now available. Geography for our present purpose is incidental merely. In a general way, it is now known that the Yana, instead of being an isolated stock, as was for many years assumed, is one unit in a widely scattered group, the "Hokan" of Kroeber and Dixon. The conclusions reached by the last mentioned writers, as far as the Yana and related stocks are concerned, are illustrated in the appended diagram (map 2). The Yana proper, whose distribution is shown in solid black on this diagram, manifestly do not derive their importance from the extent of their territory, which is very cramped. Even within this limited area, there are now recognized four separate dialects: a northern, a central, a southern, and a Yahi. Of these, Sapir mentions three in his *Yana Texts* (1910, p. 2). The existence of the

fourth, or Yahi dialect has been established on evidence made available since his paper was written.

The limits of these dialects are indicated on the appended large map, number 1.* These boundaries are only approximately correct. In fact the exact lines of demarcation must remain highly conjectural. The actual amount of divergence between these dialects, and the relations between them, does not especially concern us here. It is enough to remark that the difference in language was considerable, and that along with it went a feeling of strangeness and hostility between the dialect groups. They certainly did not feel community of language-stock as any particular bond. The term "Nozi" used by Powers probably refers to what is now called the central group. The Yana still living about Redding recognize the term and apply it to themselves. The "Kombo" of Powers are the people who call themselves Yahi. This term Yahi is itself a dialectic form of the word "Yana," and both terms mean simply, "people." The "Kombo" or Yahi were lost sight of for so long that they became at one time almost a legendary folk.

The external limits of Yana territory are also somewhat uncertain. Probably there was more or less overlapping, valley tribes going into the foothills on hunting expeditions, and the foothill peoples visiting the valley when they could, or when through starvation, they had to. There may have been extended periods of comparative quiet, when the hunting, fishing, and seed-gathering grounds were to some extent shared. At any rate, the Yana had their own names for places many miles away in the territory of other peoples, far beyond the boundaries of the country which they themselves might be said to control. For example, there is a Yana name for Fall River Mills, on Pit River.

Concerning the geographical features of the region in general, several remarks may be made. Yana

* Waterman's map 1, a foldout, was too large to be reproduced here. A somewhat less detailed map, from the illustrated edition of *Ishi* (1976), has been reproduced here instead. Waterman's references to intersecting lines on his original map have been omitted in the reprinting of this monograph.—Ed.

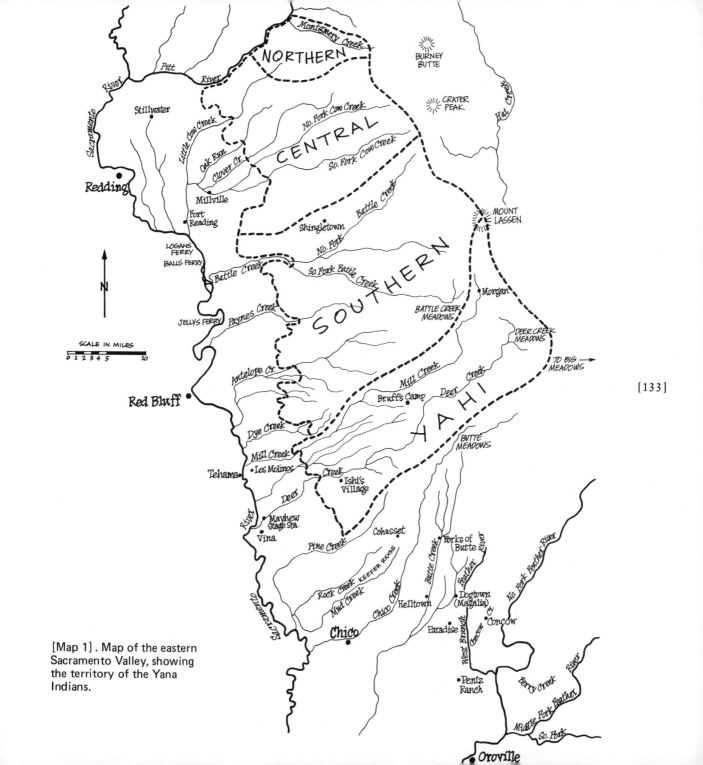

NORTHERN

Montgomery Creek

BURNEY BUTTE

CRATER PEAK

Pitt River

Sacramento River

Stillwater

Little Cow Creek

No. Fork Cow Creek

CENTRAL

Hat Creek

Oak Run

Clover Cr.

So. Fork Cow Creek

Redding

Millville

Fort Reading

Battle Creek

Shingletown

No. Fork

MOUNT LASSEN

LOGANS FERRY
BALLS FERRY

Battle Creek

So. Fork Battle Creek

SOUTHERN

Morgan

JELLYS FERRY

Paynes Creek

BATTLE CREEK MEADOWS

DEER CREEK MEADOWS

TO BIG MEADOWS →

[133]

SCALE IN MILES
0 1 2 3 4 5   10

N

Antelope Cr.

Mill Creek

Deer Creek

YAHI

Red Bluff

Bruff's Camp

Dye Creek

BUTTE MEADOWS

Mill Creek

Creek

Tehama

Los Molinos

Ishi's Village

Deer

Mayhew Stage Sta.

Cohasset

River

Vina

Pine Creek

Forks of Butte River

Rock Creek

KEEFER RIDGE

Chico Creek

Butte Creek

Feather

No. Fork Feather River

Mud Creek

Helltown

Dogtown (Magalia)

Concow Cr.

Concow

Chico

Paradise

West Branch

Berry Creek

Pentz Ranch

Middle Fork Feather River

Sacramento River

So. Fork

Oroville

[Map 1]. Map of the eastern Sacramento Valley, showing the territory of the Yana Indians.

territory stretches between two of California's best known streams, Feather River and Pit River. Both drain westward into the Sacramento. As a matter of fact, where the Pit meets the Sacramento, the Pit is the larger of the two. Above their junction the Sacramento is hardly more than a large mountain creek. This whole countryside rises gradually from the level valley bordering the Sacramento, having an elevation of three hundred or four hundred feet, to the high Sierras on the east, where the peaks reach an altitude of ten thousand five hundred. This whole region is dominated by Lassen Butte, known to the Yana as Little Mount Shasta (Wahkanupa). The character of the scenery in this part of California is largely derived from the fact that the formations are volcanic. The ancient lava flows extend clear to the level valley on the west. The southern part of the area, with which I am personally familiar, is on account of its volcanic nature extremely wild in places even today. Deer, for example, are still plentiful. The region abounds in cliffs and caves, and some of its gorges are picturesque in the extreme. Around Lassen Butte itself (called locally, by the way, as though it were "Lawson" Butte) there are still abundant signs of volcanic activity. The Lassen region was known to the Indians as P'ulp'uli, from the frequent occurrence of steaming hot springs. Quite recently, of course, Mount Lassen staged a fairly lively volcanic eruption. It is the only active volcano, I believe, anywhere in the United States. What the Indians would have thought of this eruption would be extremely interesting to find out. Unfortunately, as far as we know, none of them were left to witness it. It was through this region, by the way, that a famous emigrant road to the gold-diggings passed. It was known as the Lassen Trail, and traces of it can still be seen today. Bits of iron from the old wagons, ox shoes, and even an occasional wooden yoke are still to be found scattered along the ridges. A large number of people used it in the years just following the discovery of gold.

The large streams which bound this region, Hat Creek to the northeast, Pit River across the north, the Sacramento, and to the southeast the northern fork of Feather River, were all, I think, in the possession of peoples alien or hostile to the Yana;

except that the latter according to Sapir occupied one bank of Pit River for a short distance. Possibly the best way of describing the Yana territory would be to say that they were excluded from the valleys of the Sacramento, Pit River, Hat Creek, and the north fork of Feather River by more numerous and more happily situated Indian peoples. The boundary lines of the Yana area on the map therefore follow the watersheds between these streams. All of the places where the Yana made historical appearances (that is, where they had fights with the whites), are in the foothill region, below the line of the pine timber. This region of brush and rocks was their principal sojourning ground, and main reliance. They were emphatically a foothill people.

Authorities differ considerably concerning the border line of Yana territory in the Sacramento Valley. Powers says that their domain reached to within a mile of the Sacramento. Powell on the other hand says it stopped short ten miles from the river (1884, p. xxxvii). The truth is that no geographical features exist which would make the first of these two statements plausible. Sapir implies that the Yana dwelt in places along the river bank. In this he is almost certainly mistaken. The probability is that the strong and numerous Wintun who held the valley would not have tolerated Yana settlements. I feel convinced that the Yana territory really stopped at the line between the foothills and the valley floor, especially as the foothills are lava, and the terrain there is vastly different from that of the valley. In the absence of definite certainty on this point, I have placed the border line on the map at the thousand-foot contour. That seems to me to approximate the probable boundary line as closely as anything would, and it is at least something definite.

The total number of people speaking Yana was probably never large. Curtin speaks of three thousand. This may be in excess of the number actually existing at the time of the first white occupation, even counting all four dialects. In 1885 Curtin was able to round up about thirty Yana-speaking informants. Dr. Sapir in 1907 found only six or seven surviving. They were in the neighborhood of Redding, and around Montgomery Creek in Shasta

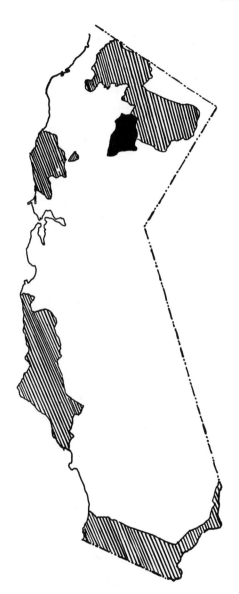

[Map 2]. The distribution of Hokan languages in California. The area occupied by the Yana is shown in solid black.

County, and could give information relative to the Northern and Central dialects. The Southern dialect was in 1907 regarded as already extinct, and the existence of a Yahi dialect was not even suspected. This latter dialect was preserved for more than forty years by a remnant of the group, not exceeding four or five, who lived by themselves hidden away in the southern part of their area. All over this region there are numerous ancient village sites, marked by the occurrence of the inevitable heap of black kitchen-earth mingled with bones and artifacts, which accompany primitive man's places of settlement the world over. Some of these Yahi middens are several yards in thickness. A great number of the caverns also show the results of long continued occupation. Such evidence of course gives no definite information on the question of population or positive antiquity. Some of the most favorable places, however, must have been occupied for many centuries. As late as 1885 some old Yahi brush lodges were standing on Little Antelope Creek though long deserted and falling by that time to decay. This place was a very old site, as shown by the existence there of a thick pile of refuse.

[135]

Early Contact with the Whites

It is really impossible to separate entirely the history of the Yana, during the early history of white occupation, from that of other groups. There was little understanding, on the part of the whites, of the linguistic and other distinctions between the Indian stocks, and little effort made to distinguish between them. In the very early chronicles of the state, the Yana do not appear by name. They existed, but they lived in the remote hills and did not visit the navigable rivers or the well-traveled routes. I should like to recount a number of incidents connected with the relation between Indians and whites in this part of the state in the "early days." The Yana were not immediately concerned in all of them, but they felt the effects indirectly. These incidents moreover show the sort of things which happened in those days, and help to explain the subsequent attitude of the Yana toward the whites.

I may say in advance that their relations as a tribe with the whites began and ended in trouble.

The earliest printed reference to Indian disturbances in this region is found in a *History of Butte County*, by Wells and Chambers, and is associated with the year 1851.

Mr. Pence (this name occurs as Pentz in the government documents and on the maps) is affronted by a "Concow" Indian, who adopts a threatening and belligerent attitude. To put down this ebullition of aboriginal ferocity, and to render Mr. Pentz's person secure, the Concow chief was executed by hanging. (Wells, p. 217).

The Concow Indians referred to in connection with this episode where the Maidu group living along Concow Creek. This same Pentz played a conspicuous part in later events. For example he next leads a party in the vicinity of Dogtown, on Little Butte Creek:

1853.—Certain "Tiger" Indians steal cattle. Our friend Pentz leads a party in pursuit of them, and twenty-five Indians are killed near Dogtown. An Indian called Express Bill is captured and hanged. The whites in Dogtown refuse to aid the party. Later, when a "raid" on the north fork of Feather River is reported, Pentz leads a party into the field, and from forty to sixty Indians are killed.

It was usually the case that, as here, the whites never proceeded against the Indians of their own neighborhood. None of the pioneer communities held any grudge against their own local aborigines. The massacres were practically always the work of a small group of unauthorized whites, acting against the Indians of some other locality. A distant Indian was a bad Indian, it seems.

A few years later the Yana proper, probably the Yahi division, appear in local history. This group, the most southerly of the Yana peoples, made their home on and about Deer Creek and Mill Creek and are often referred to as "Mill Creeks." They seem to have been, compared to other Indians, an independent and warlike group. At any rate, a party which invaded their haunts came out with that impression.

1857.—In the vicinity of Tehama, Indians raid the valley and cause much uneasiness. People are said to have been killed, houses fired, and stock driven off. A party of whites files into the hills to visit retribution on the Indians, traveling up the Lassen Trail. In the vicinity of Bluff Camp they run into an ambuscade, and make a sudden exit to the valley (Anderson, [chap. 1]). Later another party chases the Indians, who have stolen some mules, and finds them hidden in a cave near the head of Dry Creek. Although fired upon, the Indians escape. The mules, however, were killed and eaten (Anderson, [chap. 1]).*

It is, I think, worth comment that the Indians took from the whites for culinary purposes not only oxen, but also horses and mules. Such livestock was always killed and eaten. Mule meat they are said to have preferred. The author of the above account points out that when the Indians took refuge in one place, they always hid their "jerky" (dried deer or mule meat) somewhere else. If chased out of their camp, their supplies were where they could be visited and utilized later. It is said that at this time General Kibbey sent a company of United States cavalry to operate against these Indians, and that the cavalry also were surprised and chased to the valley. I can find no record of any such occurrence, but if true, it proves that these Mill Creek Indians were active and bold.

From this time on they seem to have been most belligerent. They certainly drove off and destroyed a good deal of property, and several rather atrocious murders of white people were committed by them. I want to say at the outset that these murders by the Indians, murders for example of women and children, were not one whit more cruel or pitiless than the murders of Indians by whites. I incline wholly to the belief that the whites started everything of the sort. They were certainly, in the general nature of things, the aggressors, pushing

*Waterman's references to Anderson and to Thankful Carson (reprinted above) have been changed from the original page numbers to chapter numbers, to enable the reader to find them more readily.—Ed.

constantly into Indian country. It must be remembered that as late as 1861 Indians according to California law could be indentured, that is, practically enslaved (U.S. Office of Indian Affairs, Rep. of the Com'r. for 1861, p. 147). Statements by white pioneers prove conclusively that many of their number were strangers to mercy or humanity where Indians were involved. I believe therefore that the murders the Indians committed were in the nature of plain, old-fashioned revenge. The Yahi seem to have differed from all other Indians in this part of the region in having opportunity, or seizing opportunities, for the revenge they considered themselves entitled to. In my opinion their opportunity lay in this, that they inhabited a very rough region, little traveled and unknown, with endless possibilities for hiding; and moreover, having been pressed for generations by the valley Indians, they had learned the art of "hit and run away." Every account refers to their extraordinary skill in gettting clear. This was true even of the last remnants of the stock, who lived a wild life to within the last few years. So much for the general setting. The Yahi throughout the opening period of their history were getting justice as best they could with weapons and swift legs.

In the meantime Indians far and wide were visited with blame for the acts committed by the Yahi, and many inoffensive groups were removed from the country. The Indian population rapidly dimished. I strongly suspect that the unreconstructed belligerency of the Yahi during this period was largely due to the increased difficulty of their life. Hemmed in more and more in their lava hills, and cut off more and more from acorn grounds and fishing places, they probably visited the valley and stole livestock to escape famine and actual starvation. Hounded by the whites for these offenses, they turned on pursuing parties on many occasions, profiting by surprises, and relying on their skill in evasion to get them off.

A number of such events concerning the Yana are crowded into the years 1858 and 1859. For example, one hundred and eighty-one Indians along Battle Creek were removed to the Nome Lackee Reservation, twenty miles east of Tehama on the west side of the valley (U.S. Office of Indian Affairs Rep. of Comm. for 1858, p. 289). Most of them were diseased, presumably with venereal ailments judging from the phraseology used. They probably spoke Southern Yana, and this removal may account for the disappearance of the Southern dialect from the scene. The Indians thus concentrated at Nome Lackee were scattered prior to the year 1861. The reservation buildings as a matter of fact were wrecked, and the site practically abandoned. Probably few if any of the Battle Creek people returned to their own territory. So we witness here the exit from history of one Yana dialect.

In the following year (1859) the Yahi were involved in several episodes which I should like to recount in some detail. The first one is a campaign organized against them under the name of "Mill Creek Indians."

1859.—Raids by Indians become constant. A fund of $3,000 is raised to finance a campaign against them, and placed in charge of a storekeeper named Cohen at Mayhew stage station, on Deer Creek. Three well known characters are members of one party, namely, "Hi" Good, who appears continually in subsequent chronicles, a man named Breckinridge, and R. A. Anderson, the author of a work much quoted in the present paper. The "company" moves up the Campbell trail, just north of Pine Creek, to Deer Creek flats, and then northward right through the Yahi haunts. No Indians however are seen. Moving to Black Buttes on Mill Creek, the company goes in to camp on the north side of the stream. Meanwhile a large number of the very Indians they are seeking, are camped in hiding under a point of rock a little down stream. These Indians send one of their number to shoot into the white camp with a rifle once in a while, to keep everybody's attention occupied, while the remainder of the redskins fell a tree, cross upon it to the south side of the stream, and get away. They were mostly, from the footprints, women and children.

Next day the party of whites picks up the spoor of ten or a dozen warriors, leading northward toward Paine's creek. This part of the band are pursued by the whites to Battle Creek

Meadows, then further to Lassen Butte, then clear into the cañon of Hat Creek. Here the Indians turn back, and the whites follow them over the same ground, but keeping somewhat to the west of their up-track. The Indians embrace an opportunity to kill a "bullwhacker" (ox-driver) near a sawmill northwest of Red Bluff. The whites finally halt on the Keefer ridge, between Rock Creek and Chico Creek (Anderson, [chaps. 2-4]).

Somewhere during this chase the whites were evidently thrown completely off the scent. They lost their quarry, probably somewhere in Deer Creek. They maintained however their purpose of killing some Indians. On the ridge to the south of Chico Creek, near what is now the Forest Ranch, in what is probably Maidu territory, they found a camp of Indians. That these were not the Mill Creeks they had been pursuing is amply proved by the fact that meanwhile, the Mill Creeks themselves were visiting Anderson's own farm on Deer Creek and taking away everything on the premises (Anderson, [chap. 6]). The dealings of this white force with the Indians encamped near Forest Ranch are worth recounting. To quote an eyewitness:

> "After a careful study of the ground, we returned to our camp. On this return trip we ran upon an Indian scout and after a long hard chase, killed him. We carried his scalp to camp with us, this being the first trophy we had taken in the campaign. . . .
>
> It was a weary climb out of Chico Creek cañon in the darkness, but we made it and succeeded in surrounding the hostile camp before daylight. . . . As the gray dawn melted into daylight, the outlines of the camp became clearer. It was evidently a permanent meeting place, as there were signs of its having been frequently occupied. Directly in front of me and standing something like a hundred yards apart, were two lofty pine trees, trimmed of branches except for small tufts of foliage on their tops, and, what was my surprise, as the heavens grew brighter, to behold a large American flag depending from the top of each tree. . . .
>
> Then a man emerged from a cluster of little firs and came shuffling up the trail directly toward where I lay. Captain Breckinridge had not yet given the signal to commence firing, so I slipped around my tree in order to remain hidden. As the man approached and passed me, I perceived that he was not an Indian, but a Spaniard. However, birds flocking together on this occasion were to be considered birds of a feather. The man had got but a few paces past me when Hi Good spied him. In a moment Good's rifle spoke, and the Spaniard, wounded, sprang back toward the camp. As he ran another rifle over on the other side of our circle cracked, and he fell dead.
>
> The camp was roused. In a twinkling, up the Indians sprang, men, women, and children, and as if with one impulse they swarmed up the slope directly toward where I lay. . . .
>
> Soon we came in possession of the camp. There was not a bad Indian to be found, but about forty good ones lay scattered about.
>
> Two barrels, partly filled with whiskey, were in the camp, as well as other evidences which pointed to the fact that whites had joined with the redskins in the recent celebrations" (Anderson, [chap. 4]).

It is perfectly certain that a party with women and children and two barrels of whiskey, had not been to Lassen Butte and back. Nor would the belligerent Yahi have occupied a permanent and public camp, to say nothing of getting drunk. The stealing of Anderson's horses while this is going on, gives them an alibi in any case. So the Indians killed, were not the Indians the party of whites had been chasing. An incident recounted by our author on a subsequent page explains the presence of the Indians at this resort. Going into a mining town on Butte Creek the next day, the party finds wounded Indians, and an angry storekeeper named Wallace. He says that his own squaw had been wounded in the "fight" of the day before, and that he himself had been an inmate of the camp only one day prior to the killing. In other words the whites and Indians of this vicinity had been having some sort of a "jamboree." However reprehensible their action may have been in getting drunk, there is no question but that a lot of "tame" Indians, well and favorably known to their white neighbors along Butte Creek, were shot down in cold blood. In other words, forty murders were committed.

A short time later another party of whites locates an Indian camp on Deer Creek, two miles above Tom Polk's cabin. The Indians (in this case, Yahi) when attacked, hide in water waist-deep, under an overhang of the bank. A "Doctor" Indian (who appears in various fatal episodes, apparently having as many lives as a cat) fights a lone battle and is killed. The rest surrender. The captive Yahi according to Anderson are taken to the Nome Lackee Reservation. I have been able to find no other mention of them. Meanwhile, and up to the middle of winter, other Yahi Indians uninterruptedly raid the valley, the disturbances reaching the ears of the Office of Indian Affairs (Geiger, *in* Report for 1859, p. 438). Anderson says that though many Mill Creeks were killed, their number did not grow smaller. He thinks they were continually reinforced by renegades from the outside. This is probably a mistake. The secret was that the Yahi had a knack of getting other people killed in place of themselves. On a number of occasions during this period they were seen, but I know of no incidents worth recounting.

They were, however, "making themselves felt," and this continued through several years. In the year 1862 several important events occurred, which are often spoken of in the region even yet. On the eighteenth of June a meeting was held at Forks of Butte to formulate grievances against the Mill Creek Indians. They were said to have admitted a number of murders. Twenty-four men volunteered to proceed against them *vi et armis.* Almost while this meeting was in progress, a certain Thomas Allen, teaming for J. L. Keefer, was killed by the Indians. Apparently on the same day, a party of the Yahi (probably the same individuals) ran across the children of a family named Hickok, living on Rock Creek. A girl, sixteen years of age, was shot to death with arrows, and along with her, a sister of fourteen. A boy somewhat younger was carried off (Wells, p. 218; Anderson, [chap. 10]). The boy according to Anderson was stoned to death, while Wells reports that his toes and fingers were cut off. Other authors allude vaguely to cremation. This

murder has never been forgotten to the present day. News of it at the time rang across the country side. Hi Good and another well known character, Sandy Young, boss *vaquero* for the Bidwell Ranch at Chico, went after the Indians and are said to have killed eight. (Whether the eight were Mill Creeks or not is another matter; for a few years later the Mill Creeks are still apparently as strong as ever.) Leland Stanford wrote to General Wright (of the Military Department of the Pacific) concerning these outrages, and troops were dispatched to operate against the Mill Creeks (War Records, vol. 50, part 1, p.1162). There was much talk of killing all the Indians in the country, and the U.S. troops had orders in this connection to protect peaceable tribes, such as the Big Meadows people, from hostile Indians and from unauthorized white organizations (*ibid.*, part 2, p. 28). It was not clear to the military authorities just which Indians had committed the murders spoken of. In September some United States cavalry operated through Battle Creek, Antelope Creek, Mill Creek, and Deer Creek, finding only "signs" three weeks old. The officer in command, Captain Henry B. Mellen, reports that all the settlers believed that the Indians should be utterly removed from the country. The military forces apparently did not get into contact with the Yahi, though they scouted all through their country. The Indians were evidently in hiding somewhere, and probably had the troops under observation every moment of the time.

In the meantime, in August of this year, the Yahi visited Anderson's place and took the horses from his barn, setting it on fire. When he ran out, the rocks were still wet from the wash where they had forded the creek. Being followed, they ran up Dry Creek toward the cliffs of Mill Creek. When he saw them for a moment, they were trying to repack one of the horses with "plunder" they had taken. This plunder consisted of corn and other garden truck, which would seem to indicate that the Indians were very badly off at this time. Otherwise they would not have risked their lives for the sake of a few green vegetables. Conditions after that grew rapidly worse for them. Even the Yahi were not able to escape as they had up to this time. In June of the following year (1863) they stole horses

[139]

belonging to Solomon Gore, but were followed by a party of whites. They took one of the animals up the almost perpendicular defile opposite the mouth of Sulphur Creek, in Deer Creek cañon. It is folklore in the country that the horse hung on by his teeth. The marks could be seen on the bushes!

The pursuing party crosses Little Dry Creek, Big Dry Creek, and reaches the cliff of Mill Creek cañon. From this cliff they see objects moving on the slopes below, and finally make them out to be Indian women gathering grass seeds. They hurry downward as secretly as possible, and get within a few hundred yards of the women. Suddenly an Indian lookout on the cliff behind them, gives a warning shout. The whites follow the flying squaws over the brow of the slope and come in sight of their camp. Here they are trying to pack a horse. There are a number of men. Being charged by the whites, the Indians scatter. Under a pile of new quilts the whites find an Indian boy who has slept through the battle. They leave him unharmed, and staring after them. Seven or eight Indians are killed (Anderson, [chap. 12]).

[140]

Feeling was apparently very strong at the time against redskins of all descriptions. Five Indians, affiliations unknown, were hanged at Helltown on suspicion of having committed robberies (Wells, p. 219).

In July a party of Indians "on the war path" passed through the Clear Creek country midway between Chico and Oroville. They are said to have been Mill Creek Indians (that is, Yahi) though Clear Creek is to the south of Butte Creek, and Butte Creek itself is probably outside of the Yahi range. In any case, these Indians fell upon members of the Lewis family of the neighborhood. The oldest boy was shot with a rifle, while a younger boy, along with his sister, Thankful Lewis, was carried off. The little boy soon grew leg-weary and was killed, pitiful as that may seem. His sister managed to escape, and lives today, as Mrs. Carson, in the vicinity of Chico. Luckily she has written a story of her terrible experience, about which many accounts are current in the country (see bibliography). A party of whites, roused by the incident, picked up the trail, or a trail, and followed it to Deer Creek cañon, across this cañon, and up the defile just spoken of, on to the pine flat beyond, killing one Indian. In this country the Indians scattered, taking advantage of the abundant cover, and the chase was over.

Mrs. Carson mentions [chap. 3] that two of the Indians had their heads all tarred and were "terrible to look at." It is unnecessary to discuss their pitiless behavior toward these white children. At the same time it is to be recognized that cutting the hair short and putting pitch on the head is the Indian custom when in mourning. Two Indians of this party, then, had recently lost relatives. It is possible that some of their children had been killed, and that they were bent on enslaving some white children by way of satisfaction. Otherwise it is hard to imagine why they should have gone to the trouble of dragging away the Lewis children, who could be of no practical advantage to them.

As a result of the incident involving the Lewis children, a meeting was called at Pentz's ranch, to take measures for the permanent removal of all Indians from the country. Of some three hundred and fifty Indians then concentrated at Yankee Hill, four were hanged. A pseudo-military organization known as the Oroville Guards took the field, and hanged four more Indians at Dogtown (Wells, p. 20). Mr. Lewis, father of the captives, killed two "bad" Indians at Bidwell's, one of them supposed to be a Mill Creek (Carson, [chap. 10]). This episode is also mentioned in the War Records (*ibid.*, part 2, p. 874). Meanwhile G. M. Hanson, agent for Indian Affairs for the Northern District, wrote frantically to General Wright of the Department of the Paicfic, under date of July 27, 1863, stating that there was great excitement in Chico, and asking that troops be sent to aid him in collecting, protecting and removing the Indians. Armed whites, according to Hanson, were threatening all Indians with a general extermination.

The general effect of these factors was the inauguration of measures to collect the Indian population from all the regions we have been considering, and take them away to reservations. As remarked above, Nome Lackee Reservation, twenty miles from Tehama, was by this time abolished. The project was therefore formed of collecting all the Indians (who numbered probably a thousand) and conveying them to Round Valley in Mendocino County, a reservation called at that time Nome Cult. This was actually done, after a fashion. There is some uncertainty about the identity of the people behind this enterprise. Certain army officers thought the whole idea was the work of Secessionists, and designed to embarass the government. The moving spirits in it are referred to as evil-minded. The intentions of the government in consenting were as usual, good, and even the Indian Department meant no harm. At the time the feeling among well disposed people in general was that the Indians would have no peace as long as they were mixed in with whites. The fact is however that during this agitation the Indians were hastily gotten together. Proper provision for transport was not provided; the people loudest in demanding the removal of the Indians were the most reluctant to do anything to further it, and no provision for thenewcomers was made at the reservation in Round Valley. The whole undertaking resulted in excitement, confusion, expense, discomfort for the Indians, and nothing more. Nothing was done that could in any way solve the problem. I shall not recount the details of this enforced migration. The War Records give the correspondence and reports concerning it. The liveliest part is a quarrel by letter between the army officer commanding Fort Wright, near the Agency in Round Valley, and the supervisor at that reservation; a correspondence in which the remarks of the Indian supervisor are the most dignified, but those of the army officer the most explicit and pointed. Captain Starr, who escorted the Indians on their march, left Chico with 461 Indians, and arrived at Round Valley with 277. Of the whole number, 32 died on the way, and 150 were left sick along the trail, to be brought in gradually, as their condition permitted. After all was over, General Wright, in a letter dated October 2, speaks in general of the impossibility of keeping Indians on reservations to which they may be assigned. (*Ibid.,* part 2, p. 637). Probably some of these transported Indians got back to the vicinity of Chico almost as soon as the troops did.

In the meantime the only Indians not affected by the measures taken, were the Yahi who started the trouble. Early in the year 1864, Captain Starr at Camp Bidwell, near Chico, is warned to expect an attack from them; an attack probably not to be directed against the troops themselves, but against outlying homesteads. He is directed to apprehend their leading men and send them to Alcatraz Island, to be confined in the military prison. This order was a very cool one. The captain might as well have been ordered to apprehend the Northern Lights. During the year troops did scout extensively through the hills, but did not see any Indians.

Throughout this period the people at Cherokee Flat were incensed against a group of three hundred Indians between the north and middle forks of Feather River, near Berry Creek. The Indians concerned here were undoubtedly Maidu, not Yana at all, and the probabilities are that they had never been at the bottom of any disturbances. It seems altogether likely that they got the blame for what were really Yahi activities.

About this time, in August, 1864 (Curtin, p. 517), some white people were murdered in the northern part of the Yana area. The names of Mrs. Allen and Mrs. Dirsch are mentioned in all the books. The exact location of their homes I am uncertain about. Mrs. Dirsch lived however somewhere near Millville, and according to a private informant, on the road to Ball's Ferry. In addition to the murders, a number of horses were taken, some of them, according to one informant, from "west of the river," (presumably Cow Creek). Three horses that would not swim the river were "cut all to pieces" and *shot with arrows,* and returned home in that condition. The others, according to information, were recovered in Mill Creek cañon. If all this is true, the Indians concerned were certainly Yahi. The use of arrows points in that direction. The date is somewhat uncertain. One informant places the occurrence in 1866. Curtin places it in 1864. In any case, the incident brought destruction on the heads of

[141]

the northern Yana. I am once more uncertain as to how many Indians were killed. Two companies of whites operated, and Curtin tells in detail how they shot this woman, and murdered that Indian child, and all the rest (p. 517). He says that, among other episodes, twenty Yana were killed on Cottonwood Creek, and three hundred, who were assembled for a ceremony, on Oak Run. A private informant mentions a "killing" on Bear Creek. Whatever may be the number who were actually killed at this time, the undoubted fact remains that after this period only remnants of the Yana people survived. The Indians were killed in the presence and over the protests of their white employers; women were deliberately shot down; and one white man callously exhibited four hundred dollars he had taken from the bodies of dead Indians, who were fresh from laboring in the harvest fields. A few were saved through being secreted by friendly whites.

A number of Indians were killed in the southern part of the territory as the result of the death of Mrs. Dirsch. Just north of Dye Creek and some four miles from the valley floor, there is a bold, rocky promontory. In a cave a mile or two up the ridge from this "point" of rocks, some thirty Indians were cornered, probably in the year 1867. They are said to have been caught *while returning from the Dirsch raid*. Indians located in this country were certainly members of the Yahi group, and if they really had been to the north, and had been the perpetrators of the Dirsch murder, the killing of the inoffensive northern Yana who happened to live in the vicinity of Mrs. Dirsch's home, was doubly unjustifiable. The vicinity of the cave where these Indians were killed has been called Campo Seco, or Dry Camp, because some of the Bogard family had a sheep pen here, to which water had to be transported. The details of the killing do not matter so much. The point is that the Indians were traced into the cave and shot down. The marks of the bullets are still to be seen on the rocks. In 1869 the side hill (visited at that time by Mr. Norvall) was still covered with skeletons.

At this point we may consider the history of the Yana closed, excepting only the Yahi division. After this time, the most important events happening in

the northern part of Yana territory, are the visits of ethnological investigators such as Curtin and Sapir.

The Yahi Meet Disaster

We may center our attention therefore on the Yahi. They prolong what may be called the tribal history for half a century. About this time however a catastrophe overtook even this part of the tribe. They allowed themselves to be surrounded by an armed party of whites on the upper waters of Mill Creek. The whole affair began with the killing of some white people on Concow Creek, far to the south of Yana territory. A Mrs. Workman, together with her hired man John Banks ("Scotch John"), and a Miss Rosanna Smith, a new arrival from England, were all murdered. There are said to have been atrocious details, but no one has discussed them. I can hardly imagine the Yahi proceeding so far from home for devilment, but in any case they were again credited with the outrage. About this time the peaceable Indians at Big Meadows were attacked by "wild" people, and some women carried off. The trail picked up at Big Meadows, is said to have been followed to Mill Creek. A party of seventeen whites, some of them the bitterly resentful neighbors of the murdered women, found another Yahi trail on Deer Creek flats, which they followed up. I quote subsequent occurrences from an eyewitness:

August 15, 1865.—We decided to move forward just in time to get the camp surrounded before the break of day. Hi, with six men, was left to advance upon the camp in the same manner that he and I had already adopted, while I took the balance of the force for a detour which would bring us against the Indians from the up-stream side.

We had a difficult climb for we were compelled to swing some distance up the rough hillside in order to avoid springing an alarm, but made it successfully. As day began to peep over the high walls of the cañon, I found myself lying about thirty feet above one of the three little knolls that had served us so well as landmarks. I had left orders for Hi's party to lie quiet and let us make the attack. This would throw the Indians onto the bar next the open ford where they would be completely at the mercy of both our forces.

It grew lighter and still no sound disturbed the morning excepting the incessant murmur of the nearby stream. Henry Curtis was close to my right. Suddenly he chirped like a bird. I glanced toward him and saw him pointing toward the top of the knoll. Turning my eye thither I was just in time to see the half-breed Billy Sill lowering his rifle in a line with my head. I rolled behind a tree and the half-breed knowing that he was seen sank out of sight behind a rock. I had ample time in the glimpse I caught of him to see that he still wore the white shirt.

Almost on the instant that he disappeared Good's rifle cracked and the fight was on. We crowded forward and poured a hot fire into the Indians from up stream, while Good's men hammered them from below. Into the stream they leaped, but few got out alive. Instead, many dead bodies floated down the rapid current. . . .

This battle practically ended the scourge of the Mill creeks. I had often argued with Good regarding the disposition of the Indians. He believed in killing every man or well grown boy, but in leaving the women unmolested in their mountain retreats. It was plain to me that we must also get rid of the women. On this occasion the Concow people were intensely wrought up over the horrible atrocities practiced by the Indians on the white women whom they killed, and I had told them that they were at liberty to deal with the Indians as they saw fit.

While ransacking the camp after the battle was over a little child possessing six toes on each foot was found. Hi Good at once took a notion to the child and said that he wished to take it home with him. Knowing that he had odd tastes about such things, I consented. Whereupon he declared that he must take along a squaw to carry the child. I asked Curtis what his pleasure was in the matter and after consulting with some of his own party he grudgingly agreed.

The woman selected for the purpose was slightly wounded in the heel. She packed the youngster in stolid silence up the long hill and over its crest into Twenty Mile Hollow. Here however she became sullen and refused to go a step farther. I gave her over to the Concow people and they left her to swell the number of the dead (Anderson, [chap. 14]).

Mr. W. J. Segraves, to whom I am indebted for much information, tells me that he was in person at the scene of these events some time later, and that there were forty or forty-five skeletons on the ground.

An Indian called Big-Foot Jack, who got his name from having one large and one small foot, was at the time considered to be the leader of the wild Indians. His track was never seen after this time, so the presumption is that he was killed.

The Period of Concealment

These events were considered at the time to have put an end to the Yahi people. The destruction however was not absolute. The author just quoted mentions that several men and women escaped, and he voices the opinion that at the time he wrote (in 1909) they were still living "somewhere" in the mountains. We now have positive knowledge that a group did survive. As a matter of fact I have found accounts of a good many episodes, in the period between 1865 and 1908, in which white men are described as having happened upon these Indians. I may remark that practically throughout all the latter half of the nineteenth century very persistent stories were in circulation concerning the continued existence of "wild" Indians just east of the Sacramento Valley. Some such incidents have been recounted to me by men who took part in them, men whose statements it is impossible to doubt or question in any way. Some of these I will recount in a moment. Such people told of their experiences at the time when the incidents occurred, but were mostly set down as plain liars. Accounts of encounters with wild Indians were even printed in the papers. Ethnologists such as Dixon, and later on Kroeber, were interested in similar stories, and often looked for corroboration. In general however people listened with skepticism, and all such tales, however warmly presented, were set down as mere invention or the survival of an old tradition. It is a curious example of truth seeming stranger than fiction. In dealing with the history of the Yahi I may proceed to describe therefore what might be called a period of retirement. Through their last survivor we know something of the life they led through this period, and something of their dwelling places. The main point is that the few survivors reverted more and more to their old mode of life, hunting with the bow, and keeping as much out of sight as possible. They were seen only by accident. Through this period they were probably the most nearly primitive of all the North American Indians.

Certain details of their life are interesting and may be discussed briefly here. The Indians took up their abode at first in the cañon of Mill Creek. They never were known to commit another murder, though once or twice, as we know now, they tried to: that is, they shot arrows at whites who were pursuing them. They gradually came to realize that their only chance of security lay in concealment. In the winter time they lived as best they could along Mill Creek. Fish they obtained with the spear of the usual California two-pronged type, armed with gigs. Acorns they gathered in a number of places, and when the crop was good these probably formed a very important part of their subsistence. Deer they hunted with a device consisting of a sort of a decoy, or more properly a disguise, which they wore, simulating meanwhile the actions of a deer. A deerskin blanket was part of the outfit, and on top they put a stuffed deer head. . . . They sometimes hollowed out the horns to make them light, and got the whole thing up in as convincing a manner as possible. By so disguising himself, the Yahi hunter was able to approach near enough to deer to get a "dead shot" with a bow. The last

[144]

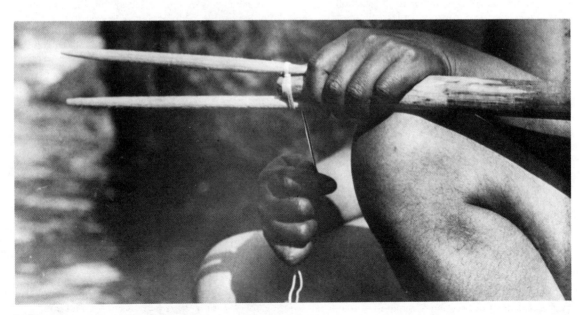

Lashing the prongs to the shaft of the salmon harpoon.

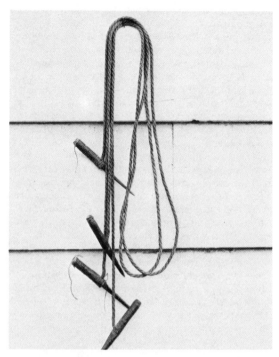

Two pairs of toggle-heads for the salmon harpoon. These specimens were found in the last Yahi camp in 1908. They are now specimens 1-19574-5 in the University of California Museum of Anthropology.

[145]

Flaying a deer.

survivor of the tribe was extremely skilful at imitating the bleat of a young fawn, and had moreover practiced himself in the art of imitating the actions of the deer in rubbing its horns on the brush. He could really put up a most plausible mimicry. I presume such devices never actually deceive the animals. They seem rather to fill them with curiosity, and they approach to see what is going on. A friend of mine who has a good deal of skill in such matters tells me that wild animals depend more on their noses than their eyes, anyway. The scent of a man will send them careening; but, on the other hand, if the hunter will approach up wind, wild creatures often exhibit the blandest naïveté. The Yana at any rate worked these methods with considerable success. They also snared deer, with a noose made of milkweed fiber. To prevent the animal from going clear through, they laced fine string across after the noose was set. They were fairly good bowmen, and killed even wildcat and bear. In the summer time they ranged as far east as the summit of Mount Lassen on the upper slopes of which they hunted, secure from intrusion. The journey took four nights' travel.

After some years they were compelled to abandon Mill Creek because of the increasing settlement of the whites. I do not know exactly when this happened, but they were on Mill Creek as late as 1894 [see below in this paper]. Toward the latter part of their history, at any rate, they were living in the cañon of Deer Creek. This whole cañon is extremely wild. The lava cliffs are very abrupt, so abrupt that in most places one can get down only with a rope. Between the cliffs and the creek, far below, the rocky and boulder-strewn slopes are covered with the densest imaginable thickets. Just at Sulphur Creek there is a gradual descent, and a trail, which crosses Deer Creek and surmounts the cañon wall a couple of miles upstream. At the junction of the two streams there is the old Speegle homestead. Upstream and downstream from this, however, the cañon is wild and comparatively impenetrable, a wilderness of rocks and undergrowth, masked by clumps of pepperwood, and encircled by the towering cliffs. This whole countryside including the cañon has been exploited only as a

stock range, and the livestock did not and could not penetrate these rough stretches. An occasional wandering cowboy or hunter might pause and view the wilderness from the edge of the cliffs above. In fact this often happened. The jungles were never actually invaded however, and both above and below Sulphur Creek the Indians had little villages. I have seen both of them, and they were so skilfully disposed among pepperwoods that they were practically invisible. The thickets in the trough of the cañon never were explored until the arrival of a new factor in the country—engineers surveying for power sites. It was due to a party of engineers that the Indians' encampments were finally discovered.

Toward the latter part of their history they were given, not to open violence, but to the robbing of cabins when the owners were away. I do not know the reason for this behavior. It involved always the risk of discovery, and the possibility of being shot down. There were some white men in the region who would have welcomed the chance to kill an Indian. I might explain that robbing cabins is more serious than it sounds. In the spring the cattlemen carry into the hills on pack trains quantities of provisions, for the subsistence of their *vaqueros* during the annual "round-up." For a number of weeks everyone is busy riding over the hills and into the gullies, and routing out the cattle for branding, and to be driven to the valley for sale. The necessary supplies are usually "cached" at long intervals at some shanty, and used as needed. Anyone, whether he is the proper owner or not, is at liberty to use this food if he needs it. Stockmen ride far and wide in their business, and there is a sort of freemasonry among them. "Grub" is more or less community property. When Indians were concerned however it was different. Aside from the fact that they were outside of this freemasonry, they never were satisfied with enjoying or pilfering a meal or two. They habitually gathered up the whole stock, which they found in a cabin, and carried it off bodily. Such incidents caused endless inconvenience and loss to the cattle owners. Often a round-up had to be interrupted, while everybody rode off to the valley for food. A delay of several weeks might be entailed, and the cattle collected might meanwhile scatter to the most inaccessible places, leaving all the work to be done over again. The Indians sometimes took even the barley intended for horse-feed. Canned stuff they avoided. It has been suggested that they may once have been poisoned by some that had spoiled; or that they did not know how to open the cans. My experience with the last survivor was that he liked nothing soft or semiliquid, and most canned provisions are of this nature. He thought such food produced a discharge from the mucous membrane, like a bad cold. His objections seemed to be based about equally on esthetic, hygienic, and moral considerations. Such a dislike as he had for gruels,

soups, sauces, eggs, milk and other soft provender amounted to a positive avoidance. It is I think highly typical of these Indians that in robbing a camp they should take away the barley, but leave behind the canned corn. In later years sheep became common in the hills, and the Indians often increased their food supply by shooting or snaring stray ones. When their village was invaded, numbers of sheepskins were found.

The Indians seem to have begun this sort of thing in 1885. At least it was habitual with them after that date. Certain camps and cabins they robbed with some regularity every spring; for example Elijah Graham's cabin on Deer Creek. Any one of

[147]

Deer snare found at "Bear's Hiding Place" in 1908. It now forms number 7 in the Stilson collection. The tapering rope is twisted of three somewhat unequal strands of milkweed or perhaps Indian hemp. The heavy end is spliced into a loop for the running noose.

View across Deer Creek cañon in the region of the camps most recently inhabited by the remnant of the Yahi.

several reasons might have driven them to this course at this time. Their best hunters may have died, for example, or the increasing number of campers and hunters, to say nothing of permanent settlers, may have made the game wilder. They seem to have committed their robberies always in the spring. This probably followed from the fact that their previous summer's supply of dried fish and acorns was always exhausted by that time, and it was still too early for their trip to Mount Lassen, which would be still covered with snow. Spring was regularly a time of scarcity with all Indians, and this small group, hemmed in by whites of whom they had a deathly fear, must have confronted utter starvation every year.

I shall proceed to recount briefly the instances where these Indians were seen, or where their traces were found, from the time of the tribal killing described on a previous page, to the breaking up of their village by surveyors in 1908. Toward the latter part of this time at least, the group consisted of Ishi, his sister or cousin, his mother, who grew to be very old, and an old man not his father. The reduction to this number was however very gradual, as the following incidents will show:

1865(?)—After the killing at the "three knolls," three Yahi women, two men, and a number of children present themselves at Hi Good's place on Dry Creek and say that they are ready to be taken to the reservation. They later run away however to the hills (Anderson, [chap. 15]).

1868.—Thirty-three wild Indians (presumably Yahi) are killed at Campo Seco. (Information from D. B. Lyon.)

March, 1870.—Mr. W. J. Segraves loses some beeves, which are "run off" at night. Having been warned against Indians, he sends for Hi Good, and the two, accompanied by George Spires and Bill Sublett, trail the Indians with dogs. Some difficulty is encountered, as the dogs sometimes follow the trail freely, and sometimes refuse to follow it at all. They finally lead the party into an Indian village or "campoodie." There are several huts in a sort of round meadow, hidden away in a clump of pepperwood (laurel). The village is . . . on Mill Creek, about 25 miles from its mouth. The huts themselves are round or oval, and made of pepperwood boughs. In the village the only live animal is a dog, who is not friendly but makes no noise, and soon vacates. Here Segraves finds the bones of his beeves. There is nothing of much interest in the camp. The Indians seem to have most of their property with them.

The next day as the party is following the trail of the Indians further up the creek, they suddenly see a considerable band, some fifteen in all, returning. Good and Segraves hide behind a tree. Several Indians leave the main party, and when they finally approach the white ambush, only six or seven women, along with one old man, are left. This man is described by Segraves as "the Old Doctor." He was very old and had only one hand. I quote the rest verbatim:

"As the Indians came abreast of us, we motioned to the squaws to squat down, so as not to be in the line of fire. One old woman, when she saw that the group was covered, immediately did so. A young woman, next in line, freed herself of her pack in a flash and started to run. The old woman grabbed her by the dress and prevented her, evidently thinking that she would be shot if she tried to escape. A little girl was also with the old woman, and was held by the hand. The Old Doctor, however, tried to get away. Good did the shooting, while I 'called' the shots. The first two missed. At the third I called 'distance!' (meaning that the range was exactly right). At the fourth shot, the Old Doctor collapsed. The weapons we used were sixteen-shot Henry repeaters, a new weapon at the time. The Indians in this party were loaded down with acorns and similar truck."

Cliffs at the rim of Deer Creek cañon, opposite mouth of Sulphur Creek. The rock and brush in the foreground are typical vegetation. The base of cliffs such as these is often from 500 to 1,000 feet above the stream.

The only Indians actually captured at this time are the two women just mentioned, and the small girl who was with them. The rest fly into the brush and disappear. A short time later an old man comes in. He evidently has failed to hear the shooting. A young fellow, said to be Ishi, is with him, but is too wild to approach closer than two hundred yards. Being unarmed, they are not fired upon. That night the party camps at the "campoodie." Next day the old man offers to bring in his relatives, and is taken back to the scene of the Old Doctor's death. The Indian, loudly calling on his people, asks permission to mount a boulder in order to look about. He seizes the opportunity to jump down on the other side of the boulder, and gets clear away.

Two weeks later the old man comes in the night-time to Segraves' cabin with eleven other people, four men and seven women. The fourth man is Ishi. He is at this time about sixteen years old and is lighter in complexion than the rest (Segraves visited Ishi at the University and positively identified him as the same person. This would make him sixty-two years old at the time of his death). The old man is thought to be Ishi's father. They make a formality of surrendering their bows to the number of five. These are about five feet long, and so strong that Segraves cannot unbend them. The whole party are taken down to Good's cabin; but he is away in Tehama. While waiting around for him to return, George Spires takes a sudden notion to weigh himself on a set of steelyards. He throws a rope over a limb to suspend the steelyards by, when the Indians take a notion that they are to be hanged. So they all run away and are never seen again. (This episode is described in Powers, but not accurately.) The only ones finally remaining in captivity are the two women and the little girl who were taken at the time of the Doctor's death.

These three are handed over to a white man named Carter, living about a mile from Acorn Hollow on Deer Creek. The young woman about this time gives birth to a baby, who is called Snowdrop (Powers gives this same incident, in highly colored form). The white man was not

[149]

her father, but one of the wild Indians. The little girl who was captured with the old woman is called "Muchacha." Both she and the mother of Snowdrop are thought by Segraves to be Ishi's sisters. Nothing is known of the final disposition of these people. (Information obtained from Mr. W. J. Segraves of Susanville, in 1915.)

1870.—An Indian boy living with Good "hooks" his cache of money. Good is very angry and threatens to "settle" with him. Shortly after that the boy murders Good with a rifle. The body he drags by the feet with a lasso from his pony, and buries it under some rocks. A Mr. Brown (who had a stage stable at the ford one mile northeast of Vina), Andy Post, and Sandy Young, previously mentioned, found the body by the odor four days later. The murdered man's hair was also sticking out between the rocks. Possibly this Indian boy is the one described above as having six toes. He was executed by Young. (Anderson, [chap. 15] ; private information from Mrs. G. W. Williams at Tehama; Wells also refers to this incident).

1870.—During this year and occasionally in after years, Mr. Norvall, working for A. C. Weed, occasionally sees sheep with arrows in them. In one case, the arrow was sticking in the sheep's wool, the sheep himself being unscratched. (Information from Mr. Norvall, 1915.)

April, 1871.—J. J. Bogard, Jim Baker, Scott Wellman, and Norman Kingsley are camped at Wild Horse Corral, in Morgan Valley. They are busy "running" cattle. They find where the Indians had wounded a steer. They follow the animal, the trail being made plain by the blood. They finally pick up a broken arrow. When they come onto the Indians, the latter "skip." Being pressed for time, instead of skinning the animal, they cut off chunks of meat, tear the hide off, and throw it into the brush. The next day the whites trail the Indians with dogs, and corner them in a cave, and kill about thirty. In this cave there is "about a ton" of dried meat.

In the cave with the meat were some Indian children. Kingsley could not bear to kill these children with his 56-calibre Spencer rifle. "It tore them up so bad." *So he did it with his 38-calibre Smith and Wesson revolver.* (Information from Mr. Norvall, 1915.)

It was evident soon afterwards that even this was not the final end of the Yahi, for the bodies of the slain Indians disappeared. The Yahi had a tribal custom of cremation. Evidently the bodies were disposed of in this or in some other way. The tender sensibilities of the fellow who preferred to shoot babies with a 38-calibre revolver are certainly worthy of remark.

1878.—Rafe Johnson, son of "old Peg Leg" Johnson, in company with Jim Melick, lassoes two squaws near Black Oak Mountain. An Indian man is shot through the thigh, and a child is shot through the ankle. One of the women "is taken to Nome Lackee, the other to Redding." [There is an evident mistake here, as the Nome Lackee Reservation was abandoned long before this. Possibly the woman was taken to Round Valley. Information from D. B. Lyon, 1915.]

February, 1885.—The Indians rob Norvall's cabin, at the head of Little Antelope Creek. At the same time they rob Girt's cabin, four miles away. (Information from Mr. Norvall, 1915.)

April, 1885.—Mr. Norvall one day approaches a cabin on Dry Creek. Hearing noises inside, he goes around in back. Four Indians were jumping out of the window. Seeing him, they all got in a row, and stood waiting for developments. A young woman is wearing three old jumpers, with the addition of little else. An old man has an old overcoat and an old rifle barrel. There are two young fellows, one of them with a crippled foot. "Rafe Johnson did that," remarks Mr. Norvall. The woman points over toward Mill Creek and says *Dos chiquitos papooses* (Spanish jargon, meaning two small children). Inside the cabin they had piled up a lot of discarded clothing, evidently preparing to carry it away. Mr. Norvall treats them in a friendly way. (Information from Mr. Norvall, 1915.)

October, 1885.—The Indians slip into Norvall's cabin while he is away, and leave two baskets. These baskets are now in the University Museum.

. . . This is probably a result of Norvall's friendly bearing in the previous episode. (Information from Mr. Norvall.)

Autumn, 1885.—Sheep are found with arrows in them. (Information from Mr. Norvall.)

1889.—Mr. D. B. Lyon, a young boy at the time, is hunting deer up Big Antelope Creek, 16 miles east of Red Bluff. He moves about an isolated patch of buckeye brush which lies in a gully, under a rock cliff. The dog hears something moving and goes in, but a moment later comes out afraid. Whatever is in the brush makes noises like tomcats fighting. (His idea at present is that the Indians did it, trying to scare him away.) Instead of running, he throws a rock into the brush to ascertain what is making the noise. The rock hits an Indian, who grunts. One thing leads to another, and Lyon finally goes in to rout out whatever is there. There is open ground all around, so the quarry insists on keeping among the buckeyes. He finally presses them close, and suddenly stumbles over packs, which they have dropped. Then he knows they are Indians. One of them has been carrying half a dozen sheep legs; the sweat from his hands is still on the wool. They also drop a sheepskin. Lyon stops and kicks this stuff over, to see what it is. They suddenly fire three arrows at him, one of them grazing his hat brim. One of these arrows breaks off against a rock just in front of him. Another he picks up and keeps. He takes time also to pick up a small cloth bag which afterwards is found to contain an interesting arrow-making outfit (the specimens are now at the University Museum). At this point Lyons considers that his curiosity is satisfied, and he very properly withdraws.

(Mr. Lyon's explanation of the incident is that the Indians were traveling across country, and hiding in this patch of brush during the daytime.)

1894.—Elijah Graham gets exasperated at the persistent robbing of his cabin, and to punish the thief, leaves there a lot of poisoned flour. To avoid accidents, he writes a plain notice that the flour is poisoned and leaves it where it must be seen. The flour nevertheless is taken. This he cites as proof that there are Indians in the country, to whom the robbing of cabins is due, but hardly anybody takes him seriously. Whether this episode reduces the number of the Yahi or not, we do not know. (Information from D. B. Lyon.)

1894.—Mr. Lyon and his brother find what they at first take for a bear track, near Mill Creek, above Avery's. It turns out to be a barefoot human track, very wide across the toes. The individual evidently has not worn shoes, for his foot is very calloused, with cracks across the bottom. They follow up his tracks, but the Indian evidently finds he is being pursued, for he jumps from the top of a bluff into the top of a tree, and escapes. Lyon remarks to his brother that he would not make the same descent for any sum. (Information from D. B. Lyon.)

1906.—The cabin at the Occidental mine, operated by Mr. Gillenwater with two employees, is robbed. Among other things, what is called in the country a "war bag," in other words, a U.S. Army dunnage bag, is taken. (Information from M. C. Polk.)

1908.—W. D. Polk and K. Crowder are camped at the Speegle place, where Sulphur Creek joins Deer Creek. They go down Deer Creek a mile or so, and anticipating an Indian visit, one of them slips back along under the edge of the bluff with a "30-30" rifle. The Indians as a matter of fact are just preparing to carry off the eatables out of the cabin. They take alarm, and dash across Deer Creek. One of them in his haste drops his headgear, which the whites pick up. Nothing is left in the cabin but a little rice and some canned stuff.

An effort is made to track them up, but they are too cunning. They step only on rocks, where they leave no footprints, and take to the water so they can not be followed with dogs.

Discovery of the Yahi Village in 1908

This brings the history of the Yahi to its final phase. The next event is the breaking up of their village. I should like to give an account of that, and tell something more of its situation. The

[151]

episode begins with a survey of the lower part of Deer Creek cañon by a party of engineers for the Oro Water, Light and Power Company. I have heard accounts of the events from several of the people who took part in it. As usual, it is somewhat difficult to get an account that is absolutely consistent and coherent.

The Power company was considering the erection of a dam just below Sulphur Creek, and were surveying a ditch which was to convey the impounded water down the cañon to a projected power plant somewhere below. This ditch was to follow the south bank of the creek, through some extremely difficult country, mentioned above. The surveying party was working some three miles below Sulphur Creek, engaged in brushing out a line. On the evening of November 9, 1908, two young men, Alf Lafferty and Ed Duensing, were returning up-stream to their camp about sunset. By the margin of the creek they suddenly saw a naked Indian standing on a rock, armed with a long-spear. The Indian was undoubtedly looking for his supper with a fish-spear, but his wild look startled both men. When he suddenly caught sight of them, being probably startled himself, he gave what they described as a vicious snarl, and brandished his spear. They had been searching for a crossing place, in order to strike an old Indian trail which leads up to the other side of the stream. When the Indian snarled, as they tell the story, any crossing place looked good to them. They waited for nothing further. When they got to camp their story was received with varying emotions. Most of the party were boundlessly pleased with the account as a work of fiction. J. M. Apperson, however, who had been convinced for a long time that Indians actually were at large in this region, went down stream early next morning to see what he could find. Along with him went Charley Herrick, who whiled away the time as they walked professing profound disbelief in the whole thing. When they went on the south side of the creek, and began working through the thick brush on the steep hillside above the stream, an

Remnants of a hut at "Bear's Hiding Place" on the south side of Deer Creek some three miles down stream from the mouth of Sulphur Creek. This is one of the three structures in which the remnant of the Yahi were discovered in 1908. The photograph was taken two years after the abandonment of the site.

arrow was shot at them, narrowly missing Apperson. After some debate they turned back.

In the meantime the surveying party went back to work, chopping out their survey line. About ten o'clock in the morning they suddenly walked into an Indian encampment or village. Two Indians, running as if for their lives, were actually seen—one of them an old man, who was helped along by a middle-aged woman. They escaped over a rock "slide" and vanished in the direction of the cliffs. This fleeting glance is all we know of these individuals. They have never been seen again. Their actual fate is still unknown. In camp was found, under some blankets, a partially paralyzed old woman, frightened nearly to death, unable to move. The whites did what they could for this old person. She asked in a few words of broken Spanish for water. Apperson gave her a drink out of a canteen which was lying there, having been filled evidently at the creek below. She trembled violently, though they did their best to reassure her. The whites then helped themselves, mainly in a spirit of curiosity, to the contents of the camp—bows, arrows, skin blankets—and after prying about, went back to camp for dinner. When they returned next day, to satisfy their further curiosity, no

Indians were about, and even the old woman was gone. Her people evidently returned and carried her away to some other shelter. Where this was, we do not know. Some effort was made later to find these Indians, but no sign of them was seen. They evidently considered that the whites were still after them, and hid themselves away.

A number of points in the arrangement of the camp and the position of the lodges may be worth mention. The village consisted of three structures. One was a shelter of pepperwood boughs, with a framework of rough poles. This was just under cover of some large laurel trees. In front and somewhat to one side, was a lurking place under some very heavy brush, where someone had sat for years making arrow-points by chipping glass. The Yahi

Framework of another house in the same camp. Also photographed after it had stood vacant and the brush-covering had been blown away.

Interior of same, showing the cross-sticks for smoking or drying food.

learned long ago that glass worked more evenly than obsidian, and the supply being more available, their arrow-points were regularly made of it. The bottles they picked up around foothill camps. A bushel or more of minute glass chips had accumulated here. Some distance to the east was another shelter, heavily smoked and showing marks of very long occupation, made of pieces of driftwood, an old wagon canvas and some odds and ends. Both structures were in the midst of a perfectly impenetrable jungle. A third structure consisted of a framework of poles, lashed together with bark, the whole very firm and strong. A few feet above the ground was a series of cross-sticks. It was evidently to be covered with a thatching of laurel. someone has suggested that it was to be used for smoking salmon. All of these lodges were of tiny proportions, but rather cunningly put together. They were of a simple *A*-shape. Between the lodges the brush was as dense as could be, but a fairly clear trail wound in and out through the undergrowth, connecting

[154]

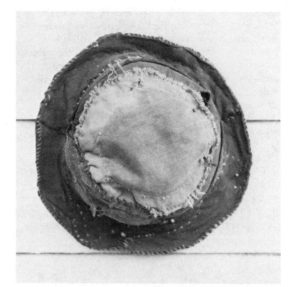

Hat patched of many fragments by a Yahi Indian and abandoned when he was surprised in an attempt to rifle a cabin on Deer Creek. This hat is now specimen number 1-19581 in the University of California Museum of Anthropology.

them. Near the first house, but somewhat closer to the creek, was a circular pit, a yard or more across and about as deep. This the Indians packed full of snow in the winter time. The melting of this snow supplied them with water for a while, and saved the labor of going to the creek, which roars along the floor of the cañon some five hundred feet below. There was also involved in every trip some risk of discovery. They called the camp in their language *Wowunupo'mu tetnA,* "Bear's Hiding Place," probably because there were bear dens in this wilderness of brush and boulders before the Indians took up their abode there. Across the creek, and less than a mile above, there is a fine little flat beside the stream with remains of old Indian house-pits. This was the Yahi village of Tcapa'launa, inhabited before the days of the Yahi troubles. Probably Indians had never lived at Bear's

[This Yahi] tray was taken at "Bear's Hiding Place" in 1908 and forms number 30 in the J. McCord Stilson collection at Chico.

Hiding Place until the last remnant of the tribe took up their abode there.

The village site has now been visited by a number of people, scientific and otherwise. I think they will all agree that the placing of the lodges was the work of people who were not only desperately anxious to hide themselves, but who knew thoroughly well how to do it. The houses were built where they were invisible from the cliffs on either side. The Indians passed down to the creek, which was very important to them on account of the fish in it, under the shelter of a growth of laurel. Thus they could move about and still remain hidden. Moreover, they avoided making visible trails, especially near the water. The little path that leads down from the lodges under and through the thicket, ramifies and disappears as it approaches the stream. In other words, they went down by different

ways, to avoid making one conspicuous pathway. In making the needful paths through the brush, they bent aside the necessary twigs. Cutting or breaking them would have made the path much more conspicuous. I doubt if an observer on the cliff would ever have seen the Indians if he had been looking directly down upon them. Altogether, the place and its selection showed considerable evidence of craft, and to the wandering hunter or rider on the mountains round about, the locality would have looked always like a genuine bear's hiding place, for all the evidence of human habitation to be seen.

Ishi it will be observed was not seen. He probably discharged the arrow which almost wounded Apperson, and was undoubtedly present, and possibly waiting for another good shot, when the camp was acutally invaded. The whites were armed with revolvers, and Ishi, being a belligerent, probably

[155]

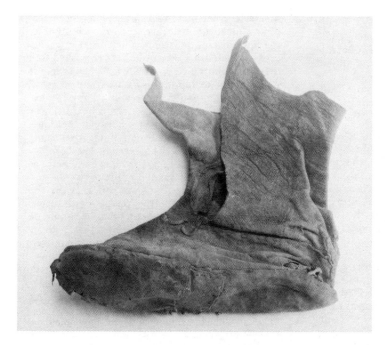

Moccasin of deerskin sewn with sinew. This was taken from the Yahi camp at "Bear's Hiding Place" in 1908. It now forms number 32 in the Stilson collection. The shoe was too small for Ishi's foot and must have been worn by one of the women of his group.

kept just out of sight, which was of course in conformity with the best military strategy. The property taken from the camp is now largely in possession of the University. The most picturesque specimen is a blanket or cape of wildcat skins. The remainder included furs, rope, bows, arrows, and baskets. It is somewhat pathetic to reflect that this material, taken in mere curiosity, may have meant the difference between survival and destruction to the poor Indians. Certain it is that as a group they were never heard of afterwards, and all of them but Ishi may have lost their lives as a result of the fatigue, hunger, and exposure entailed by leaving their camp. Apperson went through his pockets at the time trying to find something that he could leave as a present, to prove to them his friendly intentions. He had nothing however, and when he came back they were gone.

The encounter with the Indians made a considerable stir in the press. Some hope was felt at the University that the group might be found again sooner or later. It was thought that the members of the group might be able to supply many details concerning the life and culture of the Yana peoples, and would certainly supply information concerning their own language and the linguistic geography of the region. Several efforts were made to get in touch with people who might encounter the Yahi, and one expedition was sent into the field to locate them if possible.

[156]

October, 1910.—Mr. Walter Hunt and T. T. Waterman camped for three weeks in Deer Creek cañon, making a reconnaisance of the region in the hope of recovering their trail. On this occasion the little village at Bear's Hiding Place was visited, and some photographs taken. Nothing could be done in the way of following the Indians up, for they had disappeared, leaving no trace.

History of the Last Survivor

Such was the tragic end of the last remnant of the Yahi tribe. Except for one individual, our account closes here. The members of the tribe who were seen at this time seem to have perished from cold, hunger, and exposure, without ever returning to their camp.

August, 1911.—Nearly three years later, at a slaughterhouse four miles from Oroville, 32 miles away, very early one morning there suddenly appeared from nowhere a naked Indian. His only garment was an old cast-off undershirt. . . .*

There seemed to be little point in letting this individual remain in jail. He was not charged with anything, and it seemed highly desirable to bring him to the University, where facilities for recording information were better. The county authorities at Oroville were most benignantly disposed toward the Indian, and were most considerate in every way. As soon as it became evident that the "wild" man was of Yana extraction, they sent a young officer to Redding to bring down an old survivor of the Yana people there. This was Sam Batwee, who had been informant for Curtin and later for Sapir. Batwee was to be interpreter and companion for our wild man. He evinced a patronizing attitude, which developed *pari passu* with cordial symptoms of dislike on the part of Ishi. Later on it was a curious spectacle to see these two surviving representatives of an almost vanished race treating each other with the most distant politeness. They never learned to care for each other. Poor old Batwee wished to impress his importance on the "wild" man, while the wild man looked upon this civilized Indian as neither Indian nor white. He seemed to object most of all to Batwee's taste in wearing a beard. There was a good deal of divergence between their dialects, besides, which made communication somewhat laborious. Batwee had very little tact or adjustability, and Ishi regarded him as a tiresome old fool, though he was too polite to say so. A factor still more important was this, that the Yahi had learned to view all other peoples with suspicion and hostility. It was interesting that he should be readier to make friends with whites than with other Indians like himself. The Yahi had apparently been utterly isolated for a considerable time even before their tribe became so much reduced.

_____
*Waterman here repeats his narrative of Ishi's capture and his own meeting with Ishi at the Oroville jail, from "The Last Tribe of California," above. It has been omitted here.—Ed.

[At the time of Ishi's capture his apparel consisted] of an old slaughterhouse apron of canvas which the people put on him when he was first found. His strength was much reduced at this time through hardship and lack of food. He had wandered in the hills apparently living on what he could pick up as he went. For some time his most substantial food had been manzanita berries. On the point of absolute collapse, he came to the slaughterhouse to look for food. The dogs barked and attracted the butchers, who were just getting up. When first seen, Ishi was crouching on the ground in the corral, with the dogs sniffing about him. The exact route of his wanderings is still unknown. His hair he had singed off close to his scalp, throwing water on with his hands to keep from burning himself. This is (of course) the Indian custom on the death of a relative. His solitary condition seemed to indicate at the time that all his relatives had died. Aside from emaciation and some diminution of energy, his condition at that time was perfect. His feet, which had never seen a shoe, were fine examples of what the human foot should be. They were modeled in plaster by the Department of Pediatrics of the Medical School as examples of perfect and undeformed feet. Shoes, by the way, he hated, explaining that they might trip him up. He little by little recovered his spirits, and in the last years of his life was serenity personified.

I should like to tell something of my acquaintance with Ishi, especially those incidents which illustrate the character of the man and shed light on his peculiar viewpoint. I may begin by speaking of railroad trains. In bringing him down to the University, where his home was to be for the rest of his life, it was necessary to take the train. One fine morning found Ishi and myself, and an attendant Indian and some hundreds of interested pale-faces, waiting on the platform for the train to come in. As Number Five appeared in the distance and came whistling and smoking down the humming rails in a cloud of dust, Ishi wanted to hide behind something. We were standing some distance from the track as I feared that he might

be afraid of the engine. He had often seen trains. Later he told us in his own language that he had previously seen trains wandering by in the distance. But he had not known they ran on tracks. When he saw them he always lay down in the grass or behind a bush until they were out of sight. He visualized a train as some devil-driven, inhuman prodigy. Security lay not in keeping off the right-of-way, but in keeping out of sight.

Here is another fact that illustrates his personal attitude. To a primitive man, what ought to prove most astonishing in a modern city? I would have said at once, the height of the buildings. For Ishi, the overwhelming thing about San Francisco was the number of people. That, he never got over. Until he came into civilization, the largest number of people he had ever seen together at any one time was five! At first a crowd gathering around him alarmed him and made him uneasy. He never entirely got over his feeling of awe, even when he learned that everybody meant well. The big buildings he was interested in. He found them edifying, but he was not greatly impressed. The reason, as far as I could understand it, was this. He mentally compared a towering twelve-story building, not with his hut in Deer Creek which was only four feet high, but with the cliffs and crags of his native mountains. He had something in some way analogous stored up in his experience. But to see five thousand human beings alive at once was something undreamed of, and it upset him.

Generally speaking, which is to be considered more interesting and surprising, *per se,* an ordinary trolley car or an automobile? For Ishi, the trolley car, every time. I stupidly expected him to grow excited over his first automobile, as I did over mine. To Ishi, of course, both were miracles, plain and simple. Both the auto and the street car were agitated and driven about by some supernatural power; one as much as the other. The street car, however, was the bigger of the two, it had a gong which rang loudly at times, and moreover was provided with an attachment which went "shoo!" and blew the dust away when the air-brakes were released.

[157]

Ishi would watch trolley cars by the hour. Electric lights, door-knobs, safety-pins, typewriters, he considered curious or wonderful according to some mysterious standard of his own. Getting water by turning a knob pleased him boundlessly. On the whole it was a limited number of simple things that gave him most astonishment.

Aeroplanes, by the way, he took quite philosophically. We took him to Golden Gate Park to see Harry Fowler start to fly across the continent. When the plane was trundled out and the engine started, the Indian was surprised and amused at the uproar it created. The machine was finally launched, and after a long circuit, soared back over our heads. As it came overhead we particularly called his attention to it. He was mildly interested. "Saltu?" he said interrogatively, nodding toward the plane a thousand feet skyward, "White man up there?" When we said yes he laughed a bit, apparently at the white man's funny ways, and let it pass. Either he was ready to expect anything by that time, or else his amazement was too deep for any outward expression. Like most "nature-people," he was inclined to preserve his dignity in the face of the unfamiliar or the overwhelming, giving very little sign. Under equivalent stimulation of course the pale-face dances about and squeals.

Ishi was, however, jarred completely out of his equanimity by a window-shade. On the morning of his second day at the Museum, I found him trying to raise the shade to let the sunlight in. It gave me a queer feeling to realize that never in his experience, either in his cañon home or in the Oroville jail, where he spent his first thirty hours of civilization as an honored guest, had he encountered the common roller shade. He tried to push it to one side and it would not go. He pushed it up and it would not stay. I showed him how to give it a little jerk and let it run up. The subsequent five minutes he utilized for reflection. When I came back at the end of that time, he was still trying to figure out where the shade had gone.

Concerning foods he had certain prejudices which he was never able to overcome. For example he politely asked to be excused from gravies and sauces. He did not take at all kindly to the notion of boiling food. Fried, baked, roasted, broiled, or raw food he could understand. He did not like those processes which lead to semiliquids. No milk, if you please, for Ishi, and no eggs unless they were hard boiled. All such things, he said, lead to colds in the head! The real basis of his dislike seemed to be their esthetic effect. I have often wondered since just how far our eating habits might be considered messy. Ishi wanted his food dry and clean appearing. For drink he liked only transparent beverages, that could not have anything concealed about them. Tea was his idea of the proper drink. An enthusiastic chef once gave him some claret when nobody was looking. From all accounts he did not care for it. It turned out later that he thought it was medicine.

In all his personal habits he was extraordinarily neat. At his first dinner he behaved as many another man has done under similar circumstances. He waited patiently until someone let him know, by setting the example, whether a given dish was to be consumed with the aid of a spoon, a knife, some other kind of contrivance, or with the fingers. Then he calmly did likewise. His actions were always in perfectly good taste. Even during his first days in civilization, he could be taken comfortably into any company. He had a certain fastidiousness which extended to all his belongings. His effects were kept carefully in order. Not only his apparel, but his arrow-making appliances, his bow, and his other impedimenta, were always in perfect array. During the time he lived at my home a certain member of my family urged me to model my own behavior in such respects after the Indian's shining example.

Ishi moreover was remarkably clever with his hands. In his own way he was a fine workman. He made bows of perfect finish. He could chip arrow-points to perfection out of any of the materials which give a conchoidal fracture—obsidian, flint, agate, or bottle-glass. Some of his handsomest specimens were made of bromo-seltzer bottles. No more beautiful arrow-points

Ishi at the University, October, 1911.

exist than the ones he made. His finished arrow, including point, shaft, and feathering, is a model of exquisite workmanship.

On the whole he took very kindly to civilization. He seemed apprehensive at times lest we might send him back ultimately to his wilderness. Once when we were planning with much enthusiasm to take him on a camping trip, to revisit with him his foothill home, he filed a number of objections. One was that in the hills there were no chairs. A second was, that there were no houses or beds. A third was, that there was very little to eat. He had been cold and gone hungry so often in the hills, that he had few illusions left. In camp, however, he proved to be a fine companion. He could swim and wash dishes and skylark with anybody, and out-walk everybody.

He convinced me that there is such a thing as a gentlemanliness which lies outside of all training, and is an expression purely of an inward spirit. It has nothing to do with artificially acquired tricks of behavior. Ishi was slow to acquire [159] the tricks of social contact. He never learned to shake hands but he had an innate regard for the other fellow's existence, and an inborn considerateness, that surpassed in fineness most of the civilized breeding with which I am familiar.

For a number of years Ishi lived at the Museum. Finally through the action of the Regents of the University he was appointed Museum Helper; so that for the last years of his life he was self-supporting. Here he served as a ready informant. A considerable mass of material was obtained from him concerning the ethnography of his tribe. He never learned to speak English correctly or fluently, and the difficulties of mastering uninterpreted Yahi incidentally to other duties were too great for the members of the Department. In the summer of 1914 Dr. Saxton Pope and two members of the Department of Anthropology spent four weeks with Ishi in his original haunts. A good deal of information was thus obtained. Luckily for the University, Dr. Edward Sapir of the Canadian Geological Survey was enabled to work with Ishi for a number of weeks in the summer of 1915. Dr. Sapir already had some mastery of the other Yana dialects. His work with the Indian was primarily linguistic and resulted in a remarkable series of texts. Ishi's life came to an end on March 25, 1916, as the result of an oversusceptibility to tuberculosis to which he never developed the slightest immunity.

A final word about Ishi himself would be in place, but I find it difficult to say the right thing. It was patent that he liked everybody, and everybody liked him. He never wished to go back to the wilds, naturally enough, for there was nothing to go back to. He had however, to be reassured repeatedly that we had no intention of sending him back. As a matter of fact I think the closing years were far the happiest of his life.

Conclusion

It is only fair to certain of my informants to say that evidence has been advanced to prove that "wild" Indians have been at large in the Deer Creek and Mill Creek region even since Ishi came into civilization. I might give a couple of examples of this evidence:

1911.—Informant, hunting in Mill Creek cañon, finds on a sand bar a barefoot track, by a tiny smoldering fire. The sand was damp, and the track was fresh. The place was about seven miles above Avery's. The footpring was made by a person who had never worn a shoe. (Information by F. W. Grimm, of Red Bluff, 1915.)

1912.—Mr. D. B. Lyon enters a clump of heavy brush up Dry Creek. In the center he finds a bed made of twigs. The twigs had been gathered from the *inside* of the clump. There were no marks on the outside that the brush had even been entered or disturbed. No white man, according to the informant's belief, could conceivably have had any motive in preparing the bed, in its situation.

1913.—John Moke, of Chico, and his daughter find in a cave on Mill Creek signs of "Indian" occupation. In 1914 the University party took Ishi into the cave, which was as far as we know in the same condition, and he said no Indians had been there since the "old people" of former

generations had lived there, and smoked the ceiling with their cooking fires.

I presume this matter is still one in which a person is entitled to his own opinion. Personally, I cannot convince myself that any Indians survived the breaking-up of their village. Ishi says himself that his "sister" ran in one direction and he went in another, and he never saw her afterwards. He showed interest in the stories of Indians still at large, but seemed to have few hopes in that connection. Conversation on that subject always left him in a fit of depression, from which it took him some time to recover.

Sources of Information

A number of persons were good enough to supply direct information from notes and personal experiences, concerning the events mentioned in the present paper. Thanks in this connection are due Mr. Richard Gernon, Mr. F. W. Grimm, Mr. Chris Kauffman, Mrs. Ludwig, Mr. D. B. Lyon, Mr. L. L. McCoy, Mr. Norvall, and Mr. Owen, all of Red Bluff; Mr. M. C. Polk and Mr. J. McCord Stilson, of Chico; Mr. W. J. Segraves of Susanville; and Mrs. G. W. Williams of Tehama. The following list includes the printed works cited:

Anderson, R. A.
  1909. Fighting the Mill Creeks (Chico).
Carson, A. T.
  1915. Captured by the Mill Creeks (Chico?).
Curtin, Jeremiah
  1898. Creation Myths of Primitive America.
Dixon, R. B., and Kroeber, A. L.
  1913. New Linguistic Families in California, Am. Anthropologist, n. s., 15, 647-655.
Powell, J. W.
  1885. Report to Director, 6th Ann. Rep. Bur. Am. Ethn., pp. xxi-lvii.
  1886. Linguistic Families of America, north of Mexico, 7th Ann. Rep. Bur. Am. Ethn., pp. 7-139.
Powers, Stephen
  Tribes of California, U.S. Inter. Dept. Geog. and Geol. Survey, 3. Contributions to North American Ethnology.
Sapir, Edward
  1910. Yana Texts, together with Yana Myths, collected by R. B. Dixon, Univ. Calif. Publ. Am. Arch. Ethn., 10, 1-235.
  1917. The position of Yana in the Hokan Stock, Univ. Calif. Publ. Am. Arch. Ethn., 13, 1-34.

U.S.–Office of Indian Affairs
  1858. Report of Commissioner.

U.S.–War Department
  War of the Rebellion: Official records of the Union and
    Confederate Armies. Ser. 1, vol. 50, parts 1-2,
    Operations on the Pacific Coast, July 1, 1861-
    June 30, 1865.

Wells, H. L. and Chambers, W. L.
  1882. History of Butte County. 2 vols. (San Francisco).

This is A. L. Kroeber's brief chapter on the Yana and Yahi as written in 1917, when his monumental Handbook of the Indians of California *went to press. The Yana myths mentioned were recorded and published by Jeremiah S. Curtin,* Creation Myths of Primitive America *(Boston, 1898) and by Edward Sapir, "Yana Texts" (University of California Publications in American Archaeology and Ethnology, Vol. 9, No. 1 [1910]). The short section on the Yahi summarizes the historical information given earlier here, and offers new data on Yahi ethnogeography. Kroeber, writing a year after Ishi's death, is reticent on personal details about Ishi. He concludes by saying monosyllabically, "With his death the Yahi passed away." That event was a very personal and emotional one, and Kroeber's reluctance to dwell on it is understandable.*

---

4. The Yana and Yahi (1925)

A. L. Kroeber

The Yana.

ORIGIN.

The Yana are a people of fairly extensive territory but rather restricted numbers, concerning whom little general information has been extant, but to whom mystery of some kind has usually been made to attach. They were reputed of a marked physical type; their speech was not only distinctive but abnormally peculiar; in military prowess and cunning they far outshone all their neighbors; they had perhaps come from the far

Handbook of the Indians of California, Bureau of American Ethnology, Bulletin 78 (1925), Chapter 23, pp. 336-346.

east. As usual, there is a thin sediment of fact to these fancies.

As regards physical type, no measurements are available. Report makes the Yana shorter than their neighbors, and an allusion in one of their myths appears to attribute the same conviction to themselves. But they certainly are not racially anomalous to any notable degree. The few scattered survivors would pass as normal among any group of north central California.

Their warlike reputation may be due partly to the resistance offered to the whites by one or two of their bands. But whether the cause of this was actually a superior energy and courage or an unusual exasperation aided by a rough, still thinly populated, and easily defensible habitat is more doubtful. That they were feared by certain of their neighbors, such as the Maidu, argues them a hungering body of mountaineers rather than a superior stock. The hill dweller has less to lose by fighting than the wealthy lowlander. He is also less exposed, and in time of need has better and more numerous refuges available. All through California the plains peoples were the more peaceably inclined, although the stronger in numbers: the difference is one of situation reflected in culture, not of inborn quality.

[161]

The speech of the Yana disposes definitely of all theories of their remote origin. They are members of the great Hokan family. As such, their ultimate source may have been southerly; but no more and no less than that of the Achomawi, the Shasta, the Karok, the Pomo, and others. Their language, so far as its sounds and words are concerned, is perhaps somewhat nearer to the Pomo on the other side of the Sacramento Valley than to the adjacent Achomawi and Atsugewi. It has, however, certainly been long differentiated, since it has entirely lost the prefixes that are found in all other Hokan idioms, and has become a suffixing tongue. It may be added that on the chart (see Pl. 1, inset; and Fig. 17) * Yana territory looks like the end of a reflex curling movement of the interior Hokans—

* Kroeber's Plate 1 is a foldout map of the Indians of California by stocks and tribes. It is not reproduced here, nor is Fig. 17, from Kroeber's chapter on the Pomo, which shows the territory of the Pomo (on the northern California coast) and of the other Hokan speakers in California.—Ed.

Shasta, Achomawi, and Yana—from the northern end of a coastwise distribution that begins in Mexico and ends with the Pomo, Chimariko, and Karok. It is, however, possible that the Yana were once neighbors of the Pomo and became pushed apart from them as the great block of Penutians drifted up or down the Sacramento Valley. Yana tradition is silent on these questions. Like all Californians north of Tehachapi, they believe themselves to have been created in their historic seats.

MEN'S AND WOMEN'S SPEECH.

Yana speech shows one extreme peculiarity, which, as an essentially civilizational phenomenon expressed through linguistic medium, must be mentioned: The talk of men and women differed. Men spoke the women's forms when conversing with them; women always spoke female. The differences are not very great, but sufficient to disconcert one not thoroughly familiar with the tongue. Usually a suffix is clipped by women from the full male form. Thus *yana,* "person," becomes *ya* in the mouth or in the hearing of a woman; *auna,* "fire," and *hana,* "water," become *auh* and *bah.* Similarly a mortar, personified and addressed, would be called *keman-'na* if considered male, *keman-yi* if thought of as a woman. Somewhat analogous, though essentially a distinct phenomenon, is the employment of diverse roots to denote an action respectively as it is performed by men or women: *ni,* "a male goes," *ha,* "a female goes." The spring of these remarkable phenomena is unknown.

TERRITORY.

The Yana were surrounded by the Achomawi and Atsugewi, the Maidu, and the Wintun. Their holdings stretched from Pit River, on which they are said to have fronted for a distance, to Rock Creek on the south; that is, more probably, to the ridge on one or the other side of Rock Creek. In general, they ranged from the edge of the upper Sacramento Valley along the eastern tributaries of the Sacramento itself to their headwaters in the watershed beyond which the drainage flows north and south instead of westward. The summit of this divide, and the greatest landmark of the Yana country, was the ancient volcanic peak of Mount Lassen,

recently active once more: Yana Wahganupa, literally "little Mount Shasta" (Wahgala). Here the territory of two of the four Yana divisions met that of the Atsugewi and of the mountain Maidu. The whole of the Sacramento Valley in Yana latitude, east as well as west of the river, was Wintun. Yana land began with the foothills. In their lowest courses through these hills the streams often flow in narrow canyons; toward their source the beds are deep and rugged. Most of the Yana settlements were therefore in a middle belt. Those that are most accurately known and located are shown in [Map 1]. In general, Yana country was a broken and endlessly ridged and furrowed land, timbered in part, mostly covered with brush, rocky, and hard of soil.

DIVISIONS.

The Yana comprised four dialectic divisions, but the speech of the most divergent was largely intelligible. The northern dialect was called Gari'i, the central one Gata'i. The southern dialect is extinct: it may have been included in Gata'i. Beyond it was another, to which the name "Yahi" may be given, that being the term replacing Yana in the mouths of its speakers. This division is also extinct. Its recent history being a different one from that of the three other divisions, it will be treated separately. It should be admitted that the designations here applied to the four Yana groups are awkward, the "southern" one not being the most southerly. The cause is the late recognition of the Yahi division after the names of the three others had become established in print. A renaming to northeastern, northern, central, and southern would be appropriate, but would inevitably cause future confusions.

The northern group held by far the smallest territory; the drainage of Montgomery Creek into Pit River, and that of Cedar Creek, an affluent of Little Cow Creek. The northern Yana were wedged in between Wintun, Achomawi, and Atsugewi.

The Central Yana held the entire Cow Creek drainage: Cow Creek itself, Little Cow, Oak Run, Clover Creek, and North and South Forks of the Cow. To these must be added Bear Creek. The

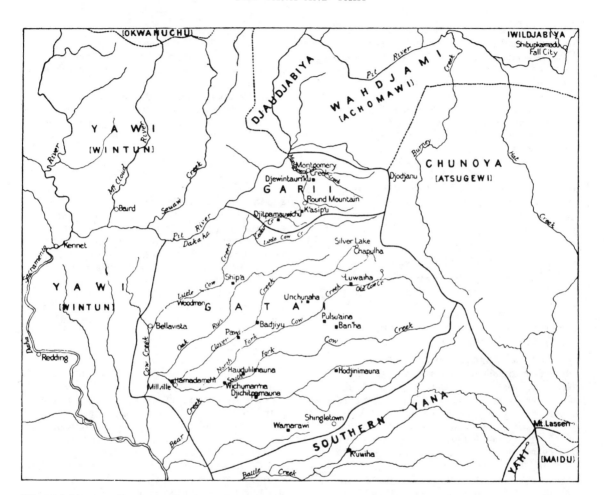

[Map 1.] Yana territory, northern part. Settlements are shown by squares; alien groups in dotted lines. Unbracketed names are Yana designations.

extreme northwestern corner of the territory shown in [Map 1] between Bellavista, Woodman, and the mouth of Squaw Creek, may have been Wintun instead of Gata'i Yana.

The southern Yana lived on Battle Creek. They also held Payne and Antelope Creeks and one or two smaller streams.

The Yahi held the course of Mill and Deer Creeks.

DESIGNATIONS AND NUMBERS.

The Yana to-day are generally known to the adjacent Indians and resident whites as Noze or Nozhi, a term of unknown origin although a Wintun source is likely. The Maidu said Kombo, although whether by this word the Yahi and southern Yana alone were meant, or all divisions of the stock, is not certain.

Sukoni-ya was a nonethnic term applied by the Yana to distant easterners: the more remote Achomawi and northeastern Maidu; perhaps also the Northern Paiute.

An average of 300 to 500 souls for each division, or 1,500 for the stock, seems a liberal computation of the pre-American numbers. To-day the two northern groups alone survive and between them can muster less than 40 full and mixed bloods, and these much scattered. The Yana as a whole suffered heavily at the hands of the whites in the first 20 years of contact, both by fighting and in massacres, and have never been even partially sheltered by reservations. None of the adjacent stocks and few of the neighboring ones, except possibly the Shasta and the Okwanuchu, have shrunk in the same ratio.

Near the central Yana village of Wichuman'na, some miles east of Millville, was a saline swamp. The dark-colored mud was taken up and dried for use as salt. Achomawi, Atsugewi, and Wintun all resorted to this place—a fact that indicates more or less chronic friendliness. This locality originated the Achomawi name for the Yana, Ti'saichi, "Salt people."

CHARACTER OF CUSTOMS.

However commendably hardy the Yana may have been, it is clear that they did not rank high among the natives of the State. They were perhaps on a level with the near-by Atsugewi and Achomawi. The little coruscations that enliven the culture of the Wintun and Maidu, for instance, are entirely lacking. Mythology, symbolism, ritual, social customs, the uses of wealth, are all of the plainest, most straightforward, and simplest character. Although bordering on both the great valley stocks, none of the Yana had any participation in the Kuksu religion that found its focus there. It is not even possible to ascribe to them any partial reflection of the valley civilization: their culture consisted of the primitive basic elements which other groups shared with them but overlaid with more special developments.

The winter house was the earth-covered one of the Modoc, Pomo, Wintun, and Maidu. They called it *igunna* and *mat'adjuwa* or *wat-guruwa.* Although

generally referred to as a "sweat house," Yana myths make clear that it was a dwelling.

Their thatched summer homes the Yana called *wawi* or *wowi,* which seems to be the generic word for house.

The Yana were situated in the region where two basketry arts meet; the northern of overlaid twining with *Xerophyllum tenax,* which they called *maha;* and the central one of coiling and twining, but without the overlay technique. The two northern divisions followed the former method chiefly if not exclusively. Their ware is scarcely distinguishable from that of the northern Wintun and the Achomawi. The Yahi coiled much like the Maidu; of what precise type their twining was, is not clear. For the southern Yana all data are lacking, but their situation suggests that the line between the two arts ran up the slope of the Sierra Nevada along their northern or southern boundary. It is possible that one or more of the Yana divisions showed an unblended mixture of the two styles, such as is found among the northeastern Maidu, although west of the Sacramento the cleavage of the arts is sharp.

Dentalia, *bahninu,* as well as clam-shell disks, *mats'ewi,* were prized as money. Again we are at the distributional border, and which form prevailed is not clear.

Brother and sister addressed each other in the plural, the singular being considered improper among them, as is the case between parents-in-law and children-in-law among several other stocks. This practice must be interpreted as an approach to a taboo on communication. Some parent-in-law taboos seem to have been observed by the Yana. In a tale, Coyote addresses his mother-in-law freely; but his erotic chracter in Indian tradition, and his actions in this story, do not allow any certain inference as to the actual custom.

A term for bastard, *wahtaurisi,* "sits at the foot of the ladder," indicates that some observance was given to social station. This position, the nearest the entrance in the earth-covered lodge, belonged to people of no moment.

The two northern divisions buried the dead. During heavy snows people were sometimes interred inside the earth lodge, to be exhumed and reburied later. The Yahi cremated.

The native dog of the Yahi was sharp-nosed, erect-eared, short-haired, of the shape and size of a coyote, but gentle and definitely domesticated since it bred in a variety of colors. It was used in hunting bear and deer, and was more or less fed on meat; but, like most American dogs, died from eating salmon. Its flesh was thought deadly poison to human beings, and was much favored by wizards for evil purposes.

Yana myths are often picturesquely told, but explain little and lack real interest in cosmogony or the origin of human institutions. Attention is concentrated on the incidents of the plot as such. Rabbit, Gray squirrel, and Lizard have been suggested as being to the Yana a creative trinity, somewhat parallel to Earth-Initiate, Father of the Secret Society, and Turtle of the Maidu, with Coyote as antithesis in each instance; but the difference in the spirit of the myths is enormous. The trivial doings of the Yana animals are devoid of all the planning and semigrandiose outlook of the acts of the Maidu gods.

The ghost dance of the early seventies is said to have reached the northern Yana from the Chico Maidu, that is, from the south.

The Yahi.

HISTORY.

The Yahi, the southernmost division of the Yana, once resident on Mill and Deer Creeks, two eastern affluents of the Sacramento, are of a peculiar interest because of their rediscovery in recent years after they had been believed extinct for 40 years.

For some reason that is still obscure, this little group, that can hardly have numbered much more than 200 or 300, became particularly embroiled with the whites and embittered against them in the period of greatest Indian unrest in northern California—the time, approximately, of the Civil War, a full dozen years after the first contact of the races. The Yahi country lay near American farms and towns, but in the early sixties did not contain permanent settlers; indeed has very few to-day. It is a region of endless long ridges and

cliff-walled canyons, of no great elevation but very rough, and covered with scrub rather than timber. The canyons contain patches in which the brush is almost impenetrable, and the faces of the hills are full of caves. There are a hundred hiding places; but there are no minerals, no marketable lumber, no rich bottom lands to draw the American. Cattle, indeed, have long ranged the region, but they drift up and down the more open ridges. Everything, therefore, united to provide the Yahi with a retreat from which they could conveniently raid. Only definite and concerted action could rout them out.

Of course, this action inevitably came. After numerous skirmishes with small parties of Americans, and at least one disastrous fight or slaughter, practically the whole remnant of the group was surrounded and exterminated in an early morning surprise attack by a self-organized body of settlers. This seems to have happened about 1865. If there were known to be survivors, they were so few and so terrified that they were obviously harmless; and no further attention was paid to them. General opinion reckoned the tribe as extinct. After a time, at intervals of years, a cattleman or hunter would report meeting a wild and naked Indian who fled like a deer. Now and then deserted cabins in the hills were rifled. A few of the local mountaineers were convinced that a handful of Indians still remained at large, but the farmers in the valley and the townspeople were inclined to scoff at their stories. In all but the immediate region the Mill Creek Indians had long been forgotten. The last printed reference to them is that of Stephen Powers, who knew them by their Maidu name of Kombo, and related how the last seen of them, in 1872 or earlier, was when two men, two women, and a child were encountered by a couple of hunters, but soon escaped into the brush. There can be little doubt that these were the only survivors.

[165]

REDISCOVERY.

At length, in 1908, a party of surveyors half way up the side of Deer Creek Canyon, a mile or two from the nearest cabin and not more than 15 miles from a trunk railroad, ran their line almost into a hidden camp in which skulked four middle-aged and elderly Indians, who fled. There was no doubt that they were untamed and living the aboriginal existence. Arrows, implements, baskets, the stored food, the huts, were purely native; such American objects and materials as there were, were all stolen. It was clear that for 43 years this household, remnant of what was once a nation, had maintained itself in this or similarly sheltered spots, smothering their camp smoke, crawling under the brush to leave no trail, obliterating their very footsteps, and running like animals at the approach of a human being. It was an extraordinary story: the ingenuity of the Indians was almost as marvelous as the secret of their long concealment.

THE LAST SURVIVOR.

The discovery broke up the existence into which the little band had settled. They had lost most of their tools; they feared to remain in the vicinity; their food supply became irregular. A year or two later the huts were found still standing, but abandoned. One after another the handful died. In 1911 a single survivor, a man with hair singed short in mourning for his relatives, remained. Solitary, weaponless, pressed by hunger, desperate and yet fearful of every white face, he wandered away from his accustomed haunts, until, in August, he was found half hiding, half approaching a house, near Oroville, 40 miles south. He was clapped into jail, but treated kindly; and, as the last wild Indian in the United States, his case aroused wide interest. There was no question of the genuineness of his aboriginal condition. He was practically naked; in obvious terror; and knew no English and but a few words of Spanish learned from his own people and considered by him part of his native tongue. He practiced all the ancient crafts, and proved an expert flint flaker and bow maker.

After a few days he was brought to San Francisco, where he remained, under the protection of the University of California, until his death in 1916. He was then about 50 or 55 years of age, and passed under the name of Ishi, an anglicization of his word for man. He refused to return to his old home or to settle on any Indian reservation,

[166]

and in clothing and personal and daily habits speedily assimilated civilized ways. He learned English very slowly and brokenly, but was volubly communicative in his own tongue on all topics except the fate of his kinsmen, where deeply ingrained sentiment imposed silence. He was industrious, kindly, obliging, invariably even tempered, ready of smile, and thoroughly endeared himself to all with whom he came in contact. With his death the Yahi passed away.

A NATIVE MAP.

A map drawn by Ishi and reproduced as [Map 2] is of interest because it proves the California Indians to have been not totally devoid of faculty in this direction. They usually refuse point-blank to make even an attempt of this kind, alleging utter inability, and it is only in the extreme south of the State that some rudiments of a sense of tracing topography appear. The Mohave readily draw streams and mountains in the sand, and the only native map ever published from California is a sketch of this type. The Diegueño ground paintings also evince some elements of cartographic endeavor, although in ritualized form. Considering the negative attitude of the northern California mind in this direction, Ishi's map is more accurate than might be expected.

YAHI GEOGRAPHICAL KNOWLEDGE.

The sketch is of further interest because Ishi appears never to have visited a considerable part of the area depicted by him, the features shown being known to him only by tradition dating back to the period before 1860.

It must be noted that Ishi applied the term "Gari'si" not to the northern Yana proper, whom he did not recognize as a separate group, but to the central Yana (the Gata'i), and to the southern Yana of Battle Creek. Actually, so far as can be judged, the southern Yana dialect is more similar to Yahi than to central Yana. Tuliyani on Mill Creek, and Yisch'inna on Deer Creek, may be names of chiefs that once lived at these villages, rather than true place names. Ishi employed the term Ga'me'si in connection with the region of these settlements. It is perhaps a designation of

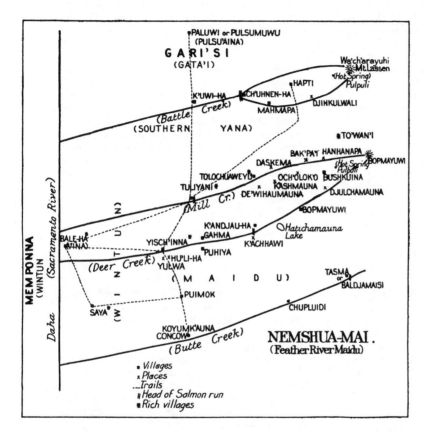

[Map 2.] Map sketched and explained by Ishi, the last Yahi.

[167]

his dialect contrasting with Gara'si for the three Yana dialects to the north. Tasma or Baldjamaisi, also Yulwa, are possibly in upper Feather River drainge, in the vicinity of Big Meadows, rather than on Butte Creek. The stream shown is, however, not intended for Feather River, of which Ishi knew by report that it had four large branches and which he had seen before his capture at Oroville, but of the ancient inhabitants of which he knew only that they were distant and unfriendly. Battle Creek he called Chuhnen-ha more frequently than by its usual northern name of K'uwi-ha.

The Memponna on the map may be named after a chief, although he mentioned Pashahi as such. At Baleha, Saik'olohna and a woman Malki were former chiefs; he also knew the group as Malkinena. At Saya, Kinnuichi was chief. North of it, where Singer Creek and Bush Creek emerge from the hills, were Munmun'i and Djaki-ha; north of these, K'aiuwi at Stevens Hollow and Bolohuwi on Mountain Branch. These seem to have been Wintun rather than Yana, but their attribution varied. The Wintun and Yahi appear to have been on friendly terms, the former coming up Deer Creek at least as far as Ya'muluk'u, near the mouth of Sulphur Creek, well in the Yahi country, to camp and hunt. Other places in or near the valley, and presumably Wintun, were Ha'wan'na, south of Deer Creek; and to the north, Eltami, on Dry Creek; Gahseha; Mukaudanchiwa; Shunhun'imaldji; Chiwa'imaldji where the Indians of Paswi lived; Dahauyap'ahdi, on Dye Creek, north of Mill Creek; and the Dachapaumi-yahi. Mimlosi is a term used in reference to the vicinity of Red Bluff, and evidently contains the Wintun stem for water, *mem.* Chupiskoto, Holok'opasna, and Dashtilaumauna are unlocated Wintun places.

Most of the Maidu groups were less known to Ishi, hostility prevailing between them and the Yahi. The Puimok, whose speech Ishi called Homoadidi—the name Puimok is Wintun—once killed two men and a child at Milshna at Six-Bit Ford on Dry Creek, between Deer and Mill Creeks. Evidently warfare between the two groups was on more even terms than the exaggerated American accounts indicate. The Daidepa-yahi seem to have been a Maidu division in the Big Meadows region, with a woman chief Yella.

The Atsugewi of Hat Creek were called Chunoya and were friendly. Three chiefs were remembered: Pumegi, Badetopi, and Kanigi, besides a woman Wamaiki. They are said to have called the Yahi and perhaps all the Yana Dip-mawi.

Ishi knew a fair number of Atsugewi, Maidu, and Wintun words, about in the proportion of this order. Since he had never met a soul of any of the three stocks, this is a fact of interest, evidencing that the California Indians in their native condition took some interest in each other and spent more or less time in the home circle telling one another about strangers and their ways.

The term "Noza" (Nozi) Ishi seems to have applied to the southern Yana, and Wailaka (Wintun: "north language") to the central Yana. Antelope Creek he called Halhala, and Tuscan Buttes Uht'anuwi.

Other group names recorded from Ishi, but only after contact with a central Yana, and therefore

not certain as a native possession, are Sasti (Shasta); Marak (Modoc); Paiuti; Sun'sona (Shoshone); Basiwi, perhaps Washo; and Shukoni, in the distant east.

While N. C. Nelson was a graduate student at Berkeley in 1912, he took the opportunity to make a careful record of the method by which Ishi produced the beautiful arrowpoints, a large collection of which are in the Lowie Museum of Anthropology at Berkeley. The accompanying two photographs were taken by Kroeber in the spring of 1914 when Ishi and his anthropologist friends returned to Deer Creek to live for a brief period the old Yahi life, hunting deer and taking salmon, and visiting the old village sites.

---

5. Flint Working by Ishi (1916)

Nels C. Nelson

Introductory

The very ancient art of producing implements from flint and allied stone substances by means of a fracturing process, though practiced almost the world over, seems to have reached a really high state of perfection in only three localities, namely, Egypt, Denmark with adjoining parts of Scandinavia, and the Pacific coast of the United States. To be sure, choice bits of workmanship are to be found elsewhere, as for example in France and in Mexico, but these appear to be exceptions rather than the rule.

Just why these seemingly sporadic occurrences of excelling technique should be localized as they are is an interesting question because the manual dexterity implied might with reason have been looked for elsewhere, unless we at once yield the point that such dexterity is not a gift peculiar to any branch of mankind or, in other words, that the human factor is not the only factor concerned.

From *Holmes Anniversary Volume: Anthropological Essays Presented to William Henry Holmes* (Washington, D.C., 1916), pp. 397-402.

For the present therefore the archaeologist in attempting to explain these isolated appearances of highly cultivated flint technique can do little more than suggest that they were conditioned to some extent at least by two interdependent factors, the first being the presence of unlimited amounts of raw material and the other a grand scale of manufacture. The larger the output and the larger the number of artisans at work the greater the possibility of an expert—an artist—whose technique, once perfected, stood some chance of being copied and handed down.

Ishi and His Work

During the early part of 1912, while connected with the University of California Museum of Anthropology, I had opportunity to observe and in a measure to direct the activities of Ishi, the lately rescued survivor of the Yahi or Southern Yana Indians. Among other things suggested to him, partly to satisfy the interest of the visiting public, was that of chipping arrowpoints, and probably nothing else that he undertook proved of equal interest and satisfaction to visitors as well as to himself. He still keeps up the work and is not at all averse to having it inspected. Whether or not Ishi is an artist might be a matter for debate, but no one will deny that he is an experienced workman. This conclusion is based partly on a comparison of his productions with the best to be found in California and also on what the English flint workers at Brandon tell us as to the time normally required to master the art.

Unfortunately, what might perhaps be considered strictly scientific procedure was sacrificed at the beginning. In the first place, no considerable amount of raw obsidian being at hand, bits of heavy plate-glass were furnished, and Ishi, finding this substance somewhat less refractory than obsidian and much more easily worked than chalcedony, agate, and the like, soon offered mild objections to using any medium except glass. This does not mean, however, that he could not be prevailed upon to work obsidian and other rocks. In the second place, Ishi, whether as a result of outside suggestions or his own intelligence I do not recall,

found tools made of iron preferable to the old-fashioned implements of Indian manufacture. But while these facts might be urged as objections to the genuineness of his art, it still remains a fact that Ishi's method is his own and was mastered by him years before, probably with tools of the same general size and shape, if not actually of iron.

That iron tools are the best, considered from the point of view of the finished product made with them, is very doubtful; it is so hard and unyielding in comparison with bone or antler as to tend to bruise the edge of the obsidian; but, on the other hand, it keeps the point better and in that way saves time. With these facts in mind let us briefly consider what actually takes place when Ishi goes to work.

The Tools Employed

Given a nodule of flint or a lump of obsidian, Ishi, in making a notched arrowpoint, let us say, employs three distinct processes, for each of which special tools ordinarily are required. The first process involves the division or breaking up of the obsidian mass to obtain suitable thin and straight flakes; the second process consists in chipping the selected flake to the size and shape of the arrowpoint desired; and the third and final process embodies, among other things, the notching of the base of the point to facilitate its attachment to the arrowshaft.

For the first process, that of dividing the obsidian mass, an ordinary hard, water-worn bowlder may do, especially if only small flakes are wanted, the obsidian being broken up or a flake struck from it by a direct blow. But if a large spearpoint or knife-blade is ultimately desired, an intermediate tool is needed. This is apparently (Ishi never made one for me to see) a short, stout, blunt-pointed piece of bone or wood serving as a sort of punch and sometimes as a lever. As a matter of fact, what is wanted in the case of producing a large implement is not the division of the obsidian mass but the trimming down of this mass by the detachment from it of all unnecessary portions. A direct blow with a hammerstone might be fatal to the obsidian core being thus shaped, while an

Plate 1. The primary process—dislodging flakes.

whole tool was nothing more nor less than a common awl.

Another necessary item was a piece of leather or hide with which to protect the hand holding the obsidian during the chipping and notching processes.

Five things therefore seem to constitute the full complement of tools and accessories used in making the average chipped artifact. But more or fewer tools may no doubt be employed under extreme conditions.

Methods of Work

Preliminary Flaking.—Unfortunately, while Ishi went through the motions of this process a number of times for me, I never photographed it, wishing first to be convinced of its feasibilities. But for reasons which I did not comprehend at the time, Ishi always refused to execute the process. Professor Kroeber has since been partly successful with him, and from his report I judge that Ishi's reluctance was due in all probability to the element of danger involved. Thus it appears that the first time Ishi was induced to try flake production he was cut about the face by flying bits of the glass-like substance and bled profusely. Quite naturally therefore the accompanying illustration of the act (Pl. 1), furnished by Professor Kroeber, shows Ishi with his eyes closed. This photograph, it should be explained, is not a mere pose; it is a selected view of the workman in action and as such tells a better story than words could do. Ishi holds a water-worn bowlder in the right hand and a lump of obsidian in the left, and is attempting to break up the latter or to dislodge flakes from it by means of repeated direct blows. From among the resulting fragments he will pick out those most readily adapted to the purpose needed, let us say arrowpoints, and proceed at once to shape them.

Secondary Flaking or Chipping.—Having selected a suitable flake, Ishi assumes a new pose. The actual disposition of flake and tool is indicated in the detail views of Pl. 2. The flake to be worked will be observed resting on a bit of leather and placed transversely across the proximal fleshy part of the left palm and there held by one or more

indirect blow, delivered through this punch, the same being held at a selected spot and angle, has some chance of success in removing the superfluous portions without shattering the whole piece to bits. A hammerstone then, or a hammerstone together with a punch, are the tools required for the preliminary rough work, namely, the production of flakes or of a flaked core.

For the secondary flaking or, as it will be termed in this paper, *chipping,* a tool was made as follows: Ishi on one occasion took a common spike and at another time a piece of iron rod about the size of a lead pencil. He ground one end down about equally on two opposing sides, making a curving, chisel-like cutting edge, lenticular in cross-section—a tool of a nature halfway between an awl and a chisel. Around the butt-end a bit of cloth was wrapped to ease the handhold, and the chipping tool was finished. The notching tool was practically a duplicate of the preceding, but much smaller. A slender nail was sharpened as before and, being too small to be held in the hand as it was, the butt-end was inserted into an improvised wooden handle. The of the finger-tips. The chipping tool, grasped firmly with the right hand, is placed on the upper side of the flake, very close to the edge, and by a quick, downward pressure a chip is removed from the under-side of the flake. That much of this seemingly simple act will be noticed by any casual observer, but it may be well to analyze the act a little so as to show that it is after all not so simple as it looks. There is, so to speak, some knack about it. First of all we may note the fact, well shown in the illustration, that the axis of the tool used and the edge of the obsidian to be worked do not meet at a right angle, although they are in nearly the same plane. Secondly, and this does not show well in the illustration, the chipping tool is so turned on its axis that the plane of its cutting edge meets the plane of the flake to be worked at nearly, if not quite, a right angle. That this turn of the chipping tool is necessary or at least deliberate is certain because Ishi employs it invariably in the later

stages of the chipping process, but not at all regularly in the early stages. Not having experimented very much, I am unable to say why Ishi proceeds as he does, but he gets results which I cannot imitate, try as I will. Ishi removes thin and fairly slender chips that extend two thirds or more across the face of the flake, while my chips are thick and short. Consequently his arrowpoints when finished are thin and shapely, while mine, much to his disgust, are thick and clumsy affairs. My work resembles the abrupt Mousterian retouch, while Ishi's is the true Solutrian technique.

As to the actual movements involved in chipping, these would be rather difficult to describe. The pressure exerted, if not too great, comes mostly from a wrist action; but if greater weight is needed the leverage is thrown back to the elbow and shoulder. The precision of the movement in the later and more delicate stage of the work is guided by placing the index finger of the tool against the

[171]

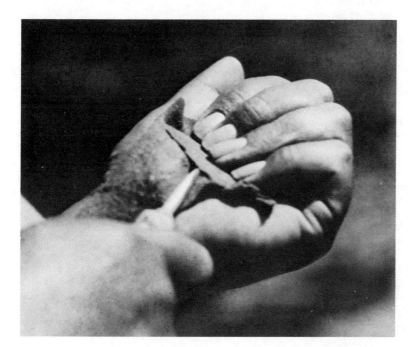

Plate 2. The secondary process—chipping.

edge of the palm on which the flake lies. The pressure is down, of course, rather than up, mainly in order to avoid the flying chips, and the chips being left in the palm of the hand absolutely necessitates the leather pad. Ishi works rapidly, reversing the flake often or not as conditions require. He begins chipping at the point on the flake nearest the tool and gradually works toward the farther end, and his best work appears to be done when he is chipping in a direction from the point end of the arrowpoint toward the base rather than when, on reversal, he must work in the opposite direction, i.e. from the base of the arrowpoint toward the point. Working in this manner Ishi can finish an arrowpoint of average size in half an hour, more or less, according to the nature of the substance he is working and also according to the adaptability of the flake originally selected. Having finished he proceeds to the final step.

Notching and Serrating.—First of all, Ishi takes his leather pad, doubles it over the end of his left thumb, and ties it in place with a string. Then he grips the arrowpoint near the base, holding it firmly between the end of the protected thumb and adjoining index finger. With the right hand he directs the point of the notching tool against the edge of the arrowpoint at the place where the notch is to be, and by a slight pressure removes a small chip. The tool is held perpendicular to the plane of the arrowpoint and is pushed forward as if to be driven into the end of the thumb. For each minute chip thus removed the arrowpoint is reversed until the notch is of the depth desired. The successful act requires some deftness, or the stem is sure to be severed from the blade of the arrowpoint. Ishi seldom fails, however, especially when working with glass, and he completes the two notches often in about half a minute's time. If the edge of the arrowpoint was to be surrated, Ishi would doubtless proceed in the same way, although I never asked him to try.

[172]

Saxton T. Pope, M.D., was on the faculty of the University of California Medical School in San Francisco. Through Ishi he became interested in *archery, learned to make and shoot bows, and wrote several books on the general subject as well as the following monograph on Yahi archery. Here, in splendid detail, is the unique account of the weapon that was in use in California for thousands of years before the Europeans appeared on the scene.*

6. Yahi Archery (1918)

Saxton T. Pope

Archery is nearly a lost art. Among civilized peoples it survives only as a game. It is well known, however, that even as late as two centuries ago the bow was a vigorous competitor with the flintlock in warfare. Benjamin Franklin at the beginning of the Revolution seriously considered the possibility of arming the American troops with the longbow, as a cheaper and more effective weapon than the flintlock[1] musket. That the archery even of the American Indian was, during the early periods of occupation, substantially as effective as the musketry of the period is attested in the historic records of some of the explorers.[2] Such aboriginal archery has, of course, undergone a great decadence since the rifle has supplanted the bow. It is now almost extinct. As a matter of fact, we have very little accurate information as to how the Indians used their weapons, and still less as to how they made them. The present paper is an attempt to present the facts concerning the archery of one tribe, the Yahi or Deer Creek Indians of north central California, the most southerly division of the Yanan[3] stock, as represented in the person of

From *University of California Publications in American Archaeology and Ethnology*, Vol. 13, No. 3 (1918), pp. 104-152, slightly abridged. Illustrations shown have been renumbered.

1. See letter from Benjamin Franklin to Major-General Lee, *in* Memoirs of the late Charles Lee, second in command in the service of the United States of America of America during the revolution. . . London, 1792, p. 240.
2. See, for example, the narrative of Cabeza de Vaca concerning the Indians of Florida, *in* Buckingham Smith, Relation of Alvar Nuñez Cabeza de Vaca, New York, 1871, p. 30.
3. Edward Sapir has published Yana Myths in volume 9 of the present series.

its last survivor, Ishi, who lived from 1911 to 1916 at the University of California. The paper will deal first with the very interesting methods of the Yahi for the manufacture of the implements of archery, and, second, their style of shooting.

It must be remembered that the performances of civilized archers, who practice with the bow as a sport, far surpass those of savages. It is a curious fact that archery was brought to perfection only after the bow became obsolete as a serious weapon. It is interesting, therefore, to compare the Yahi "style" with that of the more skilful archers who follow the rules of the modern game.

Ishi, the native informant for the present paper, comes of a tribe famous for its fighting qualities. The group lived to a considerable extent on wild game, and the bow was their glory and their delight. We have no reason to believe that their skill or the strength of their weapons was inferior to that of the average American savage. Concerning the informant himself, the following might be said:

Ishi loved his bow as he loved nothing else in his possession.

He knew what a gun was, but he had never shot one until after 1911 when he entered civilization. The bow he had used ever since boyhood. When captured he had no weapons, though a bow and many arrows were taken from his lodge by those who first discovered the camp where the remnant of his people were living. Some of these arrows we later recovered, some through the generosity of the finders and some by purchase, but his original bow is missing.

What the writer knows of Ishi's archery is based upon three years' association with him. In this period many hours were spent in making bows and arrows, in talking about shooting, in target practice, and in hunting trips in the fields and woods. During the years 1913 and 1914 there was opportunity for two extended trips in the mountains in his company. Dr. J. V. Cooke and the present writer took up the practice of archery in 1912 under Ishi's guidance, at first according to the Indian's own methods, though later we followed the English style. At first Ishi was our master in marksmanship, but at the end of a few months we were able to outdo him at target work, and to equal his performances in shooting game. This does not in any way imply greater skill on our part, but does point clearly to the actual superiority of the "civilized" methods.

In speaking of the techniques of manufacture used by Ishi, it must be remembered that he soon adopted civilized tools in this work. The jackknife and file supplanted the obsidian blade and the scraper of sandstone. He only returned to his primitive ways when requested to show the processes he formerly performed.

He was a most painstaking and finished workman. His dexterity and ingenuity were delightful to watch. No better specimens of arrowheads, shafts, and bows are contained in the Museum of the University than those made by him. Probably better ones were never made anywhere. His eye for form and symmetry was perfect.

Technical Terms

A bow has the following parts: A back, that part away from the archer; a belly, the concave side, when full drawn; a handle or hand grip, a portion near the center for holding the weapon; limbs, that part between the handle and the extremities. These extremities usually have notches, or some contrivance to maintain the string in position, called nocks. The process of bending a bow and attaching the string to the ends is called bracing it. The amount of pull on the string, necessary to draw an arrow a proper distance before discharging it from the bow, may be ascertained in pounds by means of a scale or balance. This is called the "weight" of the bow.

The Bow

Ishi called the bow *man'i.* He made bows of many woods while under observation, but upon an expedition into his country three years after his capture he showed us the tree from which the best bows were made. It was the mountain juniper. He made a stave from one of these trees on the spot, though it was later ruined.

He described another tree from which his tribe made bows, apparently the incense cedar. This, he

[173]

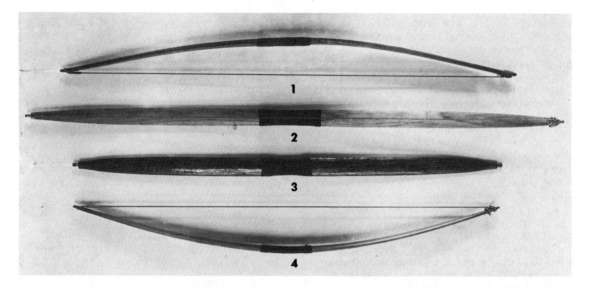

[174]

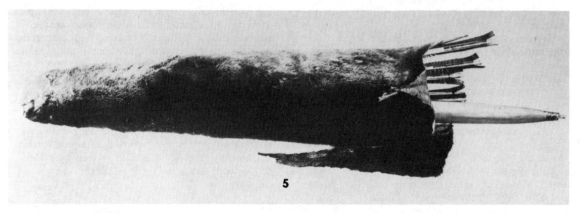

1. Hickory bow, backed with glued catgut. Made in 1914. A strong shooting bow, often used by Ishi. University of California Museum of Anthropology, specimen number 1-19867.

2. Unbacked ash bow, broken in use. It is much longer than Ishi usually made, 54 inches. Museum number 1-19451.

3. A yew bow, made on the normal proportions, backed with deer tendon. This specimen was broken in testing, before application of the backing. Museum number 1-19452.

4. Oregon yew bow, backed with thin rawhide. This was one of Ishi's best bows, used most at targets. Museum number 1-19590. Length, 44 inches. The hand grip, on all the above specimens, is woolen tape.

5. Quiver of otter skin. Specimen number 1-19566. The contained bow and arrows were made by Ishi at the Museum. The quiver is an original piece, taken when the camp of his people was discovered in 1908.

said, was chopped down by the one man in his tribe who owned an iron axe, and split with wedges of deer horn into proper-sized staves. To obtain the wood for his bow he broke a limb from the tree, which seems to have been the custom before the days of axes.

The Indian with the axe seems to have been the bow maker of the vicinity. He also owned a long knife, and was known as *Chunoyahi,* that is, Atsugewi or Hat Creek Indian. Of his prowess with the bow, Ishi told us many tales.

Juniper wood Ishi called *nogu'i.* Yew wood he did not seem to have used, though he knew of it and said that other tribes used it. His name for this was *hulogos'i.* He knew that its leaves were poisonous to eat.

While with us he used eucalyptus, tanbark oak, red cedar (*tiyun'i*), hickory, ash, juniper, and yew for his bows. All of these were of the same general shape and size, and all were backed with sinew. Yew, of course, produced the best weapon. His standard of measurement for a good bow was to hold a stave diagonally across his chest with one end in his right hand at the hip, and the left arm extended straight out at an angle of 45 degrees from the horizontal. The distance between these points was the proper length for a bow. This measured in his own case four feet and two inches. The width of the bow at the middle of each limb was three or four fingers, according to whether a light hunting bow or a powerful war bow was wanted.

The shape of his bow was a short, flat stave, with limbs wider at their center than at the handle, sometimes recurved at their outer extremity, tapering gracefully to small short nocks at the ends.

His wood, after being split or partially blocked out from a limb, was laid in a horizontal position in a warm, sheltered place. Here it seasoned. But as to what time of year to cut it, or how long to season it, Ishi seemed to have no set opinions.

The process of shaping the bow was that of scraping with flint or obsidian. With infinite patience and care he reduced the wood to the proper dimensions. In the finishing work he used sandstone. The measurements of two of his best bows are as follows:

Number 1-19590. Length, 44 inches. Diameters, at handle, 5/8 by 1 1/2 inches; at midlimb, 9/16 by 1 7/8 inches; at nock, 5/16 by 3/4 inches. Pulls 40 pounds.

Bow in possession of author. Shown in use in plate 31. Length, 54 1/2 inches. Diameters, at handle, 3/4 by 1 5/8; at midlimb, 1/2 by 1 3/4; at nock, 1/4 by 1/2 inches. Pulls 45 pounds.

He seemed to have had no great respect, as the English do, for the white sap wood of yew or cedar. Although he placed this at the back of his bow, he did not hesitate to cut through its grain to attain a symmetrical form, and just as often he would scrape most of it away, leaving only a thin stratum of white at each edge. At the handle a cross section of the bow was oval, while a section through the mid-limb was much flatter.

In some of his bows the last six inches of the limbs were recurved. This was accomplished by holding the back of the bow, at this point, on a hot rock while pressure was applied at the ends, bending the wood over the stone, shifting the bow back and forth, until the requisite curve had been obtained. Then, while the wood cooled, Ishi held it pressed against his knee, which was protected by a pad of buckskin.

After the bow was shaped and finished smoothly on the belly, the sinew was applied to the back, which had been left rather rough. As backing for his bow, Ishi used either the dorsal fascia obtained from a deer, or he teased out the long tendons, *bama,* from the hind legs. These strips were from eight to fourteen inches long, and when dry were about the thickness of parchment.

Preparatory to using this tissue he soaked it in warm water for several hours. The back of his bow, the side having the sap wood on it, he smeared thickly with glue. In his native state he made this glue, so he said, by boiling the skin of salmon and macerating it while hot. While with us he was very enthusiastic over our common liquid glue and disdained the use of hot furniture glue. He permitted this coating of glue to dry. Now, having his sinew wet, he chewed these strips until they were soft and pulpy and then carefully laid them in parallel lines down the back, overlapping the ends as he went. This process required a great deal of

[175]

tissue and much patience. Having applied the sinew, he bound it on with ribbons of maple bark running spirally about the bow. This he removed after the expiration of "one sleep." As the sinew dried, it contracted and tended to draw the ends of the bow into a reversed position. After this had happened, he applied more glue to the surface. Several days later, when all the backing was thoroughly dry and hard, he filed and scraped it very smooth, filing the overlapping margins level with the edges of his bow.

Strips of sinew during the process of "backing" were folded over the nocks of the bow. He now served or wrapped the ends of the bow with strips of tendon, covering the nock proper and running about an inch down the limb. Here he let his work rest for days or weeks, exposing it to the sunlight and permitting the wood to season fully. During this waiting period he made the bow string or *chalman'i.* The tendons used in this were of a finer quality than those used before and were obtained from the outer, more slender group of tendons in the deer's shank. These he stripped far up into their origin in the muscle bundles, tearing them free with his teeth.

If fresh, he simply chewed this tissue and teased it apart into threads no larger than floss silk. If dry, he soaked it in warm water before chewing it. He then proceeded to spin a string by fixing one end of a bundle of tendon strips to a stationary point and rolling the other end between his fingers in a single strand. As he progressed down the string he added more threads of tendon to the cord, making a very tight, simple twist one-eighth of an

inch thick. When about five feet long, he twisted and secured the proximal end, leaving his twisted cord taut between two points. The last smoothing-up stage he accomplished by applying saliva and rubbing up and down its length. The finished bow string was now permitted to dry. Its final diameter was about three thirty-seconds of an inch. After it was dry he formed a loop at one end by folding back some three inches of string, tapering it by scraping, and serving two of the three inches securely with more tendon. He seemed to have no idea of splicing, nor did he know any clever knots. Moreover, he never used glue at this point. In fact this loop was the weakest part of his string and not infrequently came apart, when, in disgust, he would tie a single loop knot and forego the finished effect of the unknotted self loop. Nor had he any idea of serving his string with any binding at the nocking point, where the arrow rests.

At this stage, Ishi was ready to string the bow. He designated the end of the stave which grew uppermost in the tree as the *chunna,* "face," and over the nock in this end he slipped the loop of his string. To fail to shoot with this end uppermost, he said, would cause the arrow to miss its mark.

In stringing the bow for the first time, he seated himself, placing the upper nock behind his left heel, the belly toward him, the handle against his right knee, the lower limb upward in his left hand. In this position he bent the bow and fastened the string about the other nock. His method of securing the string was as follows: he wound it twice around the nock, passed under the bowstring, turned backward and wound in the opposite direction

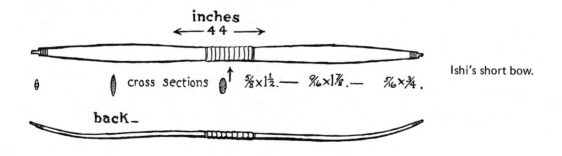

inches
← 44 →

cross sections ⬦↑ 5/8 × 1½ — 9/16 × 1⅞ — 5/16 × ¾.

back_

Ishi's short bow.

Chopping a stick of juniper into rough shape for a bow.

several laps, then fixed the end by a couple of slip knots. Usually he made his string with a tapering extremity which rendered it easier to fasten. Then he cautiously drew his bow and observed its bend. On cold days, Ishi warmed his bow over a fire before attempting to brace it. The ideal bow, to his mind, curved in a perfect arch at all points, and at full draw represented a crescent. The center bent with the limbs and was the bow's weakest point. A forty-five inch bow he drew twenty-five inches. No yew wood could stand such an arc without backing. In fact he broke two bow-staves, testing them at my request, prior to the application of sinew.

Where the contour showed the bow too strong, he filed or scraped it on the belly side, thus gradually distributing the bend evenly along the bow. About the middle he bound a ribbon of buckskin, making a hand grip some five or six inches wide. This buckskin thong was about half an inch wide and ran spirally about the bow, not overlapping,

fastened at each end by an extra wrapping of string or sinew.

Ishi showed no tendency to anoint his weapon with grease, nor to apply any protective coat, though later he learned the value of shellac in preserving his backing from dampness. The great aversion he had to shooting while any fog or moisture was in the air rather indicates that his bow was without the coverings of fat, wax, or resin so frequently used by archers in other parts of the world.

Usually Ishi made no effort to decorate his bow, though he spoke of painting it, and led me to infer that this was done only after the implement had shown some peculiar virtue, or had figured in some deed of valor. The one bow he embellished while with us he marked with three green transverse stripes just above the handle and below the nocks, and three long snaky lines running down the back. He said that red also was an appropriate color.

When finished and seasoned, these bows pulled, or "weighed," when drawn to twenty-five inches, between thirty-five and fifty pounds. His favorite hunting bow weighed forty pounds.

When not in use he kept his bows in a leather quiver, or wrapped in a cloth. The tail of a mountain lion was considered an admirable cover for a bow. The bow was always laid in a horizontal position. To stand a bow upright, according to his theories, was to keep it working; if left standing it would "sweat" and become weak. If a child touched a bow, it brought bad luck. Nor should a child step over it while it lay on the ground, for this would cause it to shoot crookedly. If a woman touched Ishi's bow, it was a serious contamination. The bow must be washed and cleaned with sand. He was most careful not to keep his bow strung too long but furnished the loop with a bit of cord, which extended from nock to loop, and served to keep the bow string from getting out of place while the bow was unbraced. After unstringing he often gave his bow a slight bend backward to restore its straightness; this is considered very bad practice by English archers.

A good bow was one whose string made a high musical note when tapped with an arrow or

[177]

Figures 1 to 3 are old Yahi arrows; 4 to 9, specimens made while Ishi was at the Museum.

1. Shaft of hazel, foreshaft of some heavier wood, possibly dogwood. There is a notch for a head, but this is missing. Buzzard wing feathers. Length, 29 3/8 inches, weight 320 grains. University of California Museum of Anthropology, number 1-19577.

2. The same type as above, feathers a trifle longer. Both are painted with alternate red and blue rings and intervening wavy lines. Museum number 1-19578.

3. The shaft is like the preceding, but the point is here preserved. It is a small serrated head of window glass. There is blood on the arrow. Museum number 1-19579.

4. A one-piece hazel shaft, feathered with turkey feathers, pointed with an obsidian head. Commercial pigments and shellac embellish this arrow. Number 1-19864.

5. This is the type of arrow Ishi adopted after living in civilization. It is made of a 5/16 birch dowel, gayly painted, feathered with blue heron feathers and is tipped with a steel head, sinew bound. Number 1-19863.

6. This is a dowel—turkey tail feathers, blue and red paint rings, obsidian head. An arrow made for show. Number 1-19866.

7. A longer type of service arrow of Japanese bamboo with short birch foreshaft and steel head. Used in early target practice and hunting. Number 1-19862.

8. A blunt-pointed arrow of native bamboo, buckeye foreshaft, gay colors, turkey tail feathers. Made for exhibition or gift. Number 1-19456.

9. Same as last, only it has an obsidian head. Length 38 inches, weight 580 grains. Number 1-19454. Similar shafts Ishi made and gave to Secretary Lane at a ceremonial occasion in San Francisco in 1914.

snapped with the fingers. It should sing the note "tin, tin, tin." This was the "chief's bow." One whose note was dead and unmusical, Ishi treated with contempt.

By placing the upper end of his braced bow at the corner of his open mouth and gently tapping the string midway between the end and center he caused clear musical notes to be produced. This sounded like our jew's-harp, and by altering the shape of the buccal cavity he was able to create a series of tones sufficient to form a melody relating to a story of wonderful deeds with the bow. He sang of a great archer who dipped his arrow point in the sea, then in the fire, drew a mighty bow, and shot at the sun. His arrow flew like the north wind, and entering the door of the sun, put out its light. Then all the world became dark, men shivered with cold, and from this time they grew feathers on their bodies to make them warm.

The Arrow

The arrow was called *sawa*.

Of all the specimens of arrows in the University Museum, scarcely any show such perfect workmanship as those of Ishi. His proportions and finish are of very high order.

At the time of the rediscovery of the remnant of the tribe, a number of arrows were secured from the huts, which doubtless represent his average work. Later, while with us, he made scores of arrows of various shapes and sizes. Apparently some arrows, those of great length, measuring a yard, and having large heads, were purely for ornamental purposes, or intended to be given as presents, or possibly to be used in time of war. His hunting shafts were of two kinds—obsidian pointed, and blunt. For shooting small game, such as birds and rabbits, the latter were used. For killing deer, bear, and predatory animals, sharp arrows were used. Here, if the object shot at were missed, a broken arrow-point resulted. The arrow shafts were made of several kinds of wood. Those obtained from his hut in Tehama County seem to be of hazel, *humoha,* and this was a favorite wood with him. A native bamboo-like reed was also a great favorite. Dogwood and mountain mahogany he

also used. Other shaft woods pointed out by him were *bakanyau'an (Philadelphus Lewisii), sawa'i* ("arrow bush," *Paeonia Brownii*), and *loko* and *habaigili'i,* unidentified. Later, as a result of a modification of ideas he underwent in our company, he adopted the commercial 5/16-inch birch dowel as the ideal material, probably because of its accessibility.

In the case of cane arrows, a wooden "foreshaft," six to eight inches long, was invariably added, and such foreshafts were sometimes added to wooden arrows. They were of hazel, buckeye *(habsi),* wild currant *(wahsu'i),* and perhaps other woods. The foreshaft was normally heavier material than the main shaft.

In general it may be said that his typical hunting arrow was a hazel stick, with a foreshaft, the entire length being 29 inches. The diameter at the middle was 11/32 inch; and the total weight was 330 grains. The feathering of the arrow consisted of three plumes from a buzzard's wing, 4 3/4 inches long, 3/8 inch wide. They were trimmed straight to the forward end, where their width was about 1/8 inch, and terminated 3/4 inch from the nock of the arrow. At each end the feathers were bound down with sinew.

In gathering wood for arrows he generally selected the tall, straight shoots of hazel where it grew in competition with other shrubs or trees, cutting them about a yard long, their greatest diameter being little more than three-eighths of an inch. These he stripped of bark with his thumb nail. He always made arrows in groups of five. Thus he would select the best of his sticks, and collecting them in groups, bind them together securely with a cord. In this bundle they were permitted to season, lying in a horizontal position. After any period from a week to a year these sticks might be used.

The first process in manufacture was that of straightening his shafts. To do this he either made a small heap of glowing embers from a fire or utilized a hot stone. He applied pressure with his thumbs on the convex side of any irregularity or bend in a shaft, and holding this near the heat, passed the wood back and forth before the stone

179]

Straightening an arrow.

or coals. When the wood was warm, it gave very readily to pressure. In less than a minute any curve or crook could be straightened out. The wood after cooling always retained its new position. Glancing down the axis of his shaft from time to time, Ishi gauged its straightness. To burn or discolor the wood was evidence of bad technique. Smoothing was accomplished by scraping and rubbing the arrow shaft between two pieces of sandstone. He sometimes finished the shaft by rolling it back and forth on the thigh with his right palm while he worked it with a piece of sandstone held in his left hand. By this means he could "turn" a shaft almost as accurately as if a lathe were used.

Where a foreshaft was to be added, the length of the main shaft was 21 inches. At the smaller end he cut a notch for the bow string with a bit of obsidian, making this nock 5/32 of an inch wide and 3/16 inch deep. In larger arrows he deepened this to 1/2 inch. The other end of the shaft was next drilled out to accommodate the foreshaft.

His method of drilling was as follows: Placing a sharp piece of bone, point up, in the ground, and steadying it with his toes, he rotated the shaft perpendicularly upon this point. The motion here was identical with that employed in making fire by means of a drill and base stick, the stick being rolled between the palms with downward pressure. The excavation averaged an inch in depth and a quarter of an inch in diameter, and ran to a point. During this drilling process the lower end of the shaft was tightly bound with sinew or cedar cord to keep it from splitting. One end of the foreshaft was formed into a spindle and made to fit this socket, leaving a slight shoulder where the two segments met. Salmon glue or resin was used to secure union, and the joint was bound with macerated tendon for the distance of an inch or more.

When a group of five arrows had been brought to this stage of completion, he painted them. His favorite colors were green and red. At first he insisted that these were the only colors to use, since they had the effect of making the arrows fly straight. After we began to excel him in marksmanship he scraped all his arrows and painted them red and blue, perhaps to change his luck. The shafts obtained from his hut were of these latter colors, but at least the blue is American pigment, perhaps secured during nocturnal prowlings in vacant cabins.

Red, he told me, came from the earth and was made with fire. Blue he obtained from a plant "like a potato"; green from a plant "like an onion"; black from the eye of salmon or trout.[4] The pigments were mixed with the gum or sap of some trees. He had no opportunity to explain the process more fully. When with us he used the ground pigments of commerce, with which he mixed an alcoholic solution of shellac.

The University Museum has a sample of red pigment obtained from the Yahi Indians before Ishi's capture, and it is the usual red ochre.

The design employed in painting usually consisted of alternating rings of red and blue a quarter of an inch wide, with a wide space between two groups of the stripes, sometimes occupied by red or blue dots, or snaky lines running lengthwise. Only that space which was later to be spanned by the feathers was painted. The design was usually three rings near the nock, then ten rings at the smaller end of the feather.

In applying his paint he used a little stick of wood, or drew a small bunch of bristles, set in resin, through a quill, making a brush. To make the rings of color he clamped the arrow shaft between his left arm and chest, while he rotated it with the left hand. In his right, which was steadied on his knee, he held the brush with its coloring matter. In making serpentine lines he used a little pattern of wood or deerhide, cut with a zigzag edge, along which he passed his brush. These figures seemed to have no symbolic meaning to him. Apparently they were simply standard designs.

When the paint was dry, he ran a broad ring of glue above and below it, at the site of the subsequent binding which holds the feathers. This he let dry.

[181]

4. Ishi designated *Lathyrus sulphurea, kununutspi'i,* as yielding a yellow paint for arrows. The "onion" from which green was obtained may have been a plant related to the lily *Fritillaria lanceolata,* which he called *t'aka,* although he declared this species to produce a salmon-colored dye. *Commandra umbellata, punentsaw'i* in his language, was also used for painting arrows.

Many kinds of feathers were used by Ishi on his arrows—eagle, hawk, owl, buzzard, wild goose, heron, quail, pigeon, flicker, turkey, bluejay. He preferred eagle feathers but admitted that they were very hard to get. While with us he used either the tail or pinion feathers from the domestic turkey. Like the best archers he put three feathers from the same wing on each arrow.

The first process of preparing the feather was to separate its laminae at the tip and split the shaft down its length by pulling it apart. Only the strip forming the posterior part of the original quill was used. He placed one end of this strip on a rock, clamping his great toe firmly upon it, and pulled it taut with the left hand, while with a sharp knife he shaved the upper surface of the aftershaft or rib to the thinness of paper. By scraping with an obsidian chip he now reduced it to translucent thinness, leaving no pith on it. Feathers so scraped are very flexible but the laminae tend to stand at an angle of thirty degrees from the perpendicular when set on the arrow. Having finished many feathers this way he collected them in groups of three, according to their similarity of form and color, and bound each group with a short bit of thread. When ready to apply them to the arrow, these sets of three, each set from the same wing, were soaked in warm water. When soft, the feathers were shaken dry, separated, and each tested for its strength by pulling its two extremities. Then, gathering about half an inch of laminae with the tip of the after-shaft and holding this end securely, he ruffled the rest of the laminae backward, in order to have a clear space over which to apply sinew in the next stage. Each feather in turn was thus made ready.

Very delicate deer tendons, having been split and soaked in water, were now chewed to a stringy pulp and drawn from the mouth in thin ribbons about a foot long. One end he held by the teeth, the other was attached to the arrow by a couple of turns near the nock. He then placed each feather in succession in its position; one perpendicular to the nock, two at its opposite edges, making equidistant spaces between them. As he rotated the shaft, the tendon being held in his teeth, he bound the rib and a half inch of laminae together down the shaft, smoothing all with his thumb nail at the last. The reversed position of the rest of the laminae at this point made his work easy. Having treated one arrow, he let it dry while he fixed each of the remaining four.

The next step was to draw the anterior extremity of the feathering down into position. Beginning at the last painted ring where the glue commenced, he stripped off the laminae in preparation for the application of tendons. Again he spun out a ribbon of tissue, and setting each feather in place, holding the top one with his left thumb, and the other two with the first and second fingers respectively, he began binding with the sinew. After proceeding a few turns, he released his hold and straightened each feather to its final position, which was about one-sixteenth of an inch off the direct line down the arrow, veering off slightly toward the concave side of the feather. Now, drawing the feathers tight and snug, he cut the rib about half an inch long and completed the binding by rotation, plus a final smoothing with his thumb nail. In applying the tendon, he was careful to make a close spiral, never overlapping his sinew except at the last few turns. Each arrow, being thus feathered, was put in the sunshine to dry. After a number of hours he would pick up a shaft and by beating it gently against his palm, restore the laminae to their natural direction, fluffing out the feathering. After having stroked the thoroughly dry feathers to settle them, he trimmed them by laying them on a flat piece of wood, using a straight stick as a ruler and running a sharp chip of obsidian along this edge. Obsidian flakes are quite as sharp as a good razor, and cut feathers better.

His feather usually had a straight edge, and had a height of $1/8$ inch at the forward end and $3/8$ or $1/2$ inch at the nock end. Sometimes they were cut in a slightly concave line, and usually no trimming was done near the nock, but the natural curve of the feather tip was left here, making a graceful finish to his work.

Instead of standing perpendicularly to the shaft, as has been recommended by our ancient English archers, Ishi's feathers were set at an angle to his arrow and tended to fall or lie closer to the shaft

Chewing sinew for arrow wrapping.

shaft with his left hand, almost in his shooting position (as described below), he cut the shaft off at the end of his left forefinger. This gave a length of about twenty-nine inches. The cutting of the shaft was done with a filing motion of an obsidian knife. Later he used a bit of broken hack-saw. The point of the shaft was then slightly rounded, and if intended for small game, bound with sinew. If obsidian points were to be used, a notch similar to that intended for the bow string was made, and so cut that when the arrow was drawn on the bow, this notch was in a perpendicular position. The idea in placing the head in a vertical plane was that in this position it entered between the ribs of an animal more readily.

Ishi did not seem to know that in flight an arrow revolves quite rapidly and necessarily must shift from its plane immediately upon leaving the bow. With the old English archers, the broad-head was placed in the same plane with the nock, for the same mistaken reason. With the English, of course, the bow is held almost perpendicular, while with most Indians, as with Ishi, the bow has a more or less horizontal position in shooting.

[183]

Arrow Points

For making arrowheads,[5] bone and obsidian and flint were used by the Yahi. Flint Ishi designated as *pana k'aina* and seemed to like it because of its varied colors. But *hahka* or obsidian was in commoner use, and among the Yahi it served even as money. Boulders of obsidian were traded from tribe to tribe throughout his country. They probably came by way of the Hat Creek Indians from Shasta County and other districts where this volcanic glass was prevalent.

A boulder of obsidian was shattered by throwing another rock on it. The chunks thus obtained were broken into smaller size by holding a short segment of deer horn or piece of bone against a projecting surface, and smartly striking it a glancing blow with a stone. The resulting flakes of obsidian best suited for arrowheads were roughly three inches

after much use or being carried in the quiver. This position does seem to have the advantage, however, of giving a better spin to the arrows in flight, which, or course, tends toward greater accuracy. Some of Ishi's feathers were not more than three inches long, and those on his exhibition or war arrows were the full length of a hawk's pinions—almost a foot.

In none of his arrows which were made in the wilds was there any evidence of glue between the feather and arrow shaft; but while with us he occasionally ran a little glue beneath his feather after binding it on.

In his native state, he seems to have used no protective over the sinew to keep out moisture—not even fat—nor did he apply any finish or varnish to the surface of his shafts.

The arrow in the condition just described was now accurately cut to a certain length. His method of measurement was to hold the butt against his own sternal notch and then, reaching along the

5. Compare the article by N. C. Nelson, Flint Working by Ishi, *in* the Holmes Anniversary Volume, Washington, 1916 [reprinted above].

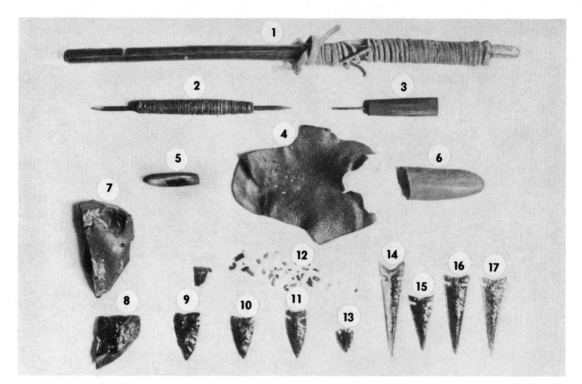

1. Aboriginal bone-pointed arrowflaker. This is from the Yurok tribe in northwestern California and illustrates the type used by the Yahi before iron was known. Length, 17 3/8 inches. University of California Museum of Anthropology, specimen number 1-2496.

2. Iron flaker made and used by Ishi while in captivity. Number 1-19591.

3. Flaker for fine retouching.

4. Leather pad to cover the ball of the hand in flaking.

5. Bone struck a glancing blow in order to detach pieces from a lump of obsidian.

6. Stone used as a mallet to strike bone.

7. Obsidian struck from a larger mass.

8. Flake as detached previous to the retouching process.

9. Obsidian arrow point taking shape.

10. Obsidian arrow nearing completion.

11. Completed obsidian arrow point.

12. Minute flakes and chips detached in the retouching.

13. A small, broad arrow point of obsidian. Length, 1 inch; width, 11/16 inch; thickness, 1/8 inch; weight, 15 grains.

14. Long, narrow arrowhead made of plate glass. Ishi made many such show pieces. They are too long and fragile for use.

15. Obsidian arrowhead. Length, 2 inches; width 15/16 inch; thickness, 1/4 inch; weight, 60 grains.

16. Glass arrowhead, made from a blue medicine bottle.

17. A glass arrowhead, made from a brown beer bottle. Length, 3 inches; width, 1 inch; thickness 3/16 inch; weight 90 grains.

long, an inch and a half wide and half an inch thick. Selecting one of these, according to its shape and grain, he began the flaking process.

Protecting the palm of his left hand by means of a piece of buckskin, and resting the left elbow on the left knee, he held the obsidian tightly against the palm by folding his fingers over it. The flaker was a piece of deer horn bound to a stick about a foot long. . . . He used deer horn for the heavier work, but while with us he chiefly employed a soft iron rod three-sixteenths of an inch in diameter and eight inches long, having a handle or padding of cloth bound about it for a distance of six inches. The tool must be a substance that will dent slightly and thus engage the sharp edge of obsidian. Tempered steel utterly fails to serve this purpose. . . .

To make a head of this type required about half an hour. He made them in all sizes and shapes. Large spike-like heads were for gift arrows and war. Medium size heads, perhaps 1 1/2 inches long, 3/4 inch wide, and 1/4 inch thick, were for ordinary

Retouching obsidian.

deer shooting, while small, flat oval heads were for shooting bear.

Apparently it was Yahi custom to do most of the making of bows and arrows away from the camp, in secluded spots particularly favorable to this employment. At least this was true of the making of arrowheads; partially so, no doubt, because of the danger entailed, and partially because it was strictly a man's job.

Ishi said that the men congregated in a circle, in a warm sunny place, painted their faces with black mud to keep the flying flakes out of their eyes, and maintained silence—either for ceremonial purposes or to avoid getting pieces of flint or glass in the mouth. Among their theories of disease, the one which they most usually invoked was the supposed presence of bits of obsidian or spines of cactus and similar sharp objects in the system. The medicine man gave support to this theory, moreover, by the "magical" extraction of such objects from his patients, by means of sucking the painful spot.

If by chance a bit of glass flew in the eye while flaking arrowheads, Ishi would pull down his lower eyelid with the left forefinger, being careful not to blink or rub the lid. Then he bent over, looking at the ground, and gave himself a tremendous thump on the crown of the head with the right hand. This was supposed to dislodge the foreign body from the eye.

After much close work he frequently suffered from eyestrain headache. His distant vision was excellent, but like many Indians he was astigmatic. He also complained of fatigue and cramp in his hands after prolonged flaking.

The arrowheads were first set in the shaft by heating pine resin, and applying it to the notched end, then moulding it about the base of the obsidian point. When firm, the point was further secured by binding it with sinew, back and forth, about the tangs and around the shaft. Three wraps were made about each notch, and the tendon was wound about the arrow for the distance of half an inch immediately below the arrowhead. After drying, this secured the head very firmly and was quite smooth. A little polishing with sandstone gave a fine finish to the binding.

[185]

Heating resin to be used on end of a shaft to affix the head on the arrow.

Sinew being applied to the arrowhead and shaft.

These heads frequently were kept in a little bag of skin, and not attached to the arrow till a few hours before the expected hunt. Extra heads were kept in readiness to substitute for those broken during use. Large oval blades were bound on short handles and used as knives. Still larger blades of the same type, on a long handle, were used as spears.

After some experience in shooting at targets, Ishi devised a substitute for the regular target arrow pile, or head. He made blunt points from thin brass tubing or steel umbrella sticks, cut into one inch lengths. He filed these with deep transverse notches across one end and pounded this portion into a blunt conical shape. These heads he set on his shafts with glue.

The Quiver

When upon a prolonged hunt, Ishi carried as many as sixty arrows with him, though his quiver seldom contained more than a score. The extra arrows he kept covered with a skin and bound with buckskin thongs, and he carried them slung over his shoulder.

His quiver, now in the University Museum, was made from the skin of an otter, the fur side out, and the hair running upward. It measures 34 inches in length, 8 inches in width at the upper end, and 4 inches at the lower. The skin had been removed whole, save for an incision over the buttocks. The hind legs had been split and left dangling, while the fore legs were two sheaths of skin inverted within the quiver. The mouth was sewn with tendon, and the split tail served as a carrying strap. Four punctures in the animal's back showed where the toggles of a salmon spear had entered and had had exit, indicating its method of capture. A strip of buckskin was also stitched to the outlet of the quiver, and, running inside, was again stitched two-thirds of the way down. Its use seems to have been as a carrying strap.

Besides his arrows he carried his bow in the quiver, and slung all over the left shoulder. It was not easy to extract arrows from the quiver quickly, so it was customary to carry a few in the hand. These, during the act of shooting, Ishi either laid on the ground or held beneath his right arm. Owing to his peculiar method of shooting, this did not interfere when he drew his bow.

Handling of the Bow

His system of shooting was as follows: Taking his bow from the quiver, he placed the lower end on his partially flexed left thigh. While he held the bow by the center with the left hand—its back was down—his right hand caught the string between forefinger and thumb. The other fingers held the upper end near the nock. Now, depressing the handle and bending the bow, he slipped the loop of the string over the nock. If, perchance, the string were too long, he unstrung the bow and twisted the string till it shortened to the proper length, when he again bent and braced his bow. When

strung, the distance between the string and the hand grip was about four and a half inches. He then would place four or five arrows beneath his right arm, points to the front, leaving one in the hand. Holding the bow diagonally across the body, the upper end to the left, he "nocked" his arrow by laying it on the right side of the bow. It crossed the middle of the bow where the first and second fingers of the left hand received it and held it from slipping; it was also a little distance away from the bow. This refinement of technique was necessary to avoid rubbing the feathers, which were longer than the space between the bow and the string. The bow itself he clamped in the notch between the thumb and fingers of the left hand. He did not grip it tightly, even when full drawn. It poised in this notch, and even when the arrow was released it was only retained from springing from the hand by a light touch of his fingers. Some Indians, he said, had a little strap on the

[187]

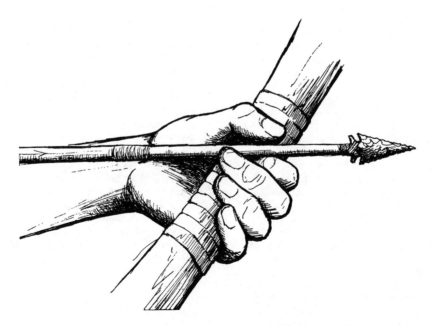

Ishi's bow hand.

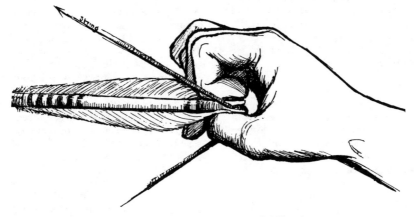

Ishi's release.

handle to prevent the bow jumping out of the hand.

The arrow, when full drawn, rested on the bow, steadied in position by the slight touch of his thumb on one side, the middle finger tip at the other. When the arrow left the string, at the moment of release, the bow revolved, or turned over completely, in his hand, so that the back of the bow was toward him.

The arrow release (the letting fly of the arrow) was a modification of that known as the Mongolian type. That is, he "drew" the bow with the right thumb flexed beneath the string. On the thumb nail he laid the end of the middle finger, to strengthen the hold. The index finger, completely flexed, rested on the arrow to keep it from slipping from the string. The extremities of the feathers, being near the nock, were neatly folded along the shaft in the grip of these fingers, to prevent them from being ruffled.

Ishi knew of several releases, saying that certain other tribes used them. The primary type, that where the arrow butt is gripped between the thumb and the flexed forefinger, he said certain Indians used, and it seemed to be a criterion of strength.

There are five known types of arrow release or methods of holding the arrow on the string while the bow is drawn. These were determined and named by E. S. Morse.[6]

The Primary release is that most naturally used by the novice. He draws the arrow by pinching it between his thumb and flexed forefinger. This is not a strong grip on the arrow, though practice undoubtedly strengthens the hold. No robust archery, according to English standards, has ever been done with this release. Yet it is the only one reported from many primitive peoples, perhaps even the method most commonly followed by uncivilized tribes.

The Secondary release is similar, but the middle finger assists in the pull by pressing on the string.

The Tertiary release holds the arrow between the thumb and straightened forefinger. It may also place other fingers on the string to assist in the pull.

The Mongolian or Asiatic release is chiefly used with the composite bow, and consists of pulling the string with the flexed thumb, more or less supported by the other fingers, while the arrow is merely steadied in position by contact with the forefinger, and by being held in the angle between the thumb and forefinger. This method reaches

6. Bulletin of the Essex Institute, Salem, XVII, 145-198, 1885.

full effectiveness when a sharp-edged thumb ring is worn to engage the string.

The Mediterranean release was known to the ancients and is that used in English archery and by the Eskimo. The first three fingers, unassisted by the thumb, draw the string, while the engaged arrow rests between the first and second fingers.

Ishi's release is of peculiar interest because its precise type has never been described before; also because the fundamental method of which it is a variety, the Mongolian, has until now not been reported in America.

A series of tests of the comparative strength of these various arrow releases, made by the writer with a spring scale attached to an arrow and cord, yields the following average pulls:

Primary, 25 pounds.
Primary, with an arrow having a grip or notch in the end to assist the draw, 35 pounds.
Secondary, 40 pounds.
Tertiary, 60 pounds.
Mongolian, 45 pounds.
Mongolian, with a Japanese-type shooting glove to protect the thumb, 55 pounds.
Mediterranean, 80 pounds.

Greater experience may have somewhat favored the result for the Mediterranean method, but there is no doubt that it is the most powerful of all known releases.

As Ishi drew with the back of his hand uppermost, he extended his bowarm horizontally and

[189]

A shot from a squatting position, a characteristic attitude in Ishi's archery.

Kneeling shot.

Nocking an arrow on the string.

Full drawn, wrist touching the chin.

After release. The bow has turned in Ishi's hand and the vibration of the string can be seen.

[191]

Ishi watching the flight of his arrow. He holds his position.

kept it straight, midway between a lateral and forward position. His right hand he drew till its back came beneath his chin, the end of his radius touching the top of his sternum. Thus he looked straight along his arrow with both eyes open. In this position his eyes were considerably above the nock of the arrow and he therefore had to allow for over-shooting his mark.

He changed the position of his drawing hand for different ranges. For near shots, his right hand was often drawn as high as his mouth. His extreme length of draw was not over twenty-six inches, while for small game and near shots he shortened this to eighteen or twenty inches. He never drew any shaft to the head. In drawing, his right arm was held close to the body, while the shoulder was markedly elevated. This gave him a hunched appearance, but it permitted him to hold arrows under his arm, and in other ways must have favored his peculiar mode of shooting. It also threw his right arm and forearm into the same plane with his bow.

Before making any careful shot it was his invariable habit to glance down his arrow and straighten with his fingers any slight curvature that might be present.

Nocking, drawing, aiming, and releasing, all were done within three seconds. He dwelt on his aim about a second, and shot entirely by intuition, not by point of aim. For long shots he attempted to assist the flight of his arrow by quickly pushing forward his bow arm as he shot.

A point blank range is that condition in aiming where the tip of the arrow seems to rest on the object to be hit. With him this was about fifty yards, and at over sixty yards his bow hand obscured his vision, so that he first aimed, then further elevated his bow hand before releasing. With the English method of shooting, where the arrow lies at the left of the bow, the hand does not interfere with the vision, unless in shots of more than a hundred yards, because the left eye can see past the hand.

After discharge of his arrow, Ishi maintained his shooting position for a second, as good archers always do. He preferred to shoot kneeling or squatting; this seems to have been the best posture for game shooting. In kneeling, he usually placed his right knee on the ground. Shooting with us, especially at targets, he stood facing the target, or turning his left side slightly toward it. His position was rather insecure, knees flexed a trifle, feet about four inches apart. His body he held quite erect, though in stalking game he shot from a crouching position.

He never used a wrist guard or "bracer" on his left arm to protect it from the string, although he nearly always pulled up his shirt sleeve. This was to avoid striking any clothing with the string, which would check the flight of the arrow. At times the string did strike his forearm, and bruise it, and after prolonged shooting his left wrist was often sore and ecchymosed. Leather protection for his forefinger he sometimes used in target shooting, but neither the glove nor bracer seemed needed for the intermittent shooting during a hunt.

In nocking his arrow, he paid no particular attention to the cock feather, or that opposite the nock. It rested against the bow as often as away from it. With nearly all modern archers, this is considered very bad technique. Since most of the feathers were soft, this however did not seem much to disturb the flight of the arrow.

Ishi's Records with the Bow

There are no records of aboriginal archery with which to compare those of civilized times. That the American Indian was a good shot is conceded by all who know him, and fiction makes him out an incomparable archer, capable of deeds outrivaling those of William Tell and the redoubtable Robin of Sherwood Forest. But no authentic scores exist. It is therefore a privilege to have been able to compare the shooting of an unspoiled American Indian with that of modern archers. . . .

There are two well recognized rounds in archery. The English or York round consists in shooting six dozen arrows at one hundred yards, four dozen at eighty yards, and two dozen at sixty yards, and adding the score thus attained. The American round consists in shooting thirty arrows at each of the distances, sixty, fifty, and forty yards. The target used is a circular straw mat four feet in diameter, four inches thick, covered with a facing on which are five concentric rings. The central ring or gold is nine and one-half inches in diameter, while each circle is one-half this in width. Their values are 9, 7, 5, 3, 1 points.

Because of the great distance, and his inability to hit the target often enough to warrant compiling a score, Ishi seldom shot the York round. But we have many records of his scores at the American round. It must be conceded that an archer may be a poor target shot and yet at the same time be a practical and accurate archer in hunting. Ishi's best scores at the American round are as follows, 30 arrows being shot at each distance:

October 23, 1914.
    60 yards,   10 hits,   32 score
    50 yards,   20 hits,   92 score, 2 golds
    40 yards,   19 hits,   99 score, 2 golds
    —   —   —

    Total . . . .49 hits, 223 score, 4 golds
May 30, 1915.
    60 yards,   13 hits,   51 score
    50 yards,   17 hits,   59 score
    40 yards,   23 hits,   95 score, 1 gold
    —   —   —

    Total . . . .53 hits, 205 score, 1 gold

A good score will total 90 hits, 500 score. My own best round is 88 hits, 538 score.

At ten and twenty yards Ishi was proportionately much more accurate, and while not consistent, he could hit objects three or four inches in diameter with such frequency that it was a commonplace event. Out of every five arrows, one or two surely would reach the mark. In his native state, his targets were small bundles of straw about the size of a rabbit or quail, or he shot at a small hoop in motion.

At shooting on the wing or at running game, he did not seem to be correspondingly adept. At so-called turtle shooting, or shooting up in the air and having the arrow strike the object in descent, he was not proficient. In rapid shooting he could just discharge his third arrow while two were in the air; unlike the alleged performance of Hiawatha,

he could not keep ten shafts aloft at once. Catlin reports that the Mandans could keep eight arrows in the air at one time.

Ishi's greatest flight shot was 185 yards. No doubt had he prepared himself for distance shooting he could have surpassed this; but using his 40-pound hunting bow and the lightest arrow in his quiver, this was his extreme length. After Ishi's death, I shot his bow, with an especially light arrow with a closely cropped feather, a distance of 200 yards. . . .

To ascertain the casting power of what Ishi considered an ideal bow, I had him select one that he considered the best, from the entire number in the Museum. This was a Yurok bow of yew heavily backed with sinew and corresponded closely in proportions to those of his own make. After warming it carefully and bracing it, Ishi shot a number of light flight arrows. His greatest cast was only 175 yards. Its weight was less than 40 pounds.

Besides the fact that Ishi, in common with all savages, failed to understand the optics and ballistics of archery, his arrows were of such unequal weight and dissimilar shape and size, that it is not surprising that his markmanship was erratic. A difference of ten grains in the weight of a shaft, or a slight difference in the height of the feathers, will cause an arrow shot sixty yards to fly several feet higher or lower than its predecessor.

The length of time required for Ishi's hunting shafts to fly 100 yards was 4 seconds. The angle of trajectory was 30 degrees. The weight of these arrows was 1 ounce; their power of penetration was sufficient to pierce our target, which consisted of a piece of oil cloth, 2 gunny sacks, and 4 inches of straw target, entirely traversing these bodies. A steel hunting point, shot from 40 yards, readily penetrated an inch into pine. On striking a tree, the entire point and an inch of the shaft were often buried in the trunk.

The angle of elevation necessary for his arrow to fly one hundred yards is much greater than that needed for our target arrows. Shooting a 48-pound bow with a five-shilling, or one-ounce arrow, my elevation is 15 degrees, while under the same conditions with a 65-pound bow it is as low as 10

[193]

1. Watching the flight of the arrow. The bow string is still vibrating. The bow has turned in Ishi's grasp in a manner that was habitual with him. He holds an extra arrow in his right armpit.

2. Carrying the bow and arrow. This is a 54-inch hunting bow of cedar, pulling 45 pounds. The arrows are steel-pointed.

degrees. The time required for a 100-yard flight of this latter is 2 2/5 seconds. The average velocity of an arrow is reckoned at 120 feet a second.

Hunting

At a very early period in our association with the Yahi, we undertook various little hunting excursions, and upon two occasions went upon extended trips into the mountains.

In shooting small game, such as quail, squirrels, and rabbits, Ishi was very proficient. His method was that of still hunting; walking over the ground very quiet and alert, always paying particular attention to wind, noise, and cover. He was indefatigable in the persistence with which he stalked game, and seldom left a clump of brush in which he knew or suspected the presence of game, until all means of getting it had been tried.

His vision was particularly well trained, and invariably he sighted the game first. This acumen was manifest also in the finding of arrows. Ishi nearly always could find a shaft in the grass or brush where we overlooked it.

He shot rabbits as close as five yards. On the other hand I have seen him shoot a squirrel through the head at forty yards. The usual killing distance was between ten and twenty yards. Game was nearly always shot while standing still, although an occasional rabbit was shot running. Arrows striking these small animals frequently passed completely through them. Death did not always result from the first shot, and one or more additional arrows were sometimes necessary to kill.

If a rabbit were shot and caught, Ishi would break all its legs with his hands, then lay it on the ground to die from the shock. This seems to have been a hunting custom, and he seemed to dislike having the animal die in his hands. Later, he adopted, with us, the more humane method of tapping his game on the head to kill it.

Animals shot at do not always become alarmed, should the arrow miss them, but often permit several shots to be made. Quail struck with an arrow in fleshy parts, sometimes fly, or attempt to fly, with the missile transfixing them, and are only detained by its catching in the brush or foliage of trees.

In hunting deer, Ishi was particularly careful in the observance of several essential precautions. He would eat no fish on the day prior to the hunt, because the odor could be detected by deer, he said; nor would he have the odor of tobacco smoke about him. The morning of the hunt Ishi bathed himself from head to foot, and washed his mouth. Eating no food, he dressed himself in a shirt, or breech clout. Any covering on the legs made a noise while in the brush, and a sensitive man rather favored cautious walking. While Ishi was proud of his shoes acquired in civilization, he said they made a noise like a horse, and he immediately discarded them when any real work in the field was encountered. In climbing cliffs, or crossing streams or trunks of trees, he first removed his shoes. So in hunting he preferred to go barefoot, and the strength of his perfectly shaped feet gave him a very definite advantage over his civilized companions.

It was a custom among his people to practice venesection before hunting expeditions. From Ishi's description, it appeared that this consisted of simple scarification over the flexor sides of the forearm and calf of the leg. This was supposed to strengthen and increase the courage of the hunter. Small chips of obsidian were used in this process.

In hunting deer, Ishi used the method of ambush. It was customary in his tribe to station archers behind certain rocks or bushes near well known deer trails. Then a band of Indians beat the brush at a mile or so distant, driving toward those in hiding. Upon our trip into Tehama County with Ishi, he showed us old deer trails near which curious small piles of rock were located at intervals hardly exceeding ten yards. These he indicated as ancient spots of ambush. They were just large enough to shield a man in a crouching position. The moss and lichen on them spoke of considerable age. One would hardly notice them in a boulder country, but the evidence of crude masonry was apparent when one's attention was called to them.

In approaching game, Ishi would rather skirt an entire mountain than come up on the wind side. His observance of this rule was almost an obsession.

He tested the wind by wetting his little finger. In travel over the country, certain places would appeal to him as ground favorable for rabbits, quail, squirrel, wildcats, or bear.

His hut in Deer Creek cañon was built on an old bear trail, many of these animals having been trapped within a few miles by an old hermit-like trapper of those parts. Years ago this same man caught an old Indian in his bear trap, maiming him for life. Ishi admitted that this Indian was his relative, perhaps his uncle or stepfather.

When in a part of the country suitable for rabbits, Ishi would hide himself behind a bush and give the

[196]

Standing shot.

rabbit call. This consists of a kissing sound, made by the lips with two fingers pressed against them. It is a shrill, plaintive squeak or cry, identical with that made by a rabbit in distress. He repeated it often, and with heart-rending pathos. He said that jackrabbits, wildcats, coyotes, and bear would come to the call. The first came to protect its young; the others came expecting food. Upon one afternoon's hunt, to test the truth of his assertions, I had Ishi repeat this call twelve times. From these dozen calls came five rabbits, and one wildcat emerged from the brush and approached us. Some rabbits came from a distance of one hundred and fifty yards, and approached within ten yards. The wildcat came within fifty yards, and permitted me to discharge five arrows at him before a glancing hit sent him into the forest.

As the game drew near, Ishi kept up a sucking sort of kiss with his lips while he adjusted an arrow on the bow. When the game was within a dozen yards, he shot.

He also used a call for deer, which he said was effective only when the does were with fawns. He took a new, tender leaf of a madrone tree, folded it lengthwise, and placing it between his lips, sucked vigorously. The sound produced was somewhat similar to that made when a small boy blows on a blade of grass held between his thumbs. It resembles the plaintive bleat of a fawn.

In decoying deer, Ishi also used a deer's head. He had one in his original camp from which the horns had been removed, and it was stuffed with leaves and twigs. This he placed on his head, and raising it above a bush, attracted the attention of his game, stimulating its curiosity while luring it within bow shot.

In none of our trips with Ishi were we able to kill a deer. Upon several occasions we secured shots, but owing to the distance, fall of the ground, or lack of accuracy, we failed to hit. The nearest shot was at sixty yards, and this is well beyond the Indian range of effectiveness. That it is possible, however, to kill large game with the bow, we proved upon a subsequent hunting expedition with Mr. W. J. Compton. We shot and killed two deer with the English long bow. One of these bucks Mr.

Calling game.

spine and probably would have caused paralysis; the third arrow entered the thorax back of the scapula, its head piercing the opposite chest wall. This also would have been fatal.[7]

In shots at buzzards, hawks, and gulls in flight, it often occurred that an arrow coming very close was dodged by these birds. To make this less possible, Ishi smeared his arrow shaft with black mud, and selected one with a close-cropped feather, that it might be less conspicuous and more silent than usual.

Our bad luck in deer hunting Ishi ascribed to the fact that I had killed a rattlesnake on the trail. He respected these reptiles, and always preferred to walk around a snake, wishing him well and leaving him unharmed.

Besides using the ambush, Ishi waited at deer licks to secure his venison. He had no special care for female deer, but considered them all good meat. He also shot fawns if needed for food. Those were the days of abundance of game, and the Indian killed only for food.

He preserved his deer meat by a process of curing in smoke, just as all hunters today make jerky. The deer hide he or more likely his female relatives, prepared by first rubbing in the brains and later by drying and scraping. Ishi himself did not seem to know how to make a fine quality of buckskin. His needlework and moccasin making were also not of an advanced type. In the University Museum we have a fur robe, previously the property of Ishi. It is composed of many wildcat and raccoon skins sewn together. Here the preparation is of a very good type. The furs are soft, fairly smooth and seem to have been smoked. This process of smoking, common among Indians, saturates the hide with creosote compounds, thus preserving the tissue from bacteria and parasites, while it renders it soft and somewhat waterproof. The absence of wounds in these skins suggests that Ishi used a trap or snare rather than the bow, to secure the pelts.

[197]

Compton shot running at 65 yards. The steel pointed arrow penetrated the chest and protruded a foot the other side, breaking off as the deer bounded through the brush. This animal died after running about 200 yards. I shot another buck at 45 yards. The arrow, penetrating just back of the diaphragm, caused an intense intra-abdominal hemorrhage, and death resulted after this deer had run a quarter of a mile. This would indicate that the Indians would have had little difficulty in striking down game. The arrows used by us were of the type of the old English broad head, 29 inches long, weighing from one ounce to an ounce and a half, heavily feathered and having steel heads one and one-half inches long by one inch wide. Mr. Compton shot a six-foot yew bow weighing 65 pounds, while mine was a sinew-backed yew bow 5 feet, 10 inches long, weighing 54 pounds.

In one deer killed with a rifle, I tested the penetrating power of Ishi's arrows. Stationed at thirty yards, he drove one arrow through the neck, half the shaft entering; the second shot struck the

7. There are interesting facts on the penetrating power of the arrow in Thomas Wilson's Arrow Wounds, *in* the American Anthropologist, n. s., III, 513-600, 1901.

[198]

Deer head. An original specimen taken from the camp which the Yahi were inhabiting in 1908. It now forms number 1-19564 in the Anthropological Museum of the University.

Ishi told us many times the methods he and his people used in killing bear. It was their ancient custom for a number of men to surround an animal, building a circle of fire about him. They then discharged arrows at him, attempting to shoot him in the mouth, and preferring to use rather small obsidian points, thinking that these made a more severe wound. If the animal charged an Indian, he defended himself with a fire brand, while the other members of the partly shot the bear with arrows. The shooting distance seems to have been twenty yards or less. The whole process seems to have been one of baiting and slowly wearing down the animal by hemorrhage and fatigue.

Among the specimens obtained by the University Museum is a skin of a cinnamon bear, which was shot by Ishi perhaps twenty-five years ago. It presents two cuts that indicate arrow and knife wounds. Ishi said that he killed this by shooting it with an arrow in the heart region, and later dispatching it with a short spear or obsidian knife. Owing to our imperfect language communication, and Ishi's natural modesty, we were unable to get minute details of this feat, but apparently the Indian killed the beast single-handed.

Shooting fish with the bow does not seem to have been one of his occupations. He used a salmon spear most expertly, and he also poisoned fish by

[199]

Cape of wildcat skins. Obtained under the same circumstances as the deer head shown in the preceding plate. The number of the specimen in the Museum is 1-19565.

putting the beaten fruit of squirting cucumber in trout pools. Fishhooks he made of bone, and wicker weirs were constructed for trout; but these things, of course, are not a part of archery.

Poisoned arrows he never used, although he knew of a method of making poison. This was to induce a rattlesnake to discharge its venom into a piece of deer liver, when, after putrefaction, the arrowheads were smeared with this combined bacterial poison and venom.

Ishi could imitate the call of many birds and small animals, and his name for these creatures had a remarkable phonetic resemblance to their call. Mountain quail he named *tsakaka;* the wild goose was *wami;* the gray squirrel, *dadichu.* These lower animals he believed fellow creatures, and all had acted human parts at times. The lizards, because of their hands, once made bows and arrows. Their bobbing motion, when on a sunny rock, was work of some sort. The yellow tendrils of the love vine or dodder were made by them at night to snare deer. The barking squirrel in the treetop told him of a near-by fox or wildcat. A story was built around every animal, and these mythical ideas he believed must be taken into consideration when hunting.

Various places had odors suggestive of certain animals. Ishi said that white men smelled bad, like a horse.

To have a bow break in the hand while shooting, Ishi considered a very serious omen and a portent of sickness. Thus he accounted for an attack of paratyphoid fever which one of us contracted. He himself had two bows shatter in his grasp, and doubtless this and several other malign influences incident to our civilization, in his mind, contributed as causes of his own last illness. During the declining days of his life, the one thing that brought that happy smile to his face which characterized him, was the subject of archery. A little work, feathering arrows or binding points on with sinew, gave him more pleasure than any diversion we could offer. Even when too weak to work, he liked to show me some little trick or method in making a shaft or backing a bow. To the last his heart was in the game. . . .

In this monograph on three Yana dialects of which Yahi was one, Sapir includes a story Ishi dictated to him in Yahi. We give the free translation of the story and Sapir's footnotes to it in full, with such of his introductory comments as refer most particularly to Ishi. It is our thought that this sampling of linguistic process will give the non-folkloristic, non-linguistic reader some sense for the process by which an unwritten language is brought onto the printed page as a written language.

Sapir made a handwritten record of Ishi's dictated story in phonetic transcription of Ishi's words. This required Ishi to speak much more slowly than he would have naturally and to suffer interruptions and repetitions, while Sapir had to take the dictation at sufficient speed and with minimal interruption in order to avoid serious distortion of Ishi's normal story flow.

This task done, the next was more tedious, that of making an interlineal translation into English, literally underneath each phoneme, word, or word cluster spoken by Ishi (see sample below). But it is the interlineal stage at which much technical linguistic information is taken and from which the literary analyst picks up numberless cues, such as individual and tribal story style; rhythm; use of repetition for emphasis, for expectancy, for sound; kind and degree of emotion conveyed; many implicit native significances no longer apparent in the final step, that of putting the story into "English" English.

A first judgment upon reading "Lizard" may be that it is diffuse, dull, without direction or point; that perhaps Ishi was an inept storyteller. Sapir's footnotes begin to bring the story into focus, but to have any idea of its meaning to the Yahi, a number of matters must be known and kept in mind: (1) that Ishi adumbrated, partly because Sapir knew only a smattering of Yahi; partly, because so familiar and favorite a tale would be known to its natural audience in full detail; (2) that Lizard was one of the two great creator gods of the Yahi, and that Long-tailed Lizard was a very modest person by comparison; (3) that one of Lizard's acts as creator was to ensure bounteous fresh pine nuts for the Yahi through all time; and (4) that Lizard's bravery, wits, strength, invulnerability, and skill with bow and arrow were long-established dogma. An encounter between Lizard and the inferior Wintun Indians could only be at one point ridiculous, until—with the day's end—the poetic imagery of the rain of unhurting arrows becomes memorable, even to our uninformed imaginations.

7. Analysis of a Yahi Text (1923)

Edward Sapir

Introductory Remarks

Of the four Yana dialects that constitute the Yanan group of Hokan languages—Northern, Central, and Southern Yana, and southernmost Yana or Yahi—texts have been secured from all but one, the Southern Yana dialect. This dialect was spoken by Sam Batwi, my Central Yana informant, in his childhood, but was exchanged early in life for the Central dialect. When I worked with him in 1907, he could give only isolated words and phrases of his old dialect, which was then extinct. The probability is strong that Southern Yana was a link between the Central and Yahi dialects, with a leaning, I surmise, to Yahi rather than to Central Yana. The Central and Northern dialects, though neatly distinct on a number of phonetic points, are mutually intelligible without difficulty. Yahi is very close in all essential respects to the two northern forms of Yana, but there are enough differences in phonetics, vocabulary, and morphology to put it in a class by itself as contrasted with the other two. It it doubtful if a Northern or Central Yana Indian could understand Yahi perfectly, but it is certain that he could make out practically all of it after a brief contact. On the whole, Yahi is the most archaic of the three

From Edward Sapir, "Text Analyses of Three Yana Dialects," *University of California Publications in American Archaeology and Ethnology,* Vol. 20 (1923). Extracts here are from pp. 263, 264-265, 282, and 283-285. Footnotes have been renumbered.

dialects; it is also appreciably harsher to the ear than the other two. Or rather, was, for with the death of Ishi, the last Indian to speak Yahi, this dialect, too, became extinct. Possibly there are still one or two Indians who know Central Yana and a handful who can speak or who know something of Northern Yana, but it can hardly be more than a matter of ten or fifteen years before Yana, like Esselen and Chimariko, becomes one of the extinct Hokan languages of California. . . .

At the time that I was working among the northern Yana survivors in 1907, the mysterious "Kombo" described by Powers were generally believed to be either a myth or safely extinct. The startling appearance on the Californian scene of Ishi in 1911 gave these old rumors an unexpected confirmation and American philology a new language with which to grapple. Little, however, was or could be done with Ishi's language till he had learned enough of the white man's ways and speech to make at least an elementary communication possible. The Yahi texts and grammatical information that are now in my hands were secured from him in the summer of 1915. Toward the end of my stay in Berkeley Ishi became ill. He never recovered. Throughout the period of my work with him, he was gentle and patient to a degree. Had he been surly, like several of the more northern Yana I have known, progress in this most nerve-racking of researches would have been impossible. It should be remembered by any one who makes a study of [the Yahi part] of this paper and who may be inclined to feel annoyance at the gaps in my analysis that Ishi's English was of the crudest. "Him's no good" did duty for "He (or it) is bad" or "That is not correct," while "sista" might mean equally "sister" or "brother." Ishi was perfectly willing to dictate and to interpret; the difficulties followed unavoidably from the circumstances. In going over his texts for interlinear translations— and it proved a difficult task to hold Ishi in leash in the matter of speed of dictation—I endeavored to use every tittle of evidence that I could muster, Ishi's "explanation" of the single words, his accompanying gestures, the context of the myth itself, and, most important of all, the analogies of

[201]

the northern dialects. Had Yahi proved to be less closely related to these dialects than it is, it is difficult to believe that it would have been feasible to secure from Ishi more than merely lexical information. As it is, Yahi not only receives abundant light from the northern dialects, but is now able to reflect light upon them on a number of fundamental points of phonology and even of morphology. As regards the purely phonetic record, I consider the Yahi material as superior, if anything, to that of the other dialects. Many of the morphological obscurities that still remain are sure to be dissipated when all the dialectic material has been systematically made available for comparison. . . .

A Story of Lizard

ʻiʹriʼ   ʻêʹbilʼ   kʻ i ʹriʼmauna
He made arrows   he was engaged in   his   arrow-making.

       kǃuʹllilʼ   niwiʹldjiʼ
He desired to turn (back).   He went west across a stream

       wiʹsduʼ   gi   iwiʹltcʻi
he went to gather pine-nuts   at   west across a stream,

       nilôʹp.djiʼ
he went westward up a mountain.

domdjawaʹldiʼ   kʻ dīʹtʻella
He put down on the ground   his   quiver.

ʻôʹkǃaudubalguʼ   gi   wêʹyumpʻa
He just cut out and pulled up   at   deer horns;

dôʹwayaltcʻidibilʼ   wêʹyumpʻa
he carried about on his shoulders as quiver   deer horns.

       bôʹtǃanʼ
He pounded out (nuts) with a rock.

Translation

(Lizard) made arrows, was busy with his arrow-making. He (put aside his work and) made up his mind to go off in another direction. He went across the river to the west,[1] went to gather pine-nuts on the western side of the river. He went westward up into the hilly country. He put his quiver down on the ground. He (had) merely cut out and pulled up the horns of a deer (for a quiver) and was

carrying them about riding his shoulder.[2] He, who was gathering pine-nuts, pounded them out with a stone. He was getting out the nuts, got them out of the cones.[3] And then he took up the nuts and, filling them in, he took up again his storage basket.[4]

The Yā́wi[5] yelled their war-whoops. (Lizard) again took up his quiver. The Yā́wi whooped.[6] He pulled a bow out of his quiver. "There's a wind blowing," he said. "It is storming," he said.[7] They rushed past him. Now he shot off his arrows and hit them straight in their faces. He returned down hill to the east. He shot off arrows to the north, he shot to the south, he shot to the east—he hit them straight in the face. He returned to the river, went back eastward over the water, and emerged from the river. The Yā́wi all scattered out of sight. Then (Lizard) went ahead on the road and came back home at nightfall. He put away his storage baskets.

Early in the morning he smooths down cane arrow-shafts. He was making arrows. He smoothed his arrow-shafts by rubbing, busied with his arrow-making. He finished. He fitted the cane shafts tight on around the foreshafts. He finished this, he socketed the foreshafts well in. He turns his arrows as he holds them down to the ground; he painted bands—(red and green)—at their butts. Now he occupied himself in this manner all day long. He feathered the arrows—finished. And then

1. The Sacramento river is meant.

2. It seems that Lizard's quiver was made of deerskin stretched on a frame of two deer horns that he had cut loose from each other at the base.
3. He first put the pine-cones over a fire to try out the pitch. When there was no more pitch left in them, he pounded out the nuts.
4. The *bǎʹnu*, an openwork, flexible receptacle for roots and nuts, made of vegetable fibres.
5. This is the term now used by the Northern and Central Yana for the Wintun. In a Central Yana myth obtained from Sam Batwi (see *Yana Texts*, p. 71) the Yā́wi are legendary, evil-minded people dwelling on the western banks of the Sacramento. . . .
6. The sound they made was a prolonged *ǎ*.
7. Apparently the Yā́wi were shooting off arrows at Lizard from all directions in the form of rain. Lizard pretended that the attack of the Yā́wi was merely a strong wind blowing.

he trimmed the vanes of the feathers—finished.
He blackened the feathers, charring them (with the
burnt point of a stick). He wrapped sinew around
the juncture of shaft and foreshaft—finished. Then
he smoothed his foreshafts with scouring rush.[8]
He put his arrows aside when it was night.

"There are not many pine-nuts to eat, it would
seem," said (Lizard), as (his people) came and stood
near, waiting for food.[9] The woman[10] gave them
all to eat. "I have no stems[11] for the making of
foreshafts," he said. "Let it be Long-tailed Lizard,[12]
pray," he said, ("who is to go for some"). "Do
go and get stems for foreshafts!" said he. And then
the one (spoken to by Lizard) went off to find a
bush for the arrow foreshafts.

---

*Even Yahi music was recorded in quantity from
Ishi on Edison wax cylinders, and later transcribed
to tapes which were used in the present study. Music
in our lives, today, is something some people
actually do, but for most it is a matter of listening.
But among the old Yahi, songs were obviously
a part of life itself, since they were connected with
hunting, curing, gambling, and the like. Here is
a glimpse into a vanished world—one rich in expression and human feeling. If it took a half-
century to finally offer this to the world, that is
a small matter because these songs are timeless.*

8. Yahi *mi'lts!imyauna.*
9. As chief, he was naturally expected to share with
his people the stock of pine-nuts he had brought home
with him from the western country. I incline to believe
that Lizard's words are to be taken in a sense opposed to
their literal meaning. He affects a chief's self-disparagement.
The true implication seems to be that there was plenty
for all. Rhetorical negatives of this type are quite common
in Yana; cf. *Yana Texts*, p. 111, 1.5, and note 166.
10. Lizard's wife.
11. The term *ba'iwak!i* seems to indicate some bush or
tree growing near the water. The stems of small ones were
used for the making of the wooden fore-shafts that fitted
in to the arrow-shafts of cane. Apparently the word indicates both the tree and the stem used in arrow-making.
12. Another species of lizard than the hero himself
(*k!a'ltc!auna*), who is named later on in the narrative.
This "Long-tailed Lizard" (*p'ā't!elwalla*) was Lizard's
little nephew.

8. The Songs of Ishi (1965)

Bruno Nettl

In 1911, one of the most famous people in
this country was Ishi, a middle-aged Yahi Indian
from Northern California, who had wandered
out of the mountains, the last survivor of a tribe
that had gone into seclusion some forty years
before. Ishi had been living in a band that never
numbered more than a dozen for all of his adolescent and adult life. His last years before discovery were spent in a group of four people, an
old man and woman, presumably his parents,
and a middle-aged woman, probably his sister.
For several months now he had been completely alone, and in 1911 he threw himself on the
mercy of the whites, fully expecting to be killed,
as had many of his compatriots. Instead, he
was taken to the Museum of Anthropology at
Berkeley and lived there for five years, serving
mainly as an informant to two eminent anthropologists, T. T. Waterman and A. L. Kroeber.
He was famed as the "last wild Indian," i.e.
the last Indian who had grown up outside the
acculturated environment typical of North
American Indian culture of the time. A number
of publications on Yahi language and culture
came about through Ishi's work, and his background as well as his years in Berkeley have
recently been described by Theodora Kroeber
in a book, *Ishi in Two Worlds.*

In the humanistic tradition of American anthropology, Waterman and Kroeber also inquired about
music, and Ishi recorded over sixty songs between
1911 and 1914. These have, to my knowledge,
never been used for research, and the present paper
is based on them, as well as on background material in the publications and notes of Waterman
and Kroeber. The recordings, made on cylinders,
were transferred to tape and sent to me through
the courtesy of Professor William Bascom, director

Musical Quarterly (New York: G. Schirmer, Inc.),
Vol. LI, No. 3 (July, 1965), pp. 460-477.

of the Lowie Museum of Anthropology at Berkeley.[1] Through these recordings, we are able to arrive at what I hope is a reasonably accurate picture of the Yahi musical style, but we may use them also in order to ask and perhaps illuminate other questions of ethnomusicological import: They represent the total repertory of a single person and, presumably, the musical idiolect of an individual. They provide a basis for comparing the songs of acculturated and unacculturated Indians. And they are, by coincidence perhaps, some interesting material for a discussion of the nature of scale and tonality in an oral tradition.

Let me mention one important limitation. Owing to the early date of these recordings, their acoustical quality is poor, and a good many details of the singing are not transmitted or are obscured by static. The quality of the transcriptions is necessarily reduced by this component.

Ishi did not use instruments, except in songs 1699 and 1700,[2] in which he accompanies himself by beating time with a stick. We have no information on Yahi instruments, but the related Yana Indians, according to Sapir and Spier,[3] had a few: a cocoon rattle, a deerhoof rattle (evidently replaced by Ishi's stick in the recordings) used in girls' puberty rites,[4] and a true vertical flute with six fingerholes.

The existence of Ishi's recordings makes it necessary to ask some questions that have broad implications. Since this is all we have available of Yahi music, can we assume that it is a representative

sample? We will never know, but we can speculate. There is a considerable variety of song functions and types, and these do not exhibit perceptible stylistic differences in spite of the relatively considerable variety in the style itself. The singing style and the musical style in general are certainly related to those of other tribes in the area, particularly the Yokuts, Modoc, and Klamath of Southern Oregon. On the other hand, we may be totally unaware of song types that Ishi may not have learned. For example, it is known that men and women used different forms of the language. These were, of course, mutually intelligible, but most words had a "male" and "female" form. Is it not possible that women, accordingly, also had a different musical style? What little evidence we have indicates that they did not, for Ishi recorded several "women doctor songs," presumably sung by female shamans, which do not differ in style from the rest. But throughout this investigation we must ask ourselves whether the singing of one informant can be regarded as an adequate sampling of a tribal repertory, especially since the informant spent most of his life in circumstances quite different from the earlier tribal life. And of course we do not know whether Ishi's singing would have been regarded as adequate, poor, or exemplary by Yahi standards.

Much of the nature of the songs—were they sacred or secular, old or new, soloistic or ensemble? —cannot readily be ascertained. We have a number of gambling songs (1682a, 1683a, 1684a, 1694, 1696a and b, 1697a, 1698a and b, 1701a, 1822, 1823, and 1825). In addition, three are labeled Atsugewi gambling songs (1816, 1817, 1818), presumably songs originating with the northeastern neighbors of the Yahi. There are several "doctor's songs" for curing various ills (1702, 1703, 1705, 1708, 1713, and 1715), and a group of "woman doctor's songs" (1701b, 1712, 1714, 1826, 1831, and 1832). Several songs are evidently hunting songs, associated with animals: deer songs (1710, 1829); fish songs (1711, 1728); owl songs (1690, 1697b). 1706 is labeled "dentalium song"; 1688a and b and 1724 are flint songs, 1707 and 1828 are thunder songs. Ceremonial songs are also found. 1725 and 1726 are "sweathouse songs," evidently

1. I am indebted to the Robert H. Lowie Museum of Anthropology, University of California, for permission to use these recordings for research and to publish my findings.

2. The numbering and arrangement of the songs is that used by the Lowie Museum. The song numbers are those of the original cylinders. This rather cumbersome numbering has been used so that reference to specific materials in other publications can be made. The recordings numbered in the 1600s and 1700s come from 1911 and 1912. Those in the 1800s, from 1914.

3. Edward Sapir and Leslie Spier, *Notes on the Culture of the Yana*, in *Anthropological Records* (University of California), III, No. 3 (1943), 259.

4. See Harold E. Driver and S. H. Riesenberg, *Hoof Rattles and Girls' Puberty Rites in North and South America*, Bloomington, Indiana University Publications in Anthropology and Linguistics, Memoir 4, 1950.

associated with the ritual sweat bath common to many Indian tribes. 1815 is labeled "dancing song of dead people," and several are songs of the girls' adolescence ceremony: 1685a, 1686a, 1687a, 1692, 1700, and 1824. In addition, 1819, 1820, and 1821 are labeled as Maidu doctor's songs, evidently from the western neighbors of the Yahi.

Of the 52 songs transcribed, eight are labeled as repetitions, made in some cases a few months and in others three years later than others, of material previously recorded in this collection. Thus, according to Ishi's own classification, we have only 44 songs plus eight duplications. In some cases, the new recording hardly even seems similar to the earlier one, while in other cases the songs are clearly variants of the earlier renditions. For example, 1710b and 1832, recorded many months apart, are obviously variants of the same song. The same is true of 1707 and 1828. On the other hand, 1683a and 1694 are similar only in the most general way, given the over-all limitations of the style. Since it is difficult to know whether "same song" means the same tune or the same text, or both, the different renditions are counted here as separate tunes. And to be sure, in our classification of tune families, discussed below, some of the duplicate renditions supposedly of the same song are related, but others are not. As in other Indian tribes, the concept of a song as a unit of musical thought may be something quite different from that held in Western art music. The duplicate recordings, as given by Ishi, are listed here:

1701b — 1832 (woman doctor's song)
1714 — 1831 (woman doctor's song)
1710 — 1829 (deer song)
1690 — 1697b (owl song)
1707 — 1828 (thunder song)
1683a — 1694 (gambling song)
1684a — 1822 (gambling song)
1700 — 1824 (girls' adolescence ceremony)

The problems of identifying songs that are genetically related, that is, of tune families, are almost insurmountable in American Indian music. These problems have been solved in at least a tentative fashion for much European folk music, where it is evident that a tune, once composed, is passed on, variants being created all the time, and except for certain variants that have changed beyond recognition, it is often possible to identify those tunes that ultimately sprang from the same parent tune.[5] In some Indian cultures, tradition does not seem to operate in the same fashion. Songs are made up from material in other songs, but rather than a linear relationship in the genealogy, there is one with crossing and criss-crossing lines of interdependence. In addition, some repertories exhibit so great a degree of homogeneity that general stylistic similarity cannot easily be distinguished from true genetic relationship.

In spite of these obstacles, it seems possible to identify at least some relationship among the tunes in Ishi's repertory. Several of these are actually labeled as "the same song," and were simply recorded at different times. Others, again, show no textual or functional relationship. In some cases, different recordings of the "same song" do not use related tunes. In a few cases, functional identity accompanies tune relationship. It must be stressed that the "tune families" here outlined are presented in the most tentative way possible. Unfortunately, since we are dealing with a closed corpus, there is no chance that further material will ever shed more light on the matter. But in view of the fact that genetic relationship has hardly been studied in American Indian music, it seems worthwhile to present even these inconclusive findings.

Thirteen groups have been identified. They comprise 39 songs, the other thirteen songs being, evidently, "families" unto themselves. We present the numberings here without further comment:

1) 1692, 1683a-1694, 1816, 1817, 1818
2) 1711, 1700-1824, 1710 (not with "same song" 1829)
3) 1688b, 1705, 1728
4) 1821, 1714-1831
5) 1708, 1701b-1832, 1823
6) 1726, 1707-1828

[205]

5. For a study of the kinds of relationship found in English folk music see Samuel P. Bayard, *Two Representative Tune Families of British Tradition*, in *Midwest Folklore*, IV (1954), 13-34.

7) 1682a, 1826, 1829 (not with "same song" 1710)
8) 1819, 1820
9) 1703, 1725
10) 1713, 1715
11) 1684a, 1697a
12) 1698a (not with "same song" 1825), 1698b
13) 1712, 1690-1697b

Songs that are related, and that are labeled as the same song on the recordings, are separated by hyphens. The decisions here have been based on general or specific similarity of melodic bits and motifs, and it should be noted that members of a hypothetical tune family do not necessarily have identical scales, forms, or rhythms.

The scales of the Yahi material are extremely limited, yet somewhat varied. 38 of the 52 songs are tritonic, twelve are tetratonic, and two, pentatonic. In a good many cases it was difficult to decide whether two separate pitches are distinct tone units or variants of a single unit. The many repetitions of a tune in each rendition were helpful in making such decisions.

The most common scale (35 songs) involves a major second at the top under which another evidently less stable interval is added. The latter is almost always more varied within the renditions of an individual song, but it is normally a major second, a minor third, or an intermediate interval. Specifically, fifteen of the songs have what we may call anhemitonic tritonic type A, ; eleven, type B, ; and nine, type C . The grouping of these three types

in one broad category is justified by the very instability of the lower interval. Characteristically, a song will be sung with the note b sometimes sharp, sometimes practically c; and when c is the lowest note, it is frequently sung flat. Here we perhaps have evidence for the supposition that an interval is, in some cultures, not a specific unit that varies only below the threshold of perception,

but rather, a range within which the singer can take liberties. We cannot assume that Ishi was unable to sing the same variant of the interval many times in one song, since the higher interval in the tritonic scales is much more stable than the lower. We must assume, rather, that we have two kinds of intervals in this little scale: one that is a more or less accurate major second, and a second one that is less stable and varies between major second and minor third (though in the transcriptions, I have for convenience used the most common manifestation in each song). If we had used a quasi-phonetic transcription, we would have had to write a scale with more tones and several microtones. Reduction of these several variant tones to one pitch unit is the kind of procedure we can call phonemic, since it corresponds roughly to the procedure, in linguistics, of reducing the many variants of a sound to one phoneme or intelligible sound in a language. Just as in certain languages it is possible that certain phonemes have many variants, or allophones, it may be that in a musical style, certain intervals tend to be varied more than others. This seems to be the case in the Yahi style.

The other type of tritonic scale has half tones:

One song has the half tone at the top, ,

and two songs, at the bottom .

The tetratonic scales fall into two broad categories. One has the range of a fifth and no halftones: type A (4 songs) , type B (one song) . The second has the range of a fourth, with the half tone at the top in two songs, in the middle in one song, and at the bottom in four songs. Two songs are pentatonic, but all tones here fall within a pentachord. Indeed, these two songs are otherwise atypical, for song 1702 has a very brief bit of sequential treatment at its beginning, and song 1686a has the form of the "rise," with a higher section occasionally appearing;

this form is discussed below, and possibly it, along with the atypical scale, is evidence that this song was a recent introduction from outside into the Yahi repertory.

The tonal aspects of the scales are somewhat baffling. It is difficult to identify main tones either by their frequency or their location in key spots. I say this is baffling because in most styles with few tones, the songs tend to be built around a single tone from which the singer deviates occasionally. While the melodic movement is, in a very general way, descending, we cannot say that the lowest tone normally appears in final position, or that the higher tones are normally initial ones. On the whole, at least two tones are used in equal degrees of importance. It is as if, within the limits of the scale, the composers of the Yahi songs tried to introduce as much variety as possible; and this is a tendency we can observe in the over-all structure of the songs also.

Melodic contour does not exhibit a high degree of specialization. One point to be mentioned is the fact that melodic intervals are almost exclusively between consecutive tones of the scales. There are hardly any skips—which would, if they occurred, almost inevitably be from the lowest to the highest tone of the scale. The lack of skips causes the middle tone of the tritonic scales to be rather prominent, something that is not typical of many other Indian styles, in which the middle of the range is frequently simply used for transitional material between the lower and higher parts of the scale, which are used for the primary melodic development.

In a very general sense, most of the melodic movement is descending. General inspection of the material gives the impression that three-fourths of the songs move downward in the most important portions. A simple count of the relationships between initial and final tones indicates that 43 of the songs begin on a higher tone than the one on which they end. In seven songs, initial and final tones are identical, and in two, the final tone is higher.

The forms of the songs are exceedingly simple, though in most cases they go beyond simple repetition of a single phrase. Each song is repeated about twenty times, but of course it is difficult to say whether or not this reflects the actual practice of the Yahi, or whether the number of renditions reflects the length of time available on one cylinder. The fact that many of the songs accompanied other activities leads us to believe that repetition was continued until the accompanying activity ceased. In North American Indian music, generally, songs in which the text is repeated in each rendition tend to be repeated until their function, for example dancing, is completed, or according to a ceremonial formula, for example four times in the case of Arapaho Peyote songs. Ishi's songs evidently fall in the former category.

In comparing the repetitions of the songs, we find that sometimes the repetitions of the total stanza differ from each other very considerably, while in other songs there is little variation. Let us examine song no. 1825 as an example of what may happen. It is one of those songs in which considerable variation appears. The nineteen repetitions are obviously versions of the first stanza, but three distinct variants of the main theme are found, and the singer gradually but increasingly departs from the variant used at the beginning. For purposes of identification, the variants are marked with letters. Variants A and B are distinguished primarily by the use of different rhythms in measure 4 (A has a half note and a quarter, B has three quarters), by a different melody in measure 1 (A moves from a to g, or remains on a; B descends from a to e) and measure 3 (A begins on a or g, and usually descends; B remains on g). Variant B has two sub-types: B^1 uses the descent from a to e at the beginning; B^2 descends only to g, as does variant A, but has the 4th measure typical of variant B. Variant C is distinct in that it has six measures instead of four, the last four of which are similar to A, but the first two of which are like B^2. The over-all pattern is one of greater diversification until the end, when C is used exclusively. If we divided the song into three equal parts, the first part would be dominated by A, the third part by C, and the middle part makes roughly equal use of A, B, and C. The structure of the variants

[207]

as a whole is AAAB^{1}AA B^{1}ACB^{1}AB^{2}A B^{2}ACCCC. Unfortunately, we do not know what would have happened next if Ishi had been allowed to continue.

The description of the internal structure of the short musical line that makes up the stanza of a Yahi song is not a simple matter, for subdivision of the song into phrases or other short units is made difficult by the very brevity of the total product. Breathing spaces cannot easily be detected in the recordings, and repetition of units does not frequently occur. Repetition of words is common and sometimes helps us to make decisions about subdividing the melody. At times, however, there is obvious conflict between verbal and musical units. Nevertheless, the forms of the Yahi songs have been analyzed with customary procedures and divided into sections marked by letters to show internal relationship. In spite of the obvious limitations of the material, there is really a great deal of variety. Compared to the songs of certain other tribes in which an individual form dominates the whole repertory, we find several types represented more or less equally.

[208]

Most numerous is a form in which two related parts are simply alternated, in the fashion of A^{1}A^2. This type of form is found, in more elaborate manifestations, in other parts of the continent. For example, the Plains Indians frequently use it, but each section itself is composed of several phrases, and A^2 is usually a slightly abbreviated version of A^1, usually minus the first phrase or two.[6] Here the difference is reflected in a difference in text, A^1 being sung with meaningless syllables, A^2 with the meaningful text. The Iroquois Eagle Dance[7] has songs using the arrangement AABAB, which is evidently similar, AAB and AB being the A^1 and A^2. Peyote songs frequently have the same general form type, and the simple songs of the Modoc,[8] a tribe not far from the Yahi, have an

arrangement similar to those described here. In Ishi's songs, the two parts, A^1 and A^2, may be either equal or unequal in length. They are roughly equal in songs nos. 1683a, 1694, 1696a, 1712, 1714, 1724, 1726, 1822, 1818, 1819, and 1831. In three songs (1684a, 1815, and 1821) the first part, A^1, is longer, and in 1688a and 1713 A^2 is longer. 1713 can be subdivided into more elaborate terms, AB^{1}AB^{2}C, the two principal sections being distinguished mainly by the addition of a sort of coda or closing measure. 1821 is a prototype of the above-mentioned Plains Indian form and, indeed, looks in some ways quite like the Iroquois Eagle Dance material: AABAB.

A related Yahi form type, found also among the Modoc, consists simply of two phrases that are not closely related, as they are in the A^{1}A^2 form described above. The relationship between them in terms of length is similar to that in the form described above and, indeed, the two types are perhaps just variations of the same basic formula. Using the label AB, we find that the two sections are about equal in length in 1690, 1697b, 1701a, and 1817. A is longer in 1702, and B in 1698a, 1706, and 1711. Of approximately equal length, also, are the components of 1703, 1715, 1819, 1820, and 1825. These, however, merit particular attention, because of the special melodic relationship between the two sections.

1703, 1819, and 1825 are distinguished in that section B is, very roughly, an inversion of A, the contour of B exhibiting motion contrary to that of A. 1715, 1819, and 1820 present a rudimentary and approximate sequence, B having the same material as A approximately a tone lower. There is, however, no question here of imitation in the specific sense of the word. Nevertheless, two points are worth raising in connection with it. First, we have here a form somewhat intermediate between AB, in which two phrases contrast, and A^{1}A^2, which is simply two variations of the same theme. New tonal material appears, but the melodic contour and the approximate intervals remain. Second, we have here a form that shows a relationship to forms used by Indian tribes in the Plains, the Pueblos, and the Eastern half of North

6. Bruno Nettl, *Musical Culture of the Arapaho,* in *The Musical Quarterly,* IV (1955), 325-31.

7. Gertrude P. Kurath, *Iroquois Music and Dance,* Washington, Bulletin 187 of the Bureau of American Ethnology, 1964, pp. 46-47.

8. Jody C. Hall and Bruno Nettl, *Musical Style of the Modoc,* in *Southwestern Journal of Anthropology,* XI (1955), 58-66.

America,[9] and which is usually described as the terrace or tile form. This consists of a gradually but markedly descending melodic contour, each phrase having its own descent and an ending on a fairly extended repeated tone. While the various phrases do not usually have a sequential relationship, they tend to exhibit sufficiently similar kinds of melodic contour to make a relationship to actual transposition as a compositional device a point worth considering.

What do Yahi songs nos. 1715, 1819, and 1820 have to do with this Plains and Eastern form? Speculation regarding origins is not our task, but a digression in that direction may be in place here. The following are possibilities: 1) The Yahi songs developed recently, from their own A^1A^2 type. 2) The Yahi songs exhibit a form type from which developed the more complex Plains form. The fact that we so frequently find a binary arrangement with an incomplete or approxiamte repetition in both areas is supporting evidence. Is is possible that we have here the prototype of the Plains form, in a state of arrested development? 3) Somehow, and in relatively recent times, the idea of sequence in a descending pattern, which was highly developed in Plains music and which is found in some songs of certain Plateau tribes, penetrated to the Yahi, who used it in a few songs. I must say that none of these hypotheses is very satisfactory to me. Alternatives 2 and 3 seem unlikely in view of the distance between the Plains and Northern California; if we knew more about California Indian music, we should be in a better position to evaluate the hypotheses. On the other hand, alternative 1 denies the common origin of what really is a group of rather specialized and similar traits. Unfortunately we will never know the answer and we will always have to rely on circumstantial evidence to support whatever hypothesis we wish to promulgate. But the fact that the exceedingly simple forms of Yahi songs show some types found in other areas of Indian culture is of great interest in other respects.

Song no. 1686a is a further illustration of the interrelationship of Yahi and other styles. Rather than consisting of two phrases alternating regularly, it has two phrases, to be sure, but phrase A usually appears two or three times together, while phrase B appears alone. This fact, plus the rather unusual circumstance of a higher range in phrase B, makes it obvious that we are dealing with an example of a form labeled by George Herzog[10] as the "rise," and characteristic of the Yuman-speaking tribes of the Southwest, and of Central California. Even so, the relationship between A and B is a close one, so that we would wish to label B as perhaps B^a to indicate the small degree to which it is new.

Several of the songs are so brief that it is necessary to regard them simply as repetitions, with variation, of one phrase: 1705, 1725, 1728, and 1685a. The remainder of the songs are best regarded as groups of three or four phrases or sections, although for several of them one could also make a case for an analysis in binary terms. Nevertheless, the slightly greater degree of complexity here justifies a more elaborate description. Nine songs have three-part forms, and of these, eight have some repetition or recurrence of material. Only 1688b is an unequivocal progressive ABC. Otherwise, we find AAB (1682a, 1697a), ABB (1708), A^1A^2B (1823, 1829), AB^aC (1826), A^1BA^2 (1687a), and AB^aC^a (1698b).

Ten songs have four distinct sections. Only one is definitely in a progressive form, ABCD (1700). The rest contain repetition or reversion, which, indeed, is usually the criterion of division into four sections. In most cases, division into two parts would also be a logical course of analysis, which shows again that the basic division into two similar but not identical sections is the root of the Yahi structure. Thus, $A^1A^2B^1B^2$, with the B's longer, is found in songs 1701b, 1707, 1828, and 1832. $A^1A^2A^2B$ is found in 1824, and $A^1A^2A^3B$ in 1696b and 1816. Four sections of equal length, $A^1A^2A^2A^3$, are found in 1710, and AB^aAC in 1692.

[209]

9. Bruno Nettl, *North American Indian Musical Styles*, Philadelphia, American Folklore Society, 1954.

10. George Herzog, *The Yuman Musical Style*, in *Journal of American Folklore*, XLI (1928), 196-98.

The over-all impression of the Yahi forms is three-fold. First, it is obvious that in most of the songs, a single basic principle determines the structure—a binary arrangement in which two sections contrast but tend to be somewhat similar or related. It is possible to divide most of the songs into two sections that can be described as $A^1 A^2$, AB^a, or AB; but because of the restricted tonal material, even the AB form does not imply total independence of the two sections. Second, within these limitations of tone material and of the basic binary principle, there is a surprising variety of forms. Few of the songs can be said to have identical forms, and our descriptions yield a total of 23 different letter formulas. Third, we occasionally find forms that, while they do not conflict with the basic binary principle, coincide with certain form types typical of Indian cultures elsewhere in North America.

The rhythmic structure of the Yahi songs also defies simple classification. The songs either were not accompanied by rattles or drums, or the accompaniment was not audible on the old recordings. In a few songs (1692, for example), a single note value dominates the whole song. In most cases, two or three note values prevail, usually in the relationship of 1:2:4. Meter can be identified in most of the songs. In about half, the metric units remain stable throughout, and there are instances of rollicking rhythm, with strong beats heavily accented, as in the 12/8 meter of 1703, or the heavy triple meter of 1821. Alternation of duple and triple measures is found in a number of the songs, for example 1715 (2/4, 3/4, 2/4, 3/4, 2/4, 3/4) or 1688a (2-2-3-, 2-2-3-2). Quintuple meter appears in individual measures, as in 1831 (6-5), 1705 (4-5), and 1832 (4-5-6-9). An unusual case of isometric seven-unit meter is 1710.

The singing is essentially in a parlando-rubato style, perhaps becuase of an emphasis on the words, but in any event conducive to fluctuations in tempo and note values. In any one song, there is considerable variation among, say, the several notes written as quarter notes. Tempo is not very stable. The tendency of notes to fluctuate in length gives rise, occasionally, to fluctuations in the metric patterns of an entire piece. Thus, both 1829 and

[210]

1696a appear in duple, triple, and intermediate forms. They begin with renditions in duple meter, but in each case the singer gradually introduces violations which eventually result in a complete change to 6/8, though the melodic material remains identical. We may have, here, a phenomenon that is perhaps analogous to the flexibility of certain intervals in the scales.

Although most or perhaps all of the songs have meaningful texts, and these were dictated by Ishi to T. T. Waterman, only ten of the recordings were clear enough to permit transcription of the texts. The underlaid texts in those songs correspond to the spoken version and do not necessarily reflect changes made in singing. It is evident that such changes do come about, and that in some cases there is considerable difference in the vowel articulation of spoken and sung versions of a word.

There seems to be a close relationship between the textual and musical structures, though this relationship does not imply automatic subservience of one or the other.

The linguistic raw material has evidently not been digested sufficiently to enable us to make a detailed analysis of the text-music relationships. In a broad sense, linguistic units such as words tend to coincide with the musical units. Thus, in songs 1690, 1713, 1821, and 1826, a word always takes up a measure. In a number of cases, the entire text is repeated once or twice within the melodic stanza. In 1819, it appears twice, each rendition of the text coinciding with one phrase of the quasi-sequential form of this melody. In 1829, the whole text is rendered three times, each time coinciding with a formal unit of the music. Within each unit, however, the end of a word does not coincide with the end of a minor musical unit. The text setting is essentially syllabic, but occasionally there are two short notes accompanying one syllable. Melismas are not used and the syllables in a song tend to take up equal amounts of time. The Yahi language, incidentally, evidently lends itself well to singing, since vowels are plentiful and words normally have vowel endings.

From Ishi's recordings, then, we learn a number of important things. We can get a picture of the Yahi style, which, it turns out, is a curious mixture of severe limitation and amazing variety. We find that even in one of the simplest Indian cultures, identification of songs learned from a neighboring tribe is known and accepted. We find evidence of some kind of contact with the music of other Indian musical areas. We can conclude that the majority of musical materials of the Yahi are closely related to those of other tribes of the Northern California plateau region, and specifically to the music of the Yokuts, Modoc, and Klamath. We find that the singing of the "last wild Indian" is in essence similar to the music of the thousands of acculturated Indians whose songs have been recorded in the last half-century.

Perhaps most important, however, these recordings are an amazing personal document. Ishi was presumably not an outstanding singer in his tribe—indeed, he did not live in a truly tribal environment. Yet he was able to sing over fifty songs, and to sing them, if the recordings are reliable, in an assured and self-confident manner. How many members of Western civilization, left alone as the only survivors of their culture, would be able to do the same?

1687a Song for girls' adolescence ceremony

1688a Flint song

1688b Flint song   1690 Owl song

1692 Song for girls' adolescence ceremony

1694 Gambling song

1696a Gambling song

1696b Gambling song

1697a Gambling song   1697b

[212]

[214]

[215]

1832 Woman doctor's song   ♪ = 144

A¹   A²   B¹   B²   *maybe

In 1955 and 1957 Martin A. Baumhoff, then attached to the University of California Archaeological Survey, excavated caves in Yahi territory—Kingsley Cave on Mill Creek and Payne Cave on Antelope Creek. The results were published in Reports No. 30 and 40 of the University of California Archaeological Survey. These are the only records of the prehistory of the Yahi, and while interesting, are too peripheral to our present concern with Ishi, the person, to be reprinted here. Attached to the second report is a list of Yahi place names taken from the notebook of T. T. Waterman, who recorded these from Ishi on the occasion of the trip back to Yahiland with Ishi in 1914. These names show how intimately Ishi was connected with the terrain in which he lived.

---

9. Yahi Place Names (1957)

Martin A. Baumhoff

During the time Ishi spent in San Francisco at the Museum of Anthropology, every effort was made to record his native lore. In this connection T. T. Waterman, A. L. Kroeber and S. T. Pope, in 1914, made a trip to Yahi territory with Ishi to record details which could only be gathered on the spot (many of the photographs shown by Waterman, 1918, were taken on that trip). Waterman recorded as many place names as he could on the trip, some of which are published (Waterman, 1918, Map 1),* others remaining until now

---

M. A. Baumhoff, "An Introduction to Yana Archaeology," *University of California Archaeological Survey Report*, No. 40 (1957), pp. 49-54.
*Waterman, 1918, in "The Yana Indians," reprinted above. As explained in an editorial footnote there, Waterman's map 1, a foldout, could not be reproduced in this volume.—Ed.

in the form of handwritten notes. In Waterman's publication and in his notes, the orthography is not explained. It seems to be the same as Sapir's (1922) for the Northern Yana.

I transcribe the notes here, preserving Waterman's orthography, and giving the names in the same sequence that Waterman recorded them. [Remarks in brackets are mine.] The sequence is occasionally important because where the location of certain features is uncertain they can sometimes be inferred from the location of the adjacent names, which must have been recorded at nearly the same time.

The place names given by Waterman are usually accompanied by his remarks on location, or other pertinent information. When the meaning of the remark is clear I have, in some cases, changed it slightly. For instance the name "tcirumau" has the remark, "knife-like ridge, below C F, N." I have changed this to read, "A knife-like ridge on the north side of the creek, below Center Ford." When the meaning is not clear to me I give it without change.

[My accompanying Map 1] was traced from the United States Geological Survey's *Mineral* Quadrangle, 1941. On this map are shown all the English place names mentioned in the text. It should be possible to locate all the Yahi place names with reference to these points. Most of the place names in English were taken from the *Mineral* Quadrangle but a few are to be found only on the United States Geological Survey's *Panther Springs* Quadrangle, 1953.

wansk!ana, Deep Hole Camp. A rock cliff west of tapanmana. [Deep Hole Camp is on the Moak Trail near the head of Little Dry Creek. I have not been able to find the word "tapanmana" recorded elsewhere, but it is probably the same word as "t'apanma'nati" below.]

tculawok. A hill north of Little Dry Creek, mineral spring.

[217]

k'emtanati, Drennan Camp.
[Drennan Camp is on Little Dry Creek about 2 miles west of Deep Hole Camp.]

man waxati. Spring.
[It is not clear whether this means spring in general or some particular spring in the neighborhood of Drennan Camp.]

putus. Cave in Lousy Gulch.
[I have not been able to locate Lousy Gulch on modern maps but it seems to be the tributary of Little Dry Creek coming in at Drennan Camp. I have so marked it on Map 1.]

ta pupati. Gully east of Lousy Gulch (runs into Little Dry.)

basyA, Devils Den.
[This is probably what is shown on modern maps as Devils Kitchen.]

matwi, Devils Parade Ground.

mardu, Cold Spring Flat. Back of deer range.
[Cold Spring Flat is not shown on my maps but Waterman shows it on his (1918, Map 1). It is not clear what his mention of a deer range refers to.]

yulwa, a creek.
[It is impossible to tell what creek this refers to. Both Dead Horse and Panther Creek are north of Deer Creek from the Cold Spring area.]

t'asma. A mountain farther north than this.
[This could be Onion Butte but there is no way to be sure.]

cunkcna, Moak Trail (?), place (?).

malama'na, Graham Pinery.

matowi, Graham's Smokey Creek. Mineral spring.
[This probably refers to Little Pine Creek rather than Smokey Creek, which is 4 or 5 miles upstream from Graham Pinery.]

basaya (pasya), Devils Den.
[These are clearly variants of the name previously given for Devils Den.]

putus. Hole north of Little Dry Creek.
[This is the same word given for the cave in Lousy Gulch. It may refer to the same place or it may be a general term for hole or cave.]

tap'upa. Tributary of Little Dry Creek.
[Waterman also marks this as "Brush Camp." He may mean the south fork of Little Dry Creek which joins at Drennan Camp.]

t'apanma'nati. Ridge north of Iron Mountain.

wolopti. First shelter up Sulphur Creek.

basiwi. Hill opposite the first shelter up Sulphur Creek.

hanmawi madu. A salt lick up Pine Creek. Probably the same as the rock finger on Deer Creek divide.
[Waterman used Pine Creek as an alternate for Wildcat Creek.]

tc'ulan'i, kinitc (after reflection), Iron Mountain.

tapupa, Big Dry Creek.

waliwa, Mt. Shasta.

k!asmat. Ridge with snow.
[It is not clear if this is a general term or if a particular place is meant.]

ba'tcapa, Sulphur Spring. On the northern part of Big Dry Creek.
[I have not been able to locate this spring.]

muk!awi. Cave on ridge above Water Hollow.

tcolawa. Saddle of a hill on northern Big Dry Creek.

an'sxa, Water Hollow.

wallmiu. A salt spring opposite Water Hollow.

woxinstca, wokinstca. A place up Dry Creek from the first night's camp on Mill Creek.
[This evidently refers to the place Ishi and Waterman camped on their trip to Mill Creek.]

——. A cave and salt spring north of Water Hollow.
[No name was recorded here. Evidently Ishi had forgotten the name.]

baiyaki. A creek west from Cave Spring hill.

tculawa. A rock west from Cave Spring hill.

puninwi. A cave west from Cave Spring hill.

p!uownwi, Boat Gunwale Creek (from Cave Spring).

payaki, Twentymile Hollow.

mak!ona. A cliff on Mill Creek.
[This cliff was probably located from somewhere near Cave Spring.]

paiyati. A hill with pine timber.
[This again was probably located from Cave Spring.]

waliwa. A snow mountain east from Cave Spring.

talaukAmwa. Center Ford on Mill Creek. T26N, R1E, Sect. 3.
[This ford is marked Blunkall Crossing on modern maps but the township and range locations show that they are the same. I have shown it as Center Ford rather than Blunkall Crossing on Map 1.]

p!inu. A big cave (with table?) 2 miles above Center Ford.
[This may read 12 miles rather than 2 miles, but if it did it would indicate a cave far out of the range of Waterman's and Ishi's travels. If it were 2 miles up from Center Ford it would be in about the right place for Kingsley Cave. Waterman later gives p!in'u as the name of a camp a quarter mile upstream from Center Ford.]

t!alap. A small pinnacle above Center Ford on the south side of the creek.

malsunmatu. A cave north of the creek a half mile below Center Ford. Buckeyes on point.

woxsuwawi. The ledge below malsunmatu.

palaupu. Buck Flat (Crag with a hole through), north side, Center Ford.
[I am not sure what this means. If it is a flat how could it be a crag with a hole through it?]

t'alusauna. Lepu gulch, cabin, and spring. T26N, R1E, SE corner Sect. 9.
[This place is not marked on the modern maps. It is evidently on the south side of Mill Creek about a half mile above the mouth of Little Mill Creek.]

huk!umi. A crag point on the north side of Mill Creek, below Center Ford.

asiwiwawi. A ledge with caves above the Lepu place.

tcirumau. A knife-like ridge on the north side of the creek above Center Ford.

k!oiyomi. The next crag below.
[Evidently the next below tcirumau.]

p!i'nu. Camp a quarter of a mile upstream from Center Ford.
[Nearly the same word was given previously as the name of a cave upstream from Center Ford.]

t!unk!aina. Rock (crag) opposite Center Ford camp.

pitsknaitea. Crag or cliff above t!unk!aina.

kulu. Juncture of Big and Little Mill Creeks. Jump crossing and cave here.

muk'autantciwa. Another leap-crossing where Mill Creek canyon comes out in valley.
[The topography indicates that this is probably just below the mouth of Little Mill Creek.]

k'uneuti (chief). Blunkall's Flat, northwest of Deadman Gulch.
[It appears that this word means chief as well as being a place name.]

t!alaukumwa. Tom's Cabin Gulch, big spring.
[Tom's Cabin Gulch does not now appear on the map. This probably refers to what is now called Buckhorn Gulch.]

xayu. A flat east of Deadman Gulch.

pitsknaitca. A chimney cave above Blunkall's cabin.

palapiuyanna. Crag or peak right above Blunkall's (also on edge of Center Ford camp).

piptc'uni. The next big point above Dead Man's Cave.

xayu, Dead Man's Cave. Double cave, side by side skeleton mat, just above Deadman Gulch on Mill Creek, close.
[It is not clear what "mat" means here. It may be an abbreviation for "material" but if so its meaning is still not clear.]

mamunpuk'u. A cave with a tiny spring above same, hole through back wall.
[This cave is probably near the mouth of Kingsley Cave. There are many small blow-outs in the cliffs here.]

batcu mamauna. Long, wall-like crag above Kingsley's Cave.
[This must refer to the cliff out of which Kingsley Cave is cut. Cf. Baumhoff, 1955, Pl. 4b.]

t!ena. Cave, Kingsley Creek, up-river side, salt spring. Cave same with baskets found in it.

[This is evidently Kingsley Cave itself. I have not seen a salt spring in that area. The baskets mentioned here may include the one described in Appendix II.] *

bunswuni. Cave, two gulches below Spring Branch. [Spring Branch is very likely one of the branch streams making up Kingsley Cove.]

wamatiwi. Table Mountain.

buncwawi. Crag to the south. Down and right from Spring Branch.

hatcawaiyu. Crag to the north.

tcarasulaiwa. Next crag above hatcawaiyu.

tawilawatcu. Spring Branch.

*Not reprinted here.—Ed.

silma, Avery Butte. [I have not been able to find such a mountain on the map. It is probably Long Point, the hill northeast of Avery Creek.]

tutma. A white hillside or ridge toward the creek from Avery Butte.

silma (?). Stone Cabin Hollow. Leads toward Avery Butte from Mill Creek. Down right from tutma. [Stone Cabin Hollow is probably what is now called Stone Corral Hollow.]

wati. Big Mineral spring. [This may be the town of Mineral, 10 or 12 miles north.]

batawi. The creek from Big Mineral Spring.

mat!oma. Across Mill Creek from Avery Butte.

[220]

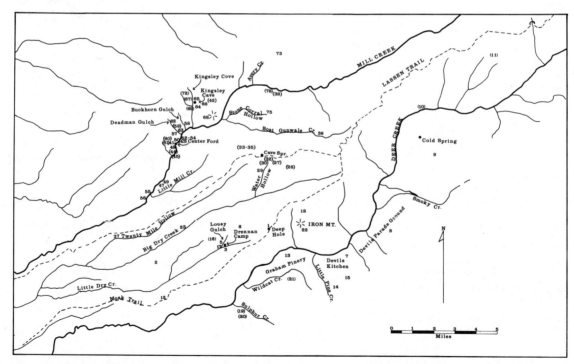

[Map 1]. Mill Creek-Deer Creek area.

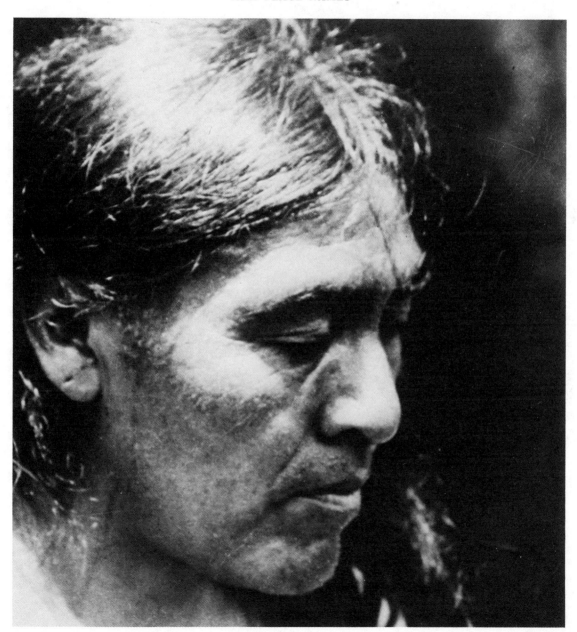

ISHI'S DEATH

ISHI'S DEATH

Reprinted here are selected extracts from Saxton Pope's longer and detailed "Medical History of Ishi," published four years after the latter's death on March 25, 1916. The cause of Ishi's death was the bovine type of tuberculosis. His final illness, medical care, and autopsy are described in detail by Pope; much of the report is too clinical to reproduce here. But Pope's observations on Ishi's personal character and medical beliefs are interesting, and these follow here, beginning with the fall of 1912.

1. Characteristics of Ishi (1920)

Saxton T. Pope

About this time I became an instructor in surgery in the University Medical School, and thus came in contact with the Indian.

From the first weeks of our intimacy a strong friendship grew up between us, and I was from that time on his physician, his confidant, and his companion in archery. He often asked if I were not part Indian, which, although it is not a fact, I naïvely admitted I was.

The Museum is near the Hospital, and since Ishi had been made a more or less privileged character in the hospital wards, he often came into the

From Saxton T. Pope, "The Medical History of Ishi," *University of California Publications in American Archaeology and Ethnology,* Vol. 13, No. 5 (1920). Extracts here are from pp. 178-193, 198, and 204-206. Footnotes and illustrations have been renumbered. References to illustrations not reproduced here have been omitted.

surgical department. Here he quietly helped the nurses clean instruments, or amused the internes and nurses by singing his Indian songs, or carried on primitive conversation by means of a very complex mixture of gesture, Yana dialect, and the few scraps of English he had acquired in his contact with us.

His affability and pleasant disposition made him a universal favorite. He visited the sick in the wards with a gentle and sympathetic look which spoke more clearly than words. He came to the women's wards quite regularly, and with his hands folded before him, he would go from bed to bed like a visiting physician, looking at each patient with quiet concern or with a fleeting smile that was very kindly received and understood.

Ishi's Medical Beliefs

Women.—Ishi had many of our own obsolete superstitions regarding women. One criticism he made of the white man's civilization was the unbridled liberty we give menstruating women. The "Sako mahale," as he designated them, were a cause of much ill luck and sickness. They should be in seclusion during this period. In fact, he often commented on the number of sick men that came to the hospital. I asked him what he thought made so many men sick. He said it was "Sako mahale, too much wowi (houses), too much automobile," and last but most important of all, the "Coyote doctor," or evil spirit.

Dogs.—Playing with dogs, and letting them lick one's hand, Ishi said was very bad. He assured me that to let babies play with dogs this way led to paralysis. It is interesting to note that Dr. R. H. Gibson of Fort Gibson, Alaska, has reported the coincidence of poliomyelitis among the Tanana Indians and the occurrence of distempers in dogs.[1]

Rattlesnakes.—Ishi's treatment for rattlesnake bite was to bind a toad or frog on the affected area. This is interesting in the light of the experiments of Madame Phisalix of the Pasteur Institute, who demonstrated the antidotal properties of salamandrin, an extract obtained from salamander skin, and the natural immunity that the salamander has to viper venom. Macht and Able have obtained a similar powerful alkaloid from the toad *Bufo nigra,* called bufogin, which has some of the properties of strychnin and adrenalin. It has been used as an arrow poison by South American aborigines. Experiments which I conducted with salamandrin as an antidote to crotalin, show that it has a pronounced protective and curative value in the immunization of guinea pigs and in their cure after being bitten by the rattlesnake. It is, however, too dangerous and potent a poison itself to be of any practical value.

[226]

When out camping we killed and cooked a rattlesnake or "kemna." Ishi refused not only to taste it, but also to eat from the dishes in which it had been cooked. We ate it, and found that it tasted like rabbit or fish. Ishi expected us to die. That we did not do so he could only explain on the grounds that I was a medicine man and used magic protection.

Moon.—Ishi held the superstition common among uneducated Caucasians, that it is unwholesome to sleep with the moon shining on one's face, so he covered his head completely under his blankets when sleeping in the open.

Hygiene.—Ishi had wholesome notions of hygiene. When out hunting he has several times stopped me from drinking water from a stream which he thought had been contaminated by dwelling houses above.

His residence in the Museum caused many misgivings in his mind. The presence of all the bones of the dead, their belongings, and the mummies

1. Journal American Medical Association, Feb. 28, 1914.

were ever a source of anxiety to him. He locked his bedroom door at night to keep out spirits. When we stored our camping provender temporarily in the Museum bone room, Ishi was not only disgusted by genuinely alarmed. It was only after the reassurance that the "bunch a mi si tee" could not enter through the tin of the cans that he was relieved.

Surgery.—On some of his visits to the University Hospital, Ishi gazed through the glass-panelled door of the operating room and watched the less grewsome scenes therein, wondering no doubt what was the meaning of this work. At times, when it seemed proper, I took him into the operating room and placed him in the visitors' stand where he could watch the entire procedure of a surgical operation. He was an attentive spectator, and his questions afterward, though few and imperfectly understood, showed that he marveled most at the anaesthetic and that he debated the advisability of such surgical work.

Once he saw me remove a diseased kidney. He viewed the sleeping man with deep wonder. He seemed interested at the methods we employed to prevent hemorrhage. For days afterwards he asked me if the patient still lived, and seemed incredulous when I said he did. When he saw an operation for the removal of tonsils he asked me why it was done. I told him of the pain and soreness which was indicative of disease, and necessitated the operation. He conveyed to me the information that among his people tonsilitis was cured by rubbing honey on the neck, and blowing ashes down the throat through a hollow stick or quill; no operations were necessary.

The only surgical operation with which he seemed familiar was scarification. This was accomplished by means of small flakes of obsidian and had as its purpose the strengthening of the arms and legs of men about to go out on a hunt.

Herbs.—His own knowledge of the use of medicinal herbs was considerable, as we learned later when he went back to Deer Creek canyon with us on a three weeks' camping trip. Here he designated scores of plants that were of technical, economic, or medicinal value. But he put very little faith in these things. The use of herbs and drugs seems to have been the province of old women in the tribe.

There was a hole in the septum of his nose which he had probably used as a receptacle for a small piece of wood, as well as for holding ornaments. When he had a cold he placed in this spot a twig of baywood or juniper, and indicated to me that this was medicine. It served very much with him as menthol inhalers do with us. Its influence was largely psychic but agreeable.

Magic.—The real medicine was magic. The mysteries of the k'uwi, or medicine man, were of much greater value than mere dosing. Their favorite charms seem to have been either the blowing of smoke and ashes in certain directions to wield a protective or curative influence, or the passing of coals of fire through themselves or their patients by means of sleight of hand. They also sucked out small bits of obsidian or cactus thorns from their clients, averring that these were the etiologic factors of sickness.

The principal cause of pain, according to Ishi, was the entrance of these spines, thorns, bee stings, or, as he called them, "pins," into the human frame. The medicine man sucked them out, or plucked them while they were floating in the air in the vicinity of the sick man. They were then deposited in a small container, usually made of the dried trachea of a bird, or of a large artery. The ends of this tube were sealed with pitch or some form of a stopper and the whole thing taken possession of by the doctor, thus keeping the "materia morbosa" where it could do no further harm.

The fact that I was able to do sleight of hand: vanish coins, change eggs into paper, swallow impossible objects at will, and perform similar parlor magic, convinced Ishi that I was a real doctor, much more than any medication or surgery at my command. He came, nevertheless, to our clinic whenever he had a headache, or a bruised member, or lumbago, and accepted our services with due faith. . . .

Ishi's Personal Habits

Sleep.—In 1915, after his first tubercular diagnosis, in order to keep him in the most favorable environment, Ishi was given a little canvas house on the hill back of the Museum. Here he slept and spent much of his time. He had to be taught to keep his windows open at night, and even this outdoor sleeping did not please him. He always preferred to sleep in his old room on the second floor of the Museum where it was warm and dry. His bed was a canvas cot and he slept between blankets in preference to sheets. He had several flannelette nightshirts but he preferred to sleep naked, taking off all his clothes in the dark after his roommate, Mr. Loud, an attaché of the Museum, had retired and extinguished the light.

Clothing.—In the daytime he most frequently wore a khaki shirt and trousers, cotton socks and army shoes. At first he was offered moccasins, but he refused to wear them. He wanted to be like other people. Usually he wore a bright colored necktie and sometimes a hat, when he was going down town. In cold weather he wore woolen underwear, but he did not seem to need it. On rare occasions he put on an old raincoat in inclement weather. A few discarded woolen suits were given him, but cotton shirts and trousers were his choice. He used a pocket handkerchief in the most approved manner, and because of his frequent colds he needed it often.

Modesty.—Ishi, strange to say, was very modest. Although he went practically naked in the wilds, and, as described by Waterman, upon his first appearance in Deer creek canyon he was seen altogether nude, nevertheless, his first request after being captured was for a pair of overalls. He was quite careful to cover his genitalia when changing clothes, assumed protective attitudes, and when swimming in the mountain streams with us wore an improvised breech clout even though his white companions abandoned this last vestige of respectability.

Toilet.—When well he bathed nearly every day, and he always washed his hands before meals. He was very tidy and cleanly in all his personal habits. When camping, he was the only man in our outfit who got up regularly and bathed in the cold mountain stream every morning.

Ishi was an expert swimmer. He used a side stroke and sometimes a modified breast stroke, but

[227]

no overhand or fancy strokes; nor did he dive. He swam under water with great facility and for long distances. The rapids of Deer creek were rather full yet he swam them, and carried my young son hanging to his hair.

When he was sick he resented being bathed except when ordered by the nurse or doctor. Like many other primitive people, he considered bathing injurious in the presence of fever. He never attempted to take a sweat bath while in civilization, but often spoke of them. I never saw him brush his teeth, but he rubbed them with his finger, and they always seemed clean. He washed his mouth out with water after meals.

His beard was sparse but he plucked it systematically by catching individual hairs between the blade of a dull jacknife and his thumb. In his native state he used a sort of tweezers made of a split piece of wood. He did this work without the use of a mirror.

He combed and brushed his hair daily. He washed it frequently, drying it by filliping it and beating it with a small stick as it hung in the sunlight. At first he had no dandruff, but after two or three years' contact with the whites he had some dry seborrhoea, and began to get a trifle gray at the temples. I offered him bay rum to use on his hair, but he never adopted this effete innovation. He said that he used grease on his scalp when in his native state; whereas bay leaves and bay nuts he said were heated and reduced to a semisolid state, when they were rubbed on the body after the sweat bath. Here they acted as a soporific, or, as he said, like whiskey, and the person thus anointed fell into a sweet slumber. The same substance was rubbed on moccasins to make them waterproof.

On one occasion he contracted ring worm, probably from a wandering cat. He was given a sulphur salve for this, and after its cure he still used the ointment to soften his hands, very much as ladies use cold cream. He assured me that it was good. He was not susceptible to "poison oak" (*Rhus diversiloba*) nor to sunburn. His skin bleached out considerably while in San Francisco, and became darker when exposed to sunlight.

[228]

Ishi swimming in Deer Creek [May, 1914].

In his clothes box he kept several cakes of soap and seemed to have the same fondness for sweet-scented soap that Orientals manifest. Even talcum powder was there, which he called "lady powder." But I never saw him use either, and I rather suspect that the powder was a gift.

His personal belongings he kept in a most orderly manner, everything in his box being properly folded and arranged with care. Articles which he kept outside of this box he wrapped in newspaper and laid in systematic arrangement on shelves in his room.

In working on arrows or flaking obsidian, he was careful to place newspapers on the floor to catch his chips. In fact, neatness and order seemed to be part of his self-education.

In the preparation of food and the washing of dishes he was very orderly and clean. In fact in the latter vocation he was by far the best artisan in our camp.

Diet.—He was, at the time I first knew him, a man of medium stature, approximately 5 feet 6 inches tall, and weighing about 165 pounds. His weight varied greatly during his four years' stay with us. This was due to his changed methods of eating and exercise. At first he rather abandoned himself to the pleasures of an unlimited food supply. He fed at the nearby Hospital and had at least two full meals daily, besides a luncheon of his own preparation. This was greatly in excess of any dietary heretofore possible to him. In consequence he increased in weight rapidly and became ungracefully fat. After a certain period of this luxury he discerned the folly of this course and began eating less, when his metabolism returned to a more normal balance. Part of this increase was due to the large quantities of water he drank. Being unaccustomed to salt, our seasoning was excessive and led to increased hydration of his bodily tissues. He had a great fondness for sweets: candy, jelly, cake, ice-cream, all were favorite articles of diet. He tried and liked nearly all kinds of foods, but seemed to have an aversion for custards, blanc manges, and similar slimy confections, nor could he be persuaded to drink milk. He contended that this was made for babies, while he said that butter ruined the singing voice. After some months of residence with us, he developed methods of preparing his own food in the basement of the Museum.

By this time he was given a small salary for his services as janitor. He purchased his articles of food at neighboring grocery stores, indicating his selection by pointing his finger at the desired object and saying, "How much money-tee?" He learned to use a small gas stove for cooking.

Matches he took up with evident delight; they were such a contrast to the laborious methods of the fire drill, or of nursing embers, which he employed in the wilds.

He bought bread, jelly, tea, coffee, sugar, canned salmon, meat, salt pork, sardines, cheese, potatoes, beans, rice, dried and fresh fruit, syrup, honey, and canned milk. This latter he took with his coffee until he discovered that it was milk, when he stopped using it.

His frugality became a little too pronounced occasionally, and it was necessary to remonstrate with him on the matter. Usually he ate three meals a day: a very early breakfast, and two other meals at the usual hours. He was influenced probably by the work and meal hours of his companions. He cooked his potatoes by boiling them with the skins on and eating them dry. His meat he boiled only about ten minutes, eating it practically without seasoning.

His own food in the wilds seems to have been fish, game, acorn meal, berries, and many roots. Prominent among these latter was the bulb of the brodiaea. The Indian could go out on an apparently barren hillside and with a sharp stick dig up enough brodiaea bulbs in an hour to furnish food for a good meal. These roots are globular in shape, with the appearance of an onion, ranging in size from a cherry to a very small potato. The flavor when raw is like that of a potato, and when cooked like a roasted chestnut.

Alcohol.—The use of alcohol soon became known to Ishi, and early in his stay with us several immature persons tried to make him intoxicated, but a stop was very promptly called in this direction and the error of their ways pointed out. Ishi himself had no liking for strong drink, although at one time he purchased a few bottles of beer and drank small quantities diluted with sugar and water. He called it medicine. His response to my query regarding whiskey was, "Whiskey-tee crazy-aunatee, die man." The sequence was strongly fixed in his mind. No temperance lectures were necessary, although several goodhearted members of the W.C.T.U. attempted to instruct his primeval mind in these matters. He had a fondness for ice-cream soda, which, with the moving pictures, constituted his entire accomplishments in debauchery.

Tobacco.—Occasionally Ishi smoked a cigarette, and he knew the use of tobacco, having had access to the native herb in the wilds. But he seldom smoked more than a few cigarettes a day, and frequently went weeks without any. He disapproved of young people smoking. He chewed tobacco at times, and spat copiously. Both of these indulgences, however, he resorted to only when invited by some congenial friend.

Etiquette.—Although uncultured, he very quickly learned the proper use of knife, fork, and spoon. His table manners were of the very best. He often ate at my home, where he was extremely diffident; watched what others did and then followed their example, using great delicacy of manner. His attitude toward my wife or any other woman member of the household was one of quiet disinterest. Apparently his sense of propriety prompted him to ignore her. If spoken to, he would reply with courtesy and brevity, but otherwise he appeared not to see her.

When he wanted to show his disapproval of anything very strongly, he went through the pantomime of vomiting. For instance, when he saw a callow youth with a mustache, for the first time, he expressed his disgust in an action which, interpreted, would correspond to our phrase "that makes me sick."

Thrift.—As janitor in the Museum, he was making a competent income, understood the value of money, was very thrifty and saving, and looked forward to the day when he could buy a horse and wagon. This seemed to be the acme of worldly possession to him. He was very happy and well contented, working a little, playing enough, and surrounded by friends.

Ishi's Disposition and Mentality

Disposition.—In disposition the Yahi was always calm and amiable. Never have I seen him vehement or angry. Upon rare occasions he showed that he was displeased. If someone who he thought had no privilege touched his belongings, he remonstrated with some show of excitement. Although he had lived in part by stealing from the cabins of men who had usurped his country, he had the most exacting conscience concerning the ownership of property. He would never think of touching anything that belonged to another person, and even remonstrated with me if I picked up a pencil that belonged to one of the Museum force. He was too generous with his gifts of arms, arrowheads, and similar objects of his handicraft.

His temperament was philosophical, analytical, reserved, and cheerful. He probably looked upon us as extremely smart. While we knew many things, we had no knowledge of nature, no reserve; we were all busy-bodies. We were, in fact, sophisticated children.

His conception of immortality was that of his tribe, but he seemed to grasp the Christian concept and asked me many questions concerning the hereafter. He rather doubted that the White God cared much about having Indians with Him, and he did not seem to feel that women were properly eligible to Heaven. He once saw a moving picture of the Passion Play. It affected him deeply. But he misconstrued the crucifixion and assumed that Christ was a "bad man."

Use of tools.—He was quite adept in the use of such simple tools as a knife, handsaw, file, and hatchet. He early discovered the advantages of a small bench vise, and it took the place of his big toe in holding objects thereafter. Larger bench tools, such as the plane, the draw knife, the auger, the level, the square, and chisels, he rarely used. His measurements were made according to some dimension of his body, such as a palm's breadth, the length of his arm, etc. But he never counted paces or used any gauge for distances. Journeys were measured by days or sleeps.

He was extremely apt at contrivance with small objects, and his hut building, as demonstrated both in civilization and by his lodges in the wilds, showed ingenuity and skill. With larger building, however, he was not conversant. He marveled greatly whenever he saw carpenters construct a house, and was awe-struck when I took him to a sawmill where large cedar logs were brought in and rapidly sawed up into small bits to be used in making lead pencils. It would have taken hours for him to fell even a small tree, and an interminable length of time to split it. But here was a miracle of work done in a few minutes. It impressed him greatly.

Use of English.—He loved to joke, and looked at the "funny pictures" in the papers, even laughing at some of the more obvious jokes. But he either could not or would not draw pictures himself.

With those whom he knew and liked he was remarkably talkative, rambling off into stories, descriptions, humorous episodes, and many unintelligible tales. When excited in his description his voice rose to a faint falsetto. He sweated with the ardor of his portraiture. He went through descriptive pantomime.

He labored with his simple tools of speech. Apparently he abbreviated his vocabulary to fit our comprehension; and I know that he sometimes changed his pronunciation to conform to our imperfect command of his dialect. If we could not get the refinements of his articulation, he often used the word as we did so that there would be no misunderstanding. In a way he spoke "broken Yahi" just as we speak "pigeon English" to foreigners.

He was a particular favorite with all small boys and from his many hours of conversation with them and with Museum visitors he learned much of his English. In consequence, his idioms had a flavor of slang, but were very expressive. When an elderly lady interested in his soul, asked him if he believed in God, he replied, "Sure, Mike!"

His English vocabularly by 1915 must have contained several hundred words and phrases. He knew the names of various peoples: English, Chinaman, Japanese, Wild Indian, Nigger, Irishman, Dutchman, policeman.

The following is an approximate of his vocabulary:

Hullo; nice day; too cole; too hot; too much water-tee; too much lazy-auna-tee; him lazy boy, smart boy; him crazy-auna-tee; hims good; hims no good; bad man; sleep; eat; work; sing; dance; I go; you go; you likey him?; lice (rice), pishy (fish); bean-us; honey; labit (rabbit); big one; little one; led (red); white; black; hat-na (hat); shoes; camisa (Spanish for shirt); mahale (mujer, Spanish for woman); lopa (rope); lopa pikta (rope picture or moving pictures); candy-tee; soda wata; whiskey-tee; smoke; doctor; big cheap (big chief); dog; kitty-tee; coyote; chicken-a-tee; egg; apple; owanga-tee; lemon; barnarna-tee; cracker; soap; powder; medicine; chair; sit down; talk; how much money-tee?; money; shoot; cut em; die man (death); sick man; ole man; lady; mama; papa; sister; papoose (baby); too much I smoke (fog); I all a time smoke; put em away; you go get em;

what's a matter-tee?; you go pretty soon; long time; automobile; horse; telephone; fire; pistol (gun); pike (fight); evelybody happy; him cry; too much pina (pain); sheep-na; paka (vaca, cow); tea; koppy (coffee); milik (milk); nipe (knife); axa (axe); hatch (hatchet); papello (paper); light; all a same.

The Indian had no set phrase of greeting as we understand it. If we insisted upon it, he would say "Hullo," and as for a parting phrase, he never said more than "You go?" If one said "Good bye" to him, he remained silent. If he was forced to speak, and in later years he seemed to understand that some response was expected, he would say "Good boy," and undoubtedly meant it as a complimentary expression. It seemed to have no such meaning as it implied in our language "God be with you."

He never learned to say "Thank you." If he valued your service, he smiled. If your present pleased him he said, "Him's good!"

Knowledge of reading and figures.—He learned to sign his name on his cheques, and I have preserved one of his signatures. No attempt was made to teach him English or reading.

[231]

He could distinguish numbers to the extent that he could be trusted to ride alone on street cars bearing certain numerals, such as car No. 6 or car No. 17, both of which carried him from the ferry to his home. In a way he could tell the time by the clock. He knew midday, and any hour one pointed out to him, and he could be depended on to act on time. He carried a cheap watch some one had given him. It had a large chain and pendants attached. He wound it faithfully every day, but it was never set properly, and consequently was more of a comfort than a help. Nevertheless he was very proud of this posession.

An estimate of character.—I once took him to Buffalo Bill's Wild West Show. He always enjoyed the circus, horseback feats, clowns, and similar performances. While at the show we were watching some Plains Indians dress for their performance. A very dignified warrior, bedecked in all his paint and feathers, approached us. The two Indians looked at each other in absolute silence for several minutes. The Sioux then spoke in perfect English, saying: "What tribe of Indian is this?" I answered, "Yana, from Northern California." The Sioux then gently picked up a bit of Ishi's hair, rolled it between his fingers, looked critically into his face, and said, "He is a very high grade of Indian." As we left, I asked Ishi what he thought of the Sioux. Ishi said, "Him's big cheap (chief)." Apparently their estimates were equally complimentary.

Clinical History, May, 1914

At the height of Ishi's physical perfection I recorded the following:

We know nothing of the parentage of our subject. He was born probably about 1860 in northern California, consequently is approximately 54 years of age, but appears about 45. There is no record of childhood diseases.

He shows no signs of chickenpox or smallpox. No suppurating glands, boils, burns, or scars of any sort. His skin is light, reddish bronze, soft, sparsely endowed with hair.

The odor of his body is faintly musty, and suggests the smell of tanned deer hide. Bones small. Musculature is well developed, with an even distribution of subcutaneous fat. The hair of his head is black, straight, and of medium weight, slightly gray at the temples; in length it reaches his shoulders, having but recently been burnt off as a sign of mourning. He wears it over his ears, tied in a single brush down his back. The scalp shows some evidence of dry seborrhoea. His head is of the brachycephalic type. The measurements are as follows:

Length of head, 193 mm.
Breadth of head, 163 mm.
Cephalic index, 84.4 mm.
Length of face, 131 mm.
Breadth of face, 152 mm.

Length of nose, 54 mm.
Breadth of nose, 42 mm.
Nasal index, mesorhynian, 77.7 mm.

The skull is strongly made, with thick supraorbital ridges, mastoid processes, and external occipital protuberance. The jaws are strong and heavy. The teeth are all present, strong, colored slightly brown, no evidence of decay or pyorrhoea. The alignment of the lower incisors is not perfect. The molars are well worn but in good condition. Ears are well formed, of good size, and the lobes are pierced for rings. The eyebrows and lashes are of moderate length and thickness. The eyes are set straight, lids Caucasian in contour. The iris is dark brown; reactions to light and accomodation are normal. The nose is strong and wide, the septum pierced just above the cutaneous margin for the insertion of a small stick.

The tongue is clean and normal in color, no coating. The tonsils are slightly hypertrophied, showing signs of past inflammation. His breath is sweet and free from the fetor common to the average white man as noted by Powers.[2]

There are no enlarged glands in the neck, the thyroid is normal. No abnormal pulsations occur in the vessels. The neck is full and strong. There is a slight pad of fat over the seventh cervical vertebra. The chest is full, normal in shape, breasts a trifle large compared to Caucasian male standards, aerola not hairy, no axillary glands are palpable.

On percussion the lungs are normal; osculation is negative. The diaphragm moves equally on the two sides. The heart outline on percussion is normal, sounds normal. The pulse is 65; blood pressure 125 mm.; arteries are soft; pulse compressible, regular, good volume.

The abdomen is negative except for some tenderness in the right hypochondriac region. There is a slight surplus of fat. No disturbances of digestion, no flatus or constipation. Good appetite, regular habits. Abdominal reflexes normal.

2. Stephen Powers, Tribes of California, Contributions to North American Ethnology, 1877, III, ch. 34, p. 403.

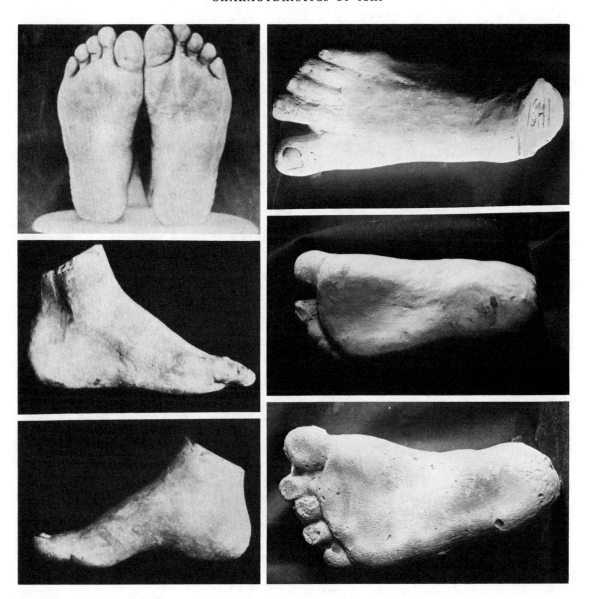

Ishi's feet from life and casts.

The genital region is normal. No hernias nor enlarged glands exist. The genitalia are rather small but of normal character; pigmentation is accentuated in this region. He gives no history of venereal infections, but knows of their existence in a vague, general way. He seems to have had little actual experience in sex function; was never married, he says, because there were no marriageable women in his tribe. There are no urinary disturbances; no nocturia; apparently he is free from perversions.

The cremasteric reflex is normal. The thighs and legs are well formed. Knee jerks normal. The feet are broad and strong. The toes are straight and unspoiled. The longitudinal and transverse arches are marvelously well preserved. His abductor pollicis is very pronounced in its development. The foot is a beautiful example of what the human foot should be. His method of locomotion is that of rather short steps, each foot sliding along the ground as it touches. Neither the heel nor the ball of the foot seems to receive the jar of the step. The foot is placed in position cautiously, not slapped or jammed down. He progresses rather pigeon-toed, and approximates crossing the line of his progress each step. He springs from the great toe, which is wonderfully strong in its plantar flexion and abduction. The plantar reflex is active. The skin of the sole is thick but not rough. The toenails are round in outline, strong, and short.

He is not an agile runner nor does he have the spring and leg action of one who in his youth had been a sprinter. His stride is rather restricted and he lacks a vigorous thrust of the legs. The knees are not drawn up well in front. He has considerable endurance, and at walking he never seems to tire.

The spine is normal in contour, with a slight drooping of the head forward. The lumbar flexion is somewhat limited and he is subject to attacks of lumbago of mild degree. The pelvis is of generous proportions, strong. The sacro-iliac joint is firm, with no evidence of relaxation.

The hands are medium size, probably a number 8 glove. The fingers are gracefully tapered, pleasing in shape, with fingernails olivoid in outline, perfect

in texture. The palms are soft and pliable. He is right handed. His grip at this time with the dynamometer registers as follows: Right hand 49 kilograms, left hand 45. These are maxima of many attempts.

He is a good informal wrestler, and scuffles with the men with evident delight. In the game in which two opponents clasp right hands, then attempt to upset the stand of the other, he is strong but awkward. He can box with the open hand in a deft though unskilled manner. He rather likes games of this sort, but no acrobatics appeal to him, nor does he ever attempt to exhibit his strength. He throws stones rather poorly, not with the strength and accuracy of one accustomed to games of ball.

About this time Ishi was successfully vaccinated, and passed through the inoculation without trouble of any sort. In fact his health seemed improved after this procedure.

Ishi was vigorous, and a good worker when working with others, but indifferent to the beauty of labor as an abstract concept. He never fully exerted himself, but apparently had unlimited endurance. When fat he perspired freely. After a three weeks' trip in the mountains he was in the pink of condition and could journey all day without effort. He was at this time—May, 1914—undoubtedly in better health than at any time during his stay with us. He had had several respiratory infections, but up to this time he showed negative tuberculine reactions and there was no premonition of the illness which later caused his death.

Every effort was made to keep him in good health. He was encouraged to stay outdoors; he was kept away from infectious diseases. His diet was ample. He was given perfect freedom. When asked if he wanted to return to the wilds, he replied that he did not, because everybody was dead, only evil spirits inhabited the places of his former pursuits, and there was not enough food to eat there. . . .

Ishi's Final Sickness, 1915-1916

Ishi's last sickness, to all visible signs, started in the summer of 1915. He had been ailing all winter and showed an increased disinclination to shoot his bow or bestir himself.

In the summer vacation of this year Ishi was moved to Berkeley, where he was studied by Dr. E. Sapir, and very valuable data were obtained on the subject of his language and mythology. For three months he was in constant communication with Dr. Sapir, living at Professor T. T. Waterman's home under most hygienic conditions with plenty of outdoor recreation, sleeping, proper food, and diversion. Nevertheless, his health suddenly began to fail, and on August 22 he was returned to the University Hospital in San Francisco, where he remained for six weeks. . . .

At the expiration of his stay in the hospital, in October, Ishi was removed to temporary quarters arranged in the Museum, where he could have a large sunny room, well ventilated, and be attended by Mr. Warburton, an attaché of the Museum. It was planned that when he became a little stronger, he should be sent to the country, somewhere near his old haunts, and several possible places were considered. Tentative arrangements were made with responsible caretakers, but he never grew strong enough to travel.

During his months of sickness in the Museum, his clinical records were faithfully kept by Mr. Warburton, and Dr. Kruse and I were his constant medical attendants. In spite of careful nursing he failed to improve. No medical treatment being indicated, he was given practically none. His appetite became more capricious and fickle. Food distressed him, and he required anodynes at times to relieve his pain. His fever persisted in a tuberculous type and weakness became extreme. For hours he lay without moving, often gazing from his window and smiling with manifest delight at the antics of the iron workers clambering up the steel construction of the new University Hospital. He would say, "All a same monkey-tee."

Some days he summoned enough strength to make a few arrows, or to talk of his life in the wilds, or discuss hunting, bow making, Indian methods of hunting, folklore, and kindred subjects.

All this time he had a moderate cough; but repeated examination failed to show tubercle bacilli. His abdomen became more sensitive, and he developed signs of pyloric obstruction. After taking food he apparently experienced great pain. Even water caused him misery and I have seen him writhe in agony, with tears running down his cheeks, yet utter no sound of complaint. At this period, when he seemed to be failing so rapidly that the end must be near, I coaxed him to get out of bed and let me take his picture once more. He was always happy to be photographed, and accommodated me. It was only after the picture was developed that I realized to what a pitiful condition he had been reduced. Had this been apparent before, I should not have asked this exertion of him.

This was his last picture, and compared with his varying poses, it records a tragic tale. We see him first as the gaunt, hunted wild man, his hair burnt

[235]

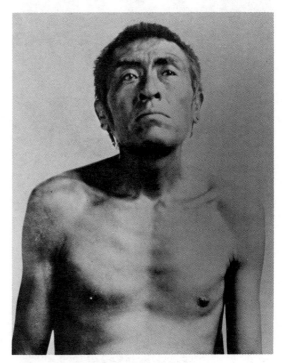

Ishi on his discovery in 1911.

Ishi in his old haunts in 1914.

In 1914 we see him at his best. On the trip to Tehama County he was undoubtedly in prime health. His stature is magnificent. Although he has lost the typical Indian litheness, there is grace and strength in every contour. For a year he was absolutely perfect. He worked, hunted, played, and enjoyed life.

Then a gradual change overcame him. His energy waned. He no longer was keen to shoot at targets with the bow. His skin became darker. He contracted another cold. He lost weight and wanted to rest most of the time. There were periods of slight improvement and we had hope that a return to his primitive mode of life might benefit him.

But as his malady increased, his cough became more distressing, fever consumed him, and eating became impossible. Our city water did not taste good to him, and he asked me to get him fresh spring water—"sweet water" he called it. We made a special effort to do this for him.

Although starving, racked with hiccough or coughing, and in more or less constant distress, he never complained. He never spoke of his suffering; never referred to death.

In March, 1916, when his weakness progressed to an extreme degree, we moved him back to the hospital where he could receive better nursing and alimentary feeding.

Shortly after reentering the hospital he had a very large pulmonary hemorrhage. This was the first complication of this sort he experienced. I was called to his side. He was very weak and faint. . . . I administered a large dose of morphia. He died soon after, at 12:20 p.m., March 25, 1916. . . .

[236]

short, his body lean and sinewy, but his legs strong and capable of great endurance. He suggests the coyote in this character.

Later, civilization agrees with him, he loses his hunted look, rounds out his shrunken frame, and is happy in his new-found friends. Then comes a period of over-feeding, the luxury of food which he himself decides is not best for him.

There follow here a series of letters exchanged between A. L. Kroeber (on sabbatical leave in Europe and in New York), T. T. Waterman, and E. W. Gifford (in San Francisco at the Museum of Anthropology) over what proved to be Ishi's terminal illness. These are personal letters, never intended for publication, but after consideration we have decided to include them in this collection in the belief that they are an essential part of the documentation of the story of Ishi.

The first letter is from Kroeber to Gifford; the next two are self-explanatory; the fourth is from Miss McMahon of the Museum staff to Gifford, who was then making field studies of the Miwok Indians. Parts of the letters that do not deal with Ishi have not been reprinted here.

2. Correspondence About Ishi (1915-1916)

7/7/15

Dear G.

Thanks for check and news. The books all came. Ponka was the one I meant. I have everything now, I think, except the Mindeleff report. Also please send a couple of these blue pads, if I haven't asked you before. I guess I have to give up my Siouan [?] relationship; I still believe it, but can't find the evidence. As to Ishi, *please* invest in a thermometer and ask Sapir or W. to keep at least fairly regular tab on afternoon temperatures and weight (general appearance counts for little) and if either shows unfavorable symptoms, shoot him over to Pope for examination. It's our responsibility and we ought to live up to it fully.

Yours,
A. L. K.

[237]

AMERICAN MUSEUM OF NATURAL HISTORY
77TH STREET AND CENTRAL PARK WEST

New York City, Aug. 28, 1915

Dear Waterman,

After my mother wrote me that Ishi had a bad cough, Gifford said he had lost weight—without giving figures. Now he reports as enclosed. I asked Gifford for the information because through proximity he knew more of the case last winter than you did; but his presentation of it now leaves me in doubt how far he grasps the significance, and in any event the ultimate responsibility will rest with you, in my absence.

We have got to handle the case. The physicians go by the book and rule, and it's up to us to apply our knowledge of the individual and our judgment to their findings and advice. He undoubtedly has had tb since last winter, though for the last 6

Death mask, March, 1916.

months it has been only latent. He crowded it back that far once, and there is no reason why he should not do so again, if things break well. But it's damn serious. At Christmas they had him buried by now. Pope alone barely admitted at last that he might have a non-important infection. I believe their diagnosis, but they didn't understand the Indian. Nor did they know what to do with him. All they could dope up was the usual prescriptions for a typical American case without money. Pope has the right imagination what to do, but I'm confident he's over optimistic, and when the Indian got better was ready to let things slide. That's why I was so particular about weight and temperature being kept without interruption, which Pope no longer bothered about and Gifford couldn't seem to see the urgency of.

We must let the doctors get their crack at him, but unless he has really broken I don't think they'll find out much. He fooled them last time, and as the present symptoms are now—in the other lung— I expect they'll be in the dark again on all essentials. If he gets back to where he was all spring, I believe the same treatment is the only one—reasonable air, exercise, and distraction, with every ready tab on the progress of the disease with scales and thermometer. If he doesn't get back that far and the disease continues active even though mild, I suggest sending him preferably to our former watchman, S. T. Clark, of Guinda, himself a lunger of ten years' standing; or if he won't have him, then to the Appersons. Pope has the only right idea, which is to handle him as a person, not as a hospital case. Even the above would be only experiments, and I'd recommend sending Gifford up after a few weeks, if you don't want to go, and if things were going well, again after a month. Whoever has him in charge should also be made to report regularly and definitely. Anyone can take temperature and weigh.

The Southwest is ideal only physiologically. Practically I'm afraid it's impossible. You couldn't keep touch, you could hardly even know what he was in, and adverse psychic factors would probably far outweigh purely physiological benefits. Besides,

[238]

the latter are at best only a chance, not a certainty. Ask Pope on this; I'm only interpreting his doctrine, I think. There's the further fact of considerable expense in the Southwest, and that the salary that supports him now might not be payable in his absence.

. . . . . .

The "few days" in the hospital are likely to spin out into a fortnight or a couple of months. That's how it went last time. I think Sapir should know, and on the other hand the doctors should know Sapir's position. They might be agreeable to let him finish up a few urgent odds and ends.

When it comes to a question of Pope against Moffitt, Allen, etc., I back Pope through in this matter.

Please advise me when you have got the information.

I sail for Europe Tuesday, if nothing breaks before—for about two months—then back here. On this matter would be glad to have you write me c/o C. Rª. Wierdsma, Calandstraat 23, Rotterdam.

. . . . . .

How's the child?

Yours,
A. L. K.

September 30, 1915.

Dear Dr. Kroeber:

To-morrow morning I leave for Miwok territory.

Work has been going at about the usual rate, which of course is not as fast as desired. However, there is no complaint.

Ishi has improved slowly, but he is a long way from being on his feet. The doctors feel that he will be better off in our building. Furthermore, he has occupied a bed for over a month, and he has received his food through the courtesy of Dr. Summersgill. The doctors say he is not in condition to move to the country.

It will therefore be necessary to try to nurse him back to health here at the museum. Waterman and I have decided to cut out the Pacific Island exhibit for awhile and give the room to Ishi. This is the sunniest room in the house. The doctors approve of this, and they think it is the best room we could possibly give him. It is far better than anything that the hospital offers. We are going to put Ishi in charge of Warburton. Loud hardly knows how to feed himself, let alone feeding a sick man? Miss McMahon has kindly volunteered to help out also. Warburton will get his breakfasts and his suppers, while Miss McMahon will attend to his lunches. It will be necessary to sponge him twice a week, which Warburton will look after. I am hoping that by the time I return on November 1 that the Indian will be in shape to move. Both Miss McMahon and Warburton thoroughly realize that they cannot give their charge too much attention. Waterman and I feel that the Indian must come first, even though we will not get as much of the other work done in caring for him. On the days that Warburton is off I have arranged that Dick is to look after him.

I am hoping that we will have an abundance of sunshine during October, so as to give our friend every chance for a quick recovery. I must say, however, that the case looks rather dubious.

As nearly as I understand from the doctors, Ishi's condition may be described as a case of concealed tubercolosis. No germs have been found in his sputum. The effusions in the left chest cavity have ceased, and most of the fluid which filled the cavity at the beginning of his illness has been absorbed. The base of the left lung seems to be affected. The hiccough occurs for a short time almost daily. Early in the month, when he first came to the hospital, there was a good deal of difficulty in checking the hiccough, which kept up for two or three days without intermission. Then hiccough, and his dislike for so many kinds of food are his two worst enemies at present. The first prevents him perhaps, from getting the proper rest, the second keeps him from building up his body, and thus getting a greater resistance to the disease. We hope to be able to overcome the second. At the museum he will be treated as Ishi. At the hospital I fear that the nurses were so busy that he was treated simply as a hospital patient, without regard for his personality.

I hope you are having a good time in Europe. I have not heard a word from you since you left New York, but I presume you are safe and sound. I am sending this letter to your New York address, and am leaving it to the judgment of your mother whether or not to forward it.

· · · · · ·

With the kindest regards, I remain
Yours sincerely,
[E. W. Gifford]

UNIVERSITY OF CALIFORNIA
MUSEUM OF ANTHROPOLOGY
Affiliated Colleges, San Francisco
December 7, 1915.

Dear Mr. Gifford:

I have written Dr. Kroeber giving an account of Ishi's temperature for the last three days, and enclose a copy of the same herewith. Is this the style report you want me to send him, or do you want me to give it more in detail?

I was up to see Ishi a little while ago. He had the hiccoughs then, but it is the first time I have noticed them in some days. He did some work on the arrows for Dr. Pope this morning, but he went to bed this afternoon. He still continues to look forward to his meals. When Mr. Warburton asked him this morning to stick out his tongue he told him that he needed medicine too. Ishi has not been weighed since he left the hospital; but Mr. Warburton says that Dr. Kruse remarked, when he examined him that day, that there was no doubt about his having gained since leaving the hospital. Ishi complained of his hand being stiff, so Mr. Warburton has been rubbing it with something Dr. Pope prescribed, and Ishi says it is all right to-day.

Richard has gone to Berkeley to-day to get Dr. Kroebers papers, etc. Dr. Waterman called up a little while ago and asked me to come to Berkeley to-morrow. He has not said anything further about the cases. He spoke about writing you to-day, and asked me for your address.

P.S. I have sent Dr. K. the envelope.
Sincerely
F. McMahon

[239]

March 24, 1916.

Dear Gifford:

I am very sorry. The temperatures made me lose hope some time ago.

Please stand by our contingently made outline of action, and insist on it as my personal wish. There is no objection to a cast. I do not however see that an autopsy would lead to anything of consequence. I might be willing to consent if it were to be a strict autopsy in the ordinary sense to determine the cause of death, but as they know that, I suspect that the autopsy would resolve itself into a general dissection. Please shut down on it. As to disposal of the body, I must ask you as my personal representative on the spot in this matter, to yield nothing at all under any circumstances. If there is any talk about the interests of science, say for me that science can go to hell. We propose to stand by our friends.

Besides, I cannot believe that any scientific value is materially involved. We have hundreds of Indian skeletons that nobody ever comes near to study. The prime interest in this case would be of a morbid romantic nature.

Please acquaint Waterman with my feelings; and convey them also to Pope, toned down in form so as not to offend him, but without concessions.

When the time comes, please see that the various people in the hospital are properly thanked. They have been more than white.

You can get an individual plot in any of the public cemeteries. Draw upon any money in our keeping, for this purpose without question or formality, on my responsibility. As to monument and care, we can see later. There is no use declaring an estate unless there is official demand. Whatever balance remains after we get through, I think should be turned over to the hospital for what they have done. All this, however, can be arranged later.

Yours,
A. L. Kroeber

[240]

March 30, 1916.

Dear Dr. Kroeber:

Your letter of March 24 with instructions concerning the disposal of Ishi's body and estate was received too late to be of use.

In disposing of his body I took the stand which you asked me to take some time ago; namely, that he have a Christian burial like any other friend. The only possible departures from your request lie in the fact that an autopsy was performed and that the brain was preserved. However, the matter, as you well know, was not entirely in my hands, as I am not the acting head of the department. In short, what happened amounts to a compromise between science and sentiment, with myself on the side of sentiment. Everything else was carried out as you would have done it yourself, I firmly believe. The Indian told Pope some time ago that the way to dispose of the dead was to burn them, so we undoubtedly followed his wishes in that matter. In the coffin were placed one of his bows, five steel pointed arrows, a basket of acorn meal, ten pieces of dentalium, a box full of shell bead money which he had saved, a purse full of tobacco, three rings, and some obsidian flakes, all of which we felt sure would be in accord with Ishi's wishes.

The remains are to be placed in a niche in the columbarium at Mount Olivet Cemetery. Pope and Waterman decided, and I agreed, that a small black Pueblo jar would be far more appropriate than one of the bronze or onyx urns which the Crematory has on sale. To-morrow afternoon Pope and I are going down to place the ashes in this jar and put it in the niche purchased.

. . . .

The funeral was private, and no flowers were brought. Waterman, Pope, Loomis, Loud, Warburton, Mason, and myself were the only people who attended. We of course went to the crematory also.

Sincerely,
[E. W. Gifford]

Ishi's funeral was attended by his closest friends, except for Kroeber, who was in New York. A number of newspapers carried reports of the funeral, and one of these is reprinted here. It is followed by Saxton Pope's account from his "Medical History of Ishi."

3. Ishi's Funeral (1916)

The body of Ishi, last of the Yano tribe of Indians, was cremated Monday at Mount Olivet cemetery. It was according to the custom of his tribe and there was no ceremony.

San Mateo Labor Index, March 30, 1916.

Death mask of Ishi.

The body was accompanied to the cemetery by several of U. of C. scientists: Professor T. T. Waterman, E. W. Gifford, assistant curator of the anthropological museum, A. W. Warburton, L. L. Loud, and Dr. Saxton Pope of the University of California medical college.

One of those who officiated as pall bearer made a few remarks at the cemetery, commenting upon the value Ishi had been to anthropologists in helping to complete a history of the tribe, incomplete until he was found. Ishi suffered with all the ills of mankind, Professor Waterman explained, and the white plague was contracted only two weeks prior to his death.

4. Conclusion (1920)

Saxton T. Pope

His body was carried to the undertakers, where it was enbalmed. No funeral services were held. Professor T. T. Waterman, Mr. E. W. Gifford, Mr. A. Warburton, Mr. L. L. Loud, of the Museum of Anthropology, and I visited the parlor, and reverently placed in his coffin his bow, a quiver full of arrows, ten pieces of dentalia or Indian money, some dried venison, some acorn meal, his fire sticks, and a small quantity of tobacco. We then accompanied the body to Laurel Hill cemetery near San Francisco, where it was cremated.* The ashes were placed in a small Indian pottery jar on the outside of which is inscribed: "Ishi, the last Yahi Indian, died March 25, 1916."

[241]

One might have thought that a somewhat more sympathetic notice would have appeared in the Chico newspaper about Ishi's death. He had become a celebrity from that area, but perhaps Chicoan pride was hurt by his having been removed

From Saxton T. Pope, "The Medical History of Ishi," *University of California Publications in American Archaeology and Ethnology,* Vol. 13, No. 5 (1920). Extract here is from p. 213.
*Ishi's ashes are at Mount Olivet, now Olivet Memorial Park, near San Francisco.—Ed.

*to San Francisco to furnish "amusement and
study to the savants at the University of California."
Apparently the old attitudes toward the "Mill
Creek Indians" as displayed in the writings of
Robert Anderson and Sim Moak, two locally renowned Indian fighters, still prevailed in the region
in 1916.*

5. Ishi's Death — A Chico Commentary (1916)

"Ishi," the man primeval, is dead. He could not
stand the rigors of civilization, and tuberculosis,
that arch-enemy of those who live in the simplicity
of nature and then abandon that life, claimed him.
Ishi was supposed to be the last of a tribe that
flourished in California long before the white man
reached these shores. He could make a fire with
sticks, fashion arrowheads out of flint, and was
familiar with other arts long lost to civilization.
He furnished amusement and study to the savants
at the University of California for a number of
years, and doubtless much of ancient Indian lore
was learned from him, but we do not believe he
was the marvel that the professors would have the
public believe. He was just a starved-out Indian
from the wilds of Deer creek who, by hiding in its
fastnesses, was able to long escape the white man's
pursuit. And the white man with his food and
clothing and shelter finally killed the Indian just
as effectually as he would have killed him with
a rifle.

Chico Record, March 28, 1916.

Picture Credits

Page 69, Native Daughters Museum, Oroville, California.

Pages 91, 112, 126, 127, 129, 144, 145, 147, 148, 149, 152, 153, 154, 155, 159, 170, 171, 174, 177, 178, 180, 183, 185, 186, 189, 190, 191, 194, 196, 197, 198, 199, 221, 228, 233, 235, 236, 237, 241, courtesy of Lowie Museum of Anthropology, University of California, Berkeley, California.

Map 1, page 163, and Map 2, page 167, from A. L. Kroeber: *Handbook of the Indians of California* (New York: Dover Publications, Inc.).

Musical notation, pages 206-216, from *Musical Quarterly*, Volume LI, Number 3, July 1965.

Designer   Dave Comstock
Composition   IBM Composer
Lithography   Thomson-Shore, Inc.
Binder   Thomson-Shore, Inc.

Text   10/10 Journal Roman
Display   Souvenir Bold